THE SOVEREIGN LADY

Photo: Neil Campbell-Sharp

Lady Webster as a 'Virgin of the Sun',
by George Romney

SONIA KEPPEL

THE
SOVEREIGN
LADY

A life of Elizabeth Vassall,
third Lady Holland, with her family

HAMISH HAMILTON
LONDON

First published in Great Britain 1974
by Hamish Hamilton Ltd
90 Great Russell Street London WC1

Copyright © 1974 by Sonia Keppel

SBN 241 02299 1

Printed in Great Britain
by T. and A. Constable Ltd, Edinburgh

To Tessa and Charlotte

CONTENTS

PART THREE: WINGS

ILLUSTRATIONS

A*

FOREWORD

As a child, living in London, my greatest treat was to spend a day at Holland House. Leaving the noise and bustle of Kensington High Street behind me, I was suddenly transported into the country. A long avenue of elm trees lay before me through which, to the left, I had a glimpse of fields. The front door of Holland House opened into a domain as thrilling as E. Nesbit's *The House of Arden* and took me straight back into the past.

In the Hall, was Elizabeth 3rd Lady Holland's sedan-chair; in the Breakfast Room, at the head of the first flight of stairs, was the bust of Charles James Fox; through the french windows, sometimes Mary Fox-Strangways and I joined the hay-makers in the field beyond. In this same field, nearly one hundred and fifty years before, Lady Sarah Lennox had made hay under the ardent gaze of the young King, George III. Still outside, in the Dutch (formerly the Portuguese) garden, Mary, her brother, Harry Stavordale, and I played hide-and-seek, using 'Roger's Seat' as sanctuary while, from his high marble plinth above us, Napoleon I looked broodingly down.

On wet days, Mary's and Harry's grandmother, Lady Ilchester (then châtelaine), allowed us, sometimes fearfully, to explore the house. Here again legend and history wove inextricably through it. Henry Rich, 1st Earl of Holland, beheaded by Cromwell's order, was said to haunt the Great Staircase and the Gilt Room, carrying his head in his hand! In the Library passage hung the fowling-piece and two pistols presented by Catherine of Russia to Charles James Fox, in 1785, for preserving peace with France.

Of all the family portraits, the one I liked least, of Augusta, 4th Lady Holland, looked to me rather sly. And the one I liked best was of Elizabeth, 3rd Lady Holland, who was painted with her dog.

This Lady Holland was linked in my mind with her sedan-chair in the Hall and seemed very remote, at first. But 'Stavey' Ilchester, Mary's and Harry's father, brought her up to date in one phrase: 'A remarkable

xi

woman, who started life in a sedan-chair and finished up in a train.'
Thereafter, the pursuit of her life-story became my aim.

Stavey devoted most of his time recording and chronicling the lives of
his forebears, the Foxes. And though he possessed another beautiful
estate, in Dorset, I think his first consideration was Holland House.
Mercifully so as, when rumours of war grew louder, in 1939, he had the
foresight to move his priceless library, china and pictures from Kensington
to Melbury. In September 1940, enemy aeroplanes dropped twenty-two
incendiary bombs on and round Holland House. The whole of the central
part of the house was gutted beyond hope of salvation. From Stavey's own
lips, I learned this fact. As his steward, together with his fellow A.R.P.
wardens, strove valiantly but vainly to contain the flames, his attention
was momentarily diverted to a large four-legged animal, slinking across the
lawn. A fox!

To the end of his life, Stavey reserved to himself the right to edit his
family papers. His erudition and industry was enormous but his efforts
were untrained. And he was jealous of his guardianship, keeping the key of
the library at Melbury in his own pocket. He died in 1959 and, a few
weeks later, Harry Stavordale, now Lord Ilchester, gave me access to the
Holland House papers. Like Aladdin, I stood alone and dumbfounded,
surrounded by 26,000 loose sheets and letters, tied together in bundles.

These, Stavey had laid out on tables in the library, in chronological order,
starting with the life and contacts of Sir Stephen Fox, and working down,
through his descendants, to Henry Richard, 3rd Lord Holland, and his
wife, Elizabeth Vassall, the object of my search. Having mapped out the
position of each table, I linked those essential to me by arrows, as I might
have done signposts to main roads. Luckily, Elizabeth Holland's Dinner
Books were there, started in 1799 and continuing until her death, in 1845.
On these, and on as much relevant material as I could absorb, I worked
very happily for years.

In his will, Stavey stipulated that the Holland House papers must
remain in England, to be housed where they could be of endless benefit to
students, at the British Museum. In November 1960, Harry Ilchester
effected this transfer, very kindly negotiating a special clause for me with
the Museum authorities whereby I was to have access to the Manuscript
Department as soon as possible. Most loyally and helpfully, these gentlemen have kept their promise to me.

Mr Hudson and his colleagues are doing a wonderful job sorting and
gradually binding the vast miscellany of the Holland House papers. But
it is by no means complete and therefore still impossible to be definitive

about foliation and exact references. Under the section headed '3rd Lord Holland' alone, there are over four hundred bound books, and others still binding.

From it, I have tried to pick out material enough to prove Elizabeth Lady Holland's infinite variety and to temper, where possible, the unflattering picture of her which has come down to posterity. I do not pretend that this is her final image, but at least, it is a first impression.

SONIA KEPPEL

Hall Place
West Meon
February, 1973

ACKNOWLEDGMENTS

My first thanks are due to Her Majesty the Queen, for her gracious permission to quote from Queen Victoria's journal, when a girl, and her unedited correspondence with Lord Melbourne. Then, to the memory of my childhood and lifelong friend, 'Harry', 7th Earl of Ilchester, for giving me *carte blanche* to work on the Holland House papers.

I am deeply grateful to Her Majesty's Librarian, Mr R. Mackworth-Young, C.V.O., for his invaluable help in sorting out relevant material for me from the Royal Archives, Windsor Castle. And to my dear friends Mr Ronald Tree and Mr R. Burdon Muller, for enlisting the kind assistance of Mr Neville Connell (Curator, Barbados Museum) and Mr David McKibban (Librarian at the Athenaeum, Boston, Mass.) to probe back into Elizabeth, 3rd Lady Holland's Vassall ancestry.

To Mr Hudson, and his team at the Manuscript Department of the British Museum, I am endlessly grateful for their unstinted help and kindness. I must thank Miss Margaret Jones and Lady Pease for their initial research at the British Museum. And Sir Bertram Long (Principal Probate Registry, Somerset House) for allowing me to transcribe Lady Holland's will. Mrs H. St George Saunders has my eternal gratitude for her expertise and patience in working on the Holland House papers for a decade. I am most grateful to Mrs P. Brayne for her excellent typing over nearly the same period and to Mrs Russell-Cobb for her help in obtaining illustrations. I must also thank Mr Stanley Gillam (Librarian, the London Library) for so kindly feeding me with material from contemporary history for this biography.

My very grateful thanks to the Dowager Countess of Bessborough and Lord Egremont for so timelessly lending their own books of family history, to work on.

I should also like to express my gratitude to Mr Richard Agnew for his great help in condensing historical material, and to Mr Guy Neville, for his able translation of several important letters in Spanish to 3rd Lord Holland and his wife.

Last but not least, I have to thank all those kind people who have so generously allowed me to reproduce their beautiful pictures in this book, Lady Theresa Agnew, Mrs E. Webster, the Countess of Chichester, Lady Howick and Lord Moyne.

PART ONE

Backcloth

CHAPTER ONE

Child Bride

DURING THE SUMMER of 1786, the poet, Richard Paul Jodrell, wrote
an ode to a beautiful girl he had seen at a masquerade:

> Imperial nymph, ill-suited is thy name
> To speak the wonders of that radiant frame,
> Where'er thy sovereign form on Earth is seen
> All eyes are vassals; thou alone art Queen.

The recipient of this panegyric was Elizabeth, daughter of Richard
Vassall, rich man of fashion living in Golden Square, Soho.

Before 1793, no portrait is known of her, but that year, Robert Fagan
(British Governor of the Ionian Isles) did a quick amateur sketch of her
in which we see the classical features which had called forth the poet's
admiration, seven years before. Fagan depicts the chestnut hair; the
sparkling eyes; the short, straight nose; the ruby-red lips. He gives a
gentle, relaxed, almost domestic impression of Elizabeth to be countered,
in 1796, by a full-length portrait of her as 'a Virgin of the Sun' by George
Romney, in which the 'imperial' qualities extolled by Richard Jodrell
are faithfully portrayed.

Almost at the same time as Jodrell's eulogy, Mrs Vassall received a
letter. (Although undated, it must have been written the same year and
was headed: Tuesday, Audley Square.)

Madam
... perhaps it may not have entirely escaped your observation the attention I have
for some time past paid to Miss Vassall. It has more than once occurred to me to
speak to you on this subject, but as I had not an opportunity except in the presence
of Miss Vassall, I was afraid of embarrassing Her, and of not being able to express
my real Sentiments of Attachment to Her, and also my Hopes that my Happiness
was not an object of perfect Indifference to Her.

I have as a necessary step asked Her permission to write to you, and have even
told Her my View in writing, she has had the goodness not to express any Disapprobation at my so doing, and from Her Delicacy I expected no more.

3

The favour I have at present to wish is, that when you judge proper, you wld ask the permission of Mr Vassall for me to be introduced to him.

I hope both Mr Vassall and yourself are convinced of my Consciousness of Miss Vassall's merits, and situation, and how highly I shall think myself honoured in not being deemed absolutely unworthy of Her Hand.

Great as Miss Vassall's personal merits are, yet with no small Part of the World Her Situation wld be a primary Object. I hope I have a Mind Superior to such considerations, and I believe Miss Vassall is convinced of the Truth of what I now say, that the Elegance of Her person, and Manners, and the Excellence of her Understanding are what have attracted me to Her.

I am not uninformed that Mr Vassall and yourself are entirely wrapped up in Miss Vassall and that Her Happiness is the Great Object of yr. Views, and wishes, and how indeed can it be otherwise with such a Daughter? It might naturally be supposed you wld not be v. ready to part with Her; but I trust that the same motives which have operated so forcibly and so happily in inducing Mr Vassall and yr.self to dedicate so much of yr. time to a purpose that has so amply repaid yr. Anxiety and Attention, will cause both Mr Vassall and you to consent to my continuing to endeavour to render myself not unworthy of having such an Honour and Happiness conferred upon me. If I at all know myself, my conduct to Mr Vassall and yourself and to Miss Vassall, will be such as to show you have not misplaced yr. Confidence.

I shall attend yr. Answer with the utmost Anxiety. I am with the Greatest Respect and Regard

> Madam,
> Yr. most obed
> most obliged Hble Servt
> Godfrey Webster

This correct approach had the desired effect, as presumably on the following Sunday, the writer is penning an unctuous epistle from Audley Square to a neighbour in Sussex (Lady George Lennox) announcing the good news.

'I have within these v. few days been promised the Hand of Miss Vassall ... You will find (her) fully worthy of yr. Esteem and Protection. Most People allow Her Merits, I naturally think them numberless; in my opinion not one of the least, is Her bearing some resemblance to (if anything can resemble) Your Family.'

He hopes that 'the Miss Lennox's will receive Her into their Friendship'. He declares: 'Her Health is v. good, but delicate, I need not say of how much Consequence for my Happiness.' So he plans to winter in Naples. 'I am sure a Winter, South of the Alps, must be both pleasant and Salutary.'

Sir Godfrey Webster's material assets were many. He had good looks, a title and assured place in Society, and was the owner of Battle Abbey, famous as having been built on the site of the Battle of Hastings, at William the Conqueror's command. At first sight, the marriage of their only child and daughter to him, fourth baronet of a distinguished line, must have seemed eminently suitable to Richard and Mary Vassall. But there were two disadvantages: Elizabeth was only fifteen years old; Sir Godfrey was forty-nine. And that self-knowledge and implied propriety of conduct about which he had written with such confidence to Mrs Vassall, before marriage, was speedily lost in a blaze of jealousy, injured dignity and bad temper after Elizabeth Vassall became his wife. On the anniversary of her wedding-day, seven years later, she made this entry in her journal: 'This fatal day seven years gave me, in the bloom and innocence of fifteen, to the power of a being who has made me execrate my life since it has belonged to him.'

She was married on 27th June 1786, by special licence granted by the Archbishop of Canterbury, in her father's drawing-room in Golden Square. The Rev. Byrne J. Aylmer, Rector of St Albans, performed the ceremony, which was witnessed by Richard Vassall and his wife, Mary, for the bride, and, for the bridegroom, Lady 'Elizabeth' Webster. Stress was laid on the fact that Elizabeth Vassall, a minor, was married 'by and with the consent of Richard Vassall, Esq., the natural and lawful father of the said minor'. Which fact reinforced the legal authority of parent or guardian established by Lord Hardwicke's Marriage Act of 1753, designed to kill the abuse of clandestine marriages contracted by parties under age.

*

Elizabeth was born on 25th March 1771, in her parents' house, in Golden Square. Nearly sixty years later, in a letter to her son, Henry Fox (dated 16th May 1828), she still remembers acutely the loneliness of the first thirteen years of her life. '. . . I have few relations in the world, never had a young associate, and only a father and mother who did not always agree with each other, and never agreed about me. The warm, ingenuous affection of youth was never drawn out, but blunted and repressed; in that my adolescence and youth was gloomy, uncheered by any tender kindred feeling. I was solitary; and till thirteen years old, no mortal seemed to think of me beyond the necessaries of life . . .' Later, in the same letter, she recalls 'the weeks, the days, in which all the hours, except those for meals, were spent by me in total solitude in a back room in a London house in the dingiest situation . . .' Then, a heaven-sent emissary penetrated her solitude, 'an old friend of my father's, struck by my looks or my character, to a degree adopted me and became my tutor'.

This friend was Anthony Morris Storer, a bibliophile and collector of prints living in the fashionable world but forced, through increasing ill-health, to play but small part in it. He was only thirty-seven when he started to instruct Elizabeth but, according to her, already 'he was an invalid sinking fast under disease, and could only, when in an interval of ease, sketch out what I should learn'. Nevertheless, throughout her life, Elizabeth looked upon Storer as her 'mental benefactor', and the outlines of his teaching inspired in her an insatiable thirst for knowledge.

As with her general education, so with her religious instruction. Though she was to temper her censure of this new neglect, no one came forward to bend her pliant mind towards belief in a Divine Authority or standards of self-discipline. Writing in her journal in 1797, she comments on the free hand she had been given in childhood to form her own opinions. 'My principles were of my own finding, both religious and moral, for I never was instructed in abstract or practical religion, and as soon as I could think at all, chance directed my studies; for though my parents were as good and as virtuous people as ever breathed, and I was always an only child, yet I was entirely left, not from system, but from fondness and inactivity, to follow my own bent.' So, from her earliest childhood, Elizabeth was forced to build up her auto-theism as a bulwark against the world.

Despite her condemnation of her parents' house as 'in the dingiest situation', as she knew it, Golden Square was an imposing octagonal Square, inhabited by people of means. True, it never attained the distinction of its neighbour, Soho (formerly King's) Square, and the streets around it remained mean and poverty stricken, a contributory reason for this being the legend that, under the turf of an adjacent field, lay the burial pit of thousands of victims of the Great Plague of London. But Golden Square was an accepted locality in which a rich man could live, and Elizabeth's father, Richard Vassall, expected to enjoy the life interest of a very considerable fortune.

Across the Oxford Road, about two miles distant, at No. 51 Wimpole Street, lived his father, Florentius Vassall, who described himself in his will (made on 20th September 1776) as 'late of Jamaica, now of Wimpole Street Parish of St Marylebone, County Middlesex, Great Britain'. Florentius had backed up his introduction to London with an impressive bank balance based on large revenues from valuable plantations in the parish of Westmoreland, County of Cornwall, Jamaica, and rich estates in New England. He became domiciled in England about 1775, in which year he built himself a family vault in the Parish Church in St Marylebone.

By his will (whereby he decreed that all his beneficiaries should add the name of Vassall to their own) he made his son, Richard, life tenant of his New England and most of his Jamaican estates, together with 'the Negro and other slaves, cattle, utensils and stock whatsoever' entailed on Richard's children. Richard had but one child, Elizabeth, who (when her grandfather died in 1779) became an heiress of note at the age of eight. That this fact made no difference whatever to her youthful unhappiness was only plain to herself.

*

To account for her family's riches, across the backcloth of its history rides a ship at full sail, the *Mayflower*, for this famous vessel formed part of the merchant fleet owned by her ancestor, Samuel Vassall.

In 1620, the voyage of the *Mayflower* to the New World, with her freight of Pilgrim Fathers, opened up for Samuel the great possibilities of future trade there as he and his brother, William, were two of the original patentees of lands in Massachusetts, New England, and were both mentioned in the first Massachusetts Charter of 1629. But, in 1624, disaster befell Samuel, and it was William alone who, as an assistant of the newly formed Massachusetts Bay Company operating from London, personally established his and his brother's claims there, in 1630.

Samuel languished for sixteen years in prison, presumably in the Tower of London, wherein he had been cast by decree of one of the last of James I's Star Chamber Courts, for his temerity in refusing to pay the tax of tonnage and poundage levied by Royal prerogative against his trading vessels. During that time, James I died and Charles I succeeded him, and, in 1635, Samuel's brother, William, apparently powerless to help him, left for New England with his wife and six children, on board the *Blessing*. William's timely departure for New England undoubtedly laid the foundations of the Vassall fortunes overseas, so perhaps Samuel himself prescribed this course. Yet, even so, he had ample time to contrast his plight, as the King's prisoner, with that of his brother, escaped to freedom across the seas; and, more poignantly still, as the penalised subject of two Stuart kings, in contrast to his father, John Vassall, living his free life in the reign of Tudor Elizabeth whose offer 'to equip and command two ships-of-war to sail with her fleet against the Spanish Armada' had been freely made and graciously accepted.

The Long Parliament of 3rd November 1640 promised to make good Samuel Vassall's losses. In July 1641, it voted him £10,455 12s 2d for his damages and 'resolved that he should be further considered for his personal sufferings'. At the end of 1640, like his father before him, he was made an alderman of London, and was elected to Parliament in the same year that his case was heard, in 1641. In 1643, he took the oath decreed by the Solemn League and Covenant and, in 1646, he was further rewarded by his appointment as Commissioner for the Kingdom of England for the conservation of peace with Scotland. His troubles seemed behind him. But Parliament substantiated nothing. In 1657, he petitioned it again, restating his grievances: sixteen years of imprisonment; his goods confiscated; his complaint that, despite the money promised him by Parliament, of it 'he had not received one penny'. And added to these, new accusations: that £2,591 17s 6d lent by him to Parliament to assist 'in their great straights in Ireland' had never been repaid; that he was owed a further £3,328 2s 7d for the services of one of his ships; and last, but not least, that his ship, the *Mayflower*, had, 'when laden and manned, been taken and made use of against the enemy, to the overthrow of his voyage and his great loss'. (Before her voyage to New England in 1620, the *Mayflower* had been used to carry cargoes of wine between English and Mediterranean ports and probably reverted to this use thereafter.)

Yet, though Samuel Vassall was not destined to enjoy the fruits of it, the pioneering voyage of the *Mayflower* to the New World charted a passage to prosperity for his family. From New England to the West Indies the Vassall trading ships proceeded: to Barbados, where his brother, William (already a rich man), migrated and became one of that island's richest settlers; and to Jamaica, where Samuel's own son, John, settled with his wife, there to amass a further fortune for his heirs. By the time Florentius Vassall was born, in 1710, two generations of Vassalls had lived in Jamaica. His grandfather, John, had died there. And his father, William, had been born and brought up on his estates.

Without doubt, the fortune of Samuel Vassall's descendants was built up on the slave trade. But, ultimately, Elizabeth Vassall's inheritance was largely dissipated by the high-minded efforts of her second husband (Henry Richard, 3rd Lord Holland) to bring such trading to an end.

*

Besides Battle Abbey, Sir Godfrey Webster owned two other important historical buildings in Sussex, the Abbey of Robertsbridge and Bodiam Castle. But, at the time of his marriage, he did not live in any of these three but in a small dower house (Rosehill) in Battle of no historical importance, down Powdermill Lane. The Abbey House was lived in by his aunt, Lady (Whistler) Webster, whose husband (the 2nd Baronet) had left it to her for life, when he died, childless, in 1779.

Sir Godfrey's father (Godfrey, 3rd Baronet) only survived his brother by one year, so that Lady (Whistler) Webster was châtelaine of the Abbey when her nephew succeeded to the title and estates, in 1780. During their tenancy, both she and her husband allowed the Abbey to deteriorate, and Sir Whistler actually destroyed the beautiful Guest House constructed by Henry VIII's Master of the Horse, Sir Anthony Browne, for the accommodation of the King's daughter, Princess Elizabeth, and many of the earlier monastery buildings besides. At the time of Sir Godfrey's marriage to Elizabeth Vassall, the ruined towers of Princess Elizabeth's Lodging soared forlornly in the foreground of his view from Rosehill, in perpetual affront to his ownership.

Since 21st March 1786, Sir Godfrey had represented the borough of Seaford at Westminster, held under the patronage of the Hon. Thomas Pelham (later, 2nd Earl of Chichester). Already, in 1785, he and a Mr Alves had stood for election 'in the Pelham interest' (under the patronage of a foregoing Sir Nicholas Pelham and, subsequently, of the Hon. Thomas Pelham) against two sitting members and two Treasury candidates. Thanks to the machinations of the bailiff, the two Treasury candidates had been returned, and lengthy legal action had been incurred before Parliament nullified that election and declared the votes equal. In 1786, Sir Godfrey stood again, alone, as Mr Alves had faded in disgust from the scene. This time the bailiff returned the two Government candidates, rejecting anyone whose name did not occur on the rates of his own party. Again, counter-petitions were presented, resulting in a declaration from the sitting members that 'it was not their intention to justify their election', and culminating in Sir Godfrey Webster's return to Parliament. The machinations of the local officials did not stop there, but at least his election gave Sir Godfrey a breathing space. For his other pursuits in the county, he was a popular Master of the East Sussex Foxhounds; he took an active interest in local affairs; he was generous to the point of extravagance with all those who knew him; he was a good gambler and, in fact, the perfect Squire. He was a club-man and a man's man, and probably it never occurred to him to provide his young wife with more than the accepted run of feminine amusement. That this was not enough was increasingly apparent as time went by.

*

It was indisputable that Elizabeth Webster was married to a man over three times her age and one who (she averred later) allowed her to languish

in solitude, in much the same way that her parents had done. But for a
time she did her best to adapt herself to her new responsibilities. Sir
Godfrey writes to Richard Vassall in an undated letter apparently written
shortly after marriage:

Eliz. is perfectly well is handsomer and in Better Spirits than ever I knew her.
She has learnt to keep the Accounts, and has been busy all the day packing up in
spite of the (Fifth?) Commandment; in short she is grown quite Notable, and quite
the Wife for a Country Squire . . .

This idyllic state was not to last for long. To counter her mounting
frustration, she made new friends and proceeded to show off, like the
child she was. Singling out a victim on whom to vent her spleen and
high spirits, she picked on her husband's aunt, subjecting her to a series of
practical jokes which left the old lady triumphantly unmoved. After which
Elizabeth had to recognise her as a worthy adversary whom she resented
as 'the usurper' of her rights, until she left Battle for good.

In 1786, Battle was a thriving little town. Since the middle of the
sixteenth century it had been the centre of the Wealden iron trade,
specialising in the making of cast-iron cannon which had been used with
effect against the Spanish Armada, and succeeding wars across the Channel.
Also, it produced a famous brand of gunpowder, at its most destructive
described by Daniel Defoe as 'the best in Europe' and, at a less lethal level,
producing the 'Battle rouser', precursor of all fireworks up to the present
day. It was well placed as a trading centre, with the mail coaches to the
coast passing regularly through it, changing horses at the 'Eight Bells' or
the 'George'. Twice a year it indulged in special festivities: on 5th
November, when great bonfires were lit to commemorate 'Guy Fawkes
Day', and the local gunpowder was put to deafening use by letting off
fireworks; and on 22nd November (St Martin's Day, by the old calendar),
when the neighbourhood rallied in force to the Abbot's Fair.

The kaleidoscopic brilliance of these rustic scenes found no favour in
young Lady Webster's eyes. Instead, a colour blindness seemed to affect
her the day she arrived in Battle, dimming her sight to the dreary mono-
chrome of boredom through which she viewed nearly every circumstance
that befell her there for the next five years. She made older and more
responsible friends, like Lady Pelham, Lady Sheffield and Lady Shelburne;
and a young married couple, William and Francis Mary Wyndham. But
the friend on whom she grew to rely more and more to relieve her tedium
was her husband's political patron, Thomas Pelham.

*

Three years passed before Lady Webster presented her husband with a son and heir, Godfrey Vassall Webster, in 1789. And when, a year later, she bore him another son, this poor little life did not survive infancy.

The year 1790 was one of disappointment for Sir Godfrey. On 11th June, Parliament was dissolved, and due to still more dubious manœuvres on the part of the Treasury candidates, he was defeated by one vote, at the subsequent polls, at Seaford.

At home, his relations with his wife grew strained and his temper frayed. And now he involved himself in his wife's financial affairs, embarking on an acrimonious correspondence with her father. He became morose and sullen, and subject to violent fits of depression. He gambled often and when he gambled he drank and, at such times, probably his wife had good grounds for complaint. She became obsessed with a desire for change of scene and hardly a day passed without her entreating her husband to take her abroad.

With his Parliamentary activities at an end, for the moment, Sir Godfrey fell in with her wishes. During the summer of 1791, in two coaches laden to bursting point with nurses, a maid, a footman, a cook, a coachman and a mountain of luggage, he and his wife and child took the road to the coast.

CHAPTER TWO

Posting Through Europe

A DIARY CAN act as lenient listener, confessional or jury, and sometimes it is designed to be used as a weapon of defence.

Lady Webster's first journal developed into this. Primarily it set out to record news, and news which, for her, only began across the Channel. Many of its earlier pages contain scrupulous records of the natural and man-made phenomena of the countries through which she passed and, had they remained at that, they would have made guidebook reading. She began by fitting scenery, events, people into the relief map of her trip across Europe, and it was only gradually that she reversed the sequence of her subject-matter. Then she hedged it in and disguised it with mountain peaks and rushing rivers, still taking care to stress that her intellectual pleasures transcended all others. Driving through a Europe rapidly succumbing to the impact of the French Revolution, she still contrived to remain untouched by it, as often happens when self-centred people move parallel with history. Anthony Storer had inspired her with a love of learning and she gravitated naturally towards the intellectual circles of the countries through which she passed. With her beauty and vivacity, and very little effort, she became Queen of an expanding court, while Sir Godfrey tagged along behind her like a drone, with only one duty.

Gradually her communications to her journal became more complex as though, despite the acclamation she was publicly accorded, in private she needed an alibi. Her self-assertion became automatic: 'I! I!' Except when she sought to vindicate her revulsion from him, to all intents and purposes her husband ceased to exist for her. But when she needed him for emphasis, she brought out damning evidence against him: she quoted the disparaging opinions of others; she implied despair. Always her auto-theism had to appear invulnerable yet, from time to time, an uneasy conscience seemed to propel her pen. For this reason, she made few references to her devoted swain, Thomas Pelham, and treated the flowering of her love for Lord Holland with oyster-like discretion, building up their increasing delight in each other's society on an edifice of ancient monuments, classical exchanges, and endless contemplation of the arts. For one whole year she ceased altogether to keep a diary, and finally recorded her marriage to him in the briefest terms. As for her extraordinary concealment of her daughter Harriet, she avoided chronicling that fact altogether until she was well enough established in her new-found security for Time to blunt the weapon of surprise.

*

Lady Webster opens her journal with a memorable phrase. 'In June 1791, I left England and went to Paris. During my stay the King and Royal Family escaped to Varennes but were brought back. I attended the debates in the National Assembly. I heard Robespierre and Maury speak. The Jacobin Club was then in embryo.' Thus, succinctly, she reduces the whole tragic canvas to terms of 'news'. No further reference to the doomed family or apprehension as to its ultimate fate; merely the recording by a cool-headed reporter of her satisfaction at being able to hear a speech in the Tribune through the good offices of the Vicomte de Noailles. 'I wanted to hear a speech and the V. de Noailles during dinner promised that he would gratify me by making one.' Thereafter, she rounds off her first paragraph with references to her companions in Paris: 'the Wyndhams', 'Mr Pelham', 'and several other English'.

On the face of it, Lady Webster's comments sound unbelievably callous as, already, King Louis XVI had suffered much. Yet, to watchful eyes on both sides of the Channel, his gradual downfall came as no surprise. Already, five years before, Daniel Hailes, British Chargé d'Affaires to Lord Dorset, British Ambassador Extraordinary to Paris, was predicting the inevitability of a revolution against the monarchy in France, due to corruption, the Queen's extravagance, the upkeep of the Royal Houses and the total inability of succeeding Ministers to administrate finance. From then on, he, Lord Dorset and visiting Englishmen such as Arthur Young, Edward Rigby and Lord John Villiers predicted pretty well every event contributing to the King's confinement in the Tuileries, with his family, by the will of the people, in October 1789. In June 1790, Lord Gower succeeded Lord Dorset as British Ambassador to Paris and continued to view the scene with the same clearsightedness. But, by this time, the great event of the preceding year, the Fall of the Bastille, was settling into its important place in the calendar and, although Lord Gower was adjured by his Sovereign to waste no time in seeking an audience with 'our good brother the most Christian King . . . to assure him of the esteem and value we have for his person', at the same time he deemed it politic to attend the anniversary of the Fall of the Bastille, the fête in the Champs de Mars.

To many the Fall of the Bastille meant death to mediaeval oppression and new life to tolerance and reason. And, at last, the Declaration of the Rights of Man and of Citizens brought recognition to the people of France, as human beings.

In England, the bloodless revolution reacted on individuals in different ways. It inspired Cowper and Blake to poetry; Charles James Fox and Edmund Burke to rhetoric; extremists to thoughts of similar revolution at home, and, in a great number of people leisured enough to travel, boundless curiosity to view it for themselves.

It became the fashion to go to France. William Wordsworth, still an undergraduate at Cambridge, went on a walking tour from Calais, down the Saône and Rhône, in August 1790; Samuel Rogers described a walk in the Tuileries Gardens (in February 1791) where he saw the Dauphin's name 'Louis Dauphin' inscribed in his little prison garden in mustard seed. Stephen Watson, an antiquary and man of letters, described the terrifying reactions of the people of Lille (in June 1791) to a messenger arriving post haste at the Hôtel de Ville with news of the apprehension of the Royal Family at Varennes. 'The whole square formed itself into a ring, and danced round like an Indian tribe, with a hoop and a halloo. All at once you saw five hundred hats in the air, and the place re-echoed with screams of joy.'

Without doubt, Lady Webster and 'several other English' were on a sightseeing spree in Paris, and she herself went into far less details of her visit there than did the daughter of her friend, Lady Sheffield. Maria Josepha Holroyd refers to the Royal prisoners in the Tuileries with the same lack of feeling, almost as though they were puppets. Writing to her aunt, Serena Holroyd (on 5th July 1791), she describes how her father, Lord Sheffield, interrogates a maid at the inn at which they dine. Where is the King? he asks, and what will they do to him? To which the maid answers, with obvious pleasure: 'Oh! Mon Dieu, on l'a bien enfermé, il n'échappera plus!'

*

Elizabeth Webster stamped her 'solitariness' on her journal and, as 'I', proceeded on her way through France to Switzerland. In Lausanne, she stayed for three months at 'Mon Repos', formerly inhabited by Voltaire.

She arrived there to find its lionising society at the feet of Edward Gibbon, returned, at long last, to the scene of his youthful romance with Suzanne Curchod. Elizabeth was annoyed by Gibbon ('His whim arranged and deranged all parties'). But we must regret that she did not meet the Neckers, living only a few miles away, or their daughter Germaine, Baroness Staël de Holstein, at that time recovering from a bout of scarlet fever under her parents' roof.

Later, Elizabeth was to meet Germaine often, and sometimes to entertain her, but she never liked her and may not the reason have been that she recognised in the Frenchwoman certain resemblances to herself? By then, many of her characteristics were identical with Madame de Staël's: her powers of conversation, her self-will, her self-absorption, her love of power. In September 1791, although only five years older than Elizabeth and married the same year, already Germaine de Staël had achieved a lasting name in French literature, a political salon of conspicuous intrigue, her only legitimate child, three—and probably four— lovers, and had become inextricably involved in the revolution in France. Germaine was always more of an actress than Elizabeth, but she lived in a world of drama and her gestures had to be extravagant to maintain her a leading part. Had Elizabeth's lot been cast in France instead of England, the chances are that she would not have acted very differently. Capable of the same impulsiveness and hero worship, and equally certain that she was always right, she too might have become an integral part of the Revolution. Her salvation lay in the fact that, where Germaine spent a lifetime looking for the man of her heart, Elizabeth found her true love early on and, with him beside her, could proclaim sympathy with the Revolution at a comfortable distance and beyond eyesight of the guillotine. For it was with the advent of Lord Holland that Elizabeth Webster discovered that she had a heart.

The rest of her journal covering Switzerland enumerates the parties she attended and the expeditions she undertook with her French and English friends. By this time, she had joined Lord and Lady Sheffield and their daughters, Maria Josepha and Louisa Holroyd; and was reunited with her cavaliere servante, Thomas Pelham.

The Sheffields and Websters were neighbours in Sussex, and Maria Holroyd herself was only two months older than Elizabeth, having been born on 3rd January 1771. At the outset of Elizabeth's married life (in 1788) Maria had so written of her to her aunt, Miss Sarah (Serena) Holroyd: 'I have no doubt but that in former Letters Mama has mentioned Lady W— in no v. favourable light. If so, it is but justice to say, three years never made a greater alteration for the better in anybody as they have made in her.' Yet, as it transpired, Lady Sheffield became devoted to Elizabeth, and Maria's magnanimous view had been largely dissipated by August 1791. As we have seen, the Sheffields had also stayed in Paris, where 'Mr Pelham' himself had been their guide and constant companion. So much so, that, on 11th July, Maria Holroyd had sung his praises to her aunt. 'Nothing can pass pleasanter than our time does, under the direction of Mr Pelham. He lays out a plan for our mornings, goes to the Play and sups with us. He is so pleasant that I hardly remember the Mr Pelham that was. Tom is quite a different man, and the most agreeable I ever saw . . .' Thomas Pelham arrived in Lausanne on 22nd July, and a few days later, Maria Holroyd has to admit his obvious preference for Lady Webster. 'On Monday, we set out for Chamony (*sic*) and the glaciers. It will be a true Party of Pleasure; in other words, the most unpleasant thing in the world. The Party consists of Sir G. and Lady Webster, Severy, and us. Sir G. is more cross than you can imagine; in short, he has just discovered that he is married, and that Mr P. has a great regard for his Lady.' Still inclined to be fair, she continues: 'I really believe that he need not have the least fear about him, and that he had much better let her quietly like a man of Honour, than one who might be less scrupulous; and like somebody, she must.' But Maria's disenchantment was complete by 11th August: 'If anybody ever offends you so grievously that you do not recollect any punishment bad enough for them, only wish them on a party of pleasure with Lady Webster! The ceremony began with irresolution in the extreme, whether they should or should not go! How and which way they should go! And everything that was proposed she decidedly determined on a contrary scheme, and as regularly altered her mind in a few hours.' Finally, she attempts to dispose of her rival: 'I think I have given words enough to this subject and will dismiss her Ladyship from my thoughts, when I have told you that the day we stayed at Geneva she passed in her Bed, à la Française, surrounded by her Beaux, the cause, Fatigue, in consequence of a Thunder Storm at Lausanne the day before.' And she vows to have nothing more to say to Thomas Pelham 'at least during Lady W's lifetime'. But Lady Webster is determined to remain on friendly terms. On 3rd November, she writes from Nice, expressing her gratitude to Maria for giving her news of Lady Sheffield. And, on 3rd December, she is writing her from Naples 'as I fear that my dear sulky Maria has already accused me of making promises I do not keep . . .' Her efforts prove fruitless. Maria Josepha is her enemy for life.

The Websters remained in Lausanne for another two months and then continued on their way to Nice. Their road through France bore increasing evidence of the Revolution and they had to by-pass Avignon because of 'the massacres'. Here the town had just succumbed to pillage and annexation by the National Assembly, barely two years old. Crossing the Esterelles, they had to have police protection against possible bandits, but they negotiated these without mishap and proceeded on to Fréjus, Antibes and Nice.

At this point, Sir Godfrey returned for a respite to England. His defeat at the polls was still under dispute, and Thomas Pelham was hopeful that another petition of protest might succeed. His wife made no effort to accompany him, but loudly complained to her journal that she had been left alone 'at twenty years old in a foreign country without a relation or any real friend'. Yet, in the very next sentence, she admitted that some of the 'most happy hours' of her life were enjoyed in Nice, that winter. Which remark she primly qualified by declaring that she lived there with great discretion 'even to prudery'.

Although, in a few months' time, Nice was to be overrun by the armies of the French Republic, that winter of 1791-92 the town still formed part of the Kingdom of Sardinia. Under its former King, Charles Emmanuel III, the prosperity of Sardinia had materially increased and Nice itself had become well established as a winter pleasure resort, largely frequented by English visitors.

During her first months there, Lady Webster lived with commendable circumspection. Only two men were allowed to visit her alone: Dr Drew, and 'a grave, married man, Mr Cowper'. In Dr Drew's company Elizabeth went back to the schoolroom. ('Drew used to spend the whole evening with me and give me lectures on chemistry, natural history, philosophy, etc., etc.') Later, Thomas Pelham was to tell her that Dr Drew had said she had 'the strongest memory united with ye most comprehensive mind he ever met and consequently that you can learn any thing you have inclination to make yourself mistress of . . .' The subjects discussed between herself and grave, married Mr Cowper she did not record.

Thomas Pelham kept Lady Webster regularly posted with news and was pathetically pleased to receive her letters. He seems to have undertaken not to see her for a space, as, in a letter written in November 1791, he says: 'I hope the Absurdity of the Promise about Time is as evident to other People as it is to you . . .' In an earlier letter he undertakes (very unwisely) to spoil her by 'the most devoted submission to yr. wishes'. As a result, and without complaint, he despatches to her, in an almost continual stream, a variety of objects ranging from a chemical laboratory

B

18 *The Sovereign Lady*

and other scientific instruments, musical instruments including a harp, domestic requirements such as tooth powder and brushes, to a riding dress and a pair of her stays retrieved from the Customs. Some friends of his, Ellis and Wallace (Charles Ellis, later created Lord Seaford, was a childhood acquaintance of Elizabeth, with the same Jamaican background) are on their way to Nice, and he commissions Wallace 'to draw a sketch of yr. house and the view from it' and, in the same letter, he tells Elizabeth that he 'wld. like also to have a plan of the House upon a card and where you sit when you are sewing, writing or reading'.

In December 1791, Thomas Pelham arrived in Paris, and from there occasionally he sent Lady Webster a cautious gift, 'a black handkerchief which is all the fashion in Paris', 'some things to put on yr. feet which will protect you from cold if you get wet'. He orders her twelve pairs of shoes and as many pairs of silk stockings. 'The Queen (Marie Antoinette) does not wear finer.' But, with this large commission he is careful to send her the bill which, together with the price paid to recover her 'corsets', comes to three hundred and seventy-four livres. In recompense for all his kindness, Lady Webster sends her adorer 'a delightful little Library' which is received with ecstatic gratitude. 'You can not bestow a favour upon a more grateful Heart or upon one more sincerely devoted to you.' Sometimes his passion gets the better of his caution. 'God bless you my dearest Friend—I feel that I love you as much as ever, it is impossible to love anybody more—', and he begs Lady Webster 'to give great assistance to joining our plans for the summer'. Then he reverts to prudence and asks her to refer to him as 'Mr Pelham' in her letters to his mother and not 'T. P.' (as she is beginning to call him) as his father likes to read her letters too. And, while Sir Godfrey is in England, he makes a point of remaining friendly with him and reporting anything unfavourable. 'Sir G. is in great spirits, he dined here on Monday and talked of you in raptures—I understand that he has been liberal in his applause of you to all yr. Friends, which is a good thing, at all Events.'

In March 1792, the quiet entertainment of Lady Webster's evenings was interrupted by the arrival in Nice of the Duchess of Devonshire and her party. Accompanying her were her mother and brother, Lady and Lord Spencer; her sister Harriet, Lady Duncannon; and her husband's mistress, Lady Elizabeth Foster. To the world, this strangely assorted family party presented an united front, surviving the calumnies such friendships engendered. Despite her own acceptance into her family of three of the Duke's illegitimate children (two of them Lady Elizabeth's), at that moment the Duchess was under sentence of exile by the Duke for her love affair with Charles Grey. And only the month before her arrival in Nice, she had had a child by her lover at Aix en Provence. A secret jealously guarded by her travelling companions, including her husband's mistress.

Beauty and high spirits automatically qualified newcomers for admittance to the Duchess's circle and, as Elizabeth Webster possessed both, she very soon found herself part of it. Thereafter, for several months, mundane pleasures supplanted nearly all else in her journal. Mr Cowper still played a part in it but, for the time being, Dr Drew went out. On rejoining his wife, Sir Godfrey's jealousy was aroused when he found her involved in a lively flirtation with Lord Spencer.

He had failed again in his petition to Parliament, and now had no valid excuse not to travel abroad. In consequence, he and his wife and the Devonshire party agreed to proceed south together, a concession which seems to have been wrung out of him with a very bad grace. Lady Webster confided to her journal that, by this time, she had experienced 'such very cruel usage from the unequal and at oftimes frantic temper of the man to whom I had the calamity to be united' that she declared that it was her mother's wish, backed up by Lady Pelham (Thomas Pelham's mother) and Lady Shelburne, that she should never go on a trip alone with her husband. Consequently, Mr Ellis and a young French emigrant called Beauval were roped in to accompany the Websters, who were to join up with the Devonshire party at various points along its route.

Elizabeth Webster's twenty-first birthday occurred on 25th March 1792, an event which remained unchronicled in her own journal, but which Thomas Pelham devotedly remembered. A week earlier, he had sent her gruesome details of an operation. He had had to have three piles removed '. . . the operation was formidable and excessively painfull (*sic*) and I must be upon my side in Bed for a week . . . even during the operation I thought of you in a manner to make me patient lest I should risk anything by moving'. Yet he got up to celebrate her birthday by sitting in a chair, which must have added acutely to his discomfort.

On 6th May 1792, Elizabeth and her oddly assorted companions left Nice on their way to Turin. She was a born sightseer. By horse-drawn carriage, imperturbably, she traversed the torrent of Paglione and struggled up through Alpine passes. She spent a night of concentrated discomfort in an inn at Tende, in one room accommodating the whole party. Owing to the dangerously melting snow, the next day her carriage had to be taken to bits to negotiate the crossing of the Col de Tende, and she herself negotiated the pass in a carrying-chair, as did her baby. Yet no word of complaint for all these physical hardships escaped her pen, and her enthusiasm remained unbounded.

On 11th May, in Turin, the Websters rejoined the Duchess of Devonshire and Lady Duncannon, and thereafter, for a month, Elizabeth savoured the distractions provided by that distinguished city. One day, she accompanied the sisters to an audience with the Prince and Princess of Piedmont; the rest of her time she spent sightseeing and attending lectures given by Bonvoisin, Professor of Chemistry. Towards the end of her stay, Count Masin gave a dinner in her honour, at which, as an appetiser to 'a fine dinner', the host treated his guests to 'the cruel experiment' of electrocution on a live frog.

*

Describing the enchanted gardens and fairy palace of Isola Bella, one of the Borromean Islands, the first breath of romance wafts through Elizabeth Webster's journal. In the Palace, as though in fulfilment of a spell, a fairy prince awaited her. Prince Augustus, Duke of Sussex and sixth son of King George III, was visiting the Palace at the same time. Elizabeth had not met him before and discreetly noted: 'He is handsome and well bred.'

Romance played no part in her next places of call, Milan and Pavia. In Milan, she spent her time with an old Barnabite monk, Padre Pini, collecting specimens of a particular form of felspar which he had found and named 'Adularia'. While in Pavia, her constant companion was the Director of the Museum, Lazaro Spallanzani, of whom she records: 'He is the man who has made some filthy experiments upon digestion.'

By this time, the heat was intense, with the thermometer varying between 92 and 96 degrees Fahrenheit. It did not unduly affect Elizabeth until it produced a thunderstorm. As Miss Holroyd had described, thunderstorms found her Achilles' heel and, at Pizzighettone, a village on the road to Mantua, no threat or abuse would budge her. Purposefully she built up her case in her journal: 'I was resolved to stay and not risk my life and my child's with hot horses near a deep river, during a heavy storm.' And, for the first time, she made a point of considering her child's welfare although, still only two, he had already forded a torrent and a river in flood and had crossed the Alps in a carrying-chair.

Once more the party prepared to negotiate a mountain pass, this time out of Italy through the Austrian Tyrol. As always, Elizabeth scrupulously recorded geographical details, but she was nervous, commenting on the narrowness of the road at one point 'with a precipice to the river undefended by a parapet'. She had an added reason for feeling frightened as, by this time, she was pregnant again.

She arrived in Munich low-spirited and unhappy. Small wonder! The drone's rights seem to have been those of which her husband had remained most conscious and we can feel sorry for her that none of her Webster children was conceived in love.

To the temporary discomfort of the reigning monarch (Frederick Augustus, first King of Saxony) in Dresden, Elizabeth Webster found no trouble in establishing her usual Court. His Court she grandly refused to attend, which high-handed action, far from alienating his family, resulted in 'a civil reproachful message' from one of his daughters, begging her 'to see them en particulier at one of their villas'.

Before conquering the Saxon Court, Elizabeth Webster had annexed a young English diplomat, Lord Henry Spencer (son of George, third Duke of Marlborough), at that time Secretary at The Hague under Lord Auckland. This gifted, witty young man was passing through Dresden on his way to deliver the congratulations of the British Government to the new Emperor of the Holy Roman Empire. He succumbed irresistibly to the charms of young Lady Webster, who herself cautiously admitted to her journal that he was the first man ever to produce 'the slightest emotion' in her heart. In his company she visited one of the Princesses whose brother, Prince Anthony, mistook her for Lord Henry's wife. Praising her looks to the supposedly infatuated husband, the Prince observed embarrassingly: 'I see by your admiration and love for her you are worthy to possess her.' This observation was made in the presence of ten people which, Lady Webster avowed, was 'too painful to bear'. Yet she recovered her equanimity quickly enough to enjoy her subsequent success in Dresden. Realising every woman's dream, she was daily entertained at special parties and dinners; guests were invited to meet 'La charmante Miladi'; her clothes were copied; her manners studiously observed.

At one of these parties, given on 2nd August, by the French Minister to the Court of Saxony, conversation kept on returning to the Duke of Brunswick's Manifesto, issued the week before against the people of Paris. Lady Webster observed that 'those present were alarmed by its injudiciousness'.

Ostensibly designed to protect the French Royal Family, the hectoring tone of the Manifesto had been miscalculated to effect the opposite. Together with the threat of almost immediate invasion, the people of Paris had been ordered to submit to their King, and those responsible for the uprising were proscribed to pay the penalty of rebellion with their lives. Too late anyway to do anything but harm, by the time the Manifesto was issued, the mob in Paris had already marched on the Tuileries, where it had placed the red bonnet of the Revolution on the King's head. On that occasion, it had shown him forbearance, but this mood was not to last for long. Less than six weeks later, its instigators incarcerated the King and his family in the Temple, whence he emerged only to face the guillotine.

For the first time, a note of concern for others pervaded the jottings in Lady Webster's journal, although it might be said that it took a revolution to produce it. Then, in an ensuing and prophetic paragraph, she proceeded to the defence of Charles James Fox.

By August 1792, Fox's advanced Liberalism and championship of the tenets of the French Revolution had blackened his name to the extent that, except for his band of devoted followers, he was ostracised in Parliament and declared by many of his compatriots to be an enemy of his country. And there were many who had already seen him as the moving spirit behind the formation of the Association of the Friends of the People, an association with his own ideal of Parliamentary Reform which had originated at a dinner party given by Lord Porchester, and which flared into prominence as the French Revolution gained momentum. Six weeks before, in a letter dated 15th June 1792, Thomas Pelham had written Elizabeth Webster a first-hand account of a conversation he had had with Fox on just this subject. In it Charles James had declared that he had never been consulted about the formation of the Association. 'He told me (what I knew to be the truth, notwithstanding what is *now* said) that he had never been consulted about it, and that, on the contrary, the Associators seemed determined *not to have any advice*, and particularly not to have *his*.' And his declaration was corroborated to Thomas Pelham by Lord Lauderdale who told him the formulators had been determined not to consult Fox 'until they saw the probability of success, in order that he might not be involved if it failed'. With this conclusive testimony to Fox's innocence, Lady Webster took up the cudgels for him, although, at that time, he was a stranger to her. Destiny seems to have guided her hand.

Her carriage rumbled on through Prague to Vienna, where again she had a royal reception and where, this time, she was gratified to attend the Emperor's Court. Countess Thüron was detailed to attend her everywhere as lady-in-waiting, and she was received in private audience by the Emperor and his Empress. Lord Henry Spencer had arrived ahead of her in Vienna and, whether by accident or design, he was in Pressburg when she visited that city (now Bratislava). She made a careful note that he and she parted on 25th or 26th September, 'not later', and it must have been at this time that he gave her her Blenheim spaniel, Pierrot.

In Venice, Mr Ellis fell dangerously ill with 'a putrid fever'. Thanks to the skill of a Jewish doctor, he recovered fairly quickly and the direction of the travellers then lay through Mantua, Parma, Bologna, on to Florence. There, Mr Ellis left them to return to England. On her first visit to Florence Lady Webster spared little time and no comment. Within a day or two, she and her companions were under way again, through Rome to Naples, which they reached during the first two weeks of October 1792.

CHAPTER THREE

Neapolitan Holiday

IN 1792, the Kingdom of Naples also comprised Sicily, over which King Ferdinand ruled under the complicated titles of Ferdinand IV of Naples, Ferdinand III of Sicily, and Ferdinand I of the Two Sicilies. In 1768, he had married the determined and politically ambitious Austrian princess, Maria Carolina. By far the stronger character of the two and astute where her husband was concerned, Maria Carolina had been quick to see that, by indulging his whims as hitherto, she could get power into her own hands without interference. Under her influence, Ferdinand first accepted the French Revolution, then repudiated it, and gradually veered towards a policy of negotiation with England and Austria, away from Spain, encouraged by his wife, his wife's English Minister, John Acton, and the English Ambassador and his wife, Sir William and Lady Hamilton.

Ties of consanguinity linked the Royal Family, in Naples, with King Louis XVI of France. The same Bourbon blood flowed in the veins of King Ferdinand IV while Queen Maria Carolina was Queen Marie Antoinette's sister.

*

By the time Elizabeth Webster reached Naples, she was five months gone with child. Yet her appetite for Society and sightseeing remained insatiable. Reunited with the Duchess of Devonshire and her sister and brother-in-law (now Earl and Countess of Bessborough as the old Earl had recently died), she found some old and some new acquaintances. Lady Spencer and Lady Elizabeth Foster were still there as was also the Duchess of Ancaster. But now Lord and Lady Palmerston (parents of the future Foreign Secretary) had joined the party, with Lady Plymouth and the faithful Mr Pelham. Together they explored the environs of Naples despite the growing menace of a French bombardment. Lady Webster commented that she made her 'grossesse' a pretext for staying at home in the evenings. But every morning she went out to see 'the objects most

24

worthy of notice', and friends in quantity visited her each evening. Dr
Drew reappeared; inevitably Mr Pelham was always there, and Italinski,
Russian Secretary of Legation at Naples, became a new and infatuated
acquaintance.

In January 1793, part of a squadron of the French fleet moored in the
Chiaia under the Websters' windows. During the same month King
Louis XVI was beheaded by his people, in Paris. Queen Maria Carolina's
detestation of the French revolutionaries had caused her to dismiss Mackau,
French Minister to the Court of Naples, and this high-handed action led
directly to the menacing appearance in the Chiaia of his Government's
Navy. For a moment the fate of Naples hung in the balance. Then Sir
John Acton's political astuteness saved the day. Mackau was reinstated
and, to the boos and execrations of King Ferdinand's still loyal subjects,
the French ships sailed away. The news of the French King's execution
plunged the Court of Naples into deep mourning, and even Mackau
himself professed concern for it. But Lady Webster makes no mention
of all this in her journal any more than she does of the declaration of war
by France on England and Austria, on 1st February. On 10th February,
she gave birth to her second son, Henry. After that she stuck to sightseeing.

On 22nd March, in company with the Palmerstons and Thomas Pelham,
the Websters started out on a three-day expedition, through the Apennines,
to Paestum, Salerno, and Pompeii. The first part of their journey followed
King Ferdinand's grand new road to his hunting-grounds, at Eboli, but,
thereafter, it took them through malaria-infested swamps wherein the
inhabitants lived in wretched poverty. Paestum's Doric temples Lady
Webster dismissed as 'too uneven', and she felt much more at ease in the
bustling, modern town of Salerno. On 25th March 1793, she celebrated
her twenty-second birthday, dining in the Temple of Isis at Pompeii.
Later, disarmingly, she refers to herself as: 'So old and yet so silly.'

The news of the death of her friend Lady Sheffield momentarily
sobered Elizabeth in her butterfly flight, long enough for her to pen a
pontifical letter of good advice to the bereaved daughter. ' . . . You now,
my dear Maria, must supply her place towards yr. Father . . . If you live
alone with yr. Father, you have the Duties of a Wife to fulfill (*sic*) . . . If
yr. Aunt shld. live with you, you will, from the many obligations you have
to her, know how to treat her as a Second Mother, and the only Substitute
Nature can give you for my Inestimable Friend.' Although this letter
may have annoyed Maria Josepha she did not destroy it.

The birth of a son to the young Emperor and Empress of Austria
decided the Queen of Naples to lift Court mourning in order to celebrate

B*

her grandson's advent. On 1st May, she gave a reception which was followed by another, four days later, given by Prince Esterhazy, Imperial Ambassador to the Court of Naples.

Lady Webster's success in Vienna acted as a laissez-passer and, at both these functions, she received most gracious attention from the Queen. '. . . her reason for liking me that I had been at Vienna and knew many of her old friends.' Indeed, at Prince Esterhazy's party, the Queen spent most of the evening in her company 'lively and entertaining in her conversation'. In sinister contrast, Lady Webster heard the rumour that 'the atrocious Marseillais' were at that moment marching on Paris to destroy Maria Carolina's sister, Marie Antoinette.

During the next two weeks almost daily Elizabeth Webster was on the road; to Posilippo, Baia, Misenum, Camaldoli. No classical allusion escaped her. Indefatigably, she pursued the footsteps of the great (those of Pollio, Julius Caesar, Cicero and other eminent members of the Senate) through their villas and out into their terraced gardens; even infamous Nero's, to his bath. Wandering amid the Elysian fields, her pleasure was cut short by one of her dreaded thunderstorms at the height of which her companions elected to cross the Stygian Lake to Misenum. But, for once, her classical knowledge sustained her. Pliny the elder had witnessed the fatal volcano from that spot; Tiberius had 'breathed out his gloomy soul' there.

The round of festivities continued, tabulated as enjoyed, with one exception: a musical party given one Saturday evening by the Hamiltons, at Caserta. As was her custom, 'Mullady' took the stage but, this time, not in her famous 'attitudes'. Less successfully, she elected to sing some arias by Paisiella. Lady Webster's comments were caustic and uncompromising. 'Her vile discordant screaming took off the whole effect of his simple melody.'

She attended three unusual parties given by the King himself; at Belvedere, and Carditello.

To the first, His Majesty commanded the Duchess of Devonshire and her usual coterie to dine with him in his hunting-box, at Belvedere. The Duchess's chronic unpunctuality caused his guests to arrive an hour late, yet, despite this breach of etiquette, the King showed himself 'v. pleasant and conversable'. Indeed, as the evening progressed, his pleasant attentions to Lady Webster became so marked that she was laughingly warned that she risked banishment to Calabria. Reputedly, this was no idle statement if the Queen's jealousy was aroused, but this time, luckily, it remained unprovoked, a tribute to Lady Webster's discreet behaviour.

The ceremony of the 'San Leucio marriages' (as spelt by Elizabeth) was one she was keen to see, in the little colony of San Lucio, near Caserta, where King Ferdinand had tried to establish a pocket Elysium. Here, by their acceptance of a strict code of conduct governing their spiritual and social lives, the inmates of the colony could be sure of good homes and certain employment. The costs of the colony, together with its factory for the manufacture of silk, were borne by the King himself, whose bounty was said by the malicious to claim certain rights. Elizabeth repeats the current gossip that the colony served for him 'the double purpose of seraglio and nursery'. Even if this gossip were true in part, there was little doubt that the King's aim had been to create a first idyllic state in San Lucio whose influence and prosperity would then gradually spread for the general betterment of his people. The code of laws on which it was founded have been variously ascribed, but he was personally cognizant of each section of it. On that Sunday in May 1793, it was evident to Elizabeth that the happy colonists attributed to the King himself all their happiness and well-being, and that he, in his turn, took a paternal interest in all of them. It was his tragedy that his altruistic scheme was only enacted at village level.

The Duchess's almost intolerable unpunctuality curtailed much of the spectacle for Elizabeth. She arrived too late to attend the marriage ceremonies at all, though still in good time to enjoy the subsequent festival. Throughout the day, a thousand happy people, dressed in their best, dined and danced round the King, blessing him for his goodness. And, as night fell, the Court was lit up while they danced what Elizabeth was pleased to call 'tarantulas'. The King's party dined on his farm, on home-produced food and wine from his vineyards. And at dinner Lady Hamilton extracted from him the code of rules that governed eligibility to the colony. Above her own signature, she added a postscript: 'Given to me by the King of Naples at the Belvedere of S. Lucio on the 19th day of May 1793 where Sir William and I dined with His Maj^ty and the Duchess of Devonshire, Lady Webster, Lady Plymouth, Lady Bessborough, Lady E. Foster, Sir G. Webster and Mr Pelham.'

*

Secure in her own good sense, before leaving Naples Lady Webster tried to caution Lady Plymouth to keep her flirtation with Lord Berwick within the bounds of discretion. Like Lady Plymouth, Lord Berwick was due to spend the whole summer in Naples and Lady Webster saw little likelihood of her advice being taken. She quotes Lord Palmerston as christening the infatuated couple 'Cymon and Iphigenia' as, before Lord Berwick fell in love, 'he was never heard to speak'. Love for Lady Plymouth unsealed his lips to her ultimate distress and disillusionment.

Elizabeth Webster herself had a touching farewell with Count Italinski and seems to have complacently enjoyed the poor man's distress at her departure. He told her that, after she had gone, he would do as Mark Antony did who wrote 'Timoleon' over his door, to show he had adopted misanthropy.

All the same, she softened enough to agree to sit for him to Robert Fagan, British Governor of the Ionian Isles. Italinski declared that Lady Webster only accorded the artist five minutes of her time so that, considering such restrictions, the result seems admirable. As already described, he depicts her curling auburn hair; her bright, questioning eyes beneath their delicately pencilled brows; her Grecian nose; her provocatively curving mouth, and the easy grace with which she leans against one of the Doric columns she condemns. She looks gentle, and compliant. But alas! for Italinski's aspirations! As an earnest of another love, Pierrot lies in her lap.

CHAPTER FOUR

Widening Hostilities

WHEN, IN THEIR turn, the Websters took the road to Rome their marital relations were strained to snapping-point. Now the scenes Sir Godfrey made assumed abnormal proportions. 'The same dreadful derangement. I shall soon become mad myself if I much longer witness his paroxysms.' At times Elizabeth was really frightened of him, and an impartial witness like Lady Palmerston went so far as to say that Sir Godfrey formed part of a trio disproving the adage that 'None are so bad but have some portion of good.' (Her other considered variants to the rule were Mrs North and the Duchess of Marlborough.)

The main reason for Sir Godfrey's bouts of temper was his wife's 'determined love for being abroad', and even she admitted that he was grossly overspending. '. . . his means are not proportioned to his expenses.' One act of conciliation on her part and her agreement to return to England, if only for a spell, might have averted many hours of acrimony. But she was obsessed by fear that, once back in England, her 'tormentor' might imprison her in the house she loathed. So she remained stubbornly unco-operative as he grew more threatening. Pigheadedly, she would not see that she was responsible for her husband's financial worries. Nor would she acknowledge her fault to her diary.

Yet, beneath all the toughness Elizabeth was acquiring (she called it 'knowledge of the world') a certain wistfulness began to creep into her journal. Sometimes she felt a longing for someone in whom she could confide; sometimes her 'selfish independence' chafed her. She sought to reassure herself, but an element of uneasiness persisted. 'The want of passion in my constitution will always save me from the calamity of letting my heart run away with my reason, but what will be my resource if both head and heart accord in their choice?' The need to find an answer to such a question was disquietingly unfamiliar.

Meantime, her social life continued, with the whole panorama of Rome rolling out before her. Arrived there, most of her English companions

29

were the same. But now she met some of the Romans, notably Princess Santa Croce, an ageing beauty who, 'without any share of cleverness', could still command the devotion of distinguished men, particularly Cardinal Bernis; and the Cardinal himself, with whom Elizabeth made friends. (To the credit of this extraordinary man, poet, statesman and former French Ambassador in Rome, when Elizabeth met him he was housing 'Mesdames', the aunts of Louis XVI of France, in defiance of the French Republican Government.) In Princess Santa Croce's drawing-room Elizabeth met again Augustus, Duke of Sussex, whom she had romantically encountered in 1792, in the fairy palace of Isola Bella. Now, in Rome a year later, romance was more scandalously coupled with his name as his associates were unaware that he had just secretly married Lady Augusta Murray.

With her usual thoroughness, Elizabeth visited the Vatican; the Borghese and Doria Palaces; the Villa Ludovici on the Pincian Hill; the Capitol. An impressively large proportion of statues and pictures was submitted to her searching and sometimes critical scrutiny. Yet she apologised to her journal for having to pass others by, due to her husband's impatience.

On 14th June the Websters proceeded on their way to Florence via Perugia and Arezzo, this time with 'good, gentleman-like' Mr Hodges as gooseberry. On arrival, bad news awaited Elizabeth. Her father was ill, and wrote to her from his sick-bed, begging her to return to see him, so that, at last, she had to make up her mind to go home.

As usual, she bombarded her journal with excuses: she was worried about her children as the weather was too hot for them to travel; the baby, Henry, had not had the smallpox; if she left them behind, to whom could she entrust them? Motive divulged itself behind excuse: she wanted a pledge that she could get back again. It took her ten days to arrange matters to her satisfaction, during which time, as usual, she entered with zest into the social life of the city. Eventually, Lady Shelley and her husband, Dr Stuart, undertook to look after the Webster children while their mother was away, during which time they were to be lodged 'in a good house with proper attendants'.

Elizabeth found Florence more forbidding than Rome, and less gay than Naples. She assigned to anxiety on her father's account her inability to enjoy 'the gallery'. On the other hand, she was fascinated by the Natural History Museum and by the personality of Professor Felix Fontana, its Director. Professor Fontana divided his considerable talents of theory and research between atheism, politics and the study of poison, in particular a viper's poison, with its effects on the human system. Also, he claimed to be able to bring worms and eels back from death. His presumptuous assertions were frowned on by the Church, which had already banned some of his findings from publication.

The usual pattern of Elizabeth's social life took shape. She became part of the circle round the English Minister, Lord Hervey, and his wife, constantly dining with them and accompanying them to the opera. Thomas Pelham and Henry Swinburne turned up in Florence; Elizabeth Foster heralded the Duchess of Devonshire's arrival there. And now Elizabeth Webster became acquainted with 'Madame d'Albany', widow of Prince Charles Edward, the Young Pretender.

In 1792, Louise, Princess of Stolberg-Gedern, Countess of Albany, had returned to live in Florence whence, in 1780, she had fled from her difficult husband into a convent. At that time she had sought and received the protection of her brother-in-law, Cardinal York. Subsequently, moving on to Rome, for four years she had lived there apart from Charles Edward before she was legally separated from him, in 1784. Another four years had had to elapse before he had died, but, by that time, Alfieri, Italy's leading dramatist, had become her inseparable companion, and together they had visited Paris and London. In London, King George III had received the Countess with great kindness, and had given her a pension from the privy purse of £1,600 a year. With this she and her lover (some said, her husband) had returned to Florence, where she had established a salon of international repute in her palazzo on the Lung' Arno.

At all available moments, we may suppose that Thomas Pelham was in devoted attendance on Elizabeth and that, like all possessive women, she did not want to share him. For Maria Josepha Holroyd was not alone in finding him attractive. On more than one occasion, Lady Bessborough herself had extolled T. P.'s virtues to her friend. In particular, in October 1792 she had written: '. . . I mean *your Pelham* he is the most angelic creature I ever met with in my life and if you do not absolutely adore him you are a vile unworthy ungratefull (*sic*) little Puss, not fit to be lov'd or kiss'd by any human being as pretty as you will . . .' which remonstrance may have decided Elizabeth to be more careful in future. At any rate, when Elizabeth Foster suggested that T. P. should accompany the Duchess and herself back to England, Elizabeth Webster advised T. P. against it, persuading him instead to 'go quietly with Swinburne'. So, when the Duchess and Lady Bessborough arrived in Florence they found their expected escort gone, an event smugly recorded by Lady Webster.

Again, she had an 'entrée' into the Court. Ferdinand III, Grand Duke of Tuscany, was not only the Emperor's brother but also his brother-in-law. Lady Webster availed herself of her letters of introduction to his Prime Minister, Manfredini, although, by so doing, she realised she would annoy her own English Minister. As England had been at war with France since February 1793, Lord Hervey now hated that country as a personal adversary. Protesting against the exportation of grain from neutral Tuscany to belligerent France, he was reputed to have just called the Grand Duke a fool and his Prime Minister a knave! Not considering her Ambassador's indiscretion as her concern, Elizabeth sailed ahead.

June 27th dawned, the date on which, seven years before, Elizabeth Vassall had married Sir Godfrey Webster. Now her transports against him became hysterical. In the darkness of the night her thoughts turned to suicide. She wrote pathetically: 'My children are yet too young to attach me to existence, and Heaven knows I have no close, no tender ties besides.' But dawn renewed her resilience.

Three days more remained to her, which she spent mainly in the Devonshire set. This now included Dr Drew who had become attached to it as travelling physician.

On the eve of the Websters' departure, Lord Hervey gave a ball at the British Embassy, at which the Countess of Albany introduced Lady Webster to Alfieri. The French Minister, La Flotte, was not invited, an omission considered by Elizabeth as 'a very marked insult at a neutral court'. Gossip had it that Lord Hervey's action was as much prompted by jealousy in the field of love as by his desire to humiliate the emissary of France. Whatever his motive, it ruined his diplomatic career, as he was recalled to England soon afterwards.

That night, Elizabeth parted from her friends with regret, but sanguine that she would see them soon again. The day after (2nd July 1793), under a burning sun, she and her husband left Florence.

*

Elizabeth reverted again to her reporter's notebook, through which the red thread of war now coursed, like an artery.

Before leaving Florence, already she had jotted down grim facts: the battle of Quesnoy (at which six thousand Frenchmen had killed four thousand Austrians); the concern of the Allies as to the position of Lord Hood who might attack the French fleet at sea; the trial of Philippe Egalité, who had voted for the French King's death; the defeat of the Royalists in Britanny. And in Florence, she had noted that an active Jacobin Club had openly rejoiced at any reverse sustained by the Allies. Now, she knew that her sensible course was not to get too close to the French lines, and yet her reporter's sense drove her to get as close as possible.

In intense heat, the carriages pursued their slow way up and over the Apennines and down into the Lombardy Plain. On 4th July they reached Parma. Lady Webster had 'seen' Parma in October 1792, so the party did not tarry there but continued its hazardous journey, involving a dozen ferries by night, to arrive at Piacenza a day later. Crossing the boundary into Milanese territory, the Websters' French cook had to pass himself off as a Swiss, since Frenchmen were no longer allowed to enter that State.

The Mt Cenis Pass having been proclaimed too close to enemy lines, the Websters decided to cross into Switzerland by the St Bernard Pass, if it were 'free of snow and French'. Their postbag reached them, containing an invitation to stay with Count Masin in his castle at the foot of the Alps, where they would find Mr and Mrs Trevor (the, British Minister in Turin), T. P. and Swinburne.

Count Masin's castle was strategically placed on a height dominating the valley of the Aosta. Behind it towered the Alps, while, to the east, Milan was distantly discernible across the Plain. Many times in history the French had besieged the castle which, hitherto, had proved impregnable. But shortly after the Websters stayed there it had to capitulate to the enemy.

July 10th saw the Websters on the road again, driving through country now in hectic preparation for defence against the French.

By the Treaty of Utrecht in 1713, the reigning Duke of Savoy and Piedmont had been made King of Sicily, but, in 1718, he had been obliged to exchange that Kingdom for Sardinia, over which he and his heirs continued to rule until they became Kings of Italy. On 10th July 1793, King Victor Amadeus III was actually touring his province of Savoy as the Websters passed through it. Elizabeth commented: 'The King of Sardinia is now making a progress through this part of his dominions. This costs him £25,000 in useless pomp, and he receives a subsidy from England of £200,000.' King Victor was a poor image of his father, Charles Emmanuel III. Through his weakness and extravagance, the Royal coffers had been emptied and the morale of his troops was so low that, only a few weeks after the Websters passed through it, Savoy was overrun by the armies of the French Republic.

Count Masin's house-party joined up again at a little village at the foot of the Alps. (Mr Trevor had delayed his return to Turin to try to ensure a safe passage for his compatriots over the mountains.) Mules would be difficult to come by as they were in short supply.

Hard by lay the combatant armies, neither more than three thousand strong. Through sickness and exposure, both sides were in poor shape, and it was reported that an epidemic of some sort had broken out among them.

At Aosta, the Websters lodged with a Baron Aviso, although this poor man had been already pronounced at death's door, a prey to the 'epidemical fever'. The hospital in the town was crammed with victims of the dire disease, and all through the night Elizabeth heard the mourning bell tolling while muffled drums proclaimed a burial, under her window. But, at this stage of her life, fears of infection did not worry her.

The morning of the next day (Friday, 13th July) was spent bargaining for mules to drag the Websters' carriage up the Pass. The exorbitant price of seventy louis for each carriage was demanded. Indignantly Elizabeth expostulated, but there seemed nothing to be done. And, even then, the Commandant had to issue an order allocating the mules to her carriages.

Before she left her dying host, unblushingly Elizabeth robbed him! With her usual enthusiasm, she had collected some pieces of 'steatites' and garnets embedded in quartz along her route. Now she helped herself to 'some specimens of minerals' from Baron Aviso's collection! In mild re-balance of this scandalous act she commented: 'My conscience smites me almost for the plunder.'

At six o'clock in the evening the cavalcade got under way, Lady Webster strapped to a mule, as her saddle had broken. It took six hours to reach St Rémy, where the travellers spent a wretched night. Then they set off to cross the St Bernard Pass, at half-past five next morning.

Elizabeth reverted to her old method of transport, a 'chaise à porteurs'. Once again, snow impeded progress, and it took three hours to reach the monastery. Here, the travellers were plied with food and strong drink and provided with a needed two-hour rest. Despite her exhaustion, Elizabeth recorded her disappointment at not seeing any of the St Bernard dogs, all out on their errands of mercy.

A still more hazardous journey awaited her, carried backwards down the mountain. Yet such was her 'indifference about life' that she felt 'neither hurt nor frightened'. And with her strangely unfeminine absorptions, she paused to look at a small, petrified body in a mortuary which, though shrivelled, had yet preserved all its features in perfect condition after a year's exposure to the rarefied air. Frogs, snakes, eels, worms, human beings: what a career in biology she might have had!

Now Italy was behind the travellers and their passage through Switzerland began. At Vevey, on 16th July, Mr Hodges met the Websters with a packet of letters. Her father was better; her children were well. As usual, T. P. supplied political news. Events in Paris were still 'disgusting and bloody'; Lord Yarmouth had gone on a diplomatic mission to Frankfurt; Lord Porchester, 'as a reward for deserting Mr Fox, whose party was breaking up apace', had been made an earl; Mr Fox's debts were to be paid by subscription from his friends, and he was to be given an annuity of £3,000 a year.

The sight of Lausanne filled Elizabeth with brief melancholy. Poor Lady Sheffield's apartment was empty; Gibbon had left for England. Across the lake from Madame Cerjat's garden, Elizabeth could see 'the detested tricolor' flag flying from the tree of Liberty at Evian. And clearly over the water, she could hear the enemy drums.

The Duchess of Ancaster (now very frail and ill) was in Lausanne, and two young Englishmen, one of them Lord Morpeth (afterward sixth Earl of Carlisle). Lady Webster found the latter very attractive and was chagrined to see that his attentions were taken up elsewhere. For a moment she considered setting herself up as the other lady's rival, but discretion prevailed. With a big sop to her journal she declared that 'a pretty woman is always sure of as many lovers as she chooses; but to me there would be more humiliation than glory in such a train'. Despite these sentiments of renunciation, Lord Morpeth was destined to become her lifelong though platonic friend.

Within earshot of the enemy, Elizabeth still contrived to amuse herself, notably one evening 'at Casanova's Ball'. In between her social engagements she inserted items of murder and bloodshed: Charlotte Corday's assassination of Marat; the continued siege of Valenciennes. She spoke up for La Fayette, then in confinement at Magdebourg, and recorded the beheading of Charlotte Corday and her heroic conduct to the last. She chronicled the terrifying hysteria with which the women of Paris had appeared before the Bar of the Convention, screaming that their children should adopt the name of Marat, and that they themselves would renounce forever all creeds and beliefs other than those taught by him and incorporated in the new Constitution. And she recorded Lord Grenville's snub to General Dumouriez in England where the General had sought asylum after his final condemnation as a traitor, by the French Convention.

Then the news of the Royalist Army improved, and some said it was within sixteen miles of Paris. Nantes had been in counter-revolution for thirty-six hours; Lyons, though full of Republicans, was supposedly hostile to the Convention. Elizabeth became impatient to reach Valenciennes before General Ferraris: otherwise, he might get there before she could witness its siege.

An ardent Mr Douglas tried to tack himself on to the Websters when they resumed their journey. but Elizabeth dealt with him coldly and he returned to Lausanne. Boredom in its extremest form attacked her at Berne, which she described as 'the neatest, dullest, cleanest town'. Grudgingly, she admitted that it was more magnificent than might have been expected of the capital of a canton about the size of an English county; also, that it had wide, clean streets, and that its houses were built on arcades 'like dear, dear Italy'. But, other than that, she would admit nothing. On she went, depressed by the thought that, with each step, she was approaching nearer to England. 'Oh I abhor the thoughts of living in that country. No friends, few relations!'

Through the canton of Lucerne the Websters took the road to Baden; crossed the Rhine at Kaiserstükl and reached Schaffhausen on 28th July. They were advised to avoid the Basle road as being too near the French frontier for safety so, travelling through the old Hercynian Forest, still inhabited by wild boar and wolves, they proceeded, through Stuttgart, to reach Mannheim, on 1st August. They found the town a centre of military activity, garrisoned by six thousand men, with troops constantly passing through it and couriers hurrying to and fro. Despite the sense of tension, Elizabeth contrived to visit the picture gallery and to examine 'some beautiful specimens of mineralogy' (carefully guarded we hope).

Having missed the siege of Valenciennes, she had the opportunity to read the Duke of York's ultimatum and Articles of Capitulation. By his Articles, members of the garrison were to be allowed to return to France but to be on parole and still to consider themselves prisoners of war. Elizabeth felt sceptical as to their abiding by these terms, adding that 'were I the Government of France, they should not' (a feminine view which accorded only too well with the French view, later). Lord Yarmouth told her that there had been a parley after the Duke had delivered his terms during which many people had fled from the beleaguered city. The first intimation he had had that they had been accepted was when the Director of the town's theatre had come out to ask him what music he desired to be played.

When the Websters departed from Mannheim they found the road crowded with cavalry, troops, ammunition and transport waggons, wounded, and all the stragglers and hangers-on of an army at war. A shortage of posthorses held them up for three hours at Worms. Following along the course of the Rhine, they found the road almost unnegotiable as a result of the heavy artillery which had been dragged along it to the siege of Mainz. Soon after, Elizabeth got her first view of a pontoon bridge. The outskirts of Mainz had been totally destroyed (its final capitulation to the Prussians had taken place on 25th July); the Cathedral was in ruins and the Electoral Palace had been converted into a hospital. Fields of sprouting corn and unpruned vines added their unkemptness to the desolate scene. Again the Websters' progress was held up for want of horses, and this time for a grimmer reason: the French had eaten many of them to stave off starvation during the siege.

Somehow, the carriages struggled on to Frankfurt; then to Königstein, always held up by the want of horses. Königstein had surrendered to the Russians after an heroic resistance of two months, finally worn down by famine. Among the people Elizabeth sensed a feeling of hatred against their former masters. The new doctrine of egalitarianism was becoming attractive to many.

On their journey from Königstein to Coblenz the Websters met some Austrian soldiers marching from Linz to Brabant. One poor boy was writhing on the ground with colic. With the best intentions, Lady Webster gave him money, on this occasion a doubtful pain-killer. Then she gave him a lift in her second carriage until she found a baggage waggon to transfer him to. No officer appeared to challenge her high-handed action, in either case.

At Düsseldorf, where the Websters found the gates shut against them, they were forced to spend the night on a floor crawling with bugs, spiders, and earwigs. Lady Webster commented that she was 'never really annoyed by any gîte before this'.

Her reporting varied. At Aix-la-Chapelle she heard the news that Marie Antoinette had been moved to the Conciergerie; Maestricht she was impressed by as a strongly fortified town (then held by the Dutch) which had resisted a siege; at Tongres, her progress was again held up through lack of horses. It took four days to reach Brussels, where the Websters arrived, on 14th August.

There, a budget of letters awaited Elizabeth, mainly from T. P. and her father; and an indiscreet one from Lord Henry Spencer, proposing to steal away from The Hague (where he was now 'en poste') to meet her in Brussels. Elizabeth was attracted by his suggestion and decided to let circumstances govern her behaviour should he arrive before she left. He was switched to Stockholm before he could do so and was destined never to see her again before his untimely death in Berlin, three years later.

Elizabeth found Brussels unchanged from the town she had visited nine years before when, as a child of thirteen, she had gone there with her father. Most of Paris society seemed to have moved there, among it Count Fersen, who came to see her. Of the English, she mentions Lord Elgin, British Minister there, later famous for his acquisition of the Elgin Marbles, who took a lot of trouble to gratify her wish to see Valenciennes; and Colonel St Leger, who had come over with many of his compatriots to take a look at the armies.

Armed with 'quantities of passports', on 20th August 1793, Elizabeth and her husband started out 'very sullenly' for Valenciennes. They went through the battlefield of Jemappes, fought over the previous November. Prosaically, Elizabeth reported that, though the plain was now covered with newly made graves, she saw no human skeletons, only those of a few horses. Enormous quantities of ammunition and army waggons were still to be seen. Just outside Valenciennes, an impressive array of artillery and cannon balls were guarded by a small company of Austrian soldiers. Valenciennes itself was almost totally destroyed, the tragic outcome of forty-three days of continual siege. On the penultimate day, a special concentration of cannon balls had been used. The devastation caused by them was decisive. Two thousand five hundred men, women and children were reported to have perished during the siege, the faint-hearted being crammed into hospital vaults so that their lamentations could not be heard by the garrison and civil defenders. Elizabeth noted that, here, Dampierre, the Citizen-General of the French, had fought to the death and his monument, 'a tree of liberty decorated with military trophies', had been erected in the nearby camp of Famars.

The Websters dined that evening in company with two Englishmen, 'Mr Hobart and Mr Meyrick', who brought them news that the Duke of York, intent on reaching Ypres, had unexpectedly encountered some Republican forces at Tourcoing. In the subsequent engagement his vanguard, composed of Dutch troops, had been forced to retire, and the detachment of 'Guards' sent to their relief had sustained a loss of two hundred men, including their Colonel killed, and many wounded.

Like Helen of Troy, Elizabeth walked on the ramparts—of Valenciennes. Here she was accosted by an Austrian grenadier, who told her that he wished she were his wife so that she could mother a future race of grenadiers. Oddly enough, the same compliment had been paid her the year before by one of his compatriots, in Prague!

On 22nd August, Elizabeth and her husband continued on their way towards the coast, still along roads crowded with troops and transport. Between St Amand and Tournai she took fright, mistaking some horsemen in the dusk for French hussars. They found the inn at Tournai full of English soldiers. The nearer they got to the seat of war, the more contradictory became the news. The Duke of York was reported to be at Ypres; then at Furnes; then at neither place. Bluntly, Elizabeth reported that they met the Dutch troops 'who had run away on the 18th', now to be used to garrison the towns, their morale being suspect in battle. At Menin she met a wounded English officer, Colonel Doyle, 'with a deep wound in his arm and a contusion on his knee'.

Although the Websters were advised not to pursue their way towards Ypres, they decided to go on. Hardly surprisingly, Lady Webster felt 'Queer, not to say frightened'. They passed within two miles of the French lines. Then they met an Englishman who said that he had just left Furnes and that the Duke's army was now preparing to lay siege to Dunkirk.

The Websters were told that the Austrians were displeased with the lenient terms of the Duke's decree of capitulation for Valenciennes. He had spared the lives of two of the deputies who had voted for the French King's death and, as Elizabeth had already anticipated, the French members of the garrison, far from considering themselves immune from further active service as prisoners of war, were at that moment reported to be hurrying to the defence of Dunkirk. Precariously, the Webster carriages traversed the road through Ypres to Furnes, at one point within a hundred yards of the enemy. At Furnes, accommodation seemed impossible, so Elizabeth prepared to spend the night in her carriage in the market square. But at that point an hospitable old woman made her welcome to her little parlour. This was devoid of furniture except for one big chair and a cupboard filled with Delft china cups, so Elizabeth lay on the floor on blankets. A small, adjacent bedroom she yielded up to Sir Godfrey to prevent him from becoming 'outrageously discontented'.

Through the night Elizabeth heard the cannon detonating before Dunkirk, and, from the belfry of the church at Furnes, she saw the horizon lit up with red flames and smoke and the conflagration from five villages. News came of the death of General (Count) 'd'Alton' and Colonel Elde. It was not altogether extraordinary that she passed 'a wretched night'. Her reporter's sense was quelled, though not for long. There was a feeling among the English officers with whom Elizabeth spoke that it was unwise to attempt to invest Dunkirk without the Austrians. (The Austrians were at that moment besieging Quesnoy, the scene of their defeat two months earlier.) And some of the officers even doubted the advantages to be gained by the capture of Dunkirk.

As though by magnet, the Websters were drawn nearer and nearer to the danger zone. Only six miles separated them from the British camp and now the road was pure sand, running between high dunes and the sea. Thirteen dead horses lay across it. These had to be dragged away to allow the carriage to pass and it was at this point that General Dalton had been killed. The English camp was still in the making as they had only captured this bit of ground the day before. Lady Webster was made welcome to Captain Cerjat's tent and then, almost as a matter of course, she went to view the corpse of General Dalton.

On hearing of her arrival, the Duke of York sent to invite her and, presumably, her husband to dinner. All his staff dined with him, and Elizabeth professed to feel 'odd' at being the only woman in such male company. At dinner, the Duke inveighed against the Duke of Richmond for failing to send the ordnance. (Later, the Duke of Richmond, Master-General of Ordnance from 1783 to 1795, blamed the Duke of York for this same failure.) To add to the troubles of the General in command, the cannon and artillery-carriages had been sent by different routes, and so did not arrive together.

After dinner, Lady Webster attended Colonel Elde's funeral, which she found 'an affecting sight'. Startled at first by the firing over the grave, after the first discharge she did not mind it. But she refused to attend another funeral, professing to be 'low-spirited'. So, to cheer her up, Colonel St Leger drove her round the camp in a cabriolet. This tour was cut dramatically short by an army chaplain, who galloped after them to warn them they were about to enter the danger zone. They walked instead upon the dunes, but again Lady Webster was warned that she was near enough to be shot at by French marksmen.

Returning to the Duke of York's tent, Elizabeth became aware of a patter, like rain, on the canvas. When the Duke's aide-de-camp burst in to say that the outposts (of Dunkirk) had been driven in and a general attack might now be expected, the Duke upbraided him for alarming the lady! Thereafter, to allay her rising panic, he gave his orders clearly. He asked Elizabeth to give the watchword which, when she declined, he gave as 'Elizabeth and Success . . . or something to that purpose'. Then, to deaden the sound of the guns, he ordered his band of musicians to play until she left. And finally, he ordered 'an escort of several light dragoons' to accompany her back to Furnes. On the field of battle surely such courtesy was unique?

*

The Websters crossed over to England from Ostend, and, on 1st September 1793, Elizabeth was reunited with her father at Windsor. Thereafter she visited the Wyndhams, at Bignor, and T. P.'s parents, at Stanmer. ('Mr Pelham was there and, of course, delighted to see me.') Nothing would induce her to go back to Sir Godfrey's house, at Battle. Instead, she lodged at the Deanery.

Her defiance was as injudicious as it was tactless. By October, Elizabeth must have realised she was again with child, and her jealous husband might well have traced back her conception to those few days at Stanmer.

CHAPTER FIVE

Introduction to Politics

BY THE TIME Lady Webster reluctantly returned to her native land, England had been at war with France for seven months. At the outset, no one had expected that war against such an undisciplined rabble as the French Armies of the Convention could last more than a few weeks. But the continued Allied reliance on traditional methods of warfare made them increasingly vulnerable to the new conscript French army, which had replaced line movements by smaller mobile forces moving at the double, unencumbered by heavy artillery and supplies.

In 1793, England had been put on a war footing, and even gentle, peace-loving T. P. had been pressed into military service with the Sussex Militia, which force he and his parents obviously expected Sir Godfrey to join, on his return. In fact, this belief had prompted Lady Pelham's invitation to Lady Webster to stay at Stanmer. Writing on 23rd August, T. P. had told Elizabeth that his mother sent her 'everything that is kind' and his father hoped she would make Stanmer her headquarters 'if you come with Sir G. to camp'. And, in the same letter, he had said he was writing 'Webster' to offer him a bed 'till he can arrange his tent etc.'

But no ties of loyalty bound Elizabeth, other than those to her sick father. To her, war meant a series of scoops for her journal, not a campaign of honour and endurance bound by treaty to allies. No ties mean no roots. After the briefest sojourn at Battle ('that detested spot where I had languished in solitude and discontent the best years of my life') she was off to stay with Lord Sheffield at Sheffield Park, near Uckfield. Sir Godfrey seems to have gone to camp for a short time and, later on, to Camberley, as T. P. escorted Lady Webster to Sheffield Park without him.

Elizabeth found Lord Sheffield still a disconsolate widower with Maria Josepha doing the honours for her father. 'The whole family were affected at seeing me.' That its feelings were mixed is revealed by Maria Josepha's letters to her friend, Ann Firth, written before and after Lady Webster's visit.

Having already announced Lady Webster's arrival in England, in a letter of 12th September 1793, Maria writes to Miss Firth: 'Lady Webster (or the Diavo-lady) will be at Stanmer this week, and (hang her!) next week she will probably do us the honour of a visit and I believe Tom (Mr Pelham) with her. I had rather see old Beelzebub a thousand times!' But later Maria admits that 'she chose to be v. amiable, affectionate and tender and, for her, as little nonsensical as one cld. reasonably expect'. Nevertheless, she mercilessly ridicules Lady Webster's account of 'the Camp, near Dunkirk' and damns as sadistic her necrological interest. 'She went to see General Dalton before he was buried and talked of the dead bodies on the field of Battle . . . with as much Rapture as any Vulture might be supposed to do. I do not give her credit for half the unfeelingness she pretends to, or I shld. begin to question if she were not really an Infernal.'

Finally, Maria Josepha tells Ann that 'Her Ladyship has entirely adopted Foreign Manners and Customs, our Family will, I suppose, never recover from the astonishment they were thrown into when they discovered André, the Italian, washed his Lady's feet when she went to Bed . . .' Devoutly, Maria Josepha concludes: 'She says she means to go abroad in ten days, and Heaven grant she may keep her Resolution . . .'

All the same, Lord Sheffield valued Lady Webster's opinion enough to consult her about remarrying. She recommended him to marry T. P.'s sister, the Hon. Lucy Pelham, which wise advice he acted on a year later, to everyone's satisfaction.

Elizabeth decided next to visit 'Brightelmstone', where the Prince of Wales, jealous of his younger brother's high command, was making great play with his regiment. The Prince went out of his way to show her attention. Vying with her recent entertainment by the Duke of York on the field of battle, his elder brother laid on a military parade to amuse Elizabeth, while she breakfasted with him in his tent.

Now back in her old rôle at Devonshire House, the Duchess warmly welcomed Lady Webster, whose real introduction to the Whig Party dates from that moment. Up till then, there is no record that she ever set out to study the rival parties of Pitt and Fox. Her one consistent loyalty in life was as a pupil and, at that time, her political mentor was Thomas Pelham. In her reporter's notebook, she had jotted down fluctuations in Fox's fortunes, as told her by T. P. Thus, her opinions had been second-hand.

Now, over a year later, Fox's continued championship of the French Revolution, despite its reign of terror and bloodshed, and his persistent harrying of Pitt's war effort, had split the Whig Party from end to end. (T. P. himself was in favour of war.) By September 1793, many of Fox's friends had deserted him, including, most notably, Edmund Burke. Yet, still, he retained one unswerving and powerful ally, Georgiana, Duchess of Devonshire.

As early as 1774, on her début in London as a great hostess, the Duchess had espoused Charles James's cause. Her allegiance had been personal before it became political, then its two facets merged together and, for thirty years, she gave him her unstinted support in any project that interested him. She entertained for him, canvassed for him, and upheld him in and out of office. And to help and amuse him she threw open the doors of Devonshire House to all sorts of people: intellectuals, gambling lowbrows, foreign emissaries, actors, playwrights—and always, without question, all his friends. When Elizabeth Webster appeared on the scene, Fox and his followers had been in Opposition for nine years. But this made no apparent difference in Devonshire House. The intrigue, the flirting, the gambling went on, and if, at the outset, Elizabeth gave to the Whig Party a largely social interpretation, she can hardly have been blamed.

During that autumn of 1793, she makes no mention of meeting Fox himself at Devonshire House, but she meets many of his associates: Lady Melbourne; the young Duke of Bedford ('Loo'), latest adherent to Charles James and his party; 'Mr Grey', just making his mark in Whig politics; Richard Brinsley Sheridan. Dazzled though she might be, she shows a certain shrewdness in describing these stars. Lady Melbourne is 'uncommonly sensible and amusing', but Elizabeth sees through her as an adventuress, comparing her to Madame de Merteuil in *Les Liaisons Dangereuses*; 'Loo' Bedford (Lady Melbourne's top favourite at this moment) she declares to be magnificently generous to everyone but 'quite brutal from the brusquerie of his manners'; and she notes Charles Grey as 'the bien aimé of the Duchess; he is a fractious and exigeant lover'. Two years before, for reasons undisclosed, Sheridan had been very rude to Elizabeth, but now, in the Duchess's drawing-room, she prepares to forgive him. The more so as she is moved to compassion for him over the recent death of his beautiful wife, Elizabeth Linley.

That autumn, in London, even in the midst of her social engagements, Elizabeth Webster discovered that Professor Higgins was giving some lectures on chemistry and, to the surprise of the Duchess's other friends, she induced Georgiana to rise early to attend them.

With commendable honesty, she told her journal that her manners had improved, and that some of her success must be due to her aura of novelty 'as coming from abroad'. Her evenings were spent attending receptions at Devonshire House; or at the theatre. And she was presented at Court by Lady George Cavendish, the Duke of Devonshire's aunt.

The contrast between ducal and Royal entertaining should have surprised Elizabeth. She had become accustomed to the large polyglot receptions at Devonshire House but, at the Court presided over by King George III and Queen Charlotte, she would have found a small unpretentious assembly, limited to the heads of patrician families and dignitaries of Church and State. Even before his illness in 1788, neither the King nor his Queen had made any attempt to keep up with the outside world, much less with the circle round the Duchess of Devonshire which, they considered, had seduced the Prince of Wales. Their talk was limited to family or domestic matters. On first acquaintance that evening, the King discussed his son Frederick Duke of York with Lady Webster and the subject he chose was the siege of Dunkirk. Lady Webster must have been pleased to attend the Court at St James's as, of all the European Courts, it was the most exclusive. And her gratification must have increased when the Queen upbraided her 'very crossly' for her determination to return to Florence.

Throughout her three months in England, her journal was filled with a record of her own outstanding success, at the very top of the social ladder. She never mentioned the execution of the French Queen, although that terrible event took place while she was in London. In fact, only once does Elizabeth refer to the war with France at all, and that was after meeting Edmund Burke at dinner, which took place in the house of Sir Gilbert Elliot, just appointed Joint Commissioner of civil affairs in Toulon.

Elizabeth found Burke full of enthusiasm over the recent surrender of Toulon to the Allies. Eloquently, he discoursed on the renewed possibility of restoring the 'Cocarde Blanche' (emblem of Bourbon kings) to that town and of once more raising the Royal Standard in France. (It was Burke's support of the Bourbon dynasty and Fox's detestation of it that had led to their final rupture.) Only one small fort stood in the way of the Allies, 'The Heights of St Ann's.' 'Aye, St Ann's is always in the way!' exclaimed Burke, referring to Charles James's home, St Anne's Hill, at Chertsey; and to his now implacably pacifist views.

*

Before starting back to Florence, Elizabeth heard that William Wyndham had been appointed to succeed the indiscreet Lord Hervey as British

Minister there; and that Lord Hervey, still not understanding the reason for his recall, was making immediate plans to return there.

Alarmed by stories of French privateers in the Channel, before leaving Dover, the Websters appealed to Admiral Peyton to detail a cutter for their protection. Then, on 2nd December 1793, they left the English coast and reached Ostend in fifteen hours, after a rough passage. 'Tormented by the impertinence and exactions of the Douane', they had no wish to tarry and, arriving in Brussels at three in the morning on 4th December, they found the town as crowded as they had left it, and had to put up again at the Belle Vue, not at all to their taste.

Various items of news assailed Elizabeth's ears, and one for which she was genuinely sorry. The Duchess of Ancaster, her companion on so many delightful trips, had recently died in Lausanne. Lord Yarmouth told Elizabeth of the hatred now existing between the combatant armies, causing many of the wounded in hospital to refuse to eat the same food 'or lie in the same room'. And, gloomily, he predicted that Toulon was untenable.

Elizabeth shocked the company at supper with Lord Elgin by her announcement that William Wyndham had been appointed to Florence. He had passed the previous winter in Brussels where he had not been popular. 'Comment donc? Ce petit polisson, ce petit Jacobin?' And Lord Elgin was himself incredulous 'that such a man could be employed'.

On 7th December Lady Webster was again entertained by Lord Elgin, this time to dinner. And before the end of the meal Lord Herbert appeared, at that time commanding the 2nd Dragoon Guards, and talked exclusively to Lady Webster for the rest of the evening. (She asserts, from eight o'clock until twelve!) He joined her in bemoaning the Duke of York's unpopularity, partly due, he thought, to his bad manners. (After the gallant way in which the Duke had behaved to her, did Lady Webster not refute this charge?) Lord Herbert told Elizabeth that no man with military experience could despise the French armies. And throughout the evening he impressed her with his sensible views.

On 9th December, the Websters were under way again, and jolted over an execrable road for the next five days. At Remagen, they caught up with six hundred Carmagnol prisoners. Many of these were boys of fifteen and sixteen, half-naked and crying from cold and exposure, their bare feet cut to pieces from the sharp flints in the roads. Huddled on top of each other, their sick and wounded were dragged along in small carts. Again Lady Webster tried to ease their sufferings with money, but the 'impitoyable' Austrian corporal kept her bounty for himself.

Despite slippery roads, wrong turnings and the final breaking of the springs of Lady Webster's carriage, her cortège reached Mannheim on 18th December, where she found the fortifications much strengthened. Bad news from Toulon soon reached Mannheim, fully justifying Lord Yarmouth's fears. For four months, Republican troops had been besieging the town, finally outnumbering the Allied garrison by more than two to one and, on 18th December, it had had to be evacuated.

Through Heidelberg Elizabeth and her husband dragged on to Stuttgart where, once again, lack of horses held them up. After Stuttgart, they spent twenty-four hours in continuous travel and, at seven o'clock on the morning of 23rd December, they lurched into Ulm.

Details of the final evacuation of Toulon caught up with the travellers. Near Verona, Lord Hervey passed them during the night, carrying the relevant despatches. Although so heavily outnumbered, the Allies had managed to evacuate the town in an orderly manner, but at Mantua, three English officers added their own tale of disillusionment to failure. All three had fought in defence of Toulon where, they contended, disaffection among the Allies had undermined their success. The inhabitants had played a double game between the besieged and besieging forces, and Burke's dream of raising the 'Cocarde Blanche' in Toulon already had faded to nothing. What the three English officers did not know was that a young artillery officer, Napoleon Bonaparte, had conducted the siege of the town.

*

On 8th January 1794, Elizabeth was reunited with her children in Florence. She found them flourishing, 'Webby' (the elder) much improved; the baby, Henry, 'as perfect a lazzarone as the Chiaia ever produced'. Rather lacking in enthusiasm, she pronounced him 'a nice child but far from pretty'. She found five letters cautioning her against taking her family to Naples where smallpox was raging. Rumour said that seven thousand children had succumbed to the virulent infection, among them Lady Plymouth's baby. So, with commendable courage, Elizabeth decided to have Henry 'inoculated' against smallpox by an Italian doctor, Gianetti.

In Florence, anti-British feeling was stronger than ever. Due to Lord Hervey's bludgeoning, the Grand Duke had agreed to dismiss the French Minister, La Flotte, and now stood committed to a breach of neutrality. Manfredini told Elizabeth that England would cause 'the ruin of Italy' which he could have saved by his own 'temporising measures'. Terror, due to French Republican successes, mounted daily and, in her journal,

Elizabeth voices her own growing admiration for the enemy troops. 'The French are successful everywhere, and will not be conquered by our vain taunts and boasts; they verify what they say of themselves: "Que la France ne sera jamais domptée, que par la France".' Fox's indoctrination, by remote control, was beginning to have its effect.

On 29th January 1794, two young Englishmen appeared in Florence: Lord Granville Leveson-Gower and Henry Richard Fox, Lord Holland. Two years before, Elizabeth had met Lord Granville in Dresden, and now described him as 'remarkably handsome and winning'. She might have been less well-disposed towards him had she known what he first said of her.

Writing to his mother, Lady Stafford, from Dresden, in August 1792, Lord Granville had told her that he had met Sir Godfrey and Lady Webster. 'He and his wife are very civil to us (to Lord Granville and his travelling companion, Lord Boringdon), by which I mean asking us to Dinner and Supper constantly, but they do not agree together, and their jarrings might as well not be made matters of publick observation. You may perhaps imagine that we should do better to cut them and live more with the natives, but the people come il faut are all out of town, and will remain in the country till the middle of September . . .' Equally, Lord Granville might have been concerned to discover how much Lady Webster already knew about him: of his sensational success in Paris, in January 1791, when, at the age of seventeen, he had been introduced to Parisian Society by Lady Sutherland as her 'beau beau-frère'; and of his initiation by her into the dangers of gambling. And he might even have been grateful to her for her refutation as 'calumny' of the scandalous gossip that his sister-in-law had fallen in love with him.

Lord Holland's looks did not impress Elizabeth. He had come to Florence after some months spent in Spain where he had become very sunburnt and 'of the Moresco hue'. But, for her, he had a disability of irresistible appeal, an ossification of the muscles of his left leg. When Professor Fontana delivered a treatise on the dangerous and sometimes fatal implications of the disease, Elizabeth was enthralled. And when Lord Holland's gaiety transcended his infirmity, she found him 'quite delightful'. But his enthusiasm for the dangerous politics of his uncle, Charles James Fox, was such that she thought him fortunate to be abroad 'out of the way of saying foolish, violent things'. (An acquaintance of Lady Stafford had already reported Holland as being 'a veritable sans culotte'.)

William Wyndham had not yet arrived. And Lady Webster was apprehensive that his tact might be no better than that of Lord Hervey.

Samuel Vassall's monument in King's Chapel,
Boston, Mass.

Anthony Morris Storer, bibliophile, Elizabeth Vassall's
'mental benefactor'. By Sir Martin Archer-Shee

Now it looked as though he could not make up his mind to leave the political arena in England. Some time before, he, Thomas Grenville and Thomas Pelham had left the Opposition ostensibly to 'uphold the Administration' of William Pitt. Rather smugly, they had named themselves 'the Virtuous Triumvirate', an empty title as thereafter they had refused to give it substance by accepting the responsibilities of office. So, while Wyndham stayed on in England, Lord Hervey continued to carry out his duties in Florence.

One of these was to retrieve Sir Gilbert Elliot from shipwreck, off Leghorn. Sir Gilbert had been on his way back to Toulon from Tuscany, where he had successfully accomplished his mission to the Grand Duke, to get him to admit Toulonese emigrants into his country. The shipwreck was not serious and, on 31st January, Sir Gilbert had informed his wife: 'I was yesterday shipwrecked but nevertheless I arrived at Leghorn without even having wetted my feet.' Lord Hervey brought him back to Florence and, on 6th February, took him to spend an evening with Lady Webster.

Some Englishmen (and Scots) undergo a metamorphosis abroad and such a man was Sir Gilbert Elliot. At home he was the most devoted of husbands. In Florence he developed a passion for Lady Webster whom he pursued with relentless vigour until one evening, returning from the Pergola, when his importunities became so pressing that she had to leave her carriage for the street. At first, she encouraged him ('Distress, awkwardness and good nature united made me act like a fool'), but she was not prepared to go beyond conventional limits. And she assured her journal that she was shocked by Sir Gilbert's hypocritical quotation: 'Pêcher en *secret*, n'est point pêcher.'

During calmer moments, his conversation was informative and he told Elizabeth that he had landed recently in Corsica, 'unlike any country in civilised Europe'. Having already suffered from attempted Jacobin infiltration, Paoli, the Island Chief, had rallied the whole population round him against the French, and now maintained his compatriots in a state of alertness and obedience, without a single officer or any military organisation. Recently, he and his islanders had offered to put themselves under the protection of England, which protection Sir Gilbert was anxious they should have, as he himself was keen to be the island's governor. (Subsequently, he achieved this ambition.) Sir Gilbert professed great admiration for the Corsicans, 'a hardy, bold and intrepid race', in which each man was equal to his neighbour with respected rights and freedoms.

c

One young Corsican had interpreted these freedoms differently. Since 1789, Napoleon Bonaparte had attributed their inspiration to the theories of Jean Jacques Rousseau. Because of this, he and his family had become suspect to Paoli and, in May 1792, they had had to flee the island. Since then, they had renounced the soil of Corsica and Napoleon Bonaparte had declared himself a Frenchman.

CHAPTER SIX

Damage Beyond Repair

AT A DISTANCE, T. P. had the courage to be censorious, in the face of Lady Webster's determination to ignore the war. For now her husband could not remain away from England indefinitely, without special leave. Sternly, T. P. writes his inamorata on 22nd January 1794:

I received very unexpectedly a letter from Sr G. dated January 5. I find that the die is cast and that he stays with you for some months at least and is proceeding with you immediately to Naples. Having given my sentiments very fully in a letter written to Florence I have only to do what I promised in that letter and I shall write to Sr G. recommending him for staying. I will do anything in my power to satisfy the D.(uke) of Richmond and those who may think it extraordinary. We are unfortunately removed at such a distance from each other that it is better to avoid any discussion of points in which we do not agree, and they are so few I hope that it will not cramp our correspondence in any degree. It requires six weeks to obtain an answer to anything that is proposed three weeks more before a reply can be received, and three weeks more before it can be known whether the reply is satisfactory so that three months will elapse before any decision is made in any subject concerning which there may be a difference of sentiment. To promote yr. happiness is so decidedly the object of my life, that the only difference or hesitation that can ever arise must be about the means. Therefore under the circumstances I shall without hesitation forward yr. wishes towards that object without exercising any judgement of my own ... God grant that yr. success in making him *stay* against his inclinations which is evidently the case may be productive of all the advantages and happiness you expect ...

The answer as to how Lady Webster induced two men of conscience to forswear their principles to please her seems to lie in the next part of T. P.'s letter.

... I have seen Mrs Wyndham this morning who has cleared up many doubts upon my mind by telling me what yr. situation is. I need not tell you whether she calmed my mind and gave me that sort of consolation which enables (me) to undergo this worry with peculiar satisfaction; I shall certainly exert myself to the utmost for you have often said that any marks of Friendship shown to Sr G. have been attended with good effects on his conduct towards you and I shall continue

51

as far as I may be able to keep him in that sort of temper as may make his séjour with you in the particular situation you are now in as comfortable as possible.

Each man believed, in his own conceit, that he fathered her coming child.

Having administered his rebuke, T. P. reverted to his usual habit of writing to Elizabeth two or three times a week, as always conscientiously numbering his letters which, gradually, began to outnumber her replies.

As we have seen, some time before, he, Thomas Grenville and William Wyndham had joined the 'Administration' of William Pitt. Now T. P. attends Parliament regularly and his letters become full of details of debates.

About the middle of January (1794), he is preparing to oppose a motion to withdraw our troops from the battlefront ('Peace is gained by War'); he has attended a meeting at Burlington House, together with Wyndham, Lord Mansfield and others 'all agree to support the war'. Again in January, he reports to Elizabeth that 'the D.(uke) of P(ortland) had seen Fox and told him very frankly that he intended to support the war and the Administration. Fox with his usual candour admitted that those who supported the war ought to resist any attempt of opposition to censure the conduct of it.' On 22nd January, T. P. assures Elizabeth that the Duke of Devonshire, too, supports the war. By every means he seeks to promote in her the patriotic loyalty of an Englishwoman.

He tries a new tack. He has dined with her parents at Golden Square. Both of them are worried that Elizabeth 'intends to settle at Naples'. T. P. begs her to set all their minds at rest that this is not so. Her mother is 'in anxiety and distress' at Elizabeth's wish that she shall join her there. She can neither leave Mr Vassall nor bring him on such a journey.

On 4th February, T. P. writes that he hopes again to bring Sir Godfrey's name forward as candidate for Seaford, where the former member had vacated his seat. He tells Elizabeth that Pitt's Budget (for 1794) is due on the following day, asking for a loan of thirteen million pounds, to be accompanied by a Bill on Bankers' foreign funds. On 16th February, he refers to alarm in the City over the possibility of a French invasion.

Lady Webster parries T. P.'s thrusts by an account of her bad headaches, and his resistance melts away at once. By 21st February, he is upbraiding her miserably for her unaccountable reticence '. . . you are not only silent about being with child but have not even insinnuated (*sic*) that Sr G. was to go with you to Naples and *resign* his commission . . . all this appears so inconsistent with the frankness and simplicity of your character that it worries me to death . . .' And, after all his strongmindedness, on

3rd March, he promises huffily never to press her again to return to England.

By this time, Elizabeth is badly behind with her numbered letters. For, in young Lord Holland, she has just found a new tutor with the fervent bias of his uncle, Charles James Fox, against the continued pursuit of war with France.

*

Once again, the Websters took the road to Naples, arriving there on 26th February. This time, they 'lodged at Severino's'. Much of her list of associates of the preceding year could have served Lady Webster a second time. Her habitual companions still were Lady Spencer, the Bessboroughs, the Palmerstons, Dr Drew, Italinski. But to them now she added the names of five young men, undergraduates from Oxford doing a grand tour of Europe, with the exception of Lord Granville Leveson-Gower, who was on furlough from his company of the Stafford-shire Militia. A new languor, amounting to laziness, pervaded Lady Webster's journal, a subtle, voluptuous languor not directly attributable to pregnancy. 'For the whole six or seven weeks I passed in that lovely spot I had not activity enough to occupy myself in any way but in lounging and talking.'

Again making her 'grossesse' her excuse, Elizabeth resumed her evenings 'at home' in her apartments. Despite possible qualms as to her social status, now Lord Granville was constantly at her side. And so, too, were Lord Holland and Lord Morpeth, whom she had so piously renounced to her journal a year earlier. Their travelling companions 'Mr Beauclerk' and 'Mr Marsh' were also admitted to Lady Webster's circle, though the former was only admitted on sufferance, because of his friendship with the rest.

For a moment, Lady Webster looked acquisitively at Lord Granville. ('My favourite, Ld. G. Leveson-Gower, used often to come to me in the evening.') But when, almost at once, this fastidious young man succumbed to Lady Bessborough's subtler charms, she switched her interest to Lord Holland without difficulty.

Already, she had found his high spirits 'delightful'. Now, she ascribed to him finer qualities as well. 'He is eager without rashness, well-bred without ceremony.' Where, only three weeks before, she had felt that Holland's outspoken political views might be condemned as violent and foolish, now she saw them as reasonable. 'His politics are warm in favour of the Revolution, and his principles are strongly tinctured with democracy.'

She attributed to his generous youth his fervour to redress the wrongs of the unfortunate. But she noted with a certain relief that he did not want to extend his revolutionary principles across the Channel to England.

Lady Bessborough conquered another heart: that of the misanthropical Mr Beauclerk. And, certainly, with Beauclerk the less successful lover of the two, Lady Webster did nothing to help redress the balance in Lady Bessborough's mind. 'I understand that I am odious to him; je me venge in feeling as much against him as he possibly can against me.'

Lord Morpeth and Mr Marsh were much more to her taste. 'Lord Morpeth improves the more he is known; I have always liked him.' And Matthew Marsh (to be ordained in 1799) established a friendship with her which lasted until death, later occupying the post of tutor to one of her sons.

A scathing reference to Sir William and Lady Hamilton proclaimed Elizabeth's continued dislike of that scheming couple. 'The Hamiltons are as tiresome as ever; he as amorous, she as vulgar.' And that this was not mere feminine prejudice is confirmed in his own memoirs by Lord Holland. 'Of all the most vulgar, vain and disagreeable women I ever saw, the fair Ambassadress is the most so.' By now, this opinion was also prevalent in Neapolitan society. After seeing Emma interpret numerous 'attitudes', one Italian lady asked: 'E quando farà Miladi?'

Elizabeth found Lady Plymouth still in Naples, doubly bereaved by the death of her child and the desertion of her beloved Lord Berwick. She maintained that Lord Berwick had behaved disgracefully towards his former love, and that now he spoke to and of her with odious familiarity.

Italinski was enchanted to be reunited with his goddess, whose portrait was still his constant joy. And he was pleased to make the acquaintance of her friend, Matthew Marsh, finding him scholarly and a good talker. By 1794, Italinski's own standard of English had improved to the extent that Sir William Hamilton had asked him to correct the English in one of his manuscripts, which had led to Mr North's sarcastic comment: 'He has made Knight as clear as Day.'

At the end of April or first week in May, Elizabeth and most of her troupe left for Rome, still unaware that a revolution had been planned and suppressed in Naples while they 'lounged and talked' there. And, while she and her companions dallied in Rome, the 'sans culotte' armies of the French advanced victoriously through Flanders. The Dutch surrendered, the Austrians retired across the Meuse and the Duke of York and his English contingent of troops fell back to the coast and re-embarked for home. Only at sea Lord Howe still flew the flag of victory at his mast-head.

*

The Websters established themselves in the Villa di Matta, on the Pincian Hills. From it they could view Rome, the Apennines and the Campagna. Most of Lady Webster's friends in Naples had moved on with her, but Lord Digby (a kinsman of Lord Holland's) and Lord Granville returned to England. She declared that 'nothing short of compulsion' would drag her back there.

An Italian nobleman placed his villa in Tivoli at the disposal of Lady Bessborough, Lady Webster and their train of young men, leaving them to supply their own cook and provisions. Events started 'with jollity'. Then, as a change from Sir Godfrey, Lord Bessborough promoted a jealous scene, citing Mr Beauclerk as the object of his displeasure. This reached such proportions that all present decided to cut the visit short, and returned to Rome.

In a mood of determined unbelief, Elizabeth saw the Pope (Pius VI) give his blessing to 'a kneeling and believing multitude' in the Church of St Peter. Paying no thought to the moments of mental agony which had led this harassed but still temperate pontiff to adopt such a rôle, that day she saw him as an actor as accomplished as Garrick. Five years later, Buonaparte's General, Berthier, took the Pope prisoner, in the Vatican.

Lord Holland's technique was irresistible. In the evenings he read aloud to Elizabeth. He introduced her to the poet Cowper, hitherto unknown to her, but whom she now found 'excellent'. When he ran out of breath 'after many hundred lines in blank verse', Matthew Marsh took over, with Murphy's translation of Tacitus. A sharp attack of gout laid Sir Godfrey low, and increased his bad temper. Yet, even so, he struggled out, rather than endure such intellectual company. By so doing, he made everything easy. 'He, however, did not mar my comfort by partaking of my tranquil society.'

Every morning, Lady Bessborough and Lady Webster went out together, sharing Lord Holland, whom they called 'Sal Volatile', so good was he at raising their spirits.

*

At long last, William Wyndham had arrived to take up his post at Florence, and Elizabeth received news from his wife that he and she had been officially received there. Regretfully parting from Lady Bessborough (who was returning home), Elizabeth hurried back to the Tuscan capital, eager to see her 'little friend'. To her dismay, she found Mrs Wyndham in great distress.

Probably, part of this was due to her husband's extraordinary behaviour at the outset of his career as a diplomat. Revenging himself on the Grand Duke's Chamberlain for doubting the authenticity of some of his news, he had horse-whipped that gentleman through the windows of a Papal Nuncio's carriage. This act of violence terminated in a duel, without much harm to the combatants but hardly conducive to better relations between the Tuscan Court and the new Minister from Great Britain. This more than justified Elizabeth's fear that William Wyndham's behaviour might not be any better than Lord Hervey's.

This time the Websters 'took a house' in the Via Maggio where, although in the last weeks of pregnancy, Elizabeth still managed to entertain. Lord Holland and even Mr Beauclerk stayed for a few days, on their way to Venice. (Delightedly, she chronicled: 'Lord H. assured me he came merely to make me a visit.') And Lady Spencer, the Palmerstons and Sir Gilbert Elliot (now under control) stayed too.

On 12th June 1794, Elizabeth gave birth to a daughter, Harriet Frances. Lady Bessborough, William and Mrs Wyndham became the godparents. The child was due to be christened at the British Embassy and, a few days before the ceremony, Lord Holland returned from Venice. Elizabeth accepted her daughter without comment. On 23rd June, from Brighton Camp, T. P. sent a fervent message: 'Thank God that all has ended so well at Florence.'

Lord Holland was awaiting Lord Wycombe, who arrived in Florence a few days later. Son and heir of the 1st Marquess of Lansdown and his first wife, Lady Sophia Carteret, Lord Wycombe was twenty-nine when Lady Webster first met him. Without wasting time, he began to make love equally to her and to Mrs Wyndham. Lord Holland told her that his sister, Caroline Fox, had been brought up by Lord Lansdown and his second wife (their aunt) Lady Louisa Fitzpatrick, and that, in the family circle, Caroline and her aunt, Elizabeth Vernon, always referred to Lord Wycombe as 'a Lovelace without his polish'. Soon afterwards, Mrs Wyndham succumbed to Lord Wycombe's advances.

The Webster ménage was breaking up. In September, Lady Webster went off alone to visit the Lucca Baths. Neither husband nor admirer accompanied her. One night, she dined and slept in the house of an Italian Marchese whom she did not know! Despite the fact that, at that time, she spoke little Italian, he and his family and friends received her most hospitably. Afterwards, she wrote in her journal: 'They must have thought of me as a strange person, young, pretty and alone, travelling merely to see the quarries of Carrara!'

At Pisa, Elizabeth was surprised to find Lord Holland and Lord Wycombe travelling with her 'farouche companion'. In their company she visited the 'Leaning Tower', the Church, the quay. And, meticulously, she noted that 'Mon. de la Condamine' had measured the tower with a plumb line, finding it out of true by thirteen feet from top to bottom. (The Chevalier de la Condamine made this observation on his tour through Italy, in 1768.) Lord Wycombe read the company one of his sonnets, and Elizabeth visited the monastery of Vallombrosa. She was not admitted within its precincts, so the Abbot compromised by bringing out some of his monks to join her and her companions, after dinner.

In October, Sir Godfrey left his wife to her own devices and departed for Turin. About the same time, Lord Holland was unwell, so he and Lord Wycombe left Florence to consult a Dr Thompson in Rome. Lady Webster vacated her palace in the Via Maggio and rented 'a delicious residence' inside the gardens of the Mattonaia. The Marchese Ginori was her landlord and she found his taste 'magnificent'. One of his rooms he had done up at a cost of 'four thousand sequins'. This he had decorated in 'rich Japan', black and gold, and had furnished it superbly.

Lady Webster was still sufficiently heartwhole to enjoy her freedom. Left to herself, she went to balls and was 'very gay'. Between them, she and Mrs Wyndham enslaved Mr Amherst (later Lord Amherst, Governor General of India). 'He was most in love with the one he saw last.' Yet, despite her frivolity, at heart she remained an intellectual. And it is to her credit as a linguist that whereas in September, she had been unable to converse in Italian with her hosts near Lucca, in October she was beginning to enjoy reading the Italian poets in the original, particularly Ariosto. She fitted in a course of lectures on chemical experiments, given her by Professor Targioni. And frequently she rode from Florence to visit the beautiful villas built on its surrounding hills. Content and happy for the first time in eight years, she had the leisure and freedom to live her life as she wished.

In November, Lord Holland and Lord Wycombe returned from Rome and, on 21st November, Lord Holland celebrated his coming-of-age by giving a ball. Thereafter, he and Lady Webster explored Florence where 'The Gallery' (which formerly she had been unable to enjoy) now became for her 'a constant source of delight'.

So happy was Elizabeth that she seemed scarcely to notice her husband's
C*

return 'about Christmas'. She recorded it in a single sentence and quickly followed it with a reference to a masquerade. But, two months later, in February 1795, she became fully conscious of him again at the time of her father's death. This put her in absolute possession of the fortune left her by her grandfather, Florentius Vassall. Her peace of mind vanished, and with misgiving she viewed her great inheritance of ten thousand pounds a year. 'Detestable gold! What a lure for a vilain (*sic*), and too dearly have I become the victim to him.'

History fails to record whether Sir Godfrey accused Lord Holland directly of stealing his wife's affections. Up to May 1795, they still went about together for, early that year, a French artist, Louis Gauffier, painted three separate, but contemporary, portraits of them, in Florence.

Elizabeth Webster's twenty-fourth birthday occurred on 25th March, which Lord Holland commemorated with some verses. He addressed his lines: 'To a lady at Florence on her birthday, 1795.'

> When twice twelve times the rolling earth
> Brought back the period of her birth,
> Thus to the Genius of the day
> A certain Dame was heard to pray:
> 'Give me, indulgent Genius, give
> 'Midst learned cabinets to live,
> 'Midst curiosities, collections,
> 'Specimens, medals and dissections.
> 'With books of every tongue and land
> 'All difficult to understand.
> 'With instruments of various sorts,
> 'Telescopes, air pumps, tubes, retorts,
> 'With friends, fair wisdom to pursue,
> 'Fontana, Macie, Blagden, Drew.'
>
> Such are thy wishes, but if kind
> The gods, and of a mortal's mind,
> These sacrifices they will spare,
> And long preserve you what you are;
> And when obdurate time besprinkles
> Your head with grey, your face with wrinkles,
> When sickness and when age shall come
> And wither transient beauty's bloom,
> Still shall the beauties of your mind,
> By reading and by time refin'd,
> Still shall thy wit and polish'd ease
> In spite of fickle nature please;
> And then th' enchanted world shall see
> Rochefoucauld's laws belied in thee,

See female merit youth outlive,
And loveliness thy charms survive.
So when old Time's relentless page
At full threescore shall mark thy age,
With equal truth but better verse
Some Bard thy merits shall rehearse,
And like myself be proud to pay
A tribute to this happy day.

Could any woman resist such easy, cheerful wooing?

In April, Elizabeth too decided to consult Dr Thompson, in Rome. She had had frequent losses of blood yet, even so, he may have correctly diagnosed her as being again with child. She made the journey alone and, on her return, her husband demanded that she should accompany him back to England. On the grounds of health, she refused. 'My health did not allow me to engage in travelling, to say the truth I made as much as I cld. of that pretext that I might not be forced to return to England, as I enjoyed myself too much here to risk the change of scene.'

Sir Godfrey gave up the unequal struggle. Again, to quote his wife: 'In May (1795) Sir G. W. set off to England as he affixed an importance to his own appearance there that I own I did not strive to convince him against.' The unhappy man had no alternative. The extended leave of absence procured by T. P.'s direct application to the Duke of York expired on 3rd May.

CHAPTER SEVEN

Slow Stages Towards Elysium

IN JUNE 1795, Elizabeth Webster took a house in Lucca and moved there with her children. Mrs Wyndham and Mr Hodges joined her soon afterwards. Lord Holland and Lord Wycombe also moved to Lucca, near enough to Lady Webster's establishment to have their meals there daily.

To this arrangement, William Wyndham strongly objected. The previous September the Grand Duke had resumed his neutrality and, by June 1795, Wyndham was beset with worries. On the one hand, to obviate Lord Hervey's mistakes, he was told by Lord Grenville to be conciliatory to the Tuscans; on the other, he knew that Tuscany was working clandestinely towards better relations with France. And, to cap it all, now he was on bad terms with his wife which clearly he put down to Lady Webster's influence. At Lucca, he picked a quarrel with Elizabeth and thereafter refused to speak to her, and he followed this up with so violent a row with his wife that she decided to leave him. Considering her own emancipated conduct, we would have expected Elizabeth to uphold her friend. Instead, she thought she behaved 'like a very silly person for her worldly concerns. She is determined to separate and quit him.'

In July, in company with Lord Holland and Mr Hodges, Elizabeth departed for a few days to Genoa. On her return, William Wyndham staged a final break with her. Although refusing to meet her, apparently he expected her to provide him with dinner, which she indignantly refused. And afterwards, she reported with satisfaction that, without his dinner, William Wyndham also had to forgo his lodging, as Lucca boasted no inn.

At the end of August, Elizabeth returned to Florence, and for the next six or seven weeks she led a quiet, ideally happy life. Driven by Lord Holland behind his team of Maremma ponies, she made delightful excursions into the country, one day visiting Pratolino, a villa belonging to the Grand Duke of Tuscany, where she took a childlike delight in watching the fountains project their columns of water into the summer air.

In the evenings, frequently she attended Countess d'Albany's salon, where now she was on intimate terms with the Countess and Alfieri, so much that the Countess gave her a self-portrait at this time, painted and signed by her own hand. Or she listened with delight to Lord Holland reading Pope's translation of Homer's *Iliad*. ('I was delighted with parts of it, but the Odyssey I could not listen to.') Each day she came more under the spell of Florence, as a centre of learning. The war in Europe was far beyond the horizon of her Utopia.

Then sadness diverted her thoughts. In October (1795) she gave birth to 'a lovely boy' who developed convulsions and died.

This time, she was vehement in her grief. 'I meant to have continued some anecdotes of the Medici, but I have undergone too much affliction since writing the above . . .' And at last her cry genuinely wrings our hearts: 'Never shall I become mother to such an infant!' This was quickly covered up by a prosaic entry: 'Lord Macartney came and dined several times with me on his way to Rome.'

A few weeks later, Elizabeth Webster had recovered her cheerful spirits, and, on 22nd November, she, Lord Holland, six-year-old Webby and 'Mr Gely' (her secretary) set out, at one o'clock in the morning, to accompany Mrs Wyndham to Bologna. There, they were to speed her on her way to Turin. Despite deep snow and frost and patches of treacherous thaw, the travellers braved the mountain road over the Apennines. It took 'twenty-three hours and a half' to reach the 'Pellegrino Inn' at Bologna, where Lord Wycombe awaited them.

Two days later, Lord Holland and Mrs Wyndham set off for Turin, leaving Lady Webster and her son to the care of Lord Wycombe and Gely. The intellectual world of Bologna closed round them, in which Lady Webster entertained freely. One lady, a Greek scholar, composed an epigram in Greek about her hostess who, for once, was unable to respond to it.

A newcomer appeared at Elizabeth's inn: Lord Bristol, the Bishop of Derry. This sophisticated prelate had had an odd career. After a flying start in the Church (he was made Bishop of Cloyne at the age of thirty-three, and Bishop of Derry a year later) he had begun to develop tastes beyond the scope of his bishopric. In particular, the arts and a collection of fine pictures began to occupy his time, carrying him beyond the confines of Ireland to the Continent. In this pursuit, his wife trailed anxiously behind him, accompanied by two sons and three daughters. With one of Lord Bristol's daughters Elizabeth Webster was well acquainted; Lady Elizabeth Foster. Also, she already knew his eldest son, Lord Hervey.

Elizabeth Webster noted that Lord Bristol arrived 'with some wretched dependents' and classified him as 'a clever, bad man'. Even so, she allowed him to dine with her. He surprised her by asking her for a copy of her picture, by Fagan. As it belonged to Italinski, she fobbed him off with a non-committal answer of which he was to make extraordinary use, a few months later.

Lord Wycombe surrendered his duties the day before Lord Holland returned. Thereafter, Elizabeth, her lover and her little son retraced their way to Florence. Snow held them up again, during which pause Gely got lost. He turned up a day and a half later. That winter of 1795, Lady Webster's salon in the Mattonaia rivalled even that of Countess d'Albany. Three times a week she entertained at dinner, and every man of note in the town came to her table. (She mentions no women.) She gives a list of her regular guests, two of whom were politically suspect, Professor Fontana and Don Nero Corsini. The others ranged through the arts and physics to engineering. Greppi, poet and playwright; Delfico, historian; Professor Fabroni, Sub-Director to Fontana of the Natural History Museum; Pignotti, Professor of Physics; Fossombroni, eminent engineer. In this company she does not list Lord Holland, preferring to keep him, in his separate though still intellectual niche, reading aloud to her English poetry; the philosophical deductions of Pierre Bailly; Larcher's translations of Herodotus. At such moments, Elizabeth is at her best, an absorbed and intelligent listener. And, though Sir Godfrey has been gone for seven months, she forbears to mention him, as though someone so gross has to be kept outside the cobweb fragility of her happiness.

From England, Lord Holland's sister, Caroline Fox, was subjecting him to a delicate but persistent pressure to induce him to return home. Six years older than he and both orphaned in 1773 (he, at the age of one), from that time she had set out to win his love and confidence. Brought up by different members of the family, the intimacy between sister and brother had been largely dependent on correspondence, but despite this obstacle, hitherto Caroline Fox had exercised considerable influence. Repeatedly, Lord Holland had been wont to tell her how much he valued her good opinion and intelligence. So, now, she had to move warily, using only the lightest weapons in her armoury.

Lord Holland's first mention of his growing infatuation for Lady Webster is in a letter from Venice to his sister dated 7th June 1794. Having put up a smoke screen eulogising Lady Bessborough's charms, he adds: 'As to another Beautiful Lady who was at Naples and Rome and whom I shall see at Florence I certainly did and am afraid still do like her a little more than is wise . . .' By 5th August he is seeking to allay Caroline's alarm: 'In dreading my return to Florence you were v. unwise for I am sure I am doing what one so much immersed in love as you imagine me to be seldom does, leading a v. rational and agreeable life. Idle with respect for exercise of the body but not at all idle as to the improvement of my mind . . . Pray do not make jokes upon my *swainery* . . .'

From this gentle rebuff Caroline took her cue, as no further reference to her brother's love affair is made by her until 13th January 1795. And that day, she softens her featherweight thrust by first praising some of his verses. She goes on to say that a young cousin at Eton, Lord Broke (son of 2nd Earl of Warwick) has been told that the main reason for Lord Holland's continued sojourn in Italy is his 'love of sweetmeats'. 'I assured him his information was good, it was the only reason for yr. staying—am I wrong?'

Charles Beauclerk had been talking indiscreetly to Caroline. In a letter to her dated 24th January, rather incoherently, Lord Holland lets off steam. 'I confess that I do not think that general abuse of her (Lady Webster) drawn from common report . . . was directed to me with yr. usual good judgment. I beg you wld. talk with Charles Beauclerk at length on the subject . . . the prejudice he had taken up has been completely done away with in his mind upon his examining the truth of a story he had heard. Do not imagine, my dearest little sister, that I am or ever can be the least angry with you but I confess I am very unhappy at hearing you abuse a person I love so much . . .' The truth is out, at last.

Caroline is quick to see that she has gone too far. In her letter of 6th March, she bites the dust. 'I cld. cry my eyes out at the idea of having hurt you . . . burn the letter my little Brother not in token of forgiveness, which I know is already granted . . . but that no trace may remain of my egregious folly . . .' She wishes she had dropped the subject 'but when I heard on all sides of the serious consequences of yr. stay; and of the duty of yr. friends to try by all possible means to convince you of this; I foolishly went on with one argument after another . . .'

Her brother does not let her off too lightly. Writing from Florence on 27th March: 'I was v. much hurt indeed and I may add *surprized* (*sic*) and even angry. However it is now over and I am writing to hope that you never cld. mean to do or say any thing that wld. give me pain . . .' He comments crushingly: 'I know you mean well . . .' And adds pugnaciously: 'I shall not return till the end of the year.'

*

Of Lady Webster's correspondents, at this time, a surprising omission is her mother. And, indeed, no letters of Mrs Vassall's have yet come to light written during Elizabeth's deliberate exile. On 15th February 1795, T. P. had already reported Richard Vassall's worsening health and Mrs Vassall's consequent anxiety. He died thirteen days later, on 28th February. Yet no word from his widow, or even T. P., establishing this fact can be found in the correspondence. An accusation of heartlessness as to Elizabeth's determination not to return home cannot have been far from Mrs Vassall's mind and, as Elizabeth was always averse to censure, in all probability she destroyed such letters. And T. P.'s too as, from February 1795, he does not mention her father again.

Over the past year, disillusionment had shown ever more plainly in T. P.'s letters to Elizabeth. True to his word to supply her with news he had plodded on, largely drawing from his military diaries. Clearly, the scales of enchantment were falling from his eyes, yet still he remained her prisoner.

He begins to play safe, and to caution reticence. Writing from Brighton, on 20th October 1794: 'I have received yr. letter of 23rd Sept. . . . I can not say all I feel or wish to say upon the subject because I am apprehensive of yr. carelessness about my letters . . . It will be impossible for me to compose a letter to you but when I sit down to converse with you in future I shall act as if somebody was in the room who might hear and perhaps join in the conversation.' When he adds that he is not altogether surprised that Elizabeth is remaining another winter abroad, it is obvious that he has 'conceived suspicions'.

Elizabeth's reply to all this is to tell T. P. his letters are becoming 'most unnatural'. But, this time, he tries to stick to his guns. While admitting that his new element of caution is 'much against my feelings and inclinations', yet still he feels 'a degree of reserve especially necessary and a sacrifice we must make for the present'. Some of his letters appear to have gone astray and again he writes: 'I am confident that many of my letters taken singly, and produced invidiously, as they certainly wld. be if produced at all, wld. not bear the scrutiny of malicious critics.' Still, as has happened so often before, he cannot sustain his prudent intentions for long and soon reverts to his usual tenderness.

He has had a corner of his rooms at Stanmer and in Stratton Street furnished in duplicate with Elizabeth's favourite books, and her portrait by Downman seems to have always travelled with him from Sussex to London. 'Writing to you in this dear little Room . . . will soon make me resume the placidity with which I should always address you.'

Despite this hope, he is obviously unhappy. He is ill, and wants to retire from politics. And, more and more, he clings to the sanctuary of his 'little library'. In the spring of 1794, the Duke of York had offered T. P. a high post on his Staff. He had refused it. Then, in March 1795, he writes to tell Elizabeth that he has accepted an appointment offered him 'by the Duke of Portland and Pitt' to go 'as Sec. to Ireland' under Lord Camden. He has made it a condition of acceptance that he need not be absent from England for long, and he begs for her good wishes. And, throwing 'studied reserve' to the winds, he ends his letter: 'Adieu, my dearest friend—God bless you and believe me unalterably yrs T. P.'

*

On 9th February 1796, Lord Holland, Lady Webster, her children and Gely left Florence on their way to Rome. Lady Plymouth had taken rooms for them in the Palazzo Corea in the Strada Pontifico, where they arrived on 18th February. Elizabeth's interest in everything in Rome was enhanced by the proximity of her lover. His praise or condemnation tempered all she saw from a colossal statue of Antinous, discovered by Sir William Hamilton, to a contemporary allegorical group by the sculptor, Sposino, 'a man who has made a lasting monument of Lord Bristol's bad taste'. Executed by command of the Bishop of Derry, this represented William Pitt as the infant Hercules, strangling the serpent heads of Lord North and Charles James Fox.

On 1st March, Elizabeth undertook another journey, this time without Lord Holland. Undeterred by the clogging presence of her three children, Gely, her cook, her French maid Hortense, and an American called Smith, she set off to visit Italinski in Naples. But an epidemic of measles in that germ-infested town decided her to leave her two younger children at Terracina. In company with Mr Smith ('an ennuyeux'), Webby and Hortense, she pursued her way to Naples.

She found Vesuvius in dangerous eruption, far worse than she had seen it. Its summit had flattened out and beneath it, molten lava flowing down from the crater had heightened the coastline by nearly fifty feet. Nevertheless, homeless inhabitants in its vicinity were optimistically rebuilding.

Elizabeth spent four days with Italinski, during which time he told her a strange story. In Naples, at that very moment, Lord Bristol was lying dangerously ill and, using his illness as a weapon, had just sent to Italinski to ask for Lady Webster's picture by Fagan. As Italinski had already refused him a copy, he asked for the original! Reluctant to refuse a dying man, Italinski had relinquished the picture and, according to rumour, now the Bishop had had it arranged on an easel at the foot of his bed, surrounded by lighted wax tapers. As an agnostic, Elizabeth was not shocked by the Bishop so sensually misdirecting his last moments. (Ultimately, he recovered his health and Italinski regained his picture.)

This time, Queen Maria Carolina invited Lady Webster to Caserta but, as some of the Royal children had measles, Lady Webster declined the honour. Instead, unexpectedly, she dined with Lady Hamilton. She found 'Mullady' altered and Sir William 'more occupied about his own digestion than in admiring the graceful turn of her head'. In a flurry to return to her loved one, Lady Webster travelled all day and night from Naples to Albano.

From there, for a few days, she returned to Florence and finally left that beautiful city on 11th April 1796. 'I bed adieu to that lovely spot, where I enjoyed a degree of happiness for a whole year that was too exquisite to be permanent.' By then, she was carrying Lord Holland's child, later to be given the names of Charles Richard Fox.

Lord Holland drove Elizabeth in his phaeton as far as Prato, and there, he behaved most unusually. Instead of accompanying her on the next stage of her journey, he allowed her to go on alone to Modena.

*

In 1793, Elizabeth had inscribed in her journal: 'The want of passion in my constitution will always save me from the calamity of letting my heart run away with my reason, but what will be my resource if both head and heart accord in their choice?' Three years later, uncontrollable passion had flooded her cold heart. To her credit, she did not cry pity on her ensuing plight or seek to minimise the seriousness of her position. In fact, at the time, she made no comment on it at all, building up her case on silence. But, as she revealed in 1799, behind her discreet pen her mind was busy.

Although Elizabeth had heard nothing of her husband for nearly a year, she realised that he must be planning revenge. Once the fact of her conception of Lord Holland's child was disclosed, certainly he would seek to deprive her of her three Webster children. The law would uphold him in this, Elizabeth had no doubt, and divorce, with inevitable disgrace, would follow. Overnight, she would be banned from the glittering world which had so universally paid her court and, forced to abandon all claim to her children, thereafter she would have to retire to some remote corner of the earth, there to live out her life in obscurity.

To mitigate her cheerless future, through her mind filtered the ingredients of a desperate plot, to kidnap her own baby and to declare its supposed death to her husband! As she disclosed later: 'The certainty of losing all my children was agonising, and I resolved to keep one in my possession, and I chose that one who, from her age and sex, required the tenderness of a mother. Besides, I was undetermined whether I could bring myself to incur the éclat and anxiety that would arise from my publicly avowing my situation, and among the visionary schemes that passed in my mind there was one I dwelt upon during my dejection with a sort of pleasure . . .' With or without Lord Holland's knowledge Elizabeth put this scheme into effect on leaving Prato.

Ostensibly bound for Modena, at Bologna she diverted 'most of her servants' to Padua. Then, with her three children, a nursery-maid, her Italian maid and this woman's child, her cook, and two footmen, she continued on her way. After a few miles, she declared that Harriet had been taken ill and that she was sure the child was developing measles. Halting in the little village of Paullo, undetected, she contrived to paint some red spots on her baby's arm, thereby convincing the nursery-maid that Harriet had, in fact, contracted the disease. Thereafter, she ordered one of her footmen to conduct her two sons, plus the nursery-maid, on to Modena. Extracting her guitar, Elizabeth filled its case with stones, covering them with a pillow on which she laid the waxen mask of a baby. This, she hoped would be taken for a small coffin, while the mask was meant to deflect the curiosity of Customs officials from too close a scrutiny of its contents. She ordered her second footman to convey the case to the British Consul in Leghorn with instructions to bury it. Turning to Harriet, she dressed her up as a boy and handed her over to her maid who, together with her own child, was told to proceed to an agreed address in Hamburg. After which, at dead of night, Elizabeth sped on to Modena to bear the sad news of her baby's supposed death to the others!

In her cover plan to her journal, she declares that her desire to visit Ariosto's tomb and relics in Ferrara had caused her to alter course, and her whole method of description deliberately implies leisure for scholarly study. In fact she never went to Ferrara at all, but drove straight on to Bologna, to consult a doctor. Then she rattled on to Padua, where 'Lord Holland overtook me from Florence'.

All Elizabeth's plans went through without a hitch, proving the meticulous forethought they had engendered. And, throughout the ensuing months, never once did her journal refer to Harriet. Only in 1799 did it divulge that she and her child had been reunited, in Hamburg. And that

Sir Godfrey had accepted Harriet as dead, while she lay in concealment in England.

*

The lovers pursued their restless way to Trieste; on through Carinthia, Styria, Upper Austria, to Vienna; through Prague, to Dresden; and northwards, to Berlin.

Outwardly, Lady Webster still moved confidently in high society, entertained to dinner by the British Ambassador in Vienna; in Dresden, dining with the Duchess of Cumberland. In Berlin, she had too much on her mind to deplore Lord Henry Spencer's untimely death at twenty-four, where Lord Elgin had just succeeded him as Envoy Extraordinary from Great Britain. Flattering, but highly inconvenient, must have been the determination of Sir Hugh Elliot (brother to Sir Gilbert, and British Minister at Dresden) to accompany her to Hamburg. And it is tantalising not to know how she dodged him there in order to recover her child.

On 4th June 1796, she left Hamburg and crossed over from Cuxhaven to Yarmouth. From thence, she proceeded directly to London where her fears were justified, as Sir Godfrey announced divorce proceedings against her.

Always up to date with her news, on 10th June, Maria Josepha Holroyd wrote to her friend, Ann Firth: 'So Lady Webster has ended with éclat as I always thought she wld . . . I am sorry for Lord H. . . .'

CHAPTER EIGHT

Elysium Attained

UNTIL 1857, only an Act of Parliament could dissolve a marriage and the right of remarriage had to be specially applied for and was not always granted. Where the wife was the guilty party, the husband brought a suit of common law against her lover, claiming damages for the material loss he estimated he had sustained. Until such a suit was resolved Lady Webster's material future lay in jeopardy.

Her main trouble was that Sir Godfrey could not make up his mind. One day, he was reported to be in tears at the thought of losing his wife; on another, he was cheerful and amenable. One day, he said he would do everything possible to help her; on another, he refused to let her have back her father's picture. His rages and reconciliations ranged up and down the scale. At one moment he felt it would be detrimental to his sons' future to go forward with the divorce. At another, he suggested a marriage between Lady Webster's spaniel Pierrot and one of his own, and went so far as to let Lord Holland know he was prepared to accept one of his terrier puppies. Nine years before, Sir Godfrey had commissioned George Romney to paint a full-length portrait of his wife. He had not accepted it and it had hung in the artist's studio ever since. Now, when Lord Holland attempted to buy it, Sir Godfrey challenged him to a duel. (There is no evidence that Lord Holland took up his challenge.) As a prerequisite to his bringing the divorce, Sir Godfrey insisted on two conditions: £6,000 down must be paid to him (from which he undertook to pay his wife an allowance of £800 a year); and no defence or damaging proofs were to be brought against him. But these conditions too were liable to cancellation at a moment's notice.

On their return to England Lord Holland had been at pains to find Lady Webster somewhere to live. Owing to his long minority, his own home, Holland House, had been let, and though it was now available again, it was not yet ready for occupation. Moreover, as his temporary estrangement with Caroline Fox had long since been bridged, now he accepted without resentment her contention that it would be lacking in taste for him to instal Lady Webster in his old home until he married her. So, he leased a house in Brompton Park, where he established himself and his mistress. There, both Lady Bessborough and Thomas Pelham begged the lovers to remain quietly until after the birth of their child, and, had they heeded this advice, much malicious criticism might have been spared them. But Charles Ellis seems to have inspired them to try to force Sir Godfrey's hand by eloping abroad, and so drove the whole affair into the open.

When he realised this, T. P. dashed off a letter to Elizabeth so agitated that it was full of scratchings-out and corrections. 'Let me entreat you therefore . . . that you will not press the Departure . . . not take any decisive steps with regard to your self or any thing else until you have time to reflect—for a few days at Lausanne—circumstances are such that an arrangement must take place between you and Sir G. For God's sake be carefull (*sic*) and circumspect in the manner of accomplishing it—consider that the world are too prone to condemn the wife without hearing any details and remember that a beautiful woman who has been so much admired on different occasions as you have has more enemies . . .' His wise counsel was ignored, but details are missing.

It took little time for the news of Lady Webster's unfortunate situation to become public knowledge. Lord Granville Leveson-Gower too was enslaved by the charms of a beautiful married woman, and his mother Lady Stafford pointed the moral to him of 'the melancholy step Lord Holland has so unwisely taken'. Mindful of public opinion (and his mother) Lord Granville 'cautioned' Lady Bessborough against associating further with Lady Webster but sweet, steadfast Lady Bessborough remained true to her friend. To Lord Granville she wrote:

You know by this time how unnecessary your cautions on poor Lady Webster's account were. I knew of her situation before her arrival in England, and when she came must have been very selfish and ungenerous could any motives of personal prudence have prevented me doing everything in my power to conceal it, to soothe her and endeavour to dissuade her from the rash step she has now taken. You will hear her very much abus'd, and certainly ye weakness she has been guilty of *always* deserves it in some measure, but indeed she does not near as much as people are inclined to think. So far from having form'd a *plan* for what has happen'd, the day I came out of town all was fix'd for an amicable separation between her and Sir G. and she was determin'd to conceal herself till after she was brought to bed. Some over nice scruple of G. (C.) Ellis's drove her to act as she did. She wrote me word of it the day before, and you may judge of my anxiety, still hoping to prevent it and dreading the event. If Sir George (Godfrey?) should follow them, the letter she left for me, and which I will some day show you, proves how falsely she is accused of braving the world and rejoicing in carrying her point. On the contrary, it is full of expressions that shew how strongly she feels all that is painful, and humiliating in her situation . . . It is impossible to say how nervous it has made me, for indeed, you know not the anxiety I have suffer'd, while I had still hopes I should succeed in my persuasion, and with the dread every moment of a discovery.

This undated letter must have been written about the end of June.

*

Caroline Fox had won back her brother's confidence and he wrote to her as freely as ever. Now he was prepared to expose his difficulties. In an undated letter written from Brompton Square, he stresses his gratitude to his sister and proceeds to an involved explanation of his behaviour:

> You are everything I cld. wish you to be to me and yr. gentleness . . . is a source of much real comfort and satisfaction to me. As to what I have done it was in some respects contrary to the advice of my friends but as her situation rendered an éclat sooner or later almost certain and any management for her character quite desperate . . . my only object was to live with her in the way most comfortable to her feelings . . . It must be at once more satisfactory to her and I think more comfortable to myself to prove that I am not forced to live with her merely and entirely by a point of honor but that the moment her reputation was materially injured my only thoughts were how to repair it and really compensate in some degree to her for her loss. It is certainly a great disadvantage to being together under such circumstances and one hardly can be justified in putting a woman in such a situation—but the fact is had I not taken that step she was in a still worse and in spite of the little credit which is to be given to the judgment of a person so infatuated as I must appear, I must repeat that we are better judges of our own temper disposition etc. than most people who have been in our situation. We have lived so entirely together for near two years that we have most made a trial sufficient to prove the probability of our happiness.

He goes on to speak most touchingly of his love and begs his sister 'not to join the common outcry against her. She may have many many faults but I am sure that the most unhappy one she has for herself is her *sincerity*.'

His unborn child is now his main concern. 'One only circumstance is yet distressing and that is the situation of our poor little child . . . You at least my Dear little Sister will be above all prejudice about it as I hope you will love it more rather than less for its misfortune . . .'

To this plea Caroline Fox made magnanimous response. By 3rd July (1796) Lord Holland is telling her how delighted both he and Lady Webster are that, should the child prove to be a girl, she is prepared to be its godmother. 'Nothing can be so gratifying to us as giving the little child shld. it be as we all hope, a girl, yr, name. In that case it shall certainly be yr. Godchild—but if it be unfortunately a boy I cannot promise as I believe Lady Besborough (*sic*) had already made the same request tho' I am in hopes I shall even in that case persuade her to wave (*sic*) it for you . . .'

Now that the die was cast, Lord Holland's close relations declared themselves (or omitted to do so) in their various ways.

His former guardians, Lord Upper Ossory (maternal uncle) and Charles James Fox (his father's brother), remained silent, but General Richard Fitzpatrick (Lord Upper Ossory's brother) showed himself warmhearted, practical and kind. Writing to his nephew on 2nd July 1796, he stresses: '. . . my affection for you makes me feel deeply interested in whatever concerns yr. happiness'. He warns him 'that the step you have taken will be condemned by prudent persons, must be expected. Its ultimate consequences however may prove such as neither you, nor those who love you, will find any reason to lament'. He follows up his kind sentiments with invitations to the young couple to his house at Sunninghill, of which they are grateful to avail themselves.

In sharp contrast, Lady Webster's one close relation, her mother, was not so generous. Much to her daughter's distress, she remained opposed to all communication with her until she was married. Lord Holland reports to Caroline: 'She (Mrs Vassall) feels no anger or sorrow but simply says that until she is my wife she can have no communication with her.' Prudent self-interest may have prompted Mrs Vassall's decision. For, on 18th July 1796, at St George's, Hanover Square, she herself was married to Sir Gilbert Affleck, Bart., of Dalham Hall, Suffolk, seventeen months after the death of her first husband.

A different person emerges from Lord Holland's description of Elizabeth to the self-centred woman portrayed in her own journal. The Elizabeth he had known so intimately for two years past is now humble and loving, anxious not to come between him and his friends and not to force her way back into a world that shuns her. Writing again from Brompton Square, Lord Holland tells his sister:

> She (Lady Webster) wishes to live as near town as possible because she wld. be v. sorry to be any impediment to my seeing so much of my friends as possible. She only wishes to be able to see all my friends and relations on my account as well as theirs and hers and as to the rest of the world she has not even the smallest wish of endeavouring to mix with it. Her being precluded the society of what is called the world is indeed a v. slight mortification to her . . . so that Holland House is of all situations that which wld. seem best to suit our plans and if there were a possibility of keeping it, we certainly wld . . .

In October, Lady Webster narrowly escaped a premature birth. But, by that time, Lord Holland's relations were gathering round him. Lord

Upper Ossory had called, and the Duke of Bedford had invited him to Woburn Abbey for the following month (an invitation which, as it might coincide with Lady Webster's confinement, Lord Holland refused).

On 6th November 1796, she bore him a son, which news Lord Holland was quick to pass on to his sister. 'This evening at a quarter past eight Lady W. was brought to bed of a boy. She and the child are so well that I cannot but feel happy . . .' He added a postscript: 'I hope you will be Godmother.' On 20th December he informed Caroline: 'They are registering the boy by the name of Vassall. It wld. be unseemly to call him Webster and this will help his claim to the (Vassall) estate. His name will be Charles Fox.'

*

In the spring of 1797, the lovers moved to Money Hill, near Rickmansworth.

The Bill petitioning Parliament to dissolve Sir Godfrey's marriage came up for first reading in the House of Lords on 9th May. It declared itself: 'An Act to dissolve the marriage of Sir Godfrey Vassall (lately called Sir Godfrey Webster) Baronet with Elizabeth Vassall his now wife and to enable him to marry again and for other Purposes therein mentioned.' On that date, the Bill was ordered to be read a second time, when Sir Godfrey was required to corroborate 'the truth of the Allegations of the Bill'. Anthony Morris Storer (that faithful friend), the doctor who had delivered the baby (Richard Croft), George Burley (Lady Webster's attorney), Joseph Rushton and four members of Lady Webster's household, past and present, were to be called as witnesses.

At the second reading, Sir Godfrey sued Lord Holland for Trespass, Assault and Criminal Conversation with his wife, and claimed damages £6,000 'besides costs of suit'. Against Elizabeth was produced the sentence of Divorce, dated 9th February 1797, passed by the Consistory Court of the Bishop of London, 'for Adultery'.

Various witnesses (including her French maid, Hortense) gave evidence of the guilty relations of Lady Webster with Lord Holland from May 1795 up to the present, to which she submitted no defence. But the Lord Chancellor (Lord Loughborough) protested violently against the jury's acceptance of Sir Godfrey's claim for damages, calling it 'iniquitous', and insisting that it should be deleted from the Bill. Upon which, Sir Godfrey threatened to drop the Bill altogether unless Lady Webster's counsel obtained 'an attendance to fight the Chancellor on this point of law'.

At this complex stage of the proceedings, Lord Holland's paternal uncle, Charles James Fox, was induced to take a hand (the first time he had appeared in the family picture). Reluctantly, he tried to divert Lord Loughborough from his purpose. But the Lord Chancellor remained adamant, proclaiming it to be his duty to protect Lady Webster from the theft of her fortune. His uncompromising attitude began to alarm Sir Godfrey who finally accepted a bond, signed by the Duke of Bedford, Charles Ellis, Sir Gilbert Affleck (who, from the day of his marriage, proved himself a helpful, kindly man) and Lord Holland, that they would be responsible if Lady Webster did not hand over her estate to her husband within two days after the Royal Assent had been given. The Lord Chancellor continued to maintain that Lady Webster was at all times entitled to her estate, divorced or not, and that the House of Lords could not ignore Florentius Vassall's will.

But freedom was too sweet to haggle over, and on 4th July 1797, Lady Webster's marriage was annulled by Parliament. Two days later, Sir Godfrey became the richer by £6,000 damages; an income of £7,000 a year from Lady Webster's West Indian estates 'with a promise of unmolested possession'; £1,000 released to him from Lady Webster's jointure; and £300 a year regained from her cancelled pin-money.

On that momentous day, even such a severe drop in her fortune did not sadden Elizabeth Webster. For, on 6th July, she and Lord Holland were married at Rickmansworth Church, his former tutor, the Rev. William Morris, officiating, and Sir Gilbert Affleck giving away his step-daughter. Jubilantly, Lord Holland confirmed the event to his sister: 'We were married this morning at Rickmansworth . . . Lady Holland (for so thank God she now is) is with her Mother at this moment. Goodbye, God bless you.'

And Lady Affleck's effusive benediction was quick in coming: 'My dearest Elizabeth . . . the pleasure I had in knowing Lord Holland and finding him so much of any thing I cd. wish, I may say as Sheba did to Solomon that much had I heard but behold the half was not told me. I hope you may both long enjoy every Blessing that a good life will afford . . . I am proud in saying I now have a Son to love and admire which is more that I cd. ever say my child yr. Mother and friend.' Nothing succeeds like success.

*

As usual in moments of crisis, Lady Webster (now Holland) had left her journal blank, in this case, for over a year. She resumed it at the moment she remarried, lamenting the difference in age between herself and her new husband: 'I was Twenty-six years old. Ld. H. was twenty-three. The difference in age is, alas! Two years and eight months—a horrid disparity.'

Gratefully, she records: 'All his family behaved to me with the utmost kindness; they came, those in town, and those in the country wrote to me.'

Lord Lansdown was the first to accord her an official welcome. On 10th July, he writes Lord Holland from Bowood: 'My dear Lord. Accept all my best wishes for yrs. and Lady Holland's happiness and be so good as to satisfye Lady Holland of my sincerity, which alone can make them worthy of yrs. and Lady Holland's acceptance. I cannot flatter myself that it will be in my power to add to yr happiness but I can with truth assure you that few things wld. add more to mine. I am ever yrs—Lansdown.' And he follows up his letter with an invitation to Bowood, arranged through Caroline Fox, for 7th August.

In her new-found spirit of humility, the prospect of meeting her husband's uncle, sister and two step-aunts, Elizabeth and Caroline Vernon, filled Lady Holland with alarm. So much so, that Lord Holland warned his sister: 'Lady Hd. is not a little nervous and awkward at the idea of going to a house without being acquainted with a single inmate of it but I shall pique her out of this nervousness as I tell her that it is only because she is ashamed of shewing herself so fat and afraid of the reputation to her beauty.'

Nevertheless, he himself shows slight apprehension about his wife's reception at Bowood, as stressed in his next letter to Caroline: 'I must entreat you to look upon the first hour of her acquaintance as a blank because like many other shy people she is extremely awkward her shyness takes the likeness almost of impudence and she says all sorts of foolish things. I feel it very necessary to say this because as you may easily believe my dear little sister I shld. feel miserable were the first impressions of her acquaintance upon yr. mind to be unfavourable.'

After their visit, Lord Holland writes again to Caroline from Holland House, where 'safe and snug' he and his family are now installed. And reading between the lines, we see clearly the degree of tact exercised by Lord Lansdown and his relations towards the newcomers at Bowood.

I wish chiefly to . . . express . . . not only my gratitude to you my Aunts and Ld. Ln. but the real comfort and pleasure I feel at the prospect of yr. intimacy with Lady Hd. Your real goodness to her wd. be unfeeling indeed not to acknowledge but that which gives me still more pleasure is that . . . she seems to me to like you all excessively. I do not know whether it is praise or censure but from a thorough knowledge of her I know that there is no person to whom it is so impossible to express what she does not feel and therefore I am really happier than I can express to find that not merely now from a sense of propriety or from a wish of saying what it wld. be wrong not to say but really from her heart she is delighted and happy at her visit to Bowood—and you all seeming to like her gives me really more pleasure than I can express . . .

To which Caroline Fox makes suitable reply. Declaring her own satisfaction that Lady Holland had enjoyed her visit, she continues:

I trust it has laid the foundation of a lasting and affectionate intimacy for I can with truth assure you that we were all pleased beyond our expectation by finding her manners accord so well with ours, and entirely free from that pedantry of affectation which idle report had taught us to expect. Indeed my little Brother she has pleased certainly as much as she has been pleased, and we are disposed to think and believe she is possessed of many very rare good qualities such as perfect sincerity and truth, with a great degree of sagacity and discernment added to real feeling without any affected display of it. This my dear little Brother is the Judgement we have formed upon a slight ackquaintance and trust a more intimate one will not prove it to be erroneous.

Lord Lansdown adds his gracious word. On 22nd August he writes: 'My dearest Ld. Holland—Why shld. you not make an inn of this house or any other use you think proper? I shall be v. sorry if you and Lady Holland do not feel it the same as Holland House . . .'

Considering her initial obstacles, Lady Holland had got off to a flying start.

CHAPTER NINE

Dynasty and a Kingdom

IN 1796, when Henry Richard, 3rd Lord Holland returned from abroad, he announced his intention to Caroline Fox possibly only to occupy Holland House 'for a year or two' and then 'to let out the property on building leases'. But, by March 1797, he had fallen so much in love with the place that he told her: 'I have determined to make it both a town and country house and my regular and permanent residence.'

No expressions of delight at the historic beauty of her surroundings were committed to Lady Holland's journal. Nor did she allow herself to evince the awe of a newcomer towards her husband's illustrious forebears but, before many weeks had passed, she realised that she had become part of a far-ranging dynasty.

*

The Foxes had played a part in English politics since the reign of Charles I. Stephen Fox, founder of their fortunes and a man of unassailable loyalty and integrity, had not only dutifully served that martyred monarch, but had later transferred his devoted allegiance to Charles Stuart in exile, which fidelity gained for him, after the Restoration, the offices of Paymaster of the Forces and Commissioner of Treasury. In the latter capacity he served under four kings. John Evelyn said of him '. . . he obtained such credit among the bankers that he was in a short time able to borrow vast sums of them upon any exigence. He is believed to be worth at least £200,000 honestly gotten and unenvied which is next to a miracle.' As a further award for his services, Stephen Fox was knighted in 1665. His son Charles, by his first marriage, and his youngest son, Henry, by his second marriage, both attained the office of Paymaster. Through the influence of their friend, Lord Hervey (elder brother of the Bishop of Derry), they both joined the ranks of Sir Robert Walpole and his Whigs. Politics came second in importance to country pursuits with Stephen, Lord Ilchester, but they played a leading part in the aspirations of his brother, Henry, and, in the hands of Henry's second son, Charles James Fox, the torch of Whiggism became a crusader's weapon.

*

In 1746, Henry Fox took Holland House on lease for twenty-two years and, the same year, he brought his bride to live there, Lady Caroline Lennox, whom he had clandestinely married two years before. (A family habit, as his elder brother, Stephen, at that time Baron and later first Earl of Ilchester, had done the same thing with the child-heiress, Elizabeth Strangways-Horner, eight years earlier.) Ambitious politician that he was, in that year too Henry Fox was created Secretary at War by Sir Robert Walpole's successor, Henry Pelham.

Horace Walpole declared that the elopement of King George II's daughter, Caroline, 'wld. not have created a greater ferment' than the runaway marriage of Henry Fox with the daughter of Charles, second Duke of Richmond. Probably it was a contributory factor to the drawing up of Lord Hardwick's Marriage Act of 1753 (which, not surprisingly, Henry Fox violently opposed in Parliament) and certainly it estranged Lady Caroline from her parents for four anxious years. But by the time she and they were reconciled (in 1748) she had already borne her husband three sons and her evident happiness and contentment proved to them that, at home at least, Henry Fox's conduct was exemplary.

In a career designed to achieve two main objectives, as large a fortune as possible and an eventual peerage, like his father and eldest brother, Henry Fox too achieved the office of Paymaster. But, regrettably, his own dubious administration of the public funds at his disposal tarnished for ever the shining example of his father. Although according to the accepted mal-practice of the time, he was within the law in claiming interest on surplus sums of public money, he used his rights too blatantly to escape scandal. Undoubtedly, this sharp practice in achieving his first objective delayed the fulfilment of his second, and it was not until 1762, two years after the accession of the new King, George III, that Henry Fox made progress towards the Upper House and then only by proxy through his wife, Lady Caroline. That year, thanks to the efforts of Lord Bute, the new Chief Minister, Lady Caroline was gazetted Baroness Holland, in her own right.

The new King was behind Lord Bute's determination to put an end to the (seven-year) war in Europe which the elder Pitt had been determined to fight to a victorious finish. But a policy of peace leading to the with-drawal of British troops from the Continent, was not yet acceptable to Parliament. To make it so, Lord Bute realised that bludgeoning methods would have to be employed and, to him, Henry Fox seemed the man to wield them. Already so publicly condemned for his lack of scruples, Fox responded to Lord Bute's appeal for help. And the result of his ensuing campaign of cajolery, bribery and blackmail against his fellow Members of Parliament was the Peace of Paris of 1763. Lord Shelburne (later created 1st Marquess of Lansdown) was his companion in crime, but his youth and inexperience in politics helped him to escape censure. After Parliament had sullenly voted for peace by a majority of five to one, it turned its wrath on Fox to such an extent that it alarmed Lord Bute into retirement. Thereby, once more there was a vacancy in the Treasury which, even then, Fox might have filled had not his wife tearfully intervened to stop him.

Under George Grenville's Ministry, at last Henry Fox achieved his peerage. On 19th April 1763, he took his seat in the Upper House as Baron Holland of Foxley, Wilts, and, in 1768, he bought the property which had inspired his title and presented it to his beloved wife, Lady Caroline.

*

Elizabeth, 3rd Lady Holland, found herself established in a house which, in 1689, William of Orange had contemplated making into a Royal residence.

About 1605 Sir Walter Cope, second Baronet, a favourite of King James I, started to build Cope Castle on that part of his property known as the Manor of Abbot's Kensington. At that time, he owned three other manors as well: West Towne, Knotting Barns (later known as Notting Hill) and Earl's Court. Subsequently he sold Knotting Barns but kept the greater part of the Abbot's Manor and a smaller part of Earl's Court. Horace Walpole was of opinion that John Thorpe was architect only of the middle block of the Castle and that Inigo Jones and Nicholas Stone altered and added to it. His theory was later discounted. Although, in 1679, Nicholas Stone designed for the Earl of Holland '2 Peeres of good Portland stone, to hang a pair of great wooden gates on . . .', neither he nor Inigo Jones is thought to have altered the main building which now is accredited to the original designs of John Thorpe, father and son.

Through the marriage of Sir Walter's daughter, Isobel, Cope Castle passed into the possession of the Rich family. Her husband, Henry Rich (son of Robert, first Earl of Warwick) was created Baron Kensington in 1622 and, in 1626, Earl of Holland. After he died, Cope Castle changed its name to Holland House. Henry Rich, Earl of Holland, commissioned Thorpe to incorporate the coronet of his newly acquired earldom into the cornice of the Hall (afterwards named: 'the Breakfast Room'). And he is supposed to have decorated 'the Gilt Room' (immediately above the Hall) in honour of the marriage of the King's son, Charles, with Henrietta Maria of France.

In 1649, the Parliamentarians beheaded the Earl for treason, but his widow was allowed to return to her home. Her son, Robert, continued to live there and his son, Edward, not only succeeded to the earldom of Holland but, on the death of his cousin, to the earldom of Warwick as well. Edward predeceased his wife who, like the widowed first Countess, continued to live on at Holland House. In her efforts to control her unsatisfactory son, Edward Henry (seventh Earl of Warwick and fourth Earl of Holland), it was said that she found him a tutor, the poet and essayist, Joseph Addison, whom later she proceeded to marry. But, as early as 1704, Addison held an office of State and by 1716, the year of his marriage, he had long been famous as a man of letters and chief contributor to the *Spectator*, so presumably was under no obligation to accept so domestic a post. Lady Warwick and Holland's dissolute son died, unmarried, in 1721, and his titles devolved on his cousin, Edward Rich (descended through the female line, from the first Earl of Holland), who died without an heir, in 1759. Thereby, both earldoms became extinct and that of Holland remained so but, almost at once, the earldom of Warwick was revived in favour of the Grevilles.

Holland House and its estates went in direct succession to William Edwardes of Haverfordwest, a grandson (again through the female line) of the second Earl of Holland. As he hardly ever lived there the property changed hands several times. As has been said, in 1689, William of Orange contemplated making Holland House into a Royal residence before finally settling on Nottingham House (thereafter renamed Kensington Palace) nearby. And, from 1768, owned by the Foxes, Holland House entered on its final and most famous phase.

*

To Elizabeth Holland, conning Fox history as she might a guide-book, her husband's grandfather must have seemed a difficult man. Having attained his objectives and withdrawn from politics, no longer should he have coveted the fruits of office. Yet, as she read on, she discovered that he expected still to collect his dues from the Paymastership. When he found himself debarred from doing so by the terms of his newly acquired peerage, he accused Lord Shelburne of misrepresenting his acceptance of it. In all probability, Lord Shelburne was innocent of such a charge, but Lord Holland never forgave him for his considered treachery. Later, Lord Bute

Photo: John Webb

Lady Webster, painted at Naples in 1793
by Robert Fagan, Governor of the Ionian Isles

The 2nd Earl of Chichester, 'T.P.', painter unknown

is supposed to have referred to him as 'the Pious Fraud', to which the first Lord Holland angrily replied: 'I can see the fraud plainly enough, but where is the piety?' He managed to hang on to the Paymastership for another two years when it was taken from him. His venom against his former close associate cost him many friends and, particularly, John, 4th Duke of Bedford, who seems to have played a leading part in ending his appointment as Paymaster.

The marriage of Lord Holland's eldest son, Stephen, to Lady Mary Fitzpatrick, niece of the Duchess of Bedford, in 1766, did little to heal the breach between the families, and there is no record that Lord Holland attended his son's wedding in the private chapel at Bedford House.

Stephen survived his father as 2nd Baron by only six months and Henry Richard, Elizabeth's husband, succeeded his father at the age of one. But, on the death of his mother, Mary, Lady Holland, in 1778, two family reconciliations were effected through the person of his sister, Caroline. Following the first three years of her orphanhood, Caroline was given into the charge of her step-aunt, Harriet Vernon, Countess of Warwick; thereafter, she was put in the care of her great-aunt, Gertrude, Duchess of Bedford; and finally, she went to live with her mother's sister, Lady Louisa Fitzpatrick, whose marriage to the 1st Lord Holland's hated colleague, Lord Shelburne, as his second wife, had taken place two years before.

At Bowood, Lord Shelburne surrounded himself with most of the advanced thinkers of the age: Jeremy Bentham and his friend and chronicler, Dumont; Joseph Jekyll, celebrated wit; the Dutch physician, Ingenhousz; Gavin Hamilton, archaeologist (who collected most of the statues for Lansdowne House); Morellet; Mirabeau. It was a scintillating circle for a child of talent to be in, and learning and a capacity to listen came easily to Caroline.

She was fourteen when she first went to live at Bowood and, meeting her shortly after she got there, Jeremy Bentham so describes her: 'She is v. prettily made, and has already a v. womanly sort of bosom . . . Her face, which I had like to have forgot, is far from an unpleasant one: but the form of it which is the Fox mouth, and a set of teeth which, tho' white, are rather large, save her from being a beauty.' Even so, later on, Caroline's looks are supposed to have charmed Bentham enough to propose marriage, and he is said to have suffered great distress when she refused him. And although twenty years older than she, and still friendly enough to write to her regularly until he reached the age of eighty, it is said that Bentham never quite forgave Caroline for her lack of response to his offer. In the same

D

category of frigidity he dumps her two step-aunts, Caroline and Elizabeth Vernon. (These sisters, daughters by a former marriage of the first Countess of Upper Ossory, were only a few years older than Caroline): 'The ice becomes more cold, I think, when the three Dianas get together: they are like snow, saltpetre and salammoniac.'

In 1784, Lord Shelburne was awarded a Marquisate for his political services and took the name of Lansdown. (He always signed his name without the 'e'.) Five years later, his wife died. For the three Dianas, the pattern of life at Bowood remained the same as, devoted to Lord Lansdown as to each other, they stayed on as triple hostesses to their foster-father's brilliant guests.

*

Now Elizabeth Holland learnt the details of her husband's empire.

The contract of purchases made by Henry Fox, 1st Baron Holland, still followed the survey of the north side of the property made, in 1694, by Edward Bostock Fuller for the first Earl of Holland. The boundary on the North was still the road to Acton and Uxbridge; on the east, still the avenue later known as Holland Walk; on the south, the 'Great Road to Brentford' (Kensington High Street); on the west, the ditch called 'the Sewer' which crossed the 'Great Road' at Counters Bridge to run into the Thames at Chelsea Creek. And this empire remained unaltered at the third Lord Holland's accession, except for one modest addition, made by his father, on the east side: a small farmstead thereafter known as 'Little Holland House'.

During Henry Richard's long minority, Holland House was let. A chapel, said to have been built by Addison's Countess of Warwick at its north-eastern corner, burnt down during that time, and, generally, the house itself deteriorated. It was not fit for occupation until the Spring of 1797 and, even then, the Hollands and their little son, Charles Richard, did not take up their residence in it until the following September. They occupied the intervening period with extensive alterations to the garden, reproducing in it Italian formal designs in topiary and clipped box hedges.

Luckily for posterity, they merely restored the interior of the house to what it had always been. The wide, shallow treads of the Great Staircase still led up to Thorpe's Breakfast Room surmounted by the carved coronets of the ill-fated first Earl of Holland; on into the Journal Room which, in its turn, led into the Green Drawing Room; through the room dedicated for ever to the memory of Joseph Addison and, finally, into the magnificent Library running the whole length of the west side of the house.

Inevitably, before the advent of the Fox family, famous names had been associated with the building: Vandyke, reputed to have spent some time there painting the first Earl of Holland; William Penn, before he emigrated overseas to found his colony of Pennsylvania; Cromwell's Lord General Fairfax. But none of these names had been reliably recorded in its history. Substance was achieved with the advent of Joseph Addison. Yet even he could only leave on his surroundings the delicate imprint of his declining years.

As shown by his gallery of portraits, Henry Fox's impression was direct and personal. Politics, as typified by two portraits of Sir Robert Walpole (one, probably by Eccardt, Henry Fox's protégé, the other, by Wootton, painted in Richmond Park); a portrait by David Morier of his thankless patron, the Duke of Cumberland, during Fox's period of office as Secretary at War. Portraits of his friends: among others, Charles, 3rd Duke of Marlborough (father of Elizabeth Webster's devoted admirer, Lord Henry Spencer); and Charles Hanbury-Williams, poet, wit and diplomat. Portraits of his family: his father and eldest half-brother, Charles, by Lely; himself, by Liotard; two of his second brother, Stephen, Earl of Ilchester, by Enoch Zeeman and Hoare of Bath; one of his cousin, 'Neddy', Lord Digby, by Battoni; another of Neddy's younger brother, 'Harry' Digby (who succeeded him as 7th Lord Digby) by Joshua Reynolds. A galaxy of beautiful pictures of his wife's family showed the measure of Lady Caroline's forgiveness by her parents for her runaway marriage to himself. Those by Verelst proclaiming Lady Caroline's royal descent from Charles II through his mistress, Louise de Kerouaille, Duchess of Portsmouth; and their son, created first Duke of Richmond. And portraits of Lady Caroline's beautiful sisters: Emily, Duchess of Leinster; Lady Louisa Connolly; and a delightful grouping by Sir Joshua, of Lady Sarah Lennox leaning from a window of Holland House to converse with Lady Susan Fox-Strangways and Charles James Fox.

All the portraits proved the 3rd Lord Holland's ready-made contacts with Whig politics, with which he was to become irresistibly involved.

*

From early childhood Elizabeth's husband had been infatuated with his brilliant uncle. All three of his uncles were devoted to him and took an interest in his upbringing: Lord Upper Ossory and his brother, Richard Fitzpatrick, and Charles James Fox. But neither of the first two had the glamour of the last. Charles James had all the talents to impress an idealistic, clever child: charm, wit, generosity, the capacity to inspire and retain friendship, altruism, scholarly attributes, the gift of oratory. By the time Henry Richard was nine years old, Charles's electric personality was vibrating through Europe, letting off sparks and administering shocks to almost anyone who came in contact with it. To a small boy, probably this capacity for dangerous fireworks made him still more exciting. By the time Henry Richard had been a year at Eton, he had invested his paternal uncle with an aura of glory. Mutual admiration had always existed in the Fox family and, in 1783, Charles James praised his nephew thus: 'Notwithstanding what I have seen of him before, I am quite surprised at him. He really seems to be both for parts and good disposition to be quite a miracle.' Later, Henry Richard sensibly played down his own progress: 'I went through Eton and Oxford without disgrace and without distinction.' He ended up in Sixth Form, but never did as well at Oxford as he had hoped.

It was when he pursued his education abroad that his uncle's political indoctrination took effect, though this merely stimulated inherited ideas. Both Henry Fox and his eldest son, Stephen, had been admirers of Voltaire, with whom the former had struck up a lifelong friendship as a young man in Paris. In 1761, Stephen and a friend, Uvedale Price, visited Voltaire (by then an old man) at Ferney, and were admitted into his presence by the magic name of Fox, which Voltaire declared was sufficient introduction. Eight years later, Charles James too met Voltaire, but by then, his own outlook had become inflamed by a newer and more violent philosophy. In Paris, in 1765, the historian David Hume, constant friend of Jean Jacques Rousseau, deplored the dissipated life Charles James was leading, but was impressed by Fox's 'knowledge, force of mind and manly way of thinking at his age'.

In 1768, jointly representing the pocket borough of Midhurst (hired for them by their indulgent fathers, Lord Holland and Lord Ilchester), Charles James and his cousin, Lord Stavordale, were returned to Parliament. At the age of twenty, Charles James was made a junior Lord of Admiralty under Lord North. But such an association proved impossible. By February 1772, Charles James was declaring his sympathy with the American Colonies against the Crown and (by then in opposition) in October 1776, he denounced Lord North for his disastrous mishandling of the American campaign and accused him of losing 'a whole continent'. By which time, he had incurred the bitter enmity of George III for his opposition to the Royal Marriage Act, and had resigned.

Fox's early association with Edmund Burke had seemed a perfect fusion of ideals, as both stood for parliamentary reform and individual liberty. But, whereas Burke sought to parcel his freedoms within the framework of the King's authority, Fox wanted drastically to weaken the King's power. Convinced that George III himself was behind Lord North in his determination to continue the American War, in 1779, Fox declared in Parliament that the King was unconstitutional in his belief that he could be his own Minister, and proceeded to draw dark parallels between George III, James II and Charles I. Secretary of State for a brief period, he held office in the Coalition Government of 1783, when he introduced the India Bill, delegating the power of appointment in India solely to Parliament. This measure so enraged the King that he made its rejection a personal issue, declaring that members of the House of Lords who voted for it, thereafter, would cease to be his friends. The Bill was thrown out, but the King dismissed his Ministers and once more Charles James was thrown back into Opposition, where he remained for twenty-three years.

It is easy to see how the anti-monarchical views of Charles James Fox took shape in the receptive mind of his nephew and how, later, his every political prejudice was reflected in the child's mind.

In 1790, at the age of 17, Henry Richard and his tutor, the Reverend William Morris, did a tour in Europe, beginning in Belgium and ending up in Paris. Mirabeau was dead and, shortly after their arrival there, the French King, Louis XVI, bowed to the new Constitution. Henry Richard was enthralled and wrote to his sister: 'I have seen the old National Assembly and hope, when I am old, *to stand on tiptoe* when it is mentioned.' He struck up a friendship with Lafayette, with whom he often dined and was in full accord, greatly swayed by the sincerity of Lafayette's belief in the need for revolution. Through the introduction of Lord Wycombe, he frequented Madame de Flahault's salon in the Louvre, where he made a friend of Machiavellian dexterity in political intrigue, Prince Talleyrand de Périgord. And so, from a distance only, Henry Richard observed the French Royal Family and neglected to attend a Court.

In the summer of 1792, again he went abroad. This time he went alone, travelling through Denmark to Berlin, there to meet his friend, Charles Beauclerk. Despite his success with the beauties of Copenhagen, from Denmark he wrote his sister that he feared his heart was 'flinty and incapable of the tender sensations which poets so beautifully describe'. But while his heart slept, his brain was active, and it was filled with thoughts of the French Revolution to the exclusion of all else.

Circumstances prevented Henry from getting to St Petersburg though he knew that the Empress Catherine had been loud in her praise of Charles James Fox, and that already she had given him concrete proof of her gratitude. In 1785, she had sent him a valuable case of firearms: a fowling-piece and two pistols, ornamented with gold and silver and platinum, and with the flints made of agate. In 1791, she had commissioned her Ambassador to England, Count Woronzov, to send her Charles James Fox's bust. The instructions she had given to her Chamberlain hung, framed, near the firearms in Holland House.

Small wonder that such a man 'whose genius was admired even by his enemies, and whose frank and generous nature gained all who approached him' should be adored and blindly followed by the nephew who so described him.

*

To the distinguished portrait gallery established by his grandfather (later augmented by his father) Henry Richard, 3rd Lord Holland, could only contribute his own portraits by Gauffier and Fabre and that of his wife, by Gauffier, all painted in Florence. Taking their furtive place beside the Verelsts, the Lelys, the Liotards, the Gainsboroughs, the Reynolds, well might their contemporaries have expected them to fade into significance in such resplendent company. Yet, by the turn of the century, Gauffier's sitters had established themselves in the forefront of their family group, and Holland House had embarked on the most renowned period of its history.

So much so that, in 1811, Hookham Frere was to scratch his appreciation on a window pane:

> May neither fire destroy nor waste impair,
> Nor time consume thee till the twentieth heir
> May taste respect thee and may fashion spare.

By which time, Elizabeth Holland was living up to her sister-in-law's nickname of 'The Sovereign Lady'; and was known throughout Europe as the hostess at Holland House.

CHAPTER TEN

Family Involvement

SAFELY ANCHORED, now Elizabeth Holland could afford to keep her journal again. She declared: 'My own individual happiness is so perfect that I can scarcely figure to myself a blessing that I do not possess'; and, indeed, she had acquired a great many. Of supreme importance, a devoted young husband, ardent yet considerate, abstemious and not a gambler. Gay where Sir Godfrey had been morose, gentle where he had been violent, and a scholar who could help and direct her search. Her love for him and her proved fidelity to anyone who could teach her augured years of happiness ahead for them both.

As Lord Holland's wife, she held a position of importance, but her divorce had made social ostracism complete. She had to accept this, though not always with a good grace. When Lord Hervey's daughter married Elizabeth's childhood friend, Charles Ellis (whose unwise advice had prompted her own elopement), Elizabeth Hervey was warned by her family that Lady Holland's company was not fit for a bride. To which Elizabeth Holland made tart comment: 'Prudery comes with an odd and questionable aspect from a Hervey.' Knowing what she did of the Bishop of Derry, and of the morals of his daughter, Lady Elizabeth Foster, the bride's aunt, her asperity seems to be justified.

Before Elizabeth Holland herself contributed to it, the percentage of runaway marriages in the Fox family had been high. Lord Ilchester's clandestine marriage to Elizabeth Strangways-Horner in 1736; Henry Fox's elopement with Lady Caroline Lennox in 1744; that of Lady Susan Strangways (Lord Ilchester's daughter) with the actor, William O'Brien, in 1764; Lady Sarah Bunbury's (Caroline, Lady Holland's sister) with Lord William Gordon in 1769, which had led to a divorce. With the exception of Lady Sarah's elopement, these marriages had turned out well, but they had formed sizeable skeletons in the Fox family's cupboard, at the time.

Most of her husband's relations, male and female, now rallied stoutly

87

to Lady Holland's side. Of her women friends, Lady Bessborough visited her regularly and the Duchess of Devonshire called occasionally, and was not above touching Lord Holland for a loan. The Duchess's passion for gambling and her consequent dependence on money-lenders led her to appeal to him 'to send 200£ for me to Drummonds', which he refused, on the grounds that 'Ldy H and myself have been obliged to retrench much more than is pleasant'. But, judging from another undated, incoherent letter, this time to Lady Holland, his wife seems to have interceded with him on the Duchess's behalf. 'You must think me mad but I was half distracted with the fright of not being in time for the demand of 200 the 15th. I hear the money was paid yesterday therefore if Ld. H. had the goodness to send it, I enclose a note for it on Monday—with many thanks and entreating you and him to excuse me . . . God bless you Dr. Ly H. . . .'

On the eve of his marriage, Lord Holland had assured his sister that his wife would have 'not the smallest wish' to mix with the rest of the world so, outwardly, Elizabeth bore her snubs with dignity. Inwardly, her resentment hardened and, dreadful to relate, it found a private scapegoat in T. P.

Still in his capacity as Secretary for Ireland, in a letter without a beginning but dated 18th July 1797, and addressed to Elizabeth Holland from Phoenix Park, Dublin, Thomas Pelham refutes her accusation that he had tried to make capital out of his friendship with her:

> I think that my esteem and veneration for you might have protected me against the imputation of so mean and wicked an intention as that of sacrificing your honour and reputation for the purposes of establishing a character for gallantry. In your present situation my Friendship will certainly be less dangerous but whether I may ever look to the enjoyment of a limited society and domestic happiness is more than the situation I am placed in and the circumstances of the world enable me to form an opinion whatever my fate may be. I hope you may never suffer so much from any future connexion, and that where you form a friendship it may be bestowed on one who values it as much as I did.

Apparently Elizabeth had been under the impression that Lord Sheffield had sided with Sir Godfrey Webster against her, and this belief too Thomas Pelham refutes. His writing becomes more agitated. He ends up: 'I must confess that your letter gave me great pain . . . That the happiness you now enjoy may be permanent will be my constant wish—(another word scratched out) it is not probable that in ye event of things I should ever have the opportunity of contributing to it but I shall not be less anxious for its existence.' (No signature.)

This letter brought Elizabeth Holland to her senses and, two months later, she seized a pretext to write to Thomas Pelham again. His answer was courteous as ever, as dutifully presenting his compliments to the new husband as he had done to the old. Moreover, he assured Elizabeth that he had not been offended by her first letter, and from then on, kept up a desultory correspondence with her. But it is doubtful if the wound she had inflicted on him ever healed.

By Society, Elizabeth Holland's censorious treatment continued, even administered by one she loved. In 1798, as a child of thirteen, Harriet Cavendish describes to her sister, Georgiana, the consternation caused to the adult members of her family party, when meeting Lady Holland at Astley's Circus. 'The first thing struck our eyes was Lady Holland seated in the box. My aunt (Lady Bessboro') moved all her *ten fingers* at once. Mr and Mrs Petersen (the Bessborough's housekeeper and butler) . . . made signs, Lady Liz (Elizabeth Foster) twisted her *shawls* with a forbidding glance . . . and I who did not know who she was thought it rather strange that a poor lady looking so demure and quiet, shld. cause such evident confusion . . .' The twisting of Lady Elizabeth's shawls may have annoyed Lady Holland, but she must have been cruelly hurt by Lady Bessborough agitating 'all her ten fingers' in public, at sight of her. And, that evening, another humiliation was still to come. After the performance, rather cavalierly, Lord Holland drove back in Lady Bessborough's already overcrowded carriage and let Lady Holland drive home alone.

*

Still, however reluctantly, now the world had to recognise Lady Holland as a respectable woman in marked contrast to her friend, Mrs Wyndham, whose desperate love affair with Lord Holland's kinsman, Lord Wycombe, had run glaringly parallel with her own, since 1794.

As we know, in November 1795, Frances Wyndham had left her husband, giving as her pretext the health of her three children, whom she took with her. Lord Wycombe joined her in Turin and together they all proceeded to Lausanne.

Ironically enough, while Caroline Fox was writing Lord Holland urging him, on behalf of Lord Lansdown, to beg Lord Wycombe to return home, a friend of Lord Lansdown's family, 'Bobus' Smith, was writing to Lord Wycombe to use his influence with Lord Holland to the same effect. Neither young man would give away the other or admit that he was under any obligation to return. In a facetious but snubbing letter to 'Bobus' Smith from Lucca (dated 12th July 1795) Lord Wycombe quotes Lord

D*

Holland as having had 'the assurance to tell me that I was egregiously deceived in the estimate which I had formed both of his importance and my own; that it was nearly a matter of indifference to the people of England whether he passed his summer in the State of Tuscany or the purlieus of a Borough . . . It was useless to argue with one who had in the wildness of imagination formed to himself opinions so eccentric. This obstinacy disgusted me so much that I determined never more to interfere in the concerns of others, a resolution which I strongly recommend to you . . .'

A year later, Lord Holland took up the reverse rôle to Caroline Fox, in a more serious vein. 'I say everything kind and grateful to Ld. L.(ansdown) (who had already sent him understanding messages about his liaison with Lady Webster). As to his questions about Ld. Wycombe. You must prevent his asking me anything on the subject—wherever Mrs W. is concerned delicacy not to say Honor must prevent me speaking to any of Wycombe's friends in the way Ld. L. wld. expect. The world no doubt looks upon their attachment as pretty decided and when you speak to me upon it it certainly wld. be ridiculous in me to draw up my face and deny it . . . Mrs W. has no separation from her husband—She cld. if she liked tomorrow rejoin him. And upon the late events in Italy she has most handsomely and generously offered to share her own little income with him as his imprudencies have reduced him almost to nothing.'

William Wyndham's 'imprudencies' were hardly of his own making as he had been crying 'Wolf, wolf!' for years to a largely heedless Lord Grenville. Even after Bonaparte's unresisted campaign through Italy had started, and after French troops had entered Bologna, he still had the presence of mind to warn Lord Hood and the British Consul to prepare to evacuate Leghorn. Thanks to Wyndham, on 27th June 1796, this evacuation was successfully effected to Porto Ferraia, in Elba, complete with Embassy archives, nearly all movable British property and a large number of emigrants besides. Bonaparte entered Florence three days later. Thereby, with his salary of £5 per day inevitably interrupted and responsible as he was for the welfare of all British emigrants, it is hardly surprising that William Wyndham's resources were reduced 'almost to nothing', at that time.

Disregarding his cataclysmic misfortunes Lord Holland continues:

. . . I know Mrs Wyndham well enough to answer that nothing nothing would induce her to take this step and that she wld. move heaven and earth to prevent it (divorce)—but this I beg you to understand is what I say *to you* . . . It is no answer to Ld. L.

Lord Wycombe's egocentricity was colossal, yielding nothing to patriotism, filial duty or fidelity to his mistresses. Yet, within the citadel of his self-centredness there was a keen intelligence, a sense of humour and a kind heart.

From November 1795, till January 1797, he found life very palatable with Mrs Wyndham, in Lausanne. On 22nd December 1796, when congratulating Lord Holland on the advent of Charles Richard, and after saying how pleased he is that 'Lady W. and the Bambino are in good health', he adds: 'Since you insist on my talking of myself I must needs own that I live in this place v. comfortably and that I am grown so fond of a rational life that I know not what wld. tempt me to quit it, short of a sufficient reason; by which we metaphysicians mean a great deal.'

Unfortunately for Mrs Wyndham, 'sufficient reason' manifested itself soon after and, in January 1797, Lord Wycombe was on his way, alone, to England with the object of straightening out his father's tangled financial affairs. A solution proved difficult as, although descended through the Lords of Kerry from Irish ancestry going back six hundred years, Lord Lansdown's main interest lay in his Wiltshire property of Bowood on which he had lavished immense sums to embellish the house and park; whereas Lord Wycombe was, by temperament and predilection, uncompromisingly Irish, and firmly against bolstering up his father's English property at the expense of his estates in County Kerry. Therefore, inevitably, the contacts between father and son were protracted and often irascible and Lord Wycombe only returned to Lausanne for a fortnight, the following June.

From Basle, on 24th June 1798, he wrote Lord Holland that he was proceeding to Ireland . . . where 'I shall endeavour to make myself as well acquainted with that country as I can which is undoubtedly material to me'. He arrived in Dublin that September and remained in Ireland, almost entirely, till 1805! Within a month, his acquaintanceship with 'the Irish girls who are strangely beautiful' was quickly established. On 20th October, he complains: 'My transgressions . . . have been few. Four days comprised them all. Yet these rare offenses drew upon me Clap and Pox which affected me conjointly.'

From the first, Lord Wycombe had begged Elizabeth (then Webster) 'to write frequently to Mrs W. who will be very much bored with Switzerland especially as it is the place she is in'. Within a week of his original departure from Lausanne, Frances Wyndham is imploring Elizabeth to give her news of 'Pretty Wicky' as she calls him: ' . . . before you receive this you will no doubt have seen Pretty Wy. and no doubt you will find him as *Pretty* and as good and as entertaining as you found him at Bologna . . . write to me about nothing but Him, for while he is about no other subject will entertain me . . . we are v. different. You like nothing so much as to feel yr. self perfectly at Liberty and there is nothing I dread more than the Freedom that arises from belonging to Nobody . . . I wish to God I was dead.'

Elizabeth Webster received this letter shortly after she had given birth to her illegitimate son, and when she herself was in a state of great apprehension as to the outcome of her divorce. Despite her protestations to the contrary, her own sensitivity to world opinion comes out as clearly as Mrs Wyndham's contempt of it although, in every other respect, she was as strongminded as Frances Wyndham was weak-willed.

On 1st February 1797, Frances Wyndham writes again:

. . . You must be content to glide into Oblivion. Why don't you do as Ly. A. does, trot about in the grounds and feed the Ducks and Chickens and be as happy as the Day is long. She lives in an old Castle in Scotd., seldom sees any Body but a few Men and sometimes a Female Society of *Emigrées*. But she is happy in the unabated affection of Ld. A. and they are both much more fond of the Boy that was born before marriage than of the Girls since. You say you wanted an object whereon to bestow yr. affections, and whose tastes were the same as yr. own?? You have found all this and yet you are unhappy. The Fact is my dear Friend you have an active mind, you cannot lead the quiet life you at times think you prefer, either you must have the Pursuit of Chemistry Minerology—or you must be Traveling (*sic*) about but I hope a few yrs. will cure this restless turn.

Just before Lord Wycombe's longed-for visit (in June 1797) Mrs Wyndham writes her friend: 'I cannot feel the least anxiety about the early termination of yr. affair you can acquire nothing by the change of name, possessing as you do everything without it . . .' But, in July and again in August, she gallantly congratulates the newly wed Lord and Lady Holland on 'a continuation of the Happiness you Possess, and which has every appearance of Durability'.

Frances Wyndham had to trim her own future to Lord Wycombe's capricious whim. During his brief visit to her in Lausanne he had made it plain that he had no intention of marrying her and she comments miserably: 'He expresses himself in the strongest terms of disapprobation, and determined to avoid the ridicule of the world . . . There remains nothing for me to do but sustain it *well* or ill as I can.' But, after Lord Wycombe's departure, she conceives a hazardous plan. On 29th June, she writes to the then Lady Webster that she is thinking of moving from Lausanne to Tuscany as she dislikes 'the *Place* the *People* the *Climate*. At Florence the Children being in their Father's house relieves my mind from so great a source of anxiety . . .' which project annoys Lord Wycombe as much as it alarms William Wyndham.

Mainly due to his correct forecasting, Wyndham's circumstances had slightly improved, but Florence was still too vulnerable a place to receive back a wife and three children. In the spring of 1797, Bonaparte offered to move his troops from Leghorn, if the British Fleet would evacuate their ships from Porto Ferraia, Elba. Wyndham pressed acceptance of this plan to which His Majesty's Government finally agreed. In April, the British Fleet sailed from Elba and, in May, the French removed their troops from Leghorn. Florence resumed its gaiety and the British Consulate re-opened in Leghorn. British merchants returned to trade with Tuscany, pressing on William Wyndham, as tokens of their gratitude for his sagacious foresight, a silver salver and a signed letter of thanks. But neither of these was sufficient guarantee for the safe return of his family, which Wyndham now fought desperately to prevent.

Lady Holland did her best to ensure fair play from Lord Wycombe for her friend. On 26th September 1797, he thanks her for a letter about 'the little woman . . .' . . . 'Who is unable to tranquillise herself. I disapproved from the first . . . of the Florence scheme . . . At the same time I did not put an absolute Negative upon anything thinking it both unjust and impracticable to govern others.' But, week by week, his annoyance increases. On 13th October, he writes: 'Little woman roars like a Bull . . .' And, on 20th October, he bursts out: 'Well, there is no governing yr. precious sex. The little woman is on the point of doing everything that is perverse and absurd . . . I advised in vain—control I cld. not and I yielded to her desire in soliciting and obtaining . . . the Passports for Italy . . . The fright that W(yndham) felt at being put to some small additional charges for the maintenance and education of his own children induced him, in the plenitude of his own selfishness, to declare that he wld. abide by none of his engagements, and to justify himself handsomely and manfully by proclaiming the misconduct of his wife; all of which though not v. creditable to W. was not v. desirable for the little woman under the circumstances.' Evidently, the thought that Lord Wycombe himself was directly responsible for the Wyndham's matrimonial upheaval did not occur to him.

Intent on leaving Lausanne, now Frances Wyndham draws upon Lord Holland for £150, which action coincides with a hasty advance from her lover 'not for her journey, but for her own comfort where she was . . .' Then, she writes him that she does not intend to take his money 'in view of what she had done the day before', which he construes as meaning that he should pay it to 'the Compère' (Lord Holland). Mrs Wyndham remains adamant 'that nothing but illness shall prevent her from setting out upon the 29th ult. for Brunswick'. Whereupon, Lord Wycombe's irritation

fizzles out and he ends on a note of compassion. 'I know not how to be
angry with the little woman who no more knows how to shift for herself
than an old caged bird.'

In January 1798 Lord Wycombe begs Lady Holland urgently to use her
influence to dissuade her friend from joining him in Ireland. Bringing out
all the conventional arguments against which he was usually wont to scoff,
he writes:

> I shld, act with great injustice both to Mrs W. and myself if I permitted myself
> to entertain a scheme of living with her in this country . . . She wld. be obliged to
> sacrifice most culpably the interests of her children . . . and that too at an age in
> which neither of us surely shld, make love the first business of our lives . . . and I
> need not comment on . . . the expense, or the extravagance . . . of her following me
> with three children from place to place, and country to country, to the utter ruin of
> a character which has not yet ceased to be respected . . .

Doughtily, Lady Holland trounces Lord Wycombe's now sanctimonious
sentiments. He replies, in three aggrieved letters, dated 27th January,
6th March and 16th March: 'I am sorry you shld. think that Mrs W. needs
any other Advocates than that within my own breast . . . no true friend of
hers will advise her coming to Ireland . . . I know not why you shld.
affect to have been ignorant of the little woman's design which if you had
been really her friend you wld. have discountenanced . . . Her disregard
of her children whom she talks of leaving between England and Ireland
is shocking. She is bent on her own destruction whilst I endeavour to
make bad better instead of worse . . .'

On 8th March, Mrs Wyndham arrived in Dublin and, a fortnight later,
Lord Wycombe is asking Lady Holland a thousand pardons for his suspicions of her. On 23rd March, he writes again: 'The little woman has been
fixed about five days in the Loutherbourg of Ireland; that is to say she is v.
creditably lodged about a mile and a half from Dublin and not a hundred
yards from the sea . . . She has left her Children with her Nurse and an
Italian coachman of Trevor's at Brunswick—with 50 Louis d'Ors and 6
Spoons and Forks to sell aux besoins! . . . Such an arrangement exceeds
my powers of comprehension. What is to become of the poor brats (of)
whom I think as *you* do . . . Yet something must be done or they will soon
be sucking their paws.'

But Mrs Wyndham's unhappy love affair was nearing its end. Reunited
at last with her lover, almost immediately her jealousy was aroused against
Lady Giffard ('a prodigious fine sow' whom Lord Wycombe eventually
married) and his maid ('my wench Rosy'). She endured it for six weeks and
then left Dublin on 23rd April, as suddenly as she had come. Although she

was to meet Lord Wycombe again in Wales and England, that autumn and in 1799, by 15th December 1798 he was unconsciously writing her obituary. In a postscript to a letter to Lord Holland he comments cruelly: 'The little woman looks like old Scratch and does not find it out.'

William Wyndham did not forget the injuries he had sustained at the hands of his wife's seducer. On 28th May 1801, Bell's *Weekly Messenger* recorded the case of 'Wyndham, Esq. v. Earl of Wycombe' in which William Wyndham sued Lord Wycombe for Criminal Conversation with his wife and damages laid at £10,000. He failed, largely because Lord Wycombe managed to produce fortuitous proof in Florence of Wyndham's own infidelity. At the end of his funds, he retired to Udine.

With her now obsessive respectability, Lady Holland urged Frances Wyndham to become reconciled with her husband. But Frances maintained her social intractability to the end. In September 1801, while admitting to Lady Holland that for her children's sake a 'decent intimacy' might still be desirable, she declared that she had suffered enough and was resolved to stand alone.

PART TWO

Floodlights

CHAPTER ELEVEN

Châtelaine

ALTHOUGH, AT THE start of her married life, Elizabeth Holland professed herself little interested in politics, within a month of her establishment in her new home she found herself presiding at what was, in effect, a Whig conference. On 14th October 1797, Charles James Fox, his kinsman 'Loo' Duke of Bedford, and other leading Whigs met at dinner at Holland House, the outcome of which was that, with the exception of George Tierney, they decided to secede from Parliament. Their reason being the failure of Charles Grey's motion for Parliamentary reform.

As an initiate, Elizabeth strongly criticised her guests for their decision, and in her first condemnation of the party system, we trace the stirrings of her unconscious search for a different form of government. 'As to the measure of secession there are many different opinions as to its expediency; but all their discussions end in the loss of time and temper, for Opposition are too unpopular to have anything left to hope for, and the system of party is obsolete. It seems astonishing to me that amidst the number of v. able men who still rally round the standard of Whiggism, not one should have discovered that the temper of the country requires another species of resistance to Administration than the old scheme of a regular Opposition with a Cavendish or a Russell at its head. There is a bigotry in their adherence to their ineffectual principles that borders upon infatuation.' And, at the other end of the scale, Lord Lansdown (whose antagonism to Charles James Fox dated back to 1783) asked Lord Holland: 'Is yr. Uncle aware what he is doing? Secession means rebellion, or it is nonsense.'

Elizabeth Holland's own impressions of her husband's uncle were twofold. First, they were made by Thomas Pelham who, while always fair, was sometimes critical of him; then Lord Holland extolled him to her, to the exclusion of all fault. So she had to resort to public opinion to balance these two views. This, she declared, was strongly in Fox's favour '. . . his v. enemies admit that he possesses more estimable qualities as an individual than falls to the share of scarcely any other'. And, once she was a member

99

of his family, she speedily and, as it were deliberately, became another victim to his charm.

In 1797, at the time of Fox's secession from Parliament, instead of a disconsolate politician raking over the ashes of his career, she found a profound scholar eager to take up again his study of Greek verse and the metaphysics of grammar in the peace and quiet of his own home, St Anne's at Chertsey, in company with his beloved mistress, Mrs Armistead. (In 1795, Charles James had, in fact, secretly married Mrs Armistead, but made no attempt to establish his lady's good name until 1802.)

Elizabeth Holland was on shaky ground when criticising the domestic irregularities of her husband's uncle, but she made it plain that she did not approve of Mrs Armistead's promiscuous past. And, as a thrifty housewife of three months' standing, she berated Mrs Armistead for her extravagance. Finally, she regretted that Charles James was to be 'lost to society', and altogether showed quite a little petulance when her brilliant new uncle seemed to prefer St Anne's to Holland House.

*

Though ostracised by the Court and the high Tories, as châtelaine of Holland House, Elizabeth began to repair her shattered ego. Her husband gave her a free rein and, for a woman who without difficulty had established a brilliant salon in Florence, it was easy to do so in Kensington. She even set up in friendly rivalry with the Duchess of Devonshire, whose social activities were restricted now by domestic tensions and increasing bad health. No gambling was permitted at Holland House. Otherwise the ingredients were the same, but used with a superior sense of application, sugaring the opinions of some guests, peppering others. Above all, on a basis of tolerance, allowing all shades of opinion to be expressed. Beside her, her husband contributed his inexhaustible good humour, charming all comers with his wit and erudition. Such a combination was irresistible. Only one art was missing, that of music. Lord Holland was not appreciative, so Elizabeth put away her guitar.

Soon a throng of interested men began to crowd through the magnificent portals designed by Nicholas Stone, including former critics: Charles Beauclerk, Lord Granville Leveson-Gower, Richard Brinsley Sheridan. (Elizabeth would have been the first to agree that the last two followed hotly in Lady Bessborough's train.) Joseph Jekyll was welcomed for his wit; Sir Philip Francis (later, the reputed author of *The Letters of Junius*) became a regular visitor; and the precociously brilliant young William Lamb made his début at Holland House. Charles Grey (now respectably married) and Lord Lauderdale fiercely argued their theories of secession with George Tierney. And Tory views were as emphatically expressed by Hookham Frere and George Canning, renegade Whig.

By 1797, Sheridan was as infamous in politics as he was famous in the theatre. With Fox, he had defended the policy of non-intervention in the war with France, and, with Fox, he had become a leader of the Devonshire House set, in opposition. Despite his love for his gentle wife Elizabeth Linley, by 1790 he had conceived a lust for Lady Bessborough which no amount of snubbing could check. With contrition, he had mourned his wife's death in 1792, and his subsequent marriage to Esther Ogle in 1795 had meant nothing to him. He continued to dog Lady Bessborough's footsteps, wherever she went, and probably his allegiance to Holland House was as much sentimental as political. Elizabeth treated his new friendliness with caution. 'About him, my reason and impulse are always at variance; reflection convinces me he ought to be despised for his private life and doubted for his political, but whenever I see him, if but for five minutes, a sort of cheerful frankness and pleasant witticism puts to flight all ye reasonable prejudices that I entertain against him.'

In 1798, 'Monk' Lewis (so called for his successful novel *Ambrosio, or the Monk*) was introduced to Holland House by Sheridan. A gruesome play, *The Castle Spectre*, which he had induced Sheridan to present at Drury Lane, had followed. Sheridan had no great opinion of it. Lewis said: 'I'll lay you the profits of my play (which, by the bye, Sheridan, you have not paid me).' To which Sheridan retorted: 'I do not like high wagers, but I'll lay you a small one, the worth of it.' Monk's plays continued lurid, but his verse was better and, by February 1799, he was asking Elizabeth Holland if he could dedicate his translation of the thirteenth Satire of Juvenal to Charles James Fox. She assured him that such a gesture would be taken as a compliment but, when the translation appeared, she noted that 'twenty-eight of the best lines are by William Lamb, a rising genius, who is to dine here for the first time today' (29th February). Lord Holland parodied some of Monk's verses and his version got into the newspapers, much to his wife's alarm. Addressed to Lord Wycombe, they dealt with the excesses of the King's forces in Ireland, hardly a subject to escape censure, if traced back to him.

Elizabeth Holland's first description of George Tierney is 'a man of whom everybody believes something against'. Of humble origin, he had married a rich wife and decided on a career in politics, as a Whig. After secession, he still continued to attend debates in the House of Commons, thereby incurring the censure of his party. But this did not preclude his becoming a regular diner at Holland House where he fell madly in love with his hostess.

It was as Pitt's Secretary of State that George Canning audaciously presented himself at Holland House. All his early education had been due to Charles James Fox, through whose influence he went to Eton. There, as a fellow student of Holland, he had shown brilliance as scholar and speaker and had contributed witty articles to the Eton chronicle, *The Microcosm*. At Oxford, he professed advanced Jacobin views. Sheridan introduced him at Devonshire House where, for a while, he was content to amuse himself. But his class-consciousness caused him to rebel against the autocratic outlook of the Whigs, and their insensitivity to the mounting horrors of the French Revolution drove him to ally himself with Pitt. As an old friend of her husband's, Elizabeth Holland received George Canning cordially but much less trustingly than her indulgent spouse. 'He is, in his heart, the veriest Jacobin there is, and wld., if he were not in power, manifest his principles in a most dangerous, innovating Opposition . . .' Still, Canning genuinely shared with Lord Holland two consuming passions: a love of the classics and a hatred of slavery.

The number of Elizabeth Holland's guests increased, sometimes amounting to fifty a day. From May 1799 she began to keep her Dinner Books.

*

Although her own love life was regularised she still retained the instinct to flirt. Now, much to the resentment of his wife, George Tierney attached himself to her as her 'shadow'. Like a cat with a mouse, Elizabeth Holland encouraged, then admonished him, not altogether displeased by his persistence. In fact, she remarked complacently on the jealousy Mrs Tierney evinced towards her at a masquerade.

Himself incapable of jealousy, Lord Holland criticised George Tierney for his attitude towards secession. He admitted that Tierney had done his best to induce Charles James and his followers not to pursue it, but felt that Tierney's own defection had ruined its chance of success. With his usual good humour Charles James proclaimed: 'We have to explain to Mr Tierney why we leave the House of Commons, not Mr Tierney to account to us for staying there.' But his followers were severe in their censure.

A new scalp was added to Lady Holland's trophies: that of Lord Hobart's step-son, 'Mr Adderley', who began to attend Lady Holland at her home and at the play. He fell into the habit of spending the night at Holland House and, besotted, mooned in the garden with his hostess, past midnight, listening to 'the harper' playing under the trees. His infatuation began to be talked of, and Elizabeth Holland grew alarmed. She resolved to make a clean breast of the whole affair to her husband whose complete understanding fully justified the risk she took. Then, a further complication arose. Lady Lucy Fitzgerald fell in love with Mr Adderley and, immediately, Elizabeth proclaimed that the unfortunate girl was 'amorously disposed'. So, perhaps it was in the best interests of all three of them that she prevailed on Mr Adderley to return for a while to his native town, Cork. Having done so, her circumspection gained her praise from an unexpected quarter. Lord Granville Leveson-Gower 'praised me for my behaviour to Add., approves of keeping friends, but checking the progress of an attachment'. No one was worse qualified than he to express such views.

Having salved her conscience by one confession, Elizabeth Holland felt it prudent to withhold any other. 'I am satisfied by reason that I ought not to disclose "gouts passagers" that are in themselves of no importance, but become so as soon as communicated.' Once again she clamped down on her journal and, next year, when a former suitor laid unsuccessful claim to her heart, she kept his name to herself.

*

To Elizabeth's surprise, towards the end of the year 1797, Caroline Vernon became engaged to Robert ('Bobus') Smith. Despite the rose-coloured spectacles through which she was determined to view the ladies of Bowood, not much sympathy had been engendered between her and the Vernon sisters, and she took a poor view of the marriage. 'In a worldly point of view it is bad, as they will be excessively poor, but the worst part is the great disparity of age; he is twenty-seven she is thirty-nine, twelve years upon the wrong side'. Later on, she became yet more disenchanted, calling Mrs Smith 'a superannuated, prudish beauty'. Lord Lansdown was horrified by the marriage and called it a 'profligate abandonment'. And yet, by 1803, he had so far revised his opinion of Bobus Smith as to advocate his appointment to be Advocate General in Bengal.

*

On 10th January 1798, Lord Holland made his maiden speech in the House of Lords. He spoke against Pitt's proposal to treble, for one year, his taxes on houses, windows, carriages and other personal possessions in order to help pay for the war with France. Although Charles James had seceded from Parliament he was delighted that 'his dear one' should go into politics and praised his initial performance. Lord Holland had drafted the Protest himself and it was bad luck that only one peer, Lord Oxford, signed it with him. His uncle comforted him: 'I think yr. speech, whether well or ill given, reads v. well indeed, but it was not the goodness of the speech only that I attended to, it was the stoutness of fighting so well, all alone against them all, and I was really delighted full as much as I said and more.'

A month later, Elizabeth Holland was taken ill and examined her condition with absorption. 'I had an alarming complaint in my stomach, the cause a total debility, the effect a deathlike, icy coldness which suspended all the functions of digestion, from which torpor nothing but the strongest cordials cld. revive me.' Her physician, Dr Parry, took a risk and bled her, which drastic treatment proved successful. After a three weeks stay in Bath, she and her husband returned to 'this delightful mansion' (Holland House). A paeon of thankfulness followed her recovery, delivered indiscriminately to God, nature or fortune. In this mood of gratitude for returned health she conceived Lord Holland's second, and first legitimate son, Stephen.

*

The same year, Tierney was commissioned by Grey to tell Lord Holland that the Prince of Wales sought an interview with the Duke of Northumberland. When this took place, the Prince 'expressed great alarms about the state of the country' and deplored 'the desperate measures of the Ministers, who were driving everything on with great violence'. He entreated the Duke to use his influence with Fox to get him to sign a declaration of adherence to Crown and State, in return for which a debate on 'a specified reform' might be agreed to. Reluctantly, the Duke passed on this idea which was immediately turned down, not only by Fox but by the whole party. And, owing to differences of opinion among themselves, a counter proposal, that the Whigs should now declare their full reasons for secession, came to nothing.

In May, Charles James and his nephew reacted violently to the news of their kinsman Lord Edward Fitzgerald's arrest in Dublin. At first, they wanted to go over to Ireland to attend his trial for treason, there to plead his cause, but later, when Lord Edward had been clapped into gaol, they decided to remain at home the better to condemn the circumstances of his capture. Lord Henry Fitzgerald came to see Lord Holland, pending an answer to his appeal to the Duke of Portland (former Viceroy of Ireland) to visit his brother, in prison. And his mother, the Duchess of Leinster, came and stayed for a while at Holland House. With relish, Elizabeth took up her rôle, as one of the mourners in this family tragedy. On marriage, she had absorbed the tone and texture of her husband's family and now upheld it against all comers. Now, she recorded that Lord Henry wrote 'a violent, reproachful letter to Ld. Camden of such a nature that personal danger may be the effect'. But she made no mention of attempting herself to appeal for clemency, to Lord Camden's Secretary of State, Thomas Pelham.

Despite the opprobrium of the Court (and perhaps because of it) on 21st June 1798, the Prince of Wales dined at Holland House. To meet him, the Hollands invited members of the Whig party: Fox, Grey, Sheridan, Whitbread, Tierney, the Dukes of Norfolk and Leinster, Lords Suffolk and Bessborough, John and William Russell. His Royal Highness arrived so early, at six o'clock, that hardly any of his fellow-guests were there to greet him. Eventually, with the exception of Sheridan, they all arrived and he joined them after dinner. Talk centred on Ireland, and the Prince declared 'that he was willing to do everything that could serve the cause of Ireland' and almost pledged himself, if Fox thought fit, to 'make a motion' in the House of Lords. While applauding his sentiments, Grey cautioned him by saying that any rash statement made by him might well imperil his right of succession.

*

As Lord Holland kept nothing from her, his wife was primed with news. Now some secret correspondence came her way, which altered the whole course of her thinking.

Since marriage, Elizabeth's journalistic sense had blunted and only rarely did the rumble of war with France obtrude itself upon her ears. When it did, the indoctrination of Charles James Fox inclined her to pacifism. Her bias in favour of the French continued and when, on 1st August 1798, Nelson destroyed the French fleet at Aboukir, she forbore to cheer. Instead, she speculated as to whether or not Bonaparte could maintain his forces in Egypt. 'Sickness and ye want of wine and clothing are the chief obstacles to a permanent establishment, but I hope and almost believe the skill of Bonaparte will baffle even those inconveniences.' So, her sympathies towards him were already aroused when copies of two or three of his letters, intercepted after the Battle of the Nile, fell into her lap.

One of them was written to his brother, Joseph Bonaparte, and Elizabeth comments: 'It places that extraordinary man in a far more amiable point

of view than I had seen him in before.' By it, she realised Napoleon
Bonaparte's fondness for his brother, and his schizophrenia between soldier
and idealist, 'disgusted with life and mankind'. Together with this letter
was another, written by Bonaparte's step-son, Eugène de Beauharnais, to
his mother. This described Bonaparte's sadness after an interview with his
general, Berthier, which confirmed his suspicions of Josephine's infidelity.
It concluded by saying that, despite this painful knowledge, Bonaparte's
kindness 'increased towards Eugène'. Elizabeth concludes: 'These letters
are not to be published; it perhaps would be as handsome if the Ministers
sent them to their respective addresses.' In fact, Pitt published them.

They made a lasting impression on Elizabeth and materially shaped her
future sympathies. She had a strong streak of hero-worship in her make-up
and, after reading them, without knowing it, she fell in love with their
concept of a superman with a human heart. In every woman there is a
primitive desire to be dominated and although Elizabeth was devoted to
her 'Holly', he was too gentle to attempt to do so by force. Rather, in
moments of passion, he was more likely to kiss her feet than to drag her
along by her hair.

*

On 18th January 1799, Elizabeth Holland gave birth to her son, Stephen.
Again, Mr Croft attended her. Everything passed off well and, two days
later, she was sufficiently recovered to receive guests. On 30th March,
five days after her twenty-eighth birthday ('Alas! Alas!') the Hollands
christened their second son. In contrast to the surreptitious baptism of their
first-born, the advent of this one occasioned great festivity. Lady Affleck,
the Duke of Bedford and Lord Upper Ossory stood sponsors, and it was
by special request of the Duchess of Leinster that the baby was called
Stephen. Just ordained, Matthew Marsh performed the ceremony. A
large dinner party followed, attended by the Duke of Bedford, the
Bessboroughs and their son, Lord Duncannon, Lord Upper Ossory,
Lord Granville Leveson-Gower, Sir Gilbert and Lady Affleck, one Miss
Vernon and 'all those in the house'. Besides its widening influence as a
political and cultural centre, now Holland House formed the background,
as of old, for frequent family gatherings.

Some time before Stephen's birth, Lady Louisa Connolly wrote to her
sister, Lady Sarah Napier (erstwhile Bunbury): '. . . what I think about
the Hollands with whom I have made a thorough acquaintance. He is,
I believe as near perfection as anybody can be . . . and as for poor Lady
Holland, she has been quite misrepresented to us. I like her of all things.

They are as happy a couple as can be, and she has excellent sense, no affectation or pretensions, many amiable qualities I am convinced, uncommonly agreable (*sic*) and in short we have taken to one another prodigiously—She is beautiful with the finest skin I ever saw, not v. healthy and in constant anxiety they both are about a v. fine little Boy that is not healthy. We are to have a family party at Holland House which I shall realy (*sic*) like from having taken so much to them . . .' The Duchess of Leinster, plus her husband, Mr Ogilvie and two daughters, Lucy Fitzgerald and 'Mimi' (Emily) Ogilvie, stayed at Holland House for a fortnight, to include Stephen's christening. At which time the hapless Lady Lucy suffered another matrimonial rebuff, when the Duchess refused to consider Matthew Marsh as her suitor. And when, to make matters worse, she had to watch the successful progress of her stepsister, Mimi's romance with Charles Beauclerk, which had her mother's approval. Lord Henry Fitzgerald and Lord Edward's son 'Eddy' (now brought up by his grandmother) stayed too. Caroline Fox and Miss Vernon were regular guests. And even Charles James spent an occasional night at Holland House, usually to speak to the Whig Club.

But two esteemed relations stayed away. Since the autumn of 1798, the Hollands had found themselves unwittingly caught up in the endless wrangles of Lord Lansdown with his elder son, both of whom were suspicious of each other's friends. Helplessly situated between two warring factions the Hollands stood unjustly condemned by both sides. But Elizabeth Holland determined to keep calm. '. . . they are both so wrong-headed, and so wide of the simple truth, that I have resolved not to say another word.' And, although Lord Wycombe remained surprisingly obdurate, before the end of April 1799, the Hollands had charmed Lord Lansdown back again.

*

A month later, Elizabeth Holland prevailed on her husband to attend a Court. Meeting Mr Adderley in the street, Lord Wycombe commented: 'So Holland has been at Court; *that* is owing to her Ladyship's activity.' When told of this remark Elizabeth showed no resentment and, thereafter, Lord Holland attended regularly on his monarch.

Provided his domestic background remained impeccable, his career as a leading Whig now seemed assured. Yet still his wife was anxious. Already, her marriage to him provided subject for scandal. What if the concealment of her daughter Harriet should be the means of ruining him?

Since her divorce, Sir Godfrey had allowed Elizabeth no access to her Webster children. In April 1799, through the connivance of her mother,

Lady Affleck, she managed to see Webby (now ten years old) three times, but all these meetings were clandestine. Elizabeth records her conflicting impressions of Webby: 'He was v. affectionate. He seems clever, but is not handsome. He is cold in his disposition, and taught by his father to be a boaster. He is at Harrow. From my window I can see the Church; often do I sigh to be nearer to him.' Had Sir Godfrey got to know of these meetings, no doubt he would have made a scene and might well have accused Elizabeth's new husband of abetting them. If, now, he became aware of Harriet's existence, how would he react? Might he not accuse Lord Holland of being an accessory to her concealment? And, if so, could Lord Holland's reputation survive a second buffeting?

Again, Elizabeth faced a crisis, and, as in the past, her adventurous spirit spurred her into action. But, whereas before it had inspired her to hide Harriet from her father, this time it inspired her to hand her back to him. Even Lady Affleck did not know of the child's existence, and to acquaint her of it now seemed of prior importance. This achieved, Elizabeth hoped that her mother would be disposed to act as intermediary between herself and Sir Godfrey, to break to him the astonishing news that the daughter he had mourned as dead had suddenly come alive! On 19th June 1799, she divulged her secret to Lady Affleck, who agreed to play her part.

Elizabeth's humble confidence to her journal reads pathetically: 'She (Harriet) was here with my mother for two days, is now gone with her and Henry, and is without exception by far the most lovely I ever beheld. She has all the beauties I had when I was v. pretty, and fewer blemishes. Her complexion is fine; she has dimples; fine hair, thick eyelashes, open chest, flat back.' With infinite relief, Elizabeth records Sir Godfrey's agreeable reaction to his long-lost daughter. 'My mother avowed the whole transaction to Sir G. W. who immediately recollected and acknowledged her; he behaved extremely well.'

Her revelations provided new material for the gossip-mongers especially when, on the exhumation of Harriet's supposed coffin, it was found to contain the body of a kid! How it got there has never been explained. Elizabeth knew fresh scandal would revolve round her but her conscience was at rest. 'I only feel I have renounced a darling child, and my heart aches afresh when I think of the separation. She is so captivating. With her I feel amused, with my others I feel gratified to see them healthy and intelligent, but her winning manners convert the duty of maternal attention into a positive enjoyment. I delight in being with her, and think her society sufficient. Wld. to God I were allowed to bring her up!'

The nine days' wonder died down. And even Maria Josepha Holroyd (newly wed to John Stanley, future Lord Stanley of Alderley) forbore to mention it.

*

On his twenty-sixth birthday (21st November 1799) Lord Holland found some verse on his dressing table, from his devoted wife:

> When thus to hail thy natal day,
> I strike my lyre and raise my song,
> 'Tis self that prompts my lips to say
> May Heaven preserve my Henry long . . .

He and she had weathered their difficult times and at last seemed to be sailing in smooth waters. Yet, several months' distress still lay ahead of them.

On Tuesday, 3rd June 1800, Sir Godfrey Webster shot himself. His family believed he died of a broken heart. Elizabeth Holland believed that he killed himself because of a gambling loss. (One of his creditors, his attorney, Mr Plummer, told her Sir Godfrey owed £17,000.) For some time, he had been depressed. A doctor had attended him for 'a low fever', but had failed to restore his spirits. Twice, he had tried to take an over-dose of laudanum and, each time, his manservant had intervened to stop him. Then, three days before his death, Sir Godfrey despatched his cousin, Whistler Webster, out of the way to fetch him some title deeds from Sussex. At nine o'clock in the morning of Tuesday, 3rd June, he went out and bought a pair of pistols from the gunsmith, Egg. At half-past four, on the same afternoon, he turned them on himself in his drawing-room in Tenterden Street.

Elizabeth was thankful he had not taken such desperate measures two years earlier. Had he done so, 'the world and my own readiness to upbraid myself would have assigned my quitting him as the cause'. His death produced fresh difficulties. Although, by it, the whole of Elizabeth's fortune would be restored to her, her estrangement from her Webster children became complete.

After Sir Godfrey had accepted Harriet back into his home, he had sent her to school, where, according to her mother, she was not happy. In December 1799, Elizabeth contrived to see her at Sir Gilbert Affleck's house, Dalham Hall, near Newmarket, but regular meetings between them were prohibited. By his will of 1786, Sir Godfrey had made his sister, Elizabeth Chaplin, and her husband, sole guardians of his children.

They were doggedly determined to carry out what they believed to be his wishes despite the kindly intervention of Lord Egremont, an old friend of Sir Godfrey's, to stop them. At the time of the funeral, with partial success, Lord Egremont removed the two Webster boys from school—Webby to Petworth, Henry to Dalham. But he was powerless to remove Harriet from her school, where she remained out of reach of her mother.

Florentius Vassall had decreed that, on his granddaughter's death, her fortune should be equally divided among her sons. As Elizabeth Holland now had four sons, two Websters and two Foxes, she had first to establish their equal rights by legally 'seizing' her property from her eldest (Webster) son, to prevent his claiming it in its entirety. But, for the third time, she found herself fighting, not for her sons, but for the welfare of her daughter, Harriet.

Whatever the outcome, when their mother died, both Webster boys were entitled to a share of her West Indian property. But Harriet stood to inherit only a portion of the moiety of £10,000 'for younger children' covenanted in Elizabeth Vassall's marriage settlement. The situation improved slightly when it was discovered that Sir Godfrey had left property 'to answer all debts'. And, a few weeks after his death, Elizabeth records in her journal that Webby would inherit £1,000 a year from his father's estate which, with his minority still ten and a half years to run, would 'be something'. Also, that Henry and Harriet would inherit £5,000 each. But nothing was assured for Harriet's future.

From writing fulsome letters of congratulation to Lady Holland at the time of her second marriage, Thomas Chaplin now became completely unco-operative, quickly making the Webster children Wards in Chancery and ignoring Lady Holland's offer to pay for Harriet's education and maintenance. Although he admitted that his promise had been made orally to Sir Godfrey, with nothing in writing, he maintained that he had given him his word that Lady Holland should not have access to her Webster children.

A letter from Webby to his brother, Henry (copied by Elizabeth Holland on to the back of one of his earlier letters to her), shows how balefully his father had influenced him against his mother. Dated 22nd June 1800, a fortnight after Sir Godfrey died, it reads:

My dearest Henry,
   The loss we have sustained will be to you and me for ever irreparable . . . But above all things my dear Henry remember never to see Lady Holland again as for me I have made up my mind never to see her or speak to her again, this my dear Henry remember for our poor father's sake and were his last wishes.

Luckily, Elizabeth had friends in plenty to help her. Henry was under Lady Affleck's immediate care (and lovingly spoilt in the process); Sir Gilbert Affleck continued in his rôle of liaison between Lady Holland and Sir Godfrey's lawyers, and some of the best legal brains were at his disposal: Lord Thurlow, Lord Erskine, and Samuel Romilly.

But the machinery of the law creaked on very slowly, running into months. And, while (with Lord Thurlow's help) Lord Holland was drafting an appeal for his wife to send to the Lord Chancellor, begging for reasonable access to her Webster children, he and she suffered a sad loss in their own home. Their baby, Stephen, died on his father's twenty-seventh birthday (21st November 1800) at Holland House. Despite her distress, Elizabeth Holland recorded his death with clinical precision: '. . . two tubercles upon the lung, and a pint of water upon the chest.'

CHAPTER TWELVE

Consul of France

BONAPARTE RALLIED FROM his defeat by Nelson at Aboukir to take Cairo and subdue Egypt, but his next opportunity came in a different field. News of the desperate plight of the Directory decided him to return to France. The *coup d'état* of the 18th Brumaire (9th November 1799) blazed his trail to glory. Shortly afterwards, he was elected First Consul of the French Republic for a period of ten years. Charles James Fox described the means Bonaparte took to reshape the French Constitution 'as military men are apt to do, by taking all the power into his own hands'.

Early in 1800, Bonaparte made an overture for peace to George III, which was haughtily refused by Pitt's government. A debate took place in Parliament. Reluctant though he was to leave the happy serenity of his home, Fox was persuaded to spend two nights at Holland House, to speak in it. In the Lords, Lord Holland spoke against rejection of Bonaparte's peace offer and Charles James spoke on the same theme, in the Commons. In the ensuing division, Fox could only muster sixty-nine supporters as against Pitt's two hundred and sixty. Pitt's Cabinet redoubled its efforts to defeat Bonaparte and Lord Holland ascribes to either George Canning or William Gifford the incautious boast that 'the idol of France tottered on his throne'. By December 1800 'the idol' had regained its balance. Bonaparte's armies caused Austria to sue for peace, and England was left alone to fight the French.

Long before this, Elizabeth Holland was complaining of the rising cost of living in England. Already, in October 1799, she had commented on the price of sugar, which had led to attempts to produce a cheaper synthetic substitute made from 'saccharine vegetables', and she had noted that a good weight of sugar had been extracted from beetroot, in Prussia. The price of West Indian sugar was down but as the Vassall revenues from it went to Sir Godfrey Webster and not to herself, Elizabeth derived a certain satisfaction from his loss of income. During the summer

112

of 1800, she observed that bread had risen to seventeen and a half pence the quartern loaf, coals sold at six guineas a cauldron, turkeys at sixteen shillings each, capons at eight shillings and sixpence, butcher's meat 'from one shilling to 14d. a pound'. To combat the rising scarcities, the Hollands adopted the regulations pertaining to the House of Lords. 'Each person in the family is limited to a quartern loaf per week, no pastry, no fine bread for breakfast.'

Charles James had a younger brother, Henry Edward Fox. He achieved a distinguished career in the Army, and by 1800 was General in the Mediterranean, with his headquarters in Minorca.

General Kléber's despatches from Egypt to the French Directorate were intercepted and brought to Fox. These gave details of dispositions and the scarcity of ammunition in the army Bonaparte had abandoned to its fate, as well as Kléber's own condemnation of Bonaparte's eve-of-departure letter to his troops. Such documents were vital weapons with which to blast open the legend of Bonaparte's invulnerability and Pitt decided to publish them, at once.

Upon which, Elizabeth Holland went to the superman's defence. 'There can be nothing more contemptible than the personal pique all ministerial people seem to feel towards him (Bonaparte). The object in publishing these letters is merely to gall him by an expression or two, and for this gratification they shabbily put in the names of individuals, which may be the means of much private ruin. They say "Aye, this will do him up!".' But, in his struggle to defeat the arch-enemy of his country, Pitt by-passed the rules of fair play, laid down by Brooks's Club.

*

Limited as they still were to exploring the beauties of their own country-side, during the late summer of 1799, the Hollands carried out an extensive tour of the West Country, progressing as far as Powys Castle, in Wales, and returning via Bowood to stay with Lord Lansdown, and then on to Lord Digby, at Sherborne and Lord Boringdon, at Saltram Park, near Exeter. But though Elizabeth Holland admitted that Tintern Abbey was 'a delicious ruin'; and declared that Saltram House was 'quite the best I ever resided in', the fact that impressed her most about the tour was the death of her Blenheim spaniel, Pierrot. 'He was the gift of Ld. Henry (Spencer). He faithfully maintained the love for me his master felt whilst living.'

Ever mindful of her distress, Lord Holland composed her little dog's epitaph:

E

Pierrot, of race, of form, of manners rare,
Envied alike in life and death lies here.
Living he proved the favourite of the fair,
And dying drew from beauty's eye a tear.

*

Sir Godfrey Webster's suicide and Webby's terrible letter may have decided Lord Holland to give his wife a wider change of scene. For, on 10th July 1800, despite the ravaged state of Europe, he and she embarked on a tour of North Germany, intending to return through France. Having received qualified approval for his journey from the Foreign Secretary, Lord Grenville (so long as he avoided Paris), Lord Holland armed himself with passports from the French Ministers to Berlin and Dresden, General Beurnonville and Monsieur de la Valette. Thereafter, he decided to risk the possible refusal of his travel permit by the Home Secretary, the Duke of Portland, and went abroad without it.

Always generous to her friends, before she left England, Elizabeth offered to send some of them presents from abroad. A graceful reply from Horace Smith, poet and author, came back to her:

Eliza, quitting Albion's shores,
Thro distant realms to roam,
Demands, to sooth the parting hour,
'What can I send you home?'
No Toys we ask, nor Dresden dishes,
Nor reams of Leipzig learning.
Oh! send to meet our utmost wishes,
The news of your returning.

The Hollands were accompanied by Charles Richard, Dr Drew, Matthew Marsh, the Bessboroughs' eldest son, Lord Duncannon, four maids (including Hortense) and five men. As a successful essay in sardine packing, Elizabeth declares: 'We manage to stuff all into a coach and postchaise.' Lord Spencer ordered a convoy to escort the travellers across the Channel but had difficulty in getting 'bigger than a cutter'. But they managed the passage uneventfully, taking 'fifty hours' to sail from Yarmouth to Cuxhaven.

Hamburg was the first town they visited where, travelling largely by sufferance of Lord Grenville, they were unwise to make dubious contacts. Lady Holland renewed her acquaintance with Dumouriez (disgraced French General whom she had briefly visited there on her trip in pursuit of Harriet, in 1796); and, ignoring the possibly regicidal association with Philippe Egalité, Duc d'Orléans, professed 'great curiosity' to meet

Madame de Genlis, 'a woman so justly celebrated for cleverness'. Madame de Genlis took care to tell Lady Holland that she had reversed her politics and was now an upholder of the Bourbons and the Church of Rome; and to boast that, recently, Bonaparte had granted her permission to return to France 'from regret that so great an ornament should seek repose in a foreign country', all of which Lady Holland jotted down in her journal, without comment. But the Frenchwoman's background was still politically suspect. Ignoring the risks they took, the Hollands dined with the Matthiessens, now harbouring the widowed Lady Edward Fitzgerald, sublimely believing in the divine right of Whig peers to go where they pleased.

In Germany, Elizabeth recaptured a little of the success she had enjoyed there, in 1792: in Brunswick, with the Grand Duchess of Brunswick-Wolfenbüttel; in Berlin, with the young King and Queen of Prussia. But the fanfare was muted. Elizabeth's condemnation by the Court of St James carried across the Channel. His Majesty's Minister to the Prussian Court (Lord Corysfort) pointedly invited only the male portion of Elizabeth's party, to dinner; and Lady Corysfort did not return her card. Elizabeth developed an eye infection and became so dispirited that she decided not to present a letter of introduction she had been given to the Dowager Duchess of Saxe-Weimar. And, at this point, Sir Hugh Elliot (still British Minister in Dresden) forwarded the Hollands a batch of letters in which was one informing Lord Holland that his application for a travel permit had been referred back by the Duke of Portland to Lord Grenville, so that he was still travelling abroad without official sanction from his own country.

The French put things right.

At Cassel, Lord Holland and Matthew Marsh presented General Beurnonville's 'laissez-passer' to the French Minister when both he and his Secretary of Legation received the English travellers with the greatest courtesy. Pandering to Lady Holland's alarm at stories of marauding deserters across the French border, they gave the Hollands an open letter to any French commander they might meet before Coblenz, demanding an escort for their protection. And, as English currency was no longer legal tender on French soil, a French banker provided the Hollands with money. For the second time, Beurnonville's passport worked wonders for, on reading it, a French General allowed Lord Holland a pass for persons and horses across the Rhine. On the French side of the Rhine, the passport was only partially effective. It failed to impress the local banker, who made difficulties about arranging funds for the Hollands to draw on, in Brussels;

but it went down well with the local mayor, who did all he could to assist.

Elizabeth threw off her depression and reported enthusiastically on the evidence of French occupation in the countryside: local juries, typifying the re-establishment of law and order; freedom of worship and speech allowed among the peasants; fields cultivated; bread (when obtainable) sold very cheap. Varying reports reached her ears as to the behaviour of the French soldiers, but the general verdict was that, since Bonaparte had taken charge, discipline had much improved.

No decisive travel permit from the Duke of Portland ever reached Lord Holland. Only a half-hearted, ungracious permit to land back in England, long after he had returned home.

*

Against what, at times, seemed overwhelming odds, Pitt managed to push through his project of union between England and Ireland. In doing so, he had to modify his original scheme to provide Catholic relief, but let it be known in Ireland that, after Union, Catholic emancipation would eventually follow. Even this half-measure lacked the support of all Pitt's Cabinet, and it met with unrelenting opposition from the King. As a result, Pitt resigned and was replaced by Addington, the Speaker of the House of Commons. But, determined to avoid a domestic upheaval at this hour of crisis in the war with France, Pitt promised Addington his full support.

Joseph Jekyll declared that to attempt to form a new Administration without Pitt was like trying to perform *The Beggar's Opera* without Macheath. On 14th February 1801, Lady Holland notes that Parliament decreed an extraordinary 'political fast during the continuance of the war'. Which drove Jekyll to verse:

> Why on this day the lot d'ye cast
> To mortify the British nation,
> When every day's a general fast
> And every hour's humiliation?

He had another crack. Asked why he did not put 'the Administration' into verse, he replied that 'it was already *inverse*'.

George Canning was outspoken in his ridicule of the new régime, but Pitt prevailed on him to write a letter of apology. Lord Holland was shown it and pronounced it to be 'fulsome in expression, but manifestly written under constraint, and at the suggestion of a third person'.

The renewed illness of the King started another round of clandestine negotiations between the Foxites and the Prince of Wales. The King recovered, and again the project of Regency was abandoned. But the policy of Whig secession was abandoned too, and Charles James was induced to resume his reluctant attendance at the House of Commons.

*

In July 1801, T. P. (now Lord Pelham) succeeded the Duke of Portland as Secretary of State for the Home Department. In 1802, very casually, Elizabeth Holland refers to him. 'Pelham is Secretary of State for the Home Department; he is married to Lady Mary Osborne, the Duke of Leeds' sister, an amiable person who will no doubt make him happy.' In fact, his wedding had taken place on 16th July 1802, and, in answer to her letter of congratulation, Elizabeth had just received back his acknowledgment and thanks.

*

For an uneasy year Addington managed to maintain his government, then, on 27th March 1802, he earned the unexpected goodwill of the Opposition by negotiating the Peace of Amiens. Lord Grenville castigated it as 'disgraceful and ruinous'; Lord Holland quotes Sir Philip Francis as saying: 'It is a peace of which everybody is glad and nobody proud.' He repeated this remark to Sheridan who, within two hours, passed it off as his own in the House of Commons. And, to his eternal discredit, in Sheridan's name, it passed down to posterity.

The peace with France began to show itself in a different form in the Dinner Book at Holland House. Frenchmen began to feature in it regularly. Charles de Calonne (former Minister of Finance to Louis XVI), Comte de Polignac, Comte Jules de Polignac, young Comte Matthieu Molé, the Duc d'Orléans (afterwards King Louis Philippe), the Duc de Montpensier (his brother). Elizabeth Holland entered each name in her untidy hand, sometimes enlivening a page with little drawings.

*

Three events of domestic importance occurred to the Hollands during the spring and summer of 1802. Another son, Henry Edward (destined to be the fourth and last Lord Holland), was born to them on 7th March; Charles James suddenly revealed to the world that he had been married to Mrs Armistead since 1795; and the Hollands acquired a new resident physician and librarian, Dr John Allen.

The regularisation of Charles James's romance was received with great satisfaction by his family, and by no member of it more than by Lady Holland. His wife's early career as a courtesan was forgotten and her fidelity to Fox, which lasted from 1783 up to his death, was universally extolled.

Dr John Allen was recommended to Lord Holland by the Rev. Sydney Smith (brother of 'Bobus') who had known him when he had taken his medical degree in the University of Edinburgh. Dr Drew's health was failing and the Hollands were seeking another resident physician to replace him, but it was as a scholar, rather than as a doctor, that Allen finally entered the household of Holland House. In his youth, he had been an ardent believer in the French Revolution and, at the University, he had declared himself an advocate of political reform. But, in later years, he moderated his political views and concentrated instead on historical research, metaphysics and philosophy. After he had accepted the post, Lord Lauderdale wrote to Elizabeth: 'Your luck in getting Allen is something more extraordinary than if you had won £20,000 in Mr Addington's three lotteries.' And for the next forty-two years the devotion of Dr (usually referred to as Mr) Allen to Lord and Lady Holland fully justified Lord Lauderdale's high praise.

*

Charles Richard nearly died of croup, during the winter of 1801, and it seemed imperative that he should pass the following winter in a warmer climate. Now, there was nothing to stop the Hollands from visiting Paris, so, on 8th July 1802, in company with both children, Frederick Howard (Lord Morpeth's younger brother), Matthew Marsh and Mr Allen, they set off, to take up their residence in luxurious apartments in the Hotel Beauveau, Faubourg St Honoré.

Twenty-four hours later, as the guests of the Secretary of State, Hugues Maret, they were witnessing a review of his troops by the First Consul, at Carrousel. The explosion of the 'infernal machine' (an attempt against the First Consul's life, on 24th December 1800) had destroyed some of the houses in its vicinity which had facilitated the widening of the court. Fifteen thousand troops could now parade. On either side of the triumphal arch the bronze horses from the Piazza di San Marco in Venice were displayed, trophies of war removed to Paris, in 1797. By contrast, the gorgeous uniforms of the officers and the trappings of their horses set off Bonaparte, on his 'fine white Arabian', plainly dressed and wearing 'an unlaced black hat'. For the first time, his corps of Mamelukes, brought back from Egypt, paraded before him. Elizabeth comments: 'Their sudden and uncombined evolutions give a wildness to their appearance that shows a little what they must be when attacking in reality.'

Early in August 1802, a rumour went round that Lord Holland had fought a duel in Paris. Such belligerent action seems unlikely, and Elizabeth Holland makes no mention of it. Prince Talleyrand is reputed to have said that it was fortunate Lord Holland's supposed adversary remained anonymous as his reputation would have been ruined had he been named for offending such a man as 'le petit Holland'.

On 4th August 1802 (11th Thermidor), Bonaparte was proclaimed Consul of France for life, with the right to nominate his successor. Lord Holland was present at what he called 'the delivery of the suffrage from the Senate to the Consul' and wrote to his sister: 'Bonaparte seemed to me affected when the passage was read and either involuntarily or by artifice had tears in his eyes.' But he repeated the current belief that no longer could anyone influence the mind or heart of the Consul. 'He consults his Ministers as he would a dictionary and employs his Generals as he does his sword. . . . His attention to the interests and grandeur of his family seems more the result of ambition and vanity than of affection and tenderness.'

On 19th August, Lord Holland's two uncles, Charles James Fox (and wife) and General Fitzpatrick, joined his party in Paris. (Charles James was seeking material from the Paris archives for his *History of the Reign of James II*). And two young men, Lord Robert Spencer (Lord Henry Spencer's younger brother) and Frederick Ponsonby (Lord Bessborough's second son) joined it soon afterwards.

Two days later, the company made an expedition to St Cloud. Much of the taste Queen Marie Antoinette had lavished on her own apartments was still apparent in the delicate gilding and carved cupids of the mouldings, but the First Consul's quasi-military 'dark and dingy style' was even more in evidence. The walls decorated at his command were hung with cloth and draped in elaborate 'particoloured fringes', usually in masculine greens and browns; the curtain rods were 'finely polished spears'. Egyptian influence was everywhere but Elizabeth much preferred the eighteenth-century French taste of the Queen's apartments to the 'broad cloth and sphinxes' of the new régime.

On 2nd September (15th Fructidor), Charles James, General Fitzpatrick and Lord Holland were received by the First Consul. Afterwards, Lord Holland was invited to dine 'by regular invitation', and Charles James, by pressing invitation from the First Consul himself. According to

Elizabeth, Bonaparte showered compliments on Fox, and addressed him
as 'the greatest man of *one* of the greatest countries in the world'. In fact,
a correspondent from Paris afterwards informed Lady Bessborough
'Buonaparte made a sort of set speech to Mr Fox on his presentation . . . that
there were but two nations in the world, the Eastern and the Western,
(and) that Europe ought to be considered as one nation'. To which
information, passed on to Lord Granville Leveson-Gower, Lady Bessborough adds her own comment: 'I do not believe he enter'd enough into
the detail of his new map to say whether he would alter the name of Europe
and have it called France.'

On 5th September, Elizabeth Holland was presented to the First Consul
and his lady. She records: 'I was presented last Sunday to the Consul
and Madame, they were both very gracious. Her figure and tournure are
perfect, her taste in dress exquisite, but her face! ghastly, deep furrows on
each side of her mouth, fallen-in cheeks, shocking, disgusting, a worn-out
hag, prematurely gone, as she is not above 40 years old. His head is out of
proportion, being too large for his figure. It is well shaped; his ears are
very neatly shaped and small, his teeth fine. The gracious smile he puts
on is not in unison with the upper part of his face: that is penetrating,
severe and unbending . . .'

In writing home to their relations (she, to her sister-in-law, Caroline
Fox, he, to his aunt, Lady Upper Ossory) both the Hollands enlarge on
the extravagance of dress displayed by the ladies in attendance at the
'Cercle'. Elizabeth writes: 'A very moderate dress costs 4 or 5 *hundred*
louis. Madame de Murat's gown at the Cercle cost 1100 and £50 sterling.
I happen to know this for a fact. A morning gown and not a costly one,
60 louis, without sleeves; a veil from 180 to 2 and 3 hundred louis. Were
I to tell you about Madame B.(s) expense, you would think I was telling
enormous fibs.' And Lord Holland too elaborates on this theme. 'When
the ladies appear, as they do at the Cercle, there are card tables and a
formal circle, but several beautiful women and an expense, a display and a
taste in dress, which it is difficult to describe, and which it is as well that
our ladies in London should be as ignorant of as they are. The sums
expended on dress are quite incredible, and the richness of the shops
in those articles, as well as in furniture, exceed not only all description we
have ever heard in England but anything the most expensive persons there
can imagine.'

To build up his new Society, it was Bonaparte's policy to conciliate
many exiled aristocrats and former political prisoners and, during the
two months of their stay in Paris, the dinner-books of the Hollands

reveal a motley collection. Lafayette, the Abbé de Cafarelli, and the Comte de Montrond had all been set at liberty by Bonaparte; the Comte de Valence had campaigned under the disgraced Dumouriez; the Abbé St Fard was the reputed father of Philippe Egalité; the Duc de Duras and Marquis de Girardin were both repatriated aristocrats; Jean Antoine Gaullois and the Marquis de Jaucourt were members of the Tribune; Louis, Comte de Narbonne, working for Bonaparte since the 18th Brumaire, had once been, for a brief period of three months and through the influence of his mistress, Madame de Staël, Minister at War during the Terror. Among the diplomats the Hollands entertained were Count Andreossy, newly appointed Ambassador to the Court of St James; and Count Markoff, erstwhile favourite of Catherine II of Russia and now accredited to the Russian Embassy in Paris (viewed by Bonaparte with deep suspicion). Poetry was represented at the table by the Abbé Casti, whose verses, Elizabeth felt, had deteriorated with age; prose, by Madame Adelaïde de Flahault.

This brilliant woman, as noted as a novelist as she was notorious as an adventuress, had just legalised a chequered career by marrying the Marquis de Souza-Botelbo, Portuguese Ambassador to France. In her salon in 1791, Lord Holland had first met her lover, Prince Talleyrand. Elizabeth Holland was inclined to crab her. '. . . her conversation consists more of a narrative of the good things she has said than in those she actually does say.' But she was much taken with Madame de Flahault's son, 'a fine open young man', declared to be the love-child of his mother and Prince Talleyrand.

In their turn, the Hollands were fêted by French hosts: Cambacères (later, Duke of Parma), Second Consul and Minister of Justice, co-architect with Bonaparte of the Civil Code; the Abbé Sièyes, provisional Consul, many of whose original ideas Bonaparte had incorporated into the new Constitution; Count Andreossy; and, of course, Prince Talleyrand.

No doubt, to Elizabeth, the glittering, new, accessible circle of the Consul of France seemed doubly resplendent after the shabby, old-fashioned, inaccessible Court of George III.

CHAPTER THIRTEEN

Spain and Portugal 1802-1805

EVER SINCE HIS first visit to Spain in 1793, Lord Holland had intended
to return there to seek material for a life of the sixteenth-century Spanish
dramatist, Lope de Vega. Now, the stimulus of their visit to Paris and the
'wanderlust' inspired by their being on foreign soil again prompted the
Hollands to extend their journey across the Pyrenees.

At the prospect, Elizabeth's old journalistic enthusiasm returned, and
she even equipped herself with a brand-new journal. But certain adverse
elements dogged her from the start. For one thing, she was eleven years
older than when she had embarked on her first exploration of Europe and,
after bearing eight children, her radiant health had waned. For another,
instead of her robust Webster children, now she was flanked by the two
delicate little boys she had borne her second husband: Charles Richard,
prone to develop croup at the slightest provocation; and Henry Edward
already with a malformation of the left leg and foot which he never out-
grew. And her own resistance had weakened. Gone was her imperturb-
ability in fording torrents, and crossing the Alps in carrying-chairs; in
marathon journeys ending with broken axles; in perilous joltings over
sand dunes within musket shot of the enemy. Now she was a prey to
apprehension of all kinds. Her second marriage had done much to soften
Elizabeth, but it had sapped her spirit of high adventure.

In 1802, the set-up of the Court of Spain resembled that of the Court
of Naples as the Hollands had known it, nine years earlier. A moronic
Bourbon monarch, Charles IV, brother of Ferdinand IV, King of Naples
and the two Sicilies, sat on the throne; a domineering Queen, Maria
Luisa, was at his side. Like her sister-in-law, Maria Carolina pursued,
though less scrupulously, her own policies through her husband's Minister
and her lover, Manuel Godoy, Duke of Alcuida, 'Prince of the Peace'.

Godoy and his masters presided over a country that was incapable of
resisting French pressure, whether diplomatic or military. And, in 1801
as in 1807, Godoy acted as Bonaparte's dupe for his intended invasion of

Portugal. Bonaparte believed that potentially Spain was a great power, if her resources were properly managed. The reality was a decadent monarchy, whose politics were a tangle of foreign diplomacy and domestic factions.

In November 1802, the Hollands, Frederick Howard (Lord Morpeth's sixteen-year-old brother), Matthew Marsh (now his tutor) and Mr Allen entered Spain.

Crossing the frontier, Lady Holland remarks: 'Fine pillars supporting the arms of Spain mark the entrance into Spain. Since the war they have not been elevated but remain overthrown, a pretty just emblem of the Kingdom they represent.'

*

For all that, the Hollands were determined to receive and return Spanish hospitality.

Although by remote control, as he himself had to be absent on Court duty in Barcelona, Admiral the Duke of Gravina had asked the Conde de Fuentes 'to show Lord Holland every civility', which he proceeded to do. As the Hollands were accommodated in a large gaunt house ('a dreary dungeon'), a kindly Dutch merchant, Mr Stembor offered to lend them his villa at Sarria, just outside the town. This offer they gratefully accepted, only to discover that the gates of Barcelona were shut against them at sundown. Whereupon the Governor was prevailed upon to open the town-gates to the Hollands 'at all hours', a right hitherto reserved exclusively for the Prince of Conti. With satisfaction, Elizabeth Holland recorded this signal honour. She was back in the world of privilege.

At the Stembors, she and her husband met the erstwhile French Consul, now rechristened 'Commissaire des Relations Commerciales'. (Elizabeth explains: '*Consul* must no longer be profaned by the vulgar'.) And a fortnight later, at their own table, the French Commissaire read the Hollands 'a flattering letter' from the Comte de Beurnonville (French General, now Ambassador to Spain) which desired the Commissaire to show them 'every civility in his power'. In Spain, as in Germany, Bonaparte's envoy went out of his way to be civil to them.

In the main, the Hollands' first visit to Spain was a social exercise, conducted regardless of expense as, in certain towns (such as Valencia), even for a tenancy of a few weeks, houses had to be bought, not leased, furnished from top to bottom, and sold again, after vacation. Passing through a maze of grandees, politicians, diplomats, men of letters and generals, they formed their conclusions and, as usual, held emphatic

views. They attended bullfights, where the slaughter of horses and bulls
was inevitably viewed with clinical interest by Lady Holland; Lord
Holland dug deeply into Spanish literature and Lady Holland, too,
became proficient in the language. They formed lasting friendships: with
the banker, Cabarrus; with Charles IV's ex-Ministers, Saavedra and
Jovellanos; with the poet, Quintana; the ill-starred courtier and soldier,
the Duke of Infantado; and many more.

*

Some time before Lord Holland's departure for France he had decided
to lease Little Holland House to his sister and step-aunt, Miss Vernon
(Aunt Ebey). There was much to do before it was habitable and, while
always careful to show gratitude for any favours, in her letters to Spain
Caroline Fox contrives to convey the impression of acute discomfort in
her future home. In a letter of 25th October 1802, she refers to the state
of 'my little mansion'. The walls are not waterproof; the bedroom window
lets in the rain so that furniture and 'the pretty bed you gave me' had to
be removed. Lord Holland is not sympathetic to his sister, and her complaints cease at once. She and Aunt Ebey then profess themselves delighted
with Little Holland House but very tardily take up residence there in
May 1804.

More serious still was the deterioration Caroline reported in Holland
House itself. Bonaiuti, the Hollands' Italian factotum, had noticed cracks
in the East Wing wherein were situated Lady Holland's rooms and the
children's nurseries. Lord Lansdown and Lord Upper Ossory advised
Lord Holland to abandon the house and develop the estate as a building
site; Sir Gilbert Affleck felt that, although no fears were expressed for the
stability of the centre block, the damaged wings should be pulled down
and rebuilt. But Caroline remained optimistic. Despite the general opinion
that it was 'ill advised to lay out money upon a crazey foundation', she
felt that 'well or ill advised many comfortable days have been passed
within the walls and many more I hope we may yet look forward to'. And
Mr Moore, Lord Holland's lawyer, supported her. In 1804, she wrote
that she believed that bad drainage was the real cause of the trouble, and
she was right. The springs, rising on the hill, were collected into one big
drain away from the house and the foundations of Holland House were
automatically strengthened.

*

After entering Spain, Charles Richard has only one severe attack of
croup in three months. But the condition of Henry Edward's leg gives

Lady Holland the greatest anxiety. She writes details to her sister-in-law. Mr Allen was reassuring in thinking the baby's spine and hip joint were not affected but, to the anxious mother, the leg hangs 'like a paralysed limb. The left knee bends as much as I have described. (She illustrates its position.) If you place yr. hand beneath the foot to feel the pressure of his body it is none.' The child is having sea water baths and is very gay despite his affliction. But, at over a year old he can neither stand nor walk. Caroline tries to comfort Lady Holland by quoting Mr Croft (her obstetric surgeon). 'With respect to yr. dear Baby he says he is quite positive that it came into the world as well formed and perfect as any Baby ever did . . . He has lately met with two instances of children who lost the use of their limbs during teething . . . use returned after.' His optimism proves misplaced.

Caroline sends the Hollands news of their relations at home, especially of the appointment of Bobus Smith to be Advocate-General in Bengal. Lady Holland had never taken to Bobus and makes some acid comments about him in her journal. 'His place is that of Advocate-General in Bengal; ye salary is £5000 pr. ann. and the gains in legal practise to a man of ambition is full double. And money was, as with him, it appears to be, the object: the temptation was irresistible. His success at home did not keep pace with his ambition. He was far fr. popular with the lawyers . . .' But she is sensible of the pain the separation will cause to Lord Lansdown, Aunt Ebey and Caroline.

*

Throughout 1802 it had become increasingly obvious that the Peace of Amiens had done little to stop French expansionist ambitions; and Addington's government declared war on 17th May 1803 before France could complete her preparations. This placed the Hollands in a precarious position. Via Granada, they had moved from Valencia to Cadiz from whence Lord Holland writes his sister, on 20th May: 'We are in great dismay at the news my little sister tho' perhaps less so than most people in this town which will suffer more perhaps than any other place in Europe by a declaration of war.' On 1st June he writes from Seville: 'As to the war I am so mad at it that it seems to me that as Addington's father made the King sound his son has made the people mad. Mad indeed they must be if they approve this war . . .' On 2nd June, Caroline writes confirming war and urges the Hollands to return home in a Lisbon packet. But now they are launched on a social season culminating in a meeting at Aranjuez with King Charles and Queen Maria Luisa.

Although the behaviour at the Spanish Court was notoriously licentious

(Maria Carolina of Naples called it 'This infamous brothel') obviously both Lord and Lady Holland were gratified by the reception accorded them by the King and Queen. Lord Holland writes Caroline: '. . . their Majesties . . . were really excessively gracious and obliging . . .' and Lady Holland confides her impressions to her journal:

On the 17th (June) I was presented to the Queen and King by the Duchess of San Teodoro. It was a private audience, which made Her Majesty dispense with my appearing in a hoop; but not even the plea of being a stranger cld. obtain a dispensation from the custom of appearing *without* gloves before his Catholic Majesty. That species of clothing produces such a sudden and violent physical effect upon him that the Queen alone chooses to encounter the consequences. White leather gloves produce similar effects upon many of the Spanish branch of the Bourbon family. The Queen's manner is uncommonly gracious. She shows great readiness in making conversation, and taste in choosing her topics; all she said was flattering, obliging, and well-expressed. The King was quite a bon homme, and his great talents lie in the skill of a garde de chasse. The Queen called her favourite child, the Infante Don Francisco, a pretty, lively boy, bearing a most indecent likeness to the P(rince) of the Peace.

The situation worsened. After England had declared war, Bonaparte ordered the arrest of all English people resident or travelling in France, and on 19th July, Lord Holland tells Caroline that he is so anxious to get home that he is willing to go via Lisbon, despite his apprehension of traversing the plains of Estremadura in midsummer 'the most scorching country in Europe'. Sickness in his family forces him to delay his plans.

On 2nd August, Lord Holland writes from Madrid to Caroline saying that his family is 'well but suffering from heat and uncertainty'. Now, he thinks that while still refusing him permission, the French might allow Lady Holland to travel home through France, which is preferable to her 'risking herself on board any ship whatever for so long a voyage'. And he extols the kindness of Comte de Beurnonville in trying to help him with his plans. With his benign but perverse capacity to see the enemy's point of view as the right one, Lord Holland adds: '. . . it is pleasant to see that two years cruel and unkind confinement by the allies last war . . . have not the least diminished the liberality of his feelings towards individuals of the nations to whom he attributes them . . .' On 11th August, Comte de Beurnonville's kind efforts are set at nought by Lady Holland suffering a severe miscarriage. Four days after it happens, Lord Holland writes to his sister: 'She is thank God better today but yesterday I was most terribly alarmed and uneasy. How long she will be recovering her strength we cannot at present guess . . .'

When he writes, on 13th September, he has had no news from England since 19th July. By which time he is enquiring about boats to Gibraltar and Lisbon, and reports that food is running short in Madrid. Three days later, Lady Holland is better and hopes to be able to travel in another ten days. Then another misfortune hits Lord Holland '. . . . this morning Lo and behold in comes Mr Gout'. By 3rd October, with Lady Holland 'low and weak' he is making for Lisbon, by road.

On 10th October Caroline writes to her brother from Bowood. 'Capt. Foley says Ld. Nelson will be particularly glad to do whatever he can for yr. accommodation and he wld. write himself to explain yr. wish and Lady Holland's in regard to a frigate if he did not think yr. own interests there wld. be quite sufficient, Ld. Nelson having a great regard and esteem for you . . .' But Lady Holland takes to her bed for another three weeks, 'swallowing alum and using nauseous styptics and astringent'. On 13th October, Lord Holland reports to Caroline that yellow fever is raging at Malaga. And he has seen 'Mr Chamberlayne', the agent of the Lisbon packets, who has told him that 'not one has reached England without fighting'. Four weeks later, he writes that 'Lady Holland's illness becomes more frequent', a few days later, developing into 'something like an ague'.

On 12th November, Spain declared war on England. But Christmas Day 1803 still found the Hollands in Madrid.

*

When they arrived in Spain, in 1802, the Hollands found a former visitor to Holland House, John Hookham Frere, as British Envoy Extraordinary at Madrid. It was as a writer and poet, though also as a friend of George Canning, that Frere had been introduced to Holland House, and the fact that, like Canning, he was also a member of William Pitt's government had not jeopardised his welcome there. With Canning, at that time Frere was editor of the *Anti-Jacobin*, and his anti-Whig views on the war with France were freely expressed. In 1799, he had succeeded Canning as Under-Secretary for Foreign Affairs when Lady Holland had commented: '. . . Since favouritism is à l'ordre du jour, I am rather glad he is a sharer tho' I think he cannot make a good man of business. He is distrait and poetical, and in lieu of a dispatch may be tempted to pen a sonnet.' In Madrid, Lady Holland did not change her opinions of Frere. She comments: '. . . his eccentricities are a source of perpetual amusement. He lives with a few obscure Spaniards and some French emigrants, who eat his dinners and fill his head with lies of counter-revolution, as he is still in hopes of some successful aristocratic Messiah, not having, from his abhorrence to the whole nation, kept up with French politics.' But she and Lord Holland think well of his brother Bartholomew (Bartle) Frere, then Secretary of Legation at Madrid.

Yet, even though his talents were more suited to literature than to foreign politics, Hookham Frere's apparently good relations with the Prince of the Peace were causing disquiet to that forgiving anglophile General Beurnonville.

Godoy realised that Spain was even worse equipped for war against France than against England, and that his only hope lay in preserving peace. So he made up to both Ambassadors, playing for time. Through Beurnonville, Bonaparte began to threaten. Either Spain must hand the British Ambassador his passports by a given date, or an army of a hundred thousand men would replace his Envoy. Still Godoy tarried. And, despite her bouts of illness, as an observant outsider, Lady Holland kept a careful day-to-day diary of events.

On 4th September she notes that French troops are massing on the frontier and that rumour has it that General St Cyr is to command them. At which 'Beurnonville was extremely irritated, and betrayed evident symptoms of his disappointment at not being named himself to the command'. Two days later she adds: 'Great anxiety prevails respecting the question of peace and war; some think the demand has already been made of passage for troops to Portugal, others that *money* is the sole object of the French Govt. The only fact that is certain is that our poetical Minister has been, and will be, completely bamboozled.'

Godoy was playing a losing game, but he was still trying to avoid a declaration of war on England. Now abruptly, he changed his tactics. Still in her memo of 13th September, Lady Holland continues: 'There is a report which the P. of the P. sedulously puts into circulation, that the French demands are insolent, and the conduct of the English so generous in allowing their money and ships to pass, that to comply with the French in declaring war against them the difficulty wld. be in finding *griefs* to make out a manifest.'

Bonaparte called Godoy's bluff. On 9th October, he exacted from Spain a new treaty whereby she undertook to pay France a monthly subsidy of six million francs; to force Portugal to maintain strict neutrality; and to make that hapless country also contribute a further crippling indemnity to France. Yet, even while ostensibly agreeing to it, Godoy assured Frere that Spain was signing the treaty under compulsion, and not from any ill will to Great Britain.

For a time Frere was prepared to be conciliatory but he could not overlook the magnitude of the subsidy. He declared: '. . . the passage of

French troops thro' the territories of Spain wld. be considered a violation of neutrality'.

Even then Godoy maintained that he sought still to combine his two objectives, to help France and keep on peaceful terms with Great Britain. But, to safeguard his own position, he repeated everything Frere said to him to Beurnonville. Immediately, Bonaparte was informed of it and, within days, supposedly word for word reports of Frere's talks with Godoy appeared in the *Moniteur*.

*

Another year passed before the Hollands left Spain for Portugal, a period of recurring ill health affecting the whole family. Time and again they were on the move only to be delayed. Lord Holland broke his right arm and lost the use of his fingers for several months; Henry Edward was critically ill again and too weak to travel; Charles Richard had further attacks of croup; Lady Holland had a second miscarriage, and in October 1804, having got as far as Valladolid on their way to Portugal, master and maids collapsed together and all the family, plus five servants, had to be admitted to hospital.

During these months, Caroline Fox adopted the same tactics as she had done in 1795, when trying to coax Lord Holland back from Italy. She played on his love of family. Lady Ossory had died of cancer, in February 1804. With almost her last breath, she had expressed her pleasure at 'yr. long letter'. Lord Henry Petty had made a brilliant maiden speech in the House of Commons and, almost at the same minute, his father, Lord Lansdown, had suffered a stroke at Lansdowne House.

Caroline tries to interest Lord Holland into giving a living to the Rev. Sydney Smith (brother of Bobus) only to discover he has already promised it to Matthew Marsh. And more than once she extols the beauties of the gardens at Holland House. 'The clump in front of the House with the sweet briar has fully answered one of the purposes for which you planted it viz. that of becoming a harbour for nightingales . . . I never saw . . . the grounds . . . in higher beauty . . . the Lilacs and Laburnhams (*sic*) have burst out at once . . . and yr. crops of hay are in the highest degree promising . . .'

Interspersed with all these tender anecdotes, already Caroline had contrived to insert a drop of acid. On 27th March 1804 she had written: 'The newspapers have been circulating idle uncomfortable reports about you, my little Brother, but as I am sure no Lisbon mail has arrived since I received a letter, they do not annoy me.'

Another domestic worry for Lady Holland was the sudden notice given her by her maid, Hortense. On 11th July, in great indignation, Lord Holland writes to Caroline: '. . . for so old and favourite a servant her manner of going is unwarrantable and in so sensible a person quite unaccountable. But Lady H. is more sorry than angry as replace her she cannot but she is moving Heaven and earth to get somebody to attend her before we sett (*sic*) off.' To which letter Lady Holland herself adds a postscript: '. . . do you remember my being v. miserable at having discovered that a child had been secretly put in to the world at H. H. and that there was a suspicion that it had been as secretly put out of it? . . . The mother was Hortense the accomplice Mary Barker. Yr. Brother out of kindness hushed up the affair . . . I suspect her husband has heard the foul story and that it is to avoid a publick disclosure that she has thus stolen away . . .'

*

In March 1804, Lady Holland recorded that the French General, Moreau, had been arrested for conspiring with General Pichergru to assassinate Bonaparte. And, early in April, she reports from Aranjuez that the *Moniteur* had printed the gist of a supposed conversation between Hookham Frere and the Prince of the Peace in which Frere was said to have justified assassination 'from the necessity of it in the deplorable state into which England is now thrown'. She adds: 'The Prince is made to use v. grand language, deprecating such doctrines, and prophecying that their effects generally recoil upon those who act upon them.' She declares that, several days before the publication of the article, Godoy had told General Beurnonville 'and others' that Frere's interest in the French conspirators was 'inconceivable'.

When Frere saw the publication he demanded a contradiction of it from Godoy from whom he received a non-committal answer, while Godoy himself continued to proclaim the veracity of his statements to General Beurnonville. Frere protested again, then got Mouravieff (Russian Ambassador to the Court of Spain) to mediate, on his behalf, with Godoy. He got a cold response. While refuting the implication that he had altered words justifying the acquiescence of foreign governments 'in a scheme of murder', then Frere admitted that he had said that 'he shld. not feel more scruples in placing a dagger in B(onaparte)'s heart than he did in sticking a knife into a leg of mutton'. Already he had remonstrated to Godoy over Spain's partiality to France in allowing her to take prize-money and sell naval armaments in Spanish harbours. Now he declared that were this practice to continue, he had express orders to end negotiations and to withdraw from Madrid.

In May, France declared herself an empire and elected Bonaparte Emperor Napoleon I.

Writing to his mother, on 1st August, George Frere, younger brother of Hookham, told her that Hookham was returning home at once and that, as Chargé d'Affaires, his brother Bartholomew was to be left behind, in Madrid. On 22nd August, Lady Holland notes in her journal: 'The last supper with poor Frere. He sets off solitarily and out of spirits to Corunna; his feelings are a mixture of indignation at the recall, and humiliation to be sacrificed to one whom he despises.'

Bartle Frere did not long survive his brother in Madrid. Early in October, the British fleet, under Sir Graham Moore, captured some Spanish treasure ships. Diplomatic relations were ruptured between the Courts of St James and Madrid and Bartle Frere applied for his passport. When the Hollands finally left for Portugal (on 14th November 1804) he went with them.

From January 1804, onwards, Mr Chamberlain had been engaged in trying to find them a house in Lisbon. Finally they chose one ('not surpassed by any in Lisbon') at a rent of six hundred Mil Reiss per annum. There, on 7th December 1804, they took up their residence.

At that moment, Lisbon was a sad place. Queen Maria had been mad for years and her son John, the Regent, lived in hourly dread of Napoleon's next move on his country. Don Antonio de Aranjo and 'Mr de Suza' (Sousa) showed the Hollands great kindness and, thanks to them, passports were issued to Lord Holland, Lady Holland 'et sua Familia', on 17th November.

Lady Holland was still very weak and her sightseeing had to be modified. But she managed to cover pretty much the same ground that William Beckford traversed in 1794, including Alcobaca and Batalha. The Lucullan delights at Alcobaca, described by Beckford, now were tempered to decorum. The Hollands were entertained by the Lord Abbot to a 'splendid dinner in the Sala de los Reyes' but the clarionet and guitar players and the minuets danced by 'young monks and young gentlemen' seem to have been eliminated from the evening's programme, as Lady Holland does not describe them.

Still, Lord Holland worries about his wife. On 3rd January 1805, he writes to Caroline: '. . . I can give you no good account of Lady Holland whose illness makes me more and more uneasy every day.' But, by 10th January he has perked up a little: 'Lady Holland is much better but you will be quite surprized (*sic*) to see her so thin. She has been complaining of being fat all her life and I long to see her so again.'

On 14th March, news came that the French fleet had escaped from Brest. Lord Robert Fitzgerald, brother of the ill-fated Lord Edward, had succeeded Hookham Frere as British Minister at Lisbon, and now he warned Lord Holland that the sailing of the next packet was imminent. For once, Lord Holland made up his mind quickly and, in thirteen hours, his whole family, including Bartle Frere, was ready to sail in the *Walsingham*. Grandiloquently, Lady Holland observes: 'We engaged the whole packet.' After a rough passage of fourteen days, on two occasions apparently pursued by enemy ships, Lord Holland's party landed safely at Falmouth.

It left behind a tangle of unsettled business for poor Mr Chamberlain. On 23rd April, he wrote that, after the 'sad confusion' the Hollands' hasty departure had caused, he had managed to get the house in Lisbon into some kind of order. He had arranged for the sale of the furniture, and reported on the results of the sale which totalled RS. 1,666 005. But there had been no bid for the mules, which were not sold till 20th September. Then, unfortunately, being Mulas (females) and not Machos (males) they sold for only 150 Moidores.

CHAPTER FOURTEEN

A Taste of Power

AT HOME MUCH had happened in politics since the Hollands had left England. Addington, not the man to ride out a crisis, had resigned in May, 1804, to be succeeded by Pitt. His desire for a comprehensive Ministry was thwarted by the King's opposition to Fox, and by the refusal of Fox and Grenville's friends to serve, other than on their own terms. But, despite his shaky political base, by August 1805, Pitt had formed a coalition with Russia and Austria, to fight Napoleon, Emperor of the French.

*

The Hollands returned to Holland House on 6th May 1805 and found Lady Affleck, Charles James Fox, Lady Bessborough and General Fitz-patrick there to greet them. Lady Bessborough declared that Lady Holland returned 'in great beauty'. With qualified enthusiasm Lady Holland herself remarks: 'I liked to see them mightily, but a *return* to this country always damps my spirits.' And one sad family event synchronised with her husband's return. Lord Lansdown died the very next day without seeing his beloved Lord Holland again. Lord Wycombe succeeded his father, tacking the 'e' on to Lansdown. On 27th May he married Lady Gifford, his mistress, whom he had once described to Lord Holland, as 'a pro-digious fine sow'.

For some time Charles James had been urging his 'Young One' in Spain to return in time to attend the Parliamentary debate on Catholic Emanci-pation; but though this was fixed in both Houses for 10th May, it proved abortive, and had no decisive outcome.

Now, Pitt was a tired, sick man, concentrating all his energies on the war with France, and flogging on his own failing steps with masochistic ferocity.

Napoleon's determination to invade England had taken active shape. A great camp, to accommodate a hundred thousand men, had been formed at Boulogne, where a flotilla of flat-bottomed boats was waiting to ferry his army across the Channel. All Napoleon asked of his naval staff was to

133

devise a plan to keep the Channel open for three clear days, perhaps even
less. Due to the vigilance and courage of Lord Nelson and Admiral
Collingwood, the plan miscarried.

*

Despite this threatening background, through the summer of 1805, the
Hollands kept open house. The dinner-books list a wide range of personali-
ties, some old, some new. Sheridan, Canning, John Whishaw, John Curran,
Henry Brougham, Samuel Romilly; Stroganoff, the Russian Ambassador
from Madrid, Souza, the Hollands' benefactor from Lisbon, the American,
James Monroe. Lord Minto is enthusiastic about the Hollands' establish-
ment. 'They live remarkably well.' Which opinion is confirmed when Lord
Lauderdale engages 'a Cuisinier and a Patissier' for Lady Holland in Paris.
'The cook asks 100 gns with aprons jackets etc. and finally settles for 110
gns; the Pastry-cook is to have 60 gns for everything . . .'

In July, the Hollands entertained the Prince of Wales at dinner, also inviting the Duke of Devonshire, the Bessboroughs, their daughter, Caroline,
and her newly-wed husband, William Lamb, Lord Morpeth, Lord Henry
Petty, Samuel Whitbread and 'Mr Allen'. In October, the Rev. Sydney
Smith most unclerically sings their praises to Sir James Mackintosh:

> With Lady Holland I believe you are acquainted. I am lately become so. She
> is very handsome, very clever, and I think very agreeable . . .
> Lord Holland is quite delightful. I hardly know a talent or a virtue that he has
> not, little or big. The Devil could not put him out of temper, nor is he any way
> superior to him in acuteness. I really never saw such a man. In addition to this,
> think of his possessing Holland House and that he reposes every evening on that
> beautiful structure of flesh and blood, Lady H.

Addington's resignation from the Cabinet, in July 1805, caused Pitt to
renew negotiations with the Foxites, in which junketings Lady Holland
suddenly evinced a lively interest. On 11th July, in one of her coded letters
to Lord Granville Leveson-Gower, in St Petersburg, Lady Bessborough
declares: 'Lord Holland is sadly indispos'd towards the marriage . . .
(coalition between Fox and Pitt); he wld. prefer medical assistance (from
ex-Dr Addington and his friends) owing, I believe, to the constant harping
of his wife on that subject, who is swayed by Mr Tierney . . .' And, on 3rd
August, she writes again: 'We din'd at Holland House yesterday. I am
afraid she will do mischief; she has taken violently to Politics lately, is a
profess'd Addingtonian, influenced by Mr Tierney, and opposes with all
her might (and certainly with might on Lord Holland's mind) all designs
of Union with Mr Pitt.'

Elizabeth Holland firmly contradicted Lady Bessborough's lighthearted insinuation that she had had a flirtation with Bartle Frere in Spain and, though she gave birth to a daughter in 1806, and was to give her husband another daughter, in 1809, according to contemporary standards she was fast approaching middle-age. Even so, she was still capable of jealousy. On 16th October 1805, rather smugly, Lady Bessborough informs Lord Granville '. . . the Hollands din'd at Chiswick yesterday. I am vex'd at what he told me—a violent quarrel between them of which I was the unconscious cause.' Nothing serious, but from that moment Lady Bessborough becomes more critical of her friend.

When Elizabeth Holland had left England three years before, Opposition was out on a limb, with Fox still enjoying a large measure of self-imposed retirement. Since the renewed outbreak of war and Pitt's gradual failure to hold back events, everything had changed and both Pitt and Addington (now Lord Sidmouth) were clearly considering overtures to the Foxites. With the fires of her youth dying down, Lady Holland thought less of personal conquests, but the chance to pull wires was a pastime she could never resist. So, what more natural than that she should turn to power-politics?

While both political groups manœuvred for position, the war on the Continent entered a new phase. Throughout August Napoleon waited in vain for his Admiral Villeneuve's invasion of England. When this plan miscarried, with incredible speed he marched the armies he had scheduled to embark for England back across Europe, to inflict a crushing defeat on the Austrians, at Ulm.

Two days later, on 21st October, the British fleet, under Lord Nelson, defeated the Franco-Spanish fleet, off Trafalgar. Thereby, although Napoleon might try to reduce the whole of land-locked Europe to subjection, Britain became absolute mistress of the seas.

*

As with the first two, the third coalition also was doomed to failure. On 2nd December 1805, Napoleon defeated the Russians and a new Austrian army, at Austerlitz.

The shattering of all his hopes of Confederation was too much for Pitt who died, after a last sharp bout of wasting sickness, on 23rd January 1806. The same day, George III called on Lord Hawkesbury to form a government, who accepted, but lacked the courage to proceed, forcing the King to consider a composite government and, with Lord Grenville at its head and Charles James Fox as Foreign Secretary, the 'Ministry of All the

Talents' was formed. William Windham became Secretary for War; Lord Spencer, Home Secretary; Charles Grey (shortly to become Lord Howick), 1st Lord of the Admiralty; Lord Henry Petty, Chancellor of the Exchequer; Sheridan, Treasurer of the Navy; and Lord Sidmouth, Privy Seal. Lord Holland gives his own version of events. 'Mr Fox and the Prince of Wales were the chief advisers of the function with Lord Sidmouth. The disunited rump of Mr Pitt's Ministry were no party, whereas Lord Sidmouth's friends, tho' few, formed a compact body, and if their leaders were inferior in talents to those of other political parties, their subalterns were more respectable than the clerks and secretaries of Mr Pitt's and Lord Melville's school . . . *It will stop up all the earths*, was Mr Fox's expression to me . . .'

For twenty-three years, George III had resisted any attempt to include Charles James Fox in a ministry. Now, confronted with the inevitable, he accepted him with a good grace. But Fox's own days were numbered and he was destined only to outlive his great political adversary by eight months.

On his return from Spain, Lord Holland had been struck 'with the change in Mr Fox's countenance'; and, as the weeks went by, it was evident that he was the victim of a grave disorder. Lord Lauderdale first pointed out the symptoms of dropsy, which were confirmed, after two examinations, by Sir Henry Halford (Vaughan). By June 1806, Charles James was unfit for any other work than signing his name, holding brief talks with his colleagues, and dictating a few letters. Yet, on 10th June, for the last time, he struggled to the House of Commons to speak for the Abolition of Slavery.

Soon after he assumed office, he told his nephew that he looked forward to the time when he could retire or, if peace could be restored, to the time when he could assume some less exacting duty in the Cabinet. Then, he gave Lord Holland to understand, he hoped to hand him over 'the seals of the Foreign Office', when he would still be near enough to 'inure' his nephew 'to business'. As his illness increased he was offered a peerage which he refused, addressing his comments to Lord Holland. 'The peerage, to be sure, seems the natural way, but that cannot be. I have an oath in Heaven against it. I will not close my politicks in that foolish way, as so many have done before me.'

Things did not work out as Fox had planned. When a new Plenipotentiary was required for Paris, to replace Lord Yarmouth and to open up discussions for peace, neither General Fitzpatrick nor Lord Holland (either of whom had been Fox's choice) was selected. Instead, Lord Howick (now in charge) sent Lord Lauderdale.

With disarming candour, Lord Holland admits to 'two minutes mortification' when he was passed over. And he had to accept, without explanation, the gratitude of his uncle for his supposed unselfishness in remaining by his bedside, 'so you would not leave me, young one, to go to Paris, but liked staying with me better—there's a kind boy'. ('He thus gave me credit for refusing what had never been offered to me and I did not like to explain the circumstances for fear he might misinterpret my explanation into an expression of disappointment at not going.')

However, in August, Lord Grenville chose Lord Auckland and Lord Holland to act as Joint-Commissioners, with an American delegation, to iron out difficulties arising from 'the arbitrary methods of the British Navy', on the high seas. James Monroe and William Pinkney were the Commissioners for the other side. To quote Lord Holland: 'These gentlemen had been sent to demand satisfaction for numerous captures made in virtue of instructions from our Admiralty, which the Government of the United States contended to be illegal.' After the death of Pitt and the advent to power of peace-loving Fox 'the (American) Mission was authorized to assume a more conciliatory tone than their original instructions seemed to breathe'. So much so that the Treaty they signed, on 31st December 1806 (leaving unsolved the impressment of British seamen from American ships), was subsequently repudiated by President Jefferson of the United States. But the credit for the Treaty could clearly be charged to the persuasion and tact of Lord Auckland and Lord Holland. And coincident with his negotiations with the American delegates, Lord Holland was made a Privy Councillor.

Since he had become Secretary of State, Charles James Fox had been living in Stable Yard, St James's. But, early in September, the surgeons had to draw the accumulated water from his system and thereafter he was too weak to return to St Anne's Hill. So his lifelong friend, William, 5th Duke of Devonshire, lent him his villa at Chiswick, halfway back to his own home. There, Charles James lay quietly, attended by his wife, his nephew, his niece, Caroline, and his secretary (Trotter). At this time too he became more demonstrative to Lady Holland, with whom he had never been on easy terms. Letters from all over the Kingdom were sent him suggesting remedial measures, including 'an exterior application of snails and . . . colewort to the belly'. Finally, early on 7th September, he grew worse and Mrs Fox sent for Lord Holland to Chiswick, where he remained. During that time Lord Holland emphasises that at least seven or eight people were by his uncle's bedside, during each day. The last coherent words Charles James uttered were: 'I die happy' and his wife's name: 'Liz'. Then he died on 13th September 1806, 'without a groan.'

Two days later, Lady Bessborough (who had herself lost her beloved sister, the Duchess of Devonshire, the previous March) gave Lord Grenville a few more details of Fox's death. 'Poor Lord H(olland) had appear'd quite calm the whole day, but then he sank down on the bed and was oblig'd to be carried out. . . . Lady Holland has not behav'd as one cld. wish, and . . . the cry against her is dreadful. A great deal of this is *manner*, and neither want of feeling or intention, but she really does act foolishly.'

Years later, Princess Liechtenstein (adopted daughter of the 4th Lady Holland) referring to Fox's death, gives this account of Elizabeth Holland's behaviour, from hearsay: '. . . Lady Holland appears to those who are waiting near the chamber of death, and answers their breathless enquiries by walking through the room with her apron thrown over her head!'

Lord Holland had planned that his uncle's remains should be committed to the family vault at Foxley, in Wiltshire; but he yielded to the pressure of Charles James Fox's friends that a petition should go forward, to bury him in Westminster Abbey. Lord Grenville offered to recommend to the King that Fox should be given a public funeral, but Lady Holland explains that it was felt 'more consistent with the simplicity and dignity of his character that he shld. be attended to the grave by his friends, public and private, without the interference of Govt. . . .' Accordingly, he was buried beside Pitt in Westminster Abbey, on 10th October 1806, but not at public expense.

When informed by Lord Howick of Fox's death, George III expressed no word of sympathy, and bitterly Lord Holland records 'the King had watched the progress of Mr Fox's disorder. He cld. hardly suppress his indecent exultation at his death.'

His widow was granted a pension of £1,200, vested in the names of Lord Holland, General Henry Edward Fox and William Adam, as Trustees.

*

After Fox's death, a rearrangement of the Ministry took place, blurred by jealousies between his followers and Lord Grenville's. The Foxites wanted Lord Holland to succeed his uncle in the Foreign Office and insisted that he should have a seat in the Cabinet. Lord Holland himself wanted to include Lord Lauderdale (his uncle's lifelong friend and colleague) in it as well as himself, but was told that only one of them could be accommodated. His uncle, General Fitzpatrick, advised him to accept the Privy Seal, with a seat in the Cabinet, reminding him that, with the figure-head of Charles James Fox no longer there, the Foxites were in no position to bargain for preferment. Yet Lord Holland still aspired to the Foreign Office and hoped that some compromise might be effected whereby, if peace with France could be achieved, he might exchange places with Lord Lauderdale, in Paris. He made these hopes plain in letters to Lord Howick and Lord Lauderdale, dated respectively 10th and 22nd September 1806.

But peace was far away and Napoleon was as intent as ever on crushing England. And first, he had to complete his plan to subjugate Europe, as only by this, could he hope to throttle British trade. On 14th October 1806, he defeated the Prussians at Jena and made his triumphant entry into Berlin. Thereafter, the way lay open for him to add Northern Germany to his empire, and to close the Baltic ports to British ships. So, from Berlin, he broadcast his plan for a Continental blockade of England, with every country in Europe agreeing to refuse her trade.

*

In a letter to Lady Bessborough, dated 24th September 1806, Lord Granville Leveson-Gower ridicules Lord Holland's acceptance of the Privy Seal, which he declares to be 'an office usually given to old retired Statesmen on account of the little labour it requires'. But Lady Bessborough replies that Lord Holland had been considered too young to be made President of the Council, so that the Privy Seal was the only Cabinet post open to him. She agrees with Lord Granville in fuming against Lord Sidmouth's appointment to be Lord President of the Council, but repeats that 'Lord Holland's youth made that place almost ludicrous for him'.

By the end of September, certain Ministerial changes had been made: Lord Howick went to the Foreign Office; Tom Grenville (Lord Grenville's son) to the Admiralty; and George Tierney became President of the Board of Control in India. To quote Lady Bessborough, Lord Howick tactfully told Lord Holland that 'he must look upon him as his locum tenens, and that whenever other arrangements made it practicable for him to have the Foreign affairs, he trusted his being in it wld. be no hindrance . . .'

Meantime, Lady Holland continued her wire-pulling.

One of the first things she did was to ask Lord Chancellor Erskine to give Sydney Smith the living of Foston-le-Clay, in Yorkshire. When Sydney went to thank him, the Lord Chancellor exclaimed: 'Oh! don't thank me, Mr Smith. I gave you the living because Lady Holland insisted on my doing so; and if she had desired me to give it to the devil, *he* must have had it.'

On 29th September, Lady Bessborough declares that Lady Holland 'is much *too* official and boasts of knowing things, which either she does not know or she proves by that very boast, that she ought not to have been told'. Further, that on being asked the nature of certain papers, Lady Holland 'put on a mysterious air, saying "Oh, those are Cabinet secrets— some papers Ld. Grenville has sent Ld. Holland to look at before they are carried to the King" '. Lady Bessborough continues: 'They say that if the Cabinet ministers' wives are to know all that passes, the country to make up for the risk of their talking ought to have the advantage of their opinions, and that it shld. be propos'd a female Cabinet shld. be call'd together consisting of Lady Sidmouth, Lady Grenville, Lady Howick, Lady Holland, Lady Sidmouth as President, full as good as my Lord. I do not know whether they wld. be for Peace abroad, but they certainly wld. produce war at home.'

Yet, despite Lady Bessborough's belittlement, undoubtedly Lady Holland knew a great deal as, daily, from the House of Lords, Lord Holland sent her little notes (usually headed 'Dearest woman') giving her blow-by-blow accounts of Cabinet affairs.

*

Sandwiched between his 'old retired Statesman's' duties, in August 1806, Lord Holland published his *Life of Lope de Vega*. It proved an outstanding success. The first edition, of five hundred copies, sold within a month, and a second edition followed immediately. He dedicated it to the Spanish poet, Don Manuel Josef Quintana, who gave it high praise, and many and varied were the congratulations he received on it. John Hookham Frere was one of the first to write, declaring that 'if the publication does you as much credit as in justice it ought I shall claim some share to myself for having exhorted and advised it'.

George Canning, Thomas Campbell, John Whishaw, Michael Payne Knight and Robert Southey voiced their admiration, not only of his knowledge of his subject but of his lucid English. In particular Knight and Southey emphasise this point. Knight writes: 'Amongst the many gratifi- cations it has afforded, the least has not been to find you sanction by yr. authority the use of plain English . . . which Johnson, Burke and Gibbon have rendered almost obsolete . . .' And Southey says: 'I have been greatly pleased by the orthodox English, both of the prose and verses . . . You are of the school to which I am attached, and have caught more of our old friend Dryden's ease and spirit than I have seen for a long time.'

Alone, Sydney Smith, who had helped to correct the proofs, takes a characteristically opposite view. 'You are naturally such an enemy to all kinds of affectation and foppery in style, that you write in an untidy, slovenly manner, and come in with yr. knees unbutton'd, vest and cravat untied, that nobody may call you a coxcomb.'

Thanks to his love of Spain and his knowledge of her language and literature, Lord Holland now added to his library an unique collection of original Lope de Vega manuscripts, together with other important Spanish authors and dramatists. (Later, Robert Southey availed himself of much of this material to write his Life of the Cid.)

*

Had Charles James Fox lived another six months he would have known the joy of achieving one of his lifelong political ambitions, that of helping to abolish the slave-trade. In 1806, Lord Grenville and he had paved the way, by introducing a Bill to put an end to British slave-trading for foreign supply. In 1807, a Bill passed both Houses of Parliament, abolishing the slave-trade as it applied to British dominions and colonies.

Lord Holland observes that 'the King and the Prince were as hostile to it (abolition) as ever' and that 'the inflexible zeal of Mr Fox and Lord Grenville carried it . . .' And he continues: 'The first time I sat in a commission to pass bills I had the satisfaction of giving the Royal assent to a measure which Mr Fox had so earnestly promoted, and which put an end to one of the greatest evils to which the human race has ever been exposed or at least our share in the guilt of it.'

Lady Holland records it too. On 2nd March 1807, she writes: 'The abolition of the Slave Trade was carried in the H. of C. by an immense majority nearly 18 to 1 . . .' And thereafter, she did not grumble, when the revenue from her Jamaican estate was greatly reduced.

*

In March 1807, the question of Catholic emancipation arose again, this time in relation to the army. The King soon withheld his limited assent and asked his Ministers to undertake never again to apply to him for such measures. Unable to agree, Lord Grenville and his colleagues resigned and, on 24th March, the 'Ministry of all the Talents' came to an end. Immediately afterwards, John Allen published the *Letters of Scaevola*, giving (to quote Lord Holland) 'a clear and concise' account of all the circumstances which led to the resignation of the Ministry. Lord Howick urged Mr Allen to continue these publications, but the last three letters were withheld. Had they not been, Lord Holland felt that 'while public curiosity was still awake on the subject of our dismissal, we shld. have had the cry, as well as the justice of the case on our side.' A new Ministry was formed by the Duke of Portland.

Despite their fall from office, on 30th July, the Hollands collected some distinguished guests to meet the Prince of Wales, at dinner. Invited to meet him were the Duke of Norfolk, Lord Albemarle, Lord Henry Petty, Lord and Lady Foley, Lady Melbourne and her son William Lamb, Sir Samuel Romilly and last but by no means least, the Rev. Sydney Smith. Although only a young curate, with cheerful effrontery Sydney Smith proceeded to challenge the Prince of Wales on the subject of 'wicked men'. He asserted: '. . . the wickedest man that ever lived was ye Regent Duke of Orleans, and he was a *Prince*'. He was trounced by the Prince of Wales. 'No, ye wickedest man who ever lived was Cardinal Dubois, the Regent's Prime Minister, and he was a *Priest*, Mr Sydney.'

*

Now the Hollands had little to do but concentrate on their own affairs. Lady Holland carefully stressed her disinterestedness to her journal. 'The loss of all interest in public affairs was the natural effect of the change of Administration to me.' Her taste of power had been brief. The Dinner Books registered a domestic note. On 25th April, Henry Edward (aged five) went to his first play: 'Mother Goose'. On the following day, he was promoted to breeches.

In May, the Hollands took a house in Southampton and, in the autumn, taking Charles and leaving Henry and the baby behind, they did a tour of the North.

In Scotland, Lord Holland received a disquieting letter from the 2nd Lord Kensington, laying claim to the property of Holland House. (In 1801, the 1st Lord Kensington had died, aged ninety.) The present baron based his claim on a supposed clause in the indenture of his father who, as William Edwardes, had sold the property to the 1st Lord Holland, in 1768. Although an Act of Parliament had been passed to obviate any such difficulties, now it seemed that the 1st Lord Kensington had inserted a clause whereby the property might revert to his son, should he be alive at the time of his own death.

Writing to Caroline Fox, on 9th September, Lord Holland tells her of his wife's agitation at the news. 'Lady H. as you wld. guess sees us all turned out homeless and houseless immediately and tho' I have no apprehension of the ultimate decision I confess I do not look forward . . . to the contest together with the expense and her agitation which will be consequences of it.' In fact, litigation dragged on till 1823 when, on the advice of James Abercrombie, later Speaker of the House of Commons, Lord Holland paid a lump sum down of £4,000 for what he described as 'this speedy, quiet and undisputed possession of what was already my own . . .'

On 28th October 1807, in a gossipy letter to Lord Granville, Lady Bessborough mentions the Hollands on their Northern trip. By now, Henry Brougham has become their intimate friend and Lady Bessborough comments: 'Think of Mr Brougham, the protégé of Ld. Holland, and apparent toad-eater and adorer of Lady Holland, abusing her violently to Corisande (St Jules) and saying he *detested* her; there never was a woman so courted, so flatter'd, so follow'd, so *obey'd*, and so *dislik'd*, as Lady Holland. Sometimes, with all her faults, it provokes me to see people who are at her feet all day, and whom she thinks adore her, come away to abuse and ridicule her . . .'

In their parents' absence, Caroline Fox had come into her own as a trusted deputy, in charge of her Fox nephews and niece. In October, she brought Henry Edward to Hinkley, in Lincolnshire, to rejoin the Hollands and there to have his leg examined by a leading surgeon, Robert Cheshire. (By this time he was wearing a surgical boot.) There, it was decided to leave him for a while to receive treatment. Lord Holland worried mainly that Henry's education would be neglected as his nurse, Scott, though 'a good body' and very attentive to the child's health and strength, was not qualified to teach.

In January 1808, Charles Richard went to Eton. And, shortly afterwards, the Hollands took a house in Pall Mall, to facilitate Lord Holland's now rather pointless attendances at the House of Lords.

As a last loving tribute to his uncle's memory, in May 1808, Lord Holland produced Charles James Fox's '*History of the Early Part of the Reign of James II*', with a preface by himself. William Miller, bookseller of Albemarle Street, bought it for £4,500. At the same time, Lord Holland announced his intention of writing his uncle's life and appealed for papers and letters to help him in his task. The response was widespread and his kinsman, John, 6th Duke of Bedford, placed all his hitherto private correspondence with Fox, at his disposal, at long last laying the ghost of the feud between his father, the 4th Duke, and the 1st Lord Holland. On 6th June, Lady Holland wrote to Lord Grey (formerly Howick, who had succeeded to the earldom on the death of his father, in 1807): 'The History succeeds far beyond our most sanguine expectations. Those even who do not perhaps agree to the sentiments allow that as a work it is excellent . . .'

The Hollands spent the summer of 1808 at Holland House.

Lady Holland genuinely loved her garden and, in May 1804, had sowed in it some dahlia seeds given her by the celebrated propagator, Cavanille, who had named the seed after the Swedish botanist, Dahl. At which time, Lord Holland had commended her enterprise, in verse:

> The Dahlia you brought to our isle
> Your praises forever should speak;
> Mid gardens as sweet as your smile,
> And in colour as bright as your cheek.

By 1806, Bonaiuti had reported over four hundred dahlia plants, in four different varieties, in her seed-beds, and had catalogued these specimens for the Natural History Museum.

From her garden, Lady Holland enthused to Lord Grey on 'the fresh air, verdure, and singing birds . . . as yet the melody of the nightingale has *only been heard* by Lauderdale. . . . These rustic pleasures have occupied and kept me out of the way of hearing much news.'

Lady Webster, painted at Florence in 1793 by Louis Gauffier. (On the back of this picture, recently discovered, are some lines to Lady Webster from the Italian poet Alfieri)

Sir Geoffrey Webster, 4th Bart., painted at
Florence in 1795 by Louis Gauffier

CHAPTER FIFTEEN

Spain 1808

IN 1807 AFTER a new secret treaty with Godoy, Napoleon had instructed
his general, Junot, to march with a large force of French and Spanish
troops to Lisbon, there to overthrow the Portuguese Royal Family. With
the help of the Royal Navy the Braganzas escaped to Brazil. But Junot's
forces remained in Lisbon, and Napoleon's plan to subdue the whole
Iberian Peninsula was under way.

Godoy fell, in March 1808, when Charles IV was forced to abdicate in
favour of his son, Ferdinand. In May, there was an uprising against the
French garrison in Madrid. A few days later, Charles and Ferdinand resigned their rights to Napoleon and a 'Junta of Regency' was proclaimed,
asking the Spanish people to accept Joseph Bonaparte as their King.

This announcement sparked off uprisings in several parts of Spain, and
national committees of resistance (juntas) sprang up all over the country.
In July the French were defeated at Baylen. Appeals for British help were
sympathetically received and Lord Castlereagh, at the War Office, began
planning military assistance.

On 8th June, members of the Asturian Junta appeared in England, and
representatives of the Junta of Oviedo quickly followed them, led by the
Vizconde de Matarrosa and Don Andreas de la Vega.

Like homing pigeons sure of their welcome, the last-named Spaniards
found their way to Holland House.

Since December 1806, the Spanish Chargé d'Affaires in England, Don
Augustin de Arguellas, had been a regular visitor to Holland House.
Through him, Lord Holland and Mr Allen dined occasionally at the
Spanish Club. In 1807, Mons. de Arguellas was still a mere dinner-guest
but, by January 1808, he was staying for four days at a time at Holland
House. In March he came again and, in June, he introduced the represen-
tatives of the Junta of Oviedo to the Hollands. On this occasion, the
Portuguese Ambassador, Mons. de Souza, was also present, a significant
factor as now resistance was breaking out in Portugal as well.

From June to October, the Spaniards were in and out of Holland House and, piecing together the events called forth by Lady Holland's erratic writing, we get a pretty clear picture of Holland House as a rallying-point.

(On 25th June) 'Ld Hd. and Mr Allen dined at Spanish Club to meet deputies of Asturias.'

(A day later) 'Ld and Ly Holland dined at Sir John Shelleys and went to see the Spaniards . . .'

On 2nd July, the dinner-list consisted of Vizconde de Matarrosa, Don Andreas de la Vega, Don Freire and, as usual, Don Augustin de Arguellas.

On 7th August a British force under Lieutenant General Sir Arthur Wellesley landed in Portugal above Leiria; and on 21st August it defeated Junot's main army at Vimiero. But the two officers in command over Wellesley, Sir Hew Dalrymple and Sir Harry Burrard, were too cautious to pursue the enemy and negotiated a truce of which Wellesley disapproved allowing the French to evacuate from Portugal with all their equipment. This 'Convention of Cintra' provoked passionate resentment in England and Spain. Meanwhile, in Lisbon, another British force under Sir John Moore awaited its orders.

*

The Hollands kept up their close contacts with the Spanish emissaries. On 18th August, they had seven members of the Seville and Oviedo Juntas to dinner; on 4th September, Lord Holland accompanied the Duke of Clarence to the Spaniards' headquarters at Bushey Park; on 11th September, the Duke of Clarence and Duke of Kent dined at Holland House to meet members of the Seville, Oviedo and Galician Juntas; and, running like a guiding thread through this maze of Spanish patriots, on 17th, 18th, 20th, 29th September and 2nd October, occurs the name of the Marques de la Romana, so soon to try to unite his Spanish troops with the British army, under Sir John Moore.

On 8th October, Lady Bessborough writes indignantly to Lord Granville Leveson-Gower:

. . . Think of the Hollands going to Spain! Why for? as Ly. Harrington wld. say. It really does appear to me v. absurd. The Spaniards have succeeded wonderfully, and I trust for the honour of human nature, and of *justice*, *will* succeed finally, and overthrow the tremendous preparation made against them; but it will be no child's play, and I shd. not think Ly. H. with all her attendants and wants, a good follower of a camp. Neither she nor Ld. H. wld. make famous warriors; and as to *counsel* in a civil capacity, much as I love Ld. Holland, I shd, be sorry to have him interfere, and still more *her*; they wld.—*she* intentionally, he possibly unintentionally—shake the confidence that is plac'd in Government, and wld. promote, I think, discussions which had better be left at peace, especially at present.

She ends naively:

After all this, if she does go and escapes without much danger, my anger will be mix'd with some envy . . .

The reasons leading up to the Hollands' decision were not far to seek. Suddenly, out of the blue, they were back in the hub of exciting politics, with Lord Holland playing the part of impresario to the epic performance about to begin in Spain. His sympathy for the Spanish people and his knowledge of their language now put him in an unique position as intermediary and, no doubt, had the Whigs been in power and his uncle still alive, Charles James would have made full use of his talents. With his sense of chivalry aroused, Lord Holland may well have thought that, in their hour of crisis, his obligation to his Spanish friends transcended party politics at home. But, unfortunately for him, the Tories were reinstated and with the death of his uncle the Whigs, once more in querulous minority, now looked on him as their spokesman in the House of Lords.

So, Lady Bessborough was only one of many who voiced their disapproval of the Hollands' plan and, at all levels, it was objected to, on moral grounds. The Hollands intended to take Charles Richard with them, but to leave Henry Edward and the baby, Mary, first, in the care of Lady Affleck and then with Caroline Fox. At first Caroline withholds her criticism, but Aunt Ebey Vernon, writing before she knew that Charles Richard was to accompany his parents, delivers a broadside:

Dear Nephew, we may differ as (to) its folly or wisdom, or right or wrong but not in good wishes or affection . . . heartily I wish you a prosperous journey but you have in my eyes increased rather than diminished the folly of it. You hardly deserve three such fine children to leave them to take a sail to Corunna to the care and inconvenience perhaps of friends. However dear little Henry E. will I hope find his aunts do all they can but indeed these are not *my* ideas of paternal or maternal feelings. Corunna might go to the devil and Spain too before I wld. leave a niece or nephew much less a child.

Yours E^y

Lord Upper Ossory too was against the Hollands' expedition, but felt it useless to protest against it. Calling them 'really worthy successors of the illustrious Knight (Don Quixote) you are going to visit' he feels 'there is no arguing upon the subject or giving advice . . . I find I have an aching at my heart to embrace and wish you all fare well before you depart on yr. wild expedition . . .'

Against this, Lord Holland won over his cousin, the Duke of Bedford, to his arguments, enough for him to agree that his son, Lord John Russell (then aged sixteen), should join his expedition. Writing from Uppark, on 9th October, the Duke declares: '. . . I place him in yr. hands in the most entire confidence not only that every care will be taken of him and that he will be highly amused and delighted, but that the time he will pass in yr. society will be most beneficially employed . . .'

Members of the Whig party were not complimentary and, in a letter from Edinburgh dated 5th October 1808, Henry Brougham (newly elected to Parliament) expresses his surprise at the Hollands' intention to go to Spain. He declares that when he had first heard the news, he had thought it a joke. Now, he 'exhorts' them not to go, considering it

a step to alienate the confidence of the people in this country from you. Be assured that however popular the Spanish cause has been or will be . . . this country does not require a man in yr. situation to run over to the patriots to shew his zeal for them . . . I must really speak plainly what I feel upon this matter. *Yr. Uncle and Pitt* are both dead, and yr. running away at the present moment is a mighty different matter from any other journey to the continent that you have formerly made. Everybody, of every party, thought you remained too long abroad last time but *now* the case is so infinitely stronger against absenting yr.self that it is not like the same thing. You will say 'What signifies the foolish talk of the publick about one's conduct'. I say it signifies nothing to a private man—and if you chuse to give up politics altogether you are right—but why do you go to the H. of Lords and make speeches and do a thousand other things which all lead towards acquiring power, through popularity? I hold it to be quite an inconsistency, at one time to court publick opinion and at another to defy it . . .'

Lord Holland's reply to this onslaught was to find it 'flattering'. Where-upon, on 28th October, Henry Brougham returns to the attack bringing up, as big guns wherewith to strengthen his argument, the adverse opinions of Lord Grey and Lord Lauderdale. (Lord Grenville too urged Lord Holland not to go to Spain.) Brougham continues:

. . . and I must say . . . that if the above design is carried into execution you will have to answer for the breaking up of yr. party . . . I entreat you not to feel so unconnected with it—you who are properly speaking its head.

On 9th October, Lord Lauderdale 'v. ill with a blister' writes to Lord Holland, from Dunbar. He 'cannot applaud yr. journey to Spain except to please yr. selves' and quotes Lord Grey who 'sees in it a thousand evils but is probably exaggerating as he is unwell'. He concludes by saying that 'there are things to decide of great importance, i.e. the Catholic subjects', at home.

It is often difficult to equate Lord Holland's seeming irresponsibility to immediate duty but, with his obvious dedication to the great causes of liberty and justice, the answer must lie in his early Rousseau-esque training. The liberation of 'the noble savage' was a world-wide concept and not confined to frontiers. Had the Whigs been in responsible office and not in the scheming opposition in which he had known them for most of his life, Lord Holland's reactions might have been more practical. As it was, now his quixotic impulse urged him to cross the Channel to the land of Don Quixote himself, where the struggle for liberty seemed to call for his particular championship.

Lord Grenville had warned him that George Canning had pronounced that he would prevent anyone who had previously held office from going to Spain and, at first, Canning was very reluctant to give Lord Holland a passport. Finally, he relented, but warned him not to make contacts with persons in authority. Lord Mulgrave (First Lord of the Admiralty) gave him permission to sail in any of His Majesty's ships and, with these two concessions, Lord Holland turned a deaf ear to the exhortations of his colleagues and the supplications of his sister. He assured Caroline that she must not consider his journey 'as a serious *going abroad* but merely as an excursion'. If things went badly, she might find him and his family back in England on New Year's Day; if well, then 'at the v. utmost in Spring April or May and Lady H. thinks most probable in February'.

*

Sir John Moore had already achieved a military career of great distinction when he landed in Portugal, in August 1808. And, in a letter of 25th September from Lord Castlereagh, he was informed that:

His Majesty, having determined to employ a corps of his troops, of not less than 30,000 infantry and 5,000 cavalry, in the North of Spain, to co-operate with the Spanish armies in the expulsion of the French from that Kingdom, has been graciously pleased to entrust to you the Command-in-Chief of this force.

He was told to leave a garrison behind him in Portugal, and to advance into Spain at the head of 20,000 men where, with a further force of between 15,000 and 20,000 men, Lieut. General Sir David Baird was to be sent out to meet him, via Corunna. Gratified though he was by the magnitude of his command ('there has been no such command since Marlborough'), Sir John found himself confronting appalling difficulties.

The army which had defeated Junot at Vimiero had deteriorated visibly in its torrid encampment at Queluz. No adequate provision had yet been made for transport. The administration of so large an army was in the hands of inexperienced men with hardly any knowledge of Spanish or Portuguese.

And, worst of all, the Treasury had not supplied Sir John with bullion, and his military chest contained only £25,000. Owing to approaching winter conditions, two roads from Lisbon over the mountains would become impassable to cavalry and heavy artillery. Which meant that he would have to send his heavy artillery and two cavalry regiments into Spain by a circuitous route to the south, through Estremadura, thus divorcing them for four or five weeks from his light artillery and infantry. However, he had reliable senior officers to carry out his orders and finally disposed them.

Sir John realised that there was no concerted effort behind the Spaniards, despite their heroic successes at Baylen and Saragossa. Each provincial junta was a law unto itself, refusing to co-operate with its fellows and unprepared to consider the Central Junta, established at Madrid, as of supreme authority. One and all of the provincial juntas made individual bids to get the lion's share of arms and ammunition from the British Government; and only one factor held them together, their self-deceiving optimism.

With his friend, George Canning, now in office as Foreign Secretary, John Hookham Frere found himself back on the active list, and, on 4th October 1808, he was appointed Minister plenipotentiary to the Central Junta, at Madrid. On 20th October, this excitable, impractical, gullible man arrived at Corunna. Again accompanied by his brother, Bartholomew, he proceeded at once to Madrid there to take over from the sensible soldier who awaited him, Lord William Bentinck.

*

On 9th October 1808, the Hollands set off for Falmouth, en route for Spain. As Lady Holland records: '. . . being resolved to take as few persons and encumbrances as possible', they travelled light 'in two carriages only' in a party consisting of themselves, Charles Richard, John Allen, Lord John Russell, two maids, and six men. One transport had already departed from Falmouth but, after a fortnight's delay, Captain Parker of the *Amazon* was induced to give the Hollands a passage. On 21st October, another of his passengers, John Ward, wrote to his friend, Mr Stewart: 'Lady H. has resolved to force herself on board it (*Amazon*) in spite of the evident reluctance of poor Capt. Parker . . .'

Although a prey to her usual nervous fears of '*strange sails*' and privateers, surprisingly, Lady Holland enjoyed the voyage. 'After a delightful passage of five days, we reached Corunna.' The date was 5th November, by which time Sir John Moore's infantry and light brigades were struggling up the terrible mountain roads, in glacial rain, towards the Spanish frontier.

Admiral de Courcy came on board the *Amazon*, to greet Lord Holland. He confirmed stories the Hollands had already heard that, for a fortnight, the local Junta of Galicia had refused to allow Lieut. General Sir David Baird (arrived in Corunna Harbour on 13th October) to disembark his troops, alleging that permission from the Central Junta had first to be obtained. Lady Holland reports that 'great difficulties also arose from want of money', as the Spaniards were no more prepared than the Portuguese to accept Government bills from England. On 20th October, Baird's situation was temporarily relieved by the arrival of John Hookham Frere at Corunna, who handed him over £42,000 from the sum of £410,000 with which he had been provided, to bolster up Spanish resistance.

Very different was the gratifying reception accorded the Hollands on their arrival on the quayside at Corunna, on 5th November. Madame Sangro (wife of a member of the Galician Junta, entertained by the Hollands in England) headed a delegation of two coach-loads of ladies, intent on escorting Lady Holland to her house. She commented: 'The house which they had procured for us was thoroughly in the Spanish fashion, spacious, but *totally* void of furniture.' In the evening, the Hollands were entertained by Madame Mosquera, and heard a first-hand account of the reception accorded the Marques de la Romana on his arrival at Corunna, on 20th October. (The same ship had brought John Hookham Frere.) The townspeople had dragged Romana's carriage through the streets, 'an honor never bestowed upon any person in Spain before', where he had been greeted with shouts of 'Viva, Viva!' 'He was quite overcome and sobbed aloud . . .'

On 26th October, Sir David Baird's troops had started to disembark, but the last detachment did not leave Corunna till 10th November, and a further five days was to elapse before the departure of the cavalry, under the command of Lieut. General Lord Paget. On 10th November, Lady Holland made his acquaintance and was much impressed ('uncommonly obliging and pleasing'). With him, she met other cavalry officers and took them to a ball, given in her honour, by Madame Mosquera. The news of General Joachim Blake's defeat at Zornosa, commanding the army of Galicia, had just come through and, at first, the ball was cancelled. Then, as a 'civility' to Lady Holland, it was allowed to take place. The Spaniards were struck by Lord Paget's beauty but found him haughty. On his part, he made little effort to fraternise with his hosts.

*

Under appalling conditions of sleet, ice and snow, the vanguard of Sir John Moore's infantry brigades crossed the Spanish frontier and staggered into Salamanca, on 13th November, and the whole of his infantry strength, of 15,000 men, assembled there, ten days later. There, his ears were assailed with tales of disaster to the Spanish armies, while Napoleon's troops were thundering through Northern Spain, to occupy Valladolid. He wrote an angry letter to John Hookham Frere, in Madrid:

I am in communication with no one Spanish army, nor am I acquainted with the intentions of the Spanish Government or any of its Generals. The imbecility of the Spanish Government exceeds belief. The goodwill of the inhabitants, whatever that may be, is of little use while there exists no ability to bring it into action.

*

On 12th November, the Hollands decided to make an excursion to Santiago. There, they visited the Cathedral and later were greeted by the Archbishop, who induced them to form part of his religious procession. Lady Holland noted that, for three years, the Archbishop (then Bishop of Avila) had been Confessor to Queen Maria Luisa. She noted further: 'Supposed to have been devoted to Godoy while he was powerful'. In the evening, she and her party were treated to a concert given by musicians from the Cathedral. During the intervals there were fireworks and acclamations of 'Viva Inglaterra' and 'George III y Fernando VIII'. To which the Hollands responded with 'Vivas' for 'Espana' and 'Fernando'.

On 16th November, they returned to Corunna. There, news had been received that, on 7th and 8th November, 13,000 troops belonging to the Army of Estremadura had reached Burgos and Lady Holland felt this news was so well authenticated that her party could proceed with 'the utmost confidence' on its journey. But three days later, the Army of Estremadura was totally defeated by Napoleon, at Gamonat.

On 17th November, Admiral de Courcy 'again and again repeated his kind and friendly offers' to put the *Tonnant* at the service of the Hollands, should they be 'compelled' to make their retreat to Corunna. They refused him and, on the day following, set out on the road to Astorga. At Betanzos, Lady Holland witnessed the ravages the cavalry horses had endured, after their seven weeks' confinement at sea. She saw several lying dead by the roadside and others too weak to get up.

At Guitiriz, the Hollands stayed at the inn already requisitioned for Lord Paget and his staff, who gallantly conceded them '*the best part*'. Then, on 19th November, they watched Lord Paget's men move off, who 'rode off with regularity', preceded by a band.

Every mile brought news. Blake's second defeat, on 10th November, at Espinosa, was soon known. Sir David was still uncertain of Sir John's whereabouts but imagined he must be at Salamanca. Now, he urged Lord Paget to join him, to take counsel with him on 'the v. critical position of affairs'. The next news of Blake confirmed that he had been driven back, with only a fragment left of his force, to Santander. General the Marques de la Romana had been detailed to supersede him, in the open field, in command of the shattered army of Galicia.

On 21st November, Lady Holland receives a further letter from Bartle Frere, dated 15th November, from Aranjuez. Diplomatically he advises the Hollands 'not to advance until something decisive is seen from the armies'. And, playing on Lady Holland's hypochondria, he complains of 'the insalubrity of Aranjuez at this season'. His ruse is successful and Lord Holland, with his dozen followers, turns about and returns to Corunna, next day.

But not before Lady Holland has committed some valorous sentiments to her journal:

> It is v. vexatious to feel it indispensable to retrograde; it really is an act of self-denial not to proceed. I am pursuaded one's courage rises in proportion as one approaches the scene of danger, and at Astorga, I should have felt less terror than I did in apprehension at Holland House.

In her letters to Caroline Fox, she consoles herself with jibes against 'Mr Ward's' pusillanimity, in not wanting to advance nearer to the battlefront. Which call forth an obvious retort from her sister-in-law.

On 21st November Caroline writes:

> ... yr. rage at Ward is rather diverting considering how much in general you are an advocate for people doing *what they like*. Aunt Ebey desires her love and bids me tell you she thinks him the wiser of the two, but for my own part I confess I think a married man could have found better reasons for coming home than a single one ... I long to hear Mr Ward's account of you, to justify himself he must be severe upon you, but what business a single man had to return to be sure one does not see so he had better be content with a woman's reason, and say honestly he came back because he did not like to stay ...

On 24th November, Sir John Moore wrote to Lord Castlereagh, again stressing his complete lack of contact with the Spanish authorities.

> The enthusiasm of which we heard so much nowhere appears ... I am at this moment in no communication with any of their generals. I am ignorant of their plans or those of their Government ... We are here by ourselves, left to manage the best way we can, without communication with any other army; no knowledge of the strength or positions of the enemy, but what we can pick up in a country where

F*

we are strangers, and in complete ignorance of the plans or wishes of the Spanish Government.

He had been at Salamanca for over a fortnight and, in all, his force now totalled 17,000 men; but he had only one battery of light guns. His heavy artillery and cavalry was still to the south, and Sir David Baird was still one hundred miles away, to the north. The next day, he heard news of the defeat of the only remaining undefeated Spanish army, at Tudela, which strengthened his conviction that retreat was the only course left open to him. Frere felt this decision would have a disastrous effect on the Spaniards but, in the meantime, Napoleon was within sight of Madrid.

On 3rd December, Sir John received a deputation from the Central Junta, full of optimism and plans for a joint campaign to relieve Madrid. To which his own reaction was that nothing was so easy as for the Junta, 'with their pens', to form armies. Frere's letters continued impertinently to admonish him for his decision to retreat and to exhort him to save the people of Madrid from the French.

At last, Moore received evidence that the Spaniards would co-operate and, although still prone to serious misgivings, on 5th December he countermanded his order to retreat. But, unknown to him, the day before, Napoleon had entered Madrid.

When this news reached him, he was not surprised. Merely, he altered his strategy. Alone, he could not hope to defeat the French in battle but, by striking east, he might act as a decoy, drawing off and preventing Napoleon's troops from advancing southwards. Could he draw the enemy northwards across the mountains, at some point beyond them, he would have to turn and run for it, to the coast. This was the only way he could help the Spaniards. Accordingly, on 11th December his army started to advance, towards Valladolid.

*

Returned to Corunna, the Hollands took the house formerly occupied by Sir David Baird, where they avidly collected news of the battle-front.

On 25th November, Admiral de Courcy arrived with bad news. 'Under the strictest seal of secrecy' he revealed that Sir David Baird had directed him to find 'a safe and proper place' wherefrom to embark troops. By and large, he had decided on Vigo. He had kindly given orders that the *Champion* should stand by, ready to take off the Hollands, should they so wish. But now, they had decided to go by road to Portugal and again refused his offer.

Lord Holland received a letter, marked 'Private' dated 24th November, from Lord Paget, from Astorga. In it he assured Lord Holland that there was 'no chance whatsoever' of his remaining in Spain. With the French at Valladolid, Sir John Moore despaired of a junction with Sir David Baird's forces and was about to retire from Salamanca, back to Portugal. Now, Sir David's troops were retreating to Villafranca. Relentlessly, Lord Paget emphasises that there are 'no reserves, no enthusiasm', and that 'there positively does not exist any Spanish corps with which any part of the British army can form a junction'. He thinks British Ministers must have been totally misled as to the state of the Spanish army and 'the disposition of its people'. He is aware that he is writing to a Spaniard (Lord Holland) but now thinks that not even he can have much to say for 'his protégés'. He ends by advising Lord and Lady Holland to return to Holland House, there to wait 'until the patriotic Spaniards are *en masse* for the expulsion of Joseph and his suite'.

Ups and downs of news varied from hour to hour, jotted down in Lady Holland's journal. On 30th November, Lord Holland received a second letter from Lord Paget, from Astorga, who now felt confident that an attempt would be made to unite Sir David Baird's forces with those of Sir John Moore. But he regretted Romana's declared intention to follow Baird's troops to Salamanca. He added a postscript: 'Most happy to tell you that our advance is decided upon . . .' 1st December was a day of doom, in Lady Holland's journal. 'All hope has vanished, and orders are given for retreating . . .' Sir David Baird had received 'positive orders' from Sir John Moore to begin his march towards the coast. He, himself, was falling back towards Ciudad Rodrigo. 'The cause of this sudden determination . . . rests upon the defeat of Castanos . . .'

Lord Paget had been to Leon to see Romana, and had not been impressed by what he found. His men were 'half-naked and starving, and unless equipped they cannot be kept together'. Nevertheless, swayed by the bias of John Hookham Frere, Lady Holland condemned Sir John Moore's decision to retreat. 'Nothing but the most *precise* and peremptory orders can justify Moore in acting as he is going to do. It is too mortifying.' Despite this, she and Lord Holland thought it 'safest to hasten to Vigo and there embark'.

On 4th December, Lady Holland notes feverish preparations for her party's departure from Corunna. 'We are hastening to Vigo, and shall set off in an hour.'

In order to ensure the transport of artillery and stores to Romana's headquarters at Leon, the Galician Junta had put an embargo on all horses and mules in the area. But Lord Holland, undeterred by scruples that he might be drawing on vital supplies for the Spanish army, successfully applied to the Junta, and was allowed a team of mules.

Two days later, the post overtook the Hollands at Santiago. It contained a letter from Admiral de Courcy, covering one from Lord William Stuart, of the *Lavinia*, offering them 'a passage to Lisbon . . . and to Cadiz where he expects to go afterwards'. This information was conveyed by Lord Holland to Caroline Fox. In a postscript to his letter of 6th December, he adds: 'They say the French are concentrating at Burgos and our army instead of joining is marching away! ! !' On 10th December, the Hollands reached Vigo, only to find that, three nights before, taking advantage of a fair wind from Corunna, the *Lavinia* had by-passed Vigo and had now arrived at Lisbon.

While Lord Holland tried to make arrangements to transfer his party, on mules and on litters, to Lisbon, he found time to write two letters to his sister.

In the first, dated 10th December, he cracks up the supposed defence of Madrid:

All private letters and public papers concur in representing the activity and determination of Madrid to be as great as possible and the people have prevailed on the Junta not to remove from Aranjuez. Every effort is making to defend the Capital and before the French can arrive there must be a considerable Spanish force in and about it. There was nothing on the 30th (November) nor I believe up to the 2nd or 3rd (Dec) between Moore and Madrid but a division of his own army amounting to 7000 under Genl. Hope and in this situation he determines to retreat—it is to abandon Spain instead of making the slightest effort to rescue the Capital . . . . I do not speak of *poor little Romana* with his shattered army at Leon who is left to stand the brunt of the French in Castile and Asturias and is to derive no sort of protection or assistance from a corps of twelve thousand British who were within twenty miles of him . . .

Four days later, still at Vigo, Lord Holland continues his obstinate forecast of heroism in Madrid:

. . . I tremble for the carnage that is likely to be exhibited at Madrid. Many coincidences make me conjecture that by this time it has been attacked and if so I trust and believe most obstinately and furiously defended. Morla who commands is a man of great talents and if his personal courage is equal to the general energy of his character and the harshness of his disposition, he is formed for the situation which he fills.

To Lord Holland, treachery in a Spaniard was inconceivable.

And neither did Sydney Smith's letter of 8th December make an impression on Lady Holland. 'Why, dear Lady Holland, do you not come home? It has been all over this month. Except in the Holland family there has not been a man of sense for some weeks who has thought otherwise. Are you fond of funerals? Do you love to follow a nation to its grave? . . .'

On 'the last day of 1808', from Weymouth, Caroline Fox replies to her brother's letters of 10th and 14th December:

Wherever the New Year dawns upon you I hope it will be propitious to you . . . Yours of the 10th from Vigo did not reach us till long after the Ministers had announced it (the fall of Madrid) to us but the winds have been very adverse to arrivals from the peninsula for the last three weeks, however now they are changed I look for letters by every post & two days ago received one of the 14th from Vigo (still ignorant of the fate of Madrid) & written on the eve of your departure for Portugal, a journey to which I confess my little Brother seems to me at this distance hazardous & consequently unwise, but I suppose you have good reason to know that you are quite safe notwithstanding the discontented & disturbed state of Portugal & that little reliance that you acknowledge is at any time to be placed upon the good faith of the Inhabitants. [Then she administers her usual quiet reproof]: The meeting of Parliament too is approaching, & if ever there was a moment in which the arguments of opposition with regard to the conduct of the war, are likely to be echoed by the publick, it is the present . . . in times like these, you ought to be *at your post*. I defended your *outset* but can say nothing in defence of this coasting expedition, when it is found impracticable to get into the interior of the Country & must continue so till the time comes when you promised to *be home*. So there you have a piece of my mind my little Brother, & you will forgive my giving you bluntly my opinion knowing that if I loved you less, I should spare myself the trouble of saying it . . .

To which, undeterred, Lord Holland replies that he is not such a Quixote as to put himself in any danger, by going to Portugal.

*

The first fifty miles of Sir John Moore's advance towards Valladolid passed auspiciously. And, on 14th December, he was brought a captured despatch from which he learnt that Marshal Soult was only 100 miles away, with 18,000 men and as yet unsupported. If he could unite with Baird and act with speed, he might defeat Soult before Napoleon's armies of nearly 300,000 could catch up with him.

On 19th December, he achieved the union with Baird, whereby he could now deploy nearly 29,000 men. But Romana's 20,000 troops had proved a myth. After a march through blinding snow, Sir John reached Sahagun on 21st December, where Paget had defeated the French in a cavalry engagement. Moore's intention was to march through the night to attack Soult, at dawn. He began his advance, then learnt that Napoleon was just behind him. Grimly, he realised that he would have to draw off his forces, before engagement, and make for the coast. That evening of 23rd December, he wrote two letters, one to Romana, one to Hookham Frere.

To Romana he wrote: 'It wld. only be losing the army to Spain and to England to persevere in my march on Soult. Single-handed I cannot pretend to contend with the superior forces the French can now bring against me.' Then, he wrote to Frere: 'If the British army were in an enemy country, it cld. not be more completely left to itself . . . The movement I am making is of the most dangerous kind. I do not only risk to be surrounded every moment by superior forces, but to have my communications intercepted. I wish it to be apparent to the whole world as it is to every individual of the army, that we have done everything in our power to support the Spanish cause, and that we do not abandon it until long after the Spaniards abandoned us.'

With a heavy heart, he re-grouped his units, and noted in his diary: 'If we can steal two marches on the French, we shall be quiet.' In sullen gloom, the men under his command received his orders to retreat.

To Lord Paget, writing confident of victory to Lord Holland, only a few hours earlier, his decision must have been heart breaking.

CHAPTER SIXTEEN

Compère and Commère

ERE HE AND HIS MOTHER took flight to Brazil the Regent, Dom Juan of Portugal, had appointed a Regency of seven. This was in abeyance while General Junot occupied Lisbon, but was reconstituted by Sir Hew Dalrymple. Sir John Cradock succeeded Sir John Moore in command of the British forces in Portugal and, under him, Sir Robert Wilson started to raise what came to be known as his 'Lusitanian Legion', a force trained to keep the peace in and around Oporto.

Despite Sir Robert's efforts to ensure the comfort of the Hollands in Oporto, within three days of her arrival there, Lady Holland is reporting adversely: 'The re-establishment of the Regency has been a most unpopular measure. . . . The persons in high office are suspected of being strongly addicted to the French cause . . .' This was a sweeping statement as the Bishop of Oporto, greatly loved and with a beneficent influence on the people, had become one of the seven members of the Regency. But she was right in thinking that the Junta of Oporto was dissatisfied with the British, feeling that Britain had not allowed it enough say in the reconstitution of the Regency.

The Hollands took rooms at the comfortable inn built into 'the Factory House', where they prepared to hold their court. Bernardino Freire de Andrada, General-in-Command of the Portuguese forces, was the first to call; he was followed by the Bishop of Oporto. The next day, Bernardino Freire called again, bringing his wife. Freire offered 'to order the monks of Grijo' to prepare to receive the Hollands, on their way to Lisbon, which offer they graciously accepted. The pattern of their reception in Spain was repeated in Portugal. In both countries, automatically, they were accorded ambassadorial status.

On 20th December 1808, at Oporto, Lady Holland makes this entry in her journal: 'Mr Butler communicated the sad and melancholy news of the capitulation of Madrid; the enemy were repulsed three times, and it must have been about the 10th that the event took place . . .' As with Lord

159

Holland, so with his wife. It was unthinkable to either of them that within twenty-four hours Madrid could have been treacherously surrendered to Napoleon by the Spaniards themselves!

The same day Lord Holland wrote to his sister, in every line revealing Hookham Frere's bias against Sir John Moore. 'Had Moore never ordered Baird to retreat even if he had not ordered him to advance till the time he did it is possible he might have relieved Madrid. What is certain is that had he marched forward on the first instead of retreating he must either have been at Madrid before it was taken or created such a diversion in Old Castile as would have prevented the French from pushing so forward.' He concludes: 'We expect to be in Lisbon in about 10 days time. . . . We have performed our journey on mules. Lady Holland riding all the way very prosperously. . . .'

Now, Mr Chamberlain was no longer in Lisbon, to make plans ahead for the Hollands' reception. He had gone with the Portuguese Royal Family to Rio de Janeiro, there to become its first British consul. But, thanks to the 'kind civility' of a Mr Bulkeley, on their arrival in Lisbon the Hollands were 'very tolerably lodged'.

Charles Villiers, British Envoy to the Portuguese Court, received Lord Holland on 3rd January 1809. And, the following day, Lord Holland breakfasted with the General-in-Command.

Lady Holland remarks that Sir John Cradock was 'very communicative and even confidential to Lord H.' According to her, he had one English infantry battalion and some Portuguese garrisoning the Fort la Lippe, at Elvas, and 'a very small English garrison, at Almeida'. Some Portuguese troops were collecting at Thomar and at Guimaranes 'but excepting these there seems *nothing* to prevent the French from penetrating when they choose to Lisbon'. In addition to this already alarming information, Lady Holland also observed that Charles Villiers had given the Factory House notice that, at any moment, it might have to evacuate its guests, all of which precautionary measures caused her to wonder whether her intended journey through Badajoz to Seville was 'quite so safe an undertaking as we had expected to find it'.

The next few days confirmed her doubts. On 5th January, she noticed 'great alarm amongst the merchants' together with much activity on their part, to despatch their property, by sea. And, fearfully, she noted that there had been 'popular commotions, excesses, and murders at Badajoz'.

Three days later, she received a letter, dated 4th January, from Bartle Frere, at Seville. In it, he gave a few near-accurate dates of the movements of Sir John Moore. Erroneously, he reported him as having left 'Carrion de los Condes' on 23rd December, to attack Soult at Saldaña. He told Lady Holland of Lord Paget's successful action at Sahagun. And he reported that, with 30,000 men, on 23rd December, Napoleon had left the Escorial, to cross the Guadarramas, in pursuit of Moore. Frere was two days out in his reckoning, and did not mention that Marshal Ney, too, was ordered to advance against Moore, from Aragon into Old Castile.

*

The mood of sullen gloom among Sir John Moore's troops persisted, rapidly degenerating, through despondency, to one of savage excess. From the moment the army started to retreat the cavalry behind it, following as its rearguard, reported arson, looting, and a breakdown of discipline. On 28th December, at Benavente, Sir John Moore called a halt.

This respite proved a prelude to Bacchanalian frenzy. As a result, Sir John issued a General Order of extreme severity, castigating officers and men alike. And he added: 'It is impossible for the General to explain to his army the motive for the movement he takes . . . When it is proper to fight a battle he will do it; and he will choose the time and place he thinks fit. . . .' The Order had a certain effect but, that night, the Convent of Benavente and the castle of the Duchess of Ossuna were looted and gutted by Moore's troops.

On 29th December the French cavalry advanced over the Esla, but were eventually put to flight by Paget's cavalry. Yet Napoleon was only 15 miles behind, and Soult was closing in on the remnants of Romana's army. Most of Moore's soldiers reached Astorga on the 29th, but he dared not pause to heed their agonised mutterings.

On 31st December, he wrote to Lord Castlereagh: 'There is no means of carriage. The people run away, the villages are deserted; and I have been obliged to destroy (a) great part of the ammunition and military stores. For the same reason I am obliged to leave the sick. In short, my sole object is to save the British army.'

He dared not remain at Astorga, for fear the French might cut off his line of retreat either to the north or to the south. So he set off with all speed to Villafranca, fifty miles nearer the coast, where there was a supply of food.

From Benavente, Napoleon wrote back derisively, to France. 'The English are running away as fast as they can . . . They have abandoned the Spaniards in a shameful and cowardly manner.' Thereafter, he decided that they were not worth pursuing himself so left the final stage of their defeat to Marshal Soult.

*

On 9th January 1809, Lady Holland records: 'A heap of good news from Sr. Robt. Wilson, but not sufficiently authenticated to justify great confidence in them.' Using his 'Lusitanian Legion' as a mobile force, about 20th December, Sir Robert Wilson had set off from Oporto and had established himself near Almeida, there to observe the French division under General Lapisse, just arrived from Benavente, after Napoleon's decision to call off his own pursuit of Moore. The same day she observes that Sir John Cradock has just decided to make 'a great effort to assist Moore' by sending him all available troops from Lisbon and collections of stores from Vizeu and Lamego. And she reports that Sir Robert Wilson, acting on his own initiative, has taken his legionaries on to Ciudad Rodrigo, bearing supplies. But she has no confidence in the British army. '... Sir Robt. Wilson has, upon his own judgment, proceeded on to Ciudad Rodrigo ... and taken with him provisions and ammunition which, as he will most likely be taken prisoner, will fall into the hands of the enemy and be of infinite service to them.'

By now, the Hollands' condemnation of any military effort other than Spanish was beginning to have its effect. It came to a head in a furious letter to Lord Holland from Lord Paget, from Sahagun, written on 23rd December, two days after his victory over the French cavalry there.

My dear Lord—I am in a violent rage with you. You are the most prejudiced man alive. You talk to a parcel of people snug upon the sea coast and who, knowing yr. enthusiasm for the Spanish cause, flatter *your misconceptions* of the state of this country, and from the language of such people you form yr. judgment of the dispositions of the Spanish nation. '*Tis one not worth saving*. Such ignorance, such deceit, such apathy, such pusillanimity, such cruelty, was never both (before) united. There is not one army that has fought at all. There is not one general who has exerted himself, there is not one province that has made any sacrifice whatever. ... We are treated like enemies. The houses are shut against us. The resources of the country are withheld from us; we are roving about the country in search of Quixotic adventures to save our own honor, whilst there is not a Spaniard who does not skulk and shrink within himself at the very name of Frenchman. I am with an army the finest in the world for its numbers, enthusiastic, equal to every exertion, burning to engage. I have been one of the most strenuous advisers to advance and to take our chance. But why have I done so? For my own sake, for that of my comrades in arms, not, believe me, not in the smallest degree for the Spaniards....

He goes on to give details of some cavalry engagements under General Stewart's command, and one in particular—

... (it is with the intensest satisfaction I relate it to you for Lady Holland's information) Captain Jones and Sir Godfrey Webster at the head of 30 men attacked 100 of the enemy, killed 20 and took 5 prisoners. 'Twas a most gallant affair.'

Then, sarcastically prefacing his next account ('as you are a great soldier') Lord Paget gives Lord Holland details of his victory at Sahagun. And he ends his letter: '. . . having begun my letter in anger I will close in good humour, sincerely congratulating Lady Holland upon the gallantry of her son. Open yr. eyes, my dear Lord, and believe me, v. faithfully yrs.— Paget.'

Like everything else he did, his postscript was valiant. 'We march tonight to attack Soult and shall beat him. We are all delighted . . . Mais à quoi bon?' (Alas! the march was stillborn.)

Lord Holland's reaction to this direct snub is unrecorded. And Lady Holland's is noncommittal.

We received a heap of letters from Coruna, Vigo, and Oporto. One from Ld. Paget, of the 23rd, at Sahagun. He mentions three brilliant affairs in which the Cavalry distinguished themselves; in one my son and Capt. Jones at the head of thirty dragoons charged 100 of the enemy, killed 20 and took five prisoners. Complains of the apathy of the Spaniards, and rallies Ld. Hd. upon his *misconceptions* in their favor, adding that they are *a people not worth saving*. He adds . . . 'We march to attack Soult to-morrow', and seemed confident of success . . .

Behind this almost prosy reporting, surely a mother's heart was torn with anxiety for her gallant son?

*

Sir John Moore's army had a nightmare march to Villafranca, which they reached on 1st January 1809. Here he made an appeal for a return to discipline which for a short time produced a good effect. Twice Paget's division repulsed the French cavalry along the River Cua but, thereafter, the road from Herrerias up Monte Cerbrero and on to Lugo became a progress to Calvary. For thirty-six hours, Sir John Moore drove his whole army to undertake a forced march yet, despite their misery, his men could not understand why he would not let them fight a battle, and the murmurs against their general's tactics grew vociferously bitter. Against them, still true to his objective of saving the British army (20,000 men against 300,000) Sir John turned a deaf ear. Always, he faced the prospect of the enemy outflanking him on the north, from Oviedo, or on the south, from Orense, and hemming him in.

At last, at Lugo, on 6th January, he decided to make a stand. The British had a promising position and, the next day, successfully repulsed the French. But, on the 8th, again he had to retire, fearing Soult's attempts to encircle him. Alone, General Paget's division kept its ranks. Otherwise, it was as a formless mass that Moore's tatterdemalion army reached Betanzos,

on 10th January. Even so, by then its men had earned their immortal title
from their opponents: 'Les squelettes féroces'.

At Betanzos, suddenly, Purgatory became Paradise. From the hilltop,
the men's tired eyes could see the sea, the snow had gone, and there was
food in plenty. And, on 14th January, they saw one hundred British
transports escorted by twelve warships sail into the harbour of Corunna
where, at last, they were warmly welcomed by the citizens of the town.
Already, Sir John Moore had reconnoitred the ground for his last stand.
His men had a further two days to recover as Marshal Soult's army, also,
had suffered distress at the rapid rate of march.

From the moment his troops engaged the enemy (on 16th January),
Moore was a man transformed, his mood changing 'from fixed gloom
bordering almost on despair, to a state of exaltation'. His army successfully
defended Corunna, and by nightfall on 17th January all his troops were
embarked, except for one covering brigade.

But Sir John Moore himself was killed, in his hour of glory.

*

Now, Lady Holland was keen to leave Portugal. ('The Portuguese begin
to murmur and complain of the English for coming among them to upset
the French, and then abandoning them to their rage.') The morale of the
clergy and the 'common people' was still high but the Regency was
alarmed and General Freire de Andrada, hitherto so unctuous, 'begins to
be insolent'. The news of the 'popular commotions' in Badajoz had been
too much for Lady Holland, who now decided to reach Seville, by sea.
But news from Seville was disquieting too. On 14th January, both Lord
Holland and she had had to swallow a bitter pill. A copy of the *Seville
Gazette*, of 6th January, had reached them, containing the gist of 'that
precious villain Morla's' letter to the Central Junta.

Charles Villiers continued to entertain them but it was plain that the
Hollands' presence in Portugal was becoming a nuisance to their compatriots. Admiral Berkeley (just arrived to take up his command, in the
Tagus) was polite but firm. He could not part 'with any force during the
actual state of affairs'. Sir John Cradock was more conciliatory, but his
offer meant an eleventh-hour change of plan. Were the Hollands to revert
to their journey by land, and to be prepared to fall in with his plans for the
British army, they could march 'with the English garrison as an escort.'
from Elvas to Seville.

On 19th January, Lady Holland makes a note: 'Sr. John Cradock is
greatly alarmed at the position of Moore's army, and expects daily to hear

of capitulation or convention.' And, three days too late, she invokes the Almighty. 'God forbid affairs should be in such a desperate state.'

The Commissary-General, Mr Rawlings, now promised to provide the Hollands with mules and carts and to go to incredible lengths to oblige them. He undertook to delay the departure of Major Stuart (aide-de-camp to General Mackenzie) with the pay-money for the troops at Elvas, to give the Hollands 'the certainty of reaching Elvas before the departure of the whole garrison'. In consequence, on 21st January, the Hollands embarked, in a Government boat, to cross the river to Aldea Gallega.

Two days later, at Arranyolos, Lord Holland received a mysterious message from Sir John Cradock. The young officer who brought it (Lt. Ellis) had orders 'not to deliver to any person' and even Lady Holland herself was not told its contents. That evening, 'a Mr Fletcher from Elvas' came to tell the Hollands that he considered the road safe, through Badajoz to Seville. On 25th January, they reached Elvas and 'marched' with the English garrison to Badajoz. Over the border, Lady Holland expressed herself 'v. happy to be once again on Spanish ground'.

The Hollands arrived in Seville, on 30th January, to find the inn full of fugitives from Madrid so, for two days, they had to content themselves with 'a v. indifferent house'. That evening they dined with Hookham Frere.

Three days later, through the agency of Charles Stuart (British liaison with the Central Junta), they moved in to Marquesa de Ariza's beautiful palace, the Casa Liria, vacated with such precipitation by herself, her sister, and her young son, the Duke of Berwick, that it still contained much of her jewellery and (to Lady Holland's advantage) 'all her plate'.

Lady Holland lost no time in catching up with the news. An old friend, Don Gaspar Jovellanos, represented Asturias on the Central Junta and he, its able secretary, Don Martin Garay, and the poet Quitnana made it their business to keep her informed, daily, of the progress of events. And, besides these three, there was Admiral Mazarredo's account of the British army, on its march to Corunna. 'He draws a most disgraceful and lamentable picture of their retreat. They had not had any action of importance with the French, but had been fortunate in all the skirmishes. They lost in their retreat their baggage, their artillery and even a portion of their money. . . .'

Now, letters in plenty were reaching Lady Holland from her Galician friends, enlarging on the acts of desperate vandalism so sternly condemned by their General-in-Command, perpetrated by the British troops. 'Terror enfurcido de nuestros aliados' (Fear spreads of our allies). And, 'in the gentlest terms' Romana added his name to the list of Sir John Moore's detractors. '. . . (He) ascribes the ruin and dispersion of his army to Sir

John Moore having deceived him; he promised to defend the pass of Villafranca, and Romana . . . made his movements with that object, but in this he was disappointed, and lost on ye 30th (at Mansilla) 2 battalions.' (As we know, Romana's attempt at self-justification was unfair and untrue.)

Saavedra (former Minister to King Charles IV) told Lady Holland that, at Salamanca, Sir John Moore had been visited by 'Escalante and another officer of high rank (Augustin Bueno) . . . sent to him from the Junta in order to urge him to advance. . . . He was cold, repulsive, scarcely civil to them, and not in the least disposed towards the cause he was employed in serving.' Events fully justified Sir John's doubts that these old men could substantiate their statements. On 9th February, Lady Holland received confirmation of Moore's death, at Corunna. 'Moore has closed the mouths of his accusers and sought the only exculpation left to him.' Yet, shortly afterwards, Marshal Soult and Romana himself were to put up a monument to his heroic stand.

On 26th February, General Sir John Cradock wrote a letter to the Under-Secretary at the War Office, Edward Cooke:

> . . . I saw a letter to-day from those shocking people Ld. and Lady Holland (I always put them together) at Seville. His Lordship says the French never had so large a force in Spain as was represented in England and, what is worse, they (the French) made our army believe it. Was not his Lordship content with the loss we sustained? (In the retreat to Corunna). I believe he would give the lives of ten English to save one Spaniard. . . .

As a serving soldier, like Lord Paget, proud of the British army and fully alive to the hardships it had had to endure in an alien, unco-operative country, his condemnation seemed justified. And we suspect that already he had put his feelings into militant language in his 'mysterious message' delivered by Lt. Ellis to Lord Holland, at Arranjolos.

Now, Lord Holland was where he wanted to be, patient in hearing his 'horrid protégés' declaim their parts, encouraging, prompting. And, beside him, his wife became their mouthpiece, committing their lines to memory and to her journal and sending back verbatim reports, in her letters home.

Despite this, the Hollands were uneasily conscious of the vacillation and lack of trust the Spaniards displayed towards each other, and disturbed by the lightning changes of mind evinced by the Central Junta. On 12th January, their friend, the Duque de Infantado, was disastrously defeated by the French, at Ucles, and immediately relieved of his command which was conferred on Urbino, Conde de Cartaojal; just over a month later (on 18th February) Cartaojal lost the Battle of Ciudad Real and, in turn, had to relinquish his command to General Cuesta. On 28th March, Cuesta lost the Battle of Medellin and, thereafter, remained on bad terms with the Central Junta. Towards the end of March, Lady Holland reports that General Blake (degraded in October 1808 and superseded, in the open field, by the Marques de la Romana) was restored to favour, as Captain General of Aragon and Valencia; while Romana himself was now very criticised, having refused to go to the help of the Portuguese general, Silveira.

Lady Holland kept her sister-in-law informed of up-to-date Spanish manœuvres, on 24th March, describing, blow by blow, the promising first stages of the battle for Medellin. But, on the same day, Lord Holland writes her, less confident of victory.

Dear little sister—It is probable that this is the last letter you will receive from me dated Seville as I do not think it impossible that you may not receive this as Cuesta by retreating to the left . . . to form a junction with Albuquerque has left the Badajoz road much exposed. . . . We shall leave this Monday or Tuesday.

By 5th April, Lord Paget's injunction to 'Open yr. eyes, my Lord' appeared to have had its effect.

. . . if a series of defeats not less than in pitched battles, a weak and slow tho' well intentioned government, intriguing ignorant and quarrelsome generals and disunited jealous and suspicious provinces can ruin Spain it is inevitably conquered by France . . .

Then Lord Holland brightens.

. . . on the other hand those said French do everything to save it not only by unaccountable folly both political and military. In short their conduct, the reports of the Austrian War, and the undiminished hatred of Frenchmen joined to the natural advantages of the Country and the approaching heats render persons on the spot and among them myself less despondent than any reasonable man at a distance from a consideration of the late events can possibly be . . . their confidence is catching. I am if you please *Spaniolated* which you tell me is Sir Philip Sidney's translation of the word Espanolada . . .

The impresario still felt that his protégés were capable of playing big parts.

As usual, the Hollands' departure was delayed by the last-minute indisposition of her Ladyship, who was pregnant again. By 7th April, she had recovered and went to say goodbye to Jovellanos, confined to his house for some weeks with an abscess on his thigh. (This account, too, he had fed to her daily, pandering to her clinical interest in it.) He seemed 'v. much concerned' that the Hollands were leaving Seville and promised to keep them regularly posted with news. Lady Holland was loath to leave Seville where she had been at the centre of events in Spain for over two months. Revealingly, she inscribes in her journal: 'It reminded me of the going out of the late Ministry, as to me the chief pleasure of their being in office was that I knew sooner and better what was going on.'

The Hollands' sojourn in Cadiz was short-lived. Arriving there on 11th April, on 13th, Lady Holland complains: 'This place so insufferable that as we cannot go by Gibraltar we have wisely determined upon returning to Seville for 10 days.' Admiral Purvis 'promised assistance about frigates, etc.' and, on 15th April, the Hollands 'set off with great satisfaction' back to Seville.

From Puerto Santa Maria, on their return journey to Seville, Lady Holland voices the Spaniards' growing discontent with Frere. 'Complaints against Frere universal; Spaniards full as much as English. They want an Ambassador and a man of consideration and rank. Mr Cranstoun said the complaints were so strong that application had already been made for his recall.'

*

On 22nd April, a British force of 26,000 men landed at Lisbon under Sir Arthur Wellesley. He had convinced the Cabinet with his contention that the Portuguese frontier could and should be defended against the French. He was successful in pushing Soult's army back through north Portugal, until he abandoned pursuit on 18th May, owing to fears of Marshal Victor.

Lady Holland continues to stress the now inevitably adverse reaction of the Central Junta to Hookham Frere.

The Govt. are somewhat displeased and a little disconcerted at Frere's behaviour in urging fresh plans of military operations, considering that Miguel Alava (later to act as intermediary between Wellesley and Cuesta) has only just been dispatched with full instructions from hence and from Cuesta to Lisbon, to concert with Genl. Wellesley for a combined plan of campaign. This conduct of his, and some expressions which he dropped inadvertently, give reason to apprehend that Wellesley's orders from home are to consider the defence of Lisbon as the chief object of his expedition.

Hookham Frere thought otherwise.

Frere, without waiting to hear the result of Alava's communication with Wellesley, is pressing a project in which the D(uque) of Albuquerque shall have an independent command in the Mancha.

But, at long last, the Central Junta had learnt its lesson. '. . . the Junta very judiciously reject all such plans until they hear what are to be the movements of the English army.'

On 3rd May, Lady Holland observes:

Gen. Wellesley is marching on towards Oporto, and carries every soldier, Portuguese and English, he can gather. Alava writes in praise of his activity and frankness, but seems disappointed that no *positive* promise of assistance is made to support Cuesta.

Spanish antipathy to British generals cropped up again. Quoting Lady Holland: 'Gen. Cuesta . . . expresses great ill-humour against the English, whose armies, he says, are never exposed.' This because of a cautious letter he had had from Sir Arthur Wellesley belying 'the flattering expectations which had been raised by Don Miguel Alava's first report'.

On 10th May, Lord Holland received a letter from Admiral Purvis, informing him that the *Ocean* had arrived in Cadiz harbour under orders to proceed with despatches to England, and urging Lord Holland to join her forthwith. So, once again, the Hollands decided to leave Seville.

The next day, their journey to Cadiz was dramatically interrupted, first, by the attempted murder of their coachman by one of their musketeers and next, by a night of terror in an inn, in an area infested by bandits. In Puerta Santa Maria, they managed to secure a private house, where they were visited by Tom Sheridan (Richard Brinsley's son) and his wife. From them, the Hollands learned that Hookham Frere had been recalled and that Lord Wellesley (Sir Arthur's elder brother) had been appointed in his stead.

An unexpected visitor came to call, no less a person than Sir John Cradock, come to complain of his shabby treatment by the British Government. Lord Castlereagh had appointed Sir Arthur Wellesley over his head, to command the British army in Portugal, and had attempted to allay Sir John Cradock's indignation by appointing him Governor of Gibraltar. Despite its confidential nature, Sir John did not hesitate to show the Hollands Lord Castlereagh's despatch 'and private letter' which Lady Holland roundly condemns as

written in a most disgusting manner, full of the jargon of the House of Commons. . . . By way of consoling Cradock he tells him that the eyes of Europe will be diverted towards Gibraltar. . . . A thorough false, tricking letter. Cradock with feeling and spirit declines the inactive station of Gibraltar.

Sir John felt the withdrawal of his command as 'a cruel mortification', as he contended that when Lord Castlereagh's despatch arrived 'he was actually on his march towards Soult'.

On 18th May, the Hollands moved to Cadiz where, for another six weeks,

they watched the barometer of Spanish fortunes rise and fall. Romana's luck
was out but Blake's was in. 'Romana, foolish fellow, instead of collecting
and reinforcing his army with the troops he might draw from the Asturias,
was on the 12th of this month (May) at Oviedo, squabbling and disputing
with the Civil Government. . . . Blake has taken Alcaniz, and the whole
plan and conduct of affairs was judicious and brilliant.'

General Cuesta still faced Marshal Victor at Merida, which had not yet
been reoccupied by French troops. Impatient though he was to engage
the enemy, he assured Don Miguel Alava that he would keep his word to
Sir Arthur Wellesley, not to attack until Wellesley had dealt with Soult.
On 5th June, Jovellanos told Lady Holland that Cuesta had gone down
with tertian fever and that he had been too ill to see two English colonels,
sent by Sir Arthur Wellesley to his headquarters, to discuss plans for
concerted action. He expressed himself very dissatisfied with Wellesley's
dilatoriness. The same day, Lady Holland herself provides the answer.
'The English army was to leave Coimbra on 1st June, but from the badness
of the roads and the want of shoes it would not arrive till the 15th or 16th.'
The old history of unfounded Spanish mistrust of the British army was
repeating itself.

Two days later, Jovellanos sent Lady Holland an extract from the
Moniteur (dated 11th May) announcing Lord Holland's appointment as
Ambassador to Vienna. He gave no further news of General Cuesta's con-
dition but told her that General Equia had taken over command, pro tem.
By 14th June, Cuesta had recovered and was writing to say that Sir
Arthur Wellesley had assured him of his active co-operation.

From that moment, some form of censorship was imposed on the movements of the Allies as, although Lady Holland continued faithfully to report
local engagements, she was clearly unaware of the wider background to the
second phase of the Peninsular campaign.

History relates that Wellesley's proposal to Cuesta to march on Madrid
via the Tagus, was joyfully received by the Central Junta, which promised
to undertake transport and supplies. On 27th June, Wellesley marched to
join Cuesta, at Piasencia. There, he was shocked to find an army whose
complete lack of training, discipline, and equipment Sir John Moore had
come to look upon as inevitable. And to find in Cuesta a general who was
old, ill, incompetent and pig-headed. But it was too late to turn back and,
on 17th July, the two armies started to advance.

Marshal Victor fell back before the Allies until reinforced by Joseph
Bonaparte. Then, it was the allies' turn to fall back, the Spaniards turning
their retreat into a panic flight. On 27th July, with much difficulty, Sir

Arthur Wellesley managed to stem the panic tide and to take up a position at Talavera. In the ensuing battle the toll was heavy on each side. But, with the arrival of the Light Brigade to reinforce him, two days later, Sir Arthur was eager to advance again.

Fortunately for the Allies, General Cuesta refused. For, on 1st August, Marshal Soult bore down on the Tagus through the Baños Pass which, despite Wellesley's earlier entreaties, Cuesta had neglected to defend. In the nick of time, Wellesley abandoned his wounded and managed to cross the bridge of Arzobispa. Thereafter, in a retreat very reminiscent of Sir John Moore's, he led his starving troops back across the frontier, at Badajoz, into Portugal. He arrived back there with one firm resolve: never again to rely upon the Spaniards.

*

By 18th June, yet again the Hollands had had to change their plans, this time because the two English admirals, Berkeley and Purvis, had quarrelled and would not allow their respective ships to leave their stations. As a result, the Hollands' plan to sail from Cadiz had to be abandoned and the prospect opened up again of proceeding by land to Lisbon, via Seville. By 24th June, they were back in the Marquesa de Ariza's palace, in Seville, en route for Portugal.

Back in the centre of things, Lady Holland found that Blake was in disgrace, having lost his army at Belchite, and her sympathy towards him was powerfully aroused. General the Duque de Albuquerque, 'in a pet', had thrown up his command which, as Lady Holland rightly observes, 'considering that he is in face of the enemy, is scandalous'. Further, she declares him as 'discontented with Cuesta and angry with the Junta for not giving him a separate supreme command'. In this ambition he was still aided and abetted by Hookham Frere 'who never ceases to urge the Junta to make him C.-in-Chief'. It was not surprising that Jovellanos continued to be 'displeased' with Frere. The epic of Spanish resistance, so romantically conceived by Lord Holland, in 1808, was, through lack of qualified actors and expert promoting, degenerating to the level of village theatricals.

The road between Seville and Badajoz was now open and, on 30th June, the Hollands arrived at Fuente de Cantos. They stayed with the Conde de Casa Chaves, a member of the Junta of Badajoz. Their host owned a big flock of merino sheep, subsequently introduced by Lord Holland into England. At Fuente de Cantos, Lord Holland received a letter from his future hosts at Badajoz, asking for precise information as to his time of arrival 'in order to receive him in a manner suitable to his rank'. (Lady Holland professed to find this 'terribly disagreeable, and entails great ennui for me'.)

On 31st July, at Santa Marta, a guard of honour on horseback, sent from the Junta at Badajoz, advanced to meet the Hollands while, nearer that city, two members of the Junta, 'in a coach and six' attended by a troop of Dragoons, were awaiting them. These gentlemen descended to deliver a set speech to Lord Holland and to invite him and his lady to transfer to their coach. Lady Holland declined the honour but Lord Holland had to endure it. Crowds greeted the Hollands' arrival in Badajoz and cheers accompanied their entrance into the house of 'the late Conde Torre Fresno' which had been prepared for them. An evening reception had been laid on, attended by 'all classes and descriptions of persons', including the President of the Badajoz Junta; then, fireworks and a concert. The day following, Lady Holland escaped a further round of gaiety on the plea of a bad cold but Lord Holland had to attend a dinner of thirty, dominated by noisy patriotic toasts, more 'fireworks, drums, etc.'

On the 5th July, terrified of one of the final honours reserved for her, a salvo of cannon, despite her five-months' pregnancy, Lady Holland left Badajoz at full gallop, leaving Lord Holland to travel by coach with the two deputies delegated to accompany him to the frontier. The instigator of all this pomp and circumstance had been Garay, Secretary to the Central Junta.

Once more in Portugal, at Evora, the Archbishop lodged the Hollands in his palace, where he regaled them with stories of looting by Junot's troops. At Setubal, Captain Smith told them that the reason for Sir Arthur Wellesley's slow start had been his distrust of the Portuguese which had caused him to concentrate a large camp at Lisbon, before he started his advance.

On 13th July, Charles Villiers' carriage awaited the Hollands, at Betem, to escort them back to his house in Lisbon. Three days later, they embarked on board the *Lively*, commanded by Captain McKinley, and had a pleasant passage home.

On 31st July, Lord Wellesley arrived in Cadiz harbour to replace the discredited Hookham Frere. With the tenacity he had displayed in 1804 at the end of his brother's first tenure of office in Spain, Bartholomew Frere remained on to serve as secretary to the newly appointed British Ambassador.

The Hollands reached Portsmouth on 10th August 1809, 'in a most boisterous gale and high sea'.

On landing back in their own country, no coach loads of ladies or civic dignitaries attended by cavalry were there to greet them, such as had cheered their arrival in, and departure from, Spain. To a Tory government, the Hollands had only a pronounced nuisance value, augmented by their one-sided criticism of the British army on its retreat to Corunna, under the generalship of Sir John Moore.

CHAPTER SEVENTEEN

Picking up the Threads

LADY AFFLECK (widowed again since July 1808), Henry Edward and Mary Fox greeted the Hollands at Holland House, also 'the Petty's and Beauclerks'. Lord Henry Petty had married Lady Louisa Fox-Strangways, daughter of second Earl of Ilchester, in 1807, so now double ties of consanguinity united them with the Hollands; Mimi Ogilvie, daughter of Emily, formerly Duchess of Leinster, had been married to Charles Beauclerk since 1799, an equally happy marriage sponsored by Holland House. In addition to these members of their family, Lady Holland notes that 'many of our friends came from the country to see us . . .' Yet a short time after her return, Lady Bessborough declares to Lord Granville Leveson-Gower that she has received a communication from Lady Holland, 'drawn up like a certificate with two witnesses' which reads: 'This is to certify that E. V. Holland is now alive and inhabiting H. H. in the Parish of Kensington, and has done so for some time past, tho' wholly neglected by her friends.'

Thanks to the devotion displayed by Lady Affleck, Caroline Fox and Elizabeth Vernon, the two younger Fox children (Henry Edward, now seven, and Mary, aged three) were happy and well, though Henry still had to have treatment for his leg and continued to walk with a limp.

Lord Upper Ossory received back the Hollands with his usual affection. 'Welcome, thrice welcome my nephew and niece, welcome Charles and John (Russell) by this time I hope you are in your old mansion and all recovering the fatigues of so long a passage.'

One happy result of the Spanish expedition was the lasting affection it inspired in the heart of young John Russell, particularly for Lady Holland who, thereafter, treated him like her son.

On 7th November, Lady Holland gave birth to her second daughter, Georgiana Anne, and Lord John wrote to congratulate her. 'I wish you joy of your new daughter—of course she is remarkably like you and Lord

Holland, and I suppose she is pretty sensible and good-humoured. I hope
you like her.'

On 14th November, Lord Lansdowne (erstwhile Lord Wycombe) died
of dropsy and his half-brother, Lord Henry Petty, succeeded him. To the
end, he resisted any attempt at reconciliation from his heir, and writing to
Lady Holland, Lord Henry ruefully declares: 'I am glad you have written
to Lady Lansdowne but I am sorry to say she must be indeed changed if
anything amiable or even reasonable can be expected from her, in what
relates to me or the family affairs.'

The wasted talents of this highly intelligent misanthrope called forth
Caroline Fox's comment: 'Alas! alas! poor human nature! Many people
might think it hypocrisy, when I said that I felt more sorrow than indignation in considering what he was and what he might have been.'

*

The Hollands returned to find a divided and unhappy Cabinet under
the ailing Duke of Portland's leadership, in which Canning and Lord
Castlereagh were at loggerheads, with Canning working actively for his
colleague's downfall. Yet, as a Cabinet Minister, Canning had endorsed
the return of Sir Arthur Wellesley to the Iberian Peninsula, and Castlereagh's ill-fated project of the Walcheren expedition. But after its failure
he ranged himself with its critics. Discovering his perfidy, Castlereagh
challenged him to a duel.

Lady Holland records the famous duel.

'Mr Canning and Lord Castlereagh fought on 21st September. Lord
Wellesley has accepted his recall.' For, in engineering his fellow-Minister's
dismissal, Canning accomplished his own as, after only two months as
Ambassador to Spain, Lord Wellesley was recalled to succeed Canning at
the Foreign Office.

Through ill-health, a few weeks before the duel, the Duke of Portland
had resigned the Premiership and, two months later, he died. Not without
misgiving, Spencer Perceval undertook to form a Cabinet, retaining the
Chancellorship of the Exchequer in his own hands. Fully aware that
Canning had his eyes fixed on the Premiership, Perceval was quietly
determined to prevent this but, at the same time, he was anxious to
broaden the administration and made rather maladroit overtures to the
leaders of the Opposition, Lords Grey and Grenville. To a man, the
Whigs refused to play with him. In consequence, Perceval re-balanced his
own party: Lord Wellesley succeeded Canning, as Foreign Secretary; and
Lord Liverpool replaced Lord Castlereagh at the War Office.

As usual, the Whigs were caught in disarray. In the Lords, Lord Grey could not be lured from his home in Northumberland to deal with any business, except by letter; and by the elevation of Lord Henry Petty to the peerage, the party's mainstay in the Commons had gone.

Picking up the threads again, whether consciously or unconsciously, Lord Holland used practically the selfsame argument, to Lord Grey, that Brougham had used to him before his departure for Spain. He warned Grey that, unless definite leadership in the Whig party was re-established it might well split into two, one side even deciding to join Canning in forming a third party for, at that moment, Canning was threatening to oppose his former colleagues. The Prince of Wales was consulted but remained non-committal and Sheridan made suspicious visits to Holland House. Finally, Lord Grey induced Lord Holland to encourage Samuel Whitbread to assert himself more forcefully in the Commons, and Lord Holland himself resumed his attendance in the Lords.

In December 1809, the Whig Corporation of Nottingham accorded Lord Holland 'the honour of choosing him their Recorder', a post left vacant by the death of the Duke of Portland, and which he accepted. He expressed his pleasure at their selection to his sister: '. . . for never was a body of men more attached to freedom or devoted to my uncle . . .' Lady Holland 'did not much relish the notion of a trip to share his civic honours' and did not accompany him to Nottingham. But, on New Year's Day 1810, Caroline Fox expresses her 'entire and v. flattering approbation' of Lord Holland's inaugural speech as Recorder.

*

Before the end of the year 1809, two weddings of note took place in the Hollands' circle of friends. On 19th October, the Duke of Devonshire married Lady Elizabeth Foster and, on 24th December, Lord Granville Leveson-Gower married the Duke's daughter, Lady Harriet Cavendish.

Lady Holland records that the new Duchess visited Holland House, on 23rd November, and that words of congratulation stuck in her throat. ('I could not utter a congratulation upon the occasion.') But, when, two years later, the Duke died suddenly without providing for his second wife in his will, Lady Holland (always apprehensive of her own future) professed quick sympathy with his widow.

The wedding of Harriet Cavendish meant heartbreak for her aunt, Lady Bessborough, who had loved Lord Granville for sixteen years, from the time in 1793 when she and Lady Holland (then Webster) had flirted so lightly with their troupe of young men, in Naples. But she accepted it with

Henry Richard Fox, 3rd Lord Holland, painted
at Florence in 1795 by Louis Gauffier

Holland House, south side, circa 1800

The Portuguese Garden,
Holland House, showing
Canova's bust of
Napoleon I

unaltered affection and dignity. As his Egeria Lord Granville spared her nothing, giving her details of his interview with the Duke ('I told him about my former follies, of which he was not ignorant, but which I did not *intend* to persevere in . . .') and even writing to her, three days after his marriage, extolling the virtues of his bride. '. . . She is indeed a perfect angel.'

With her usual discretion, Elizabeth Holland does not mention Harriet's wedding. Later, an affectionate relationship was established between herself, Harriet Leveson-Gower and Harriet's sister, Lady Morpeth, but, at this moment, her silent sympathy is undoubtedly focussed on Lady Bessborough, who had proved herself such a steadfast friend to Elizabeth Webster, in her own hour of need.

*

With his reputation for gallantry in battle personally vouched for by his general, Lord Paget, Sir Godfrey Webster returned home to display it in a different field. To Lady Holland's dismay he started up a lively flirtation with Lady Bessborough's daughter, Lady Caroline Lamb.

From childhood, Caroline had had the run of Holland House, wherein she had established herself in the dual character of humming-cum-mocking bird, flitting brilliantly from subject to subject, to amuse her hostess. She loved audacious impersonations. 'I have been much amused having put on a boy's shoe buckles a red Emery (?) wig a Boarding School frock so that I looked like a boy dressed up for a girl and in that character I told everyone that I personated Lady Caroline Lamb—had died my hair red and I jumped like a Harliquin' (*sic*). Then she 'slipped behind a curtain' . . . and emerged as the Rev. Sydney Smith!

Often, Caroline had given Lady Holland instances of her affection and admiration. On one occasion she had begged her to accompany her to 'Argyll St', a fashionable place of entertainment run by Henry Greville wherein dances, 'burlettas' and dramatic performances took place, and had declared: 'You shall be like the Persian Ambassador and I will accompany you in whatever shape you please.' Sometimes, she just wrote her up-to-date items of gossip. Her brother-in-law, Frederick Lamb, had been appointed a member of Lord Wellesley's staff, at Seville. 'He is there with Lord Wellesley, and seems quite dazzled by his splendour and magnificence.' She reacted badly to the Duke of Devonshire's marriage to Lady Elizabeth Foster. 'I hope you think Mama has behaved as she always does with the greatest kindness and strength of mind in this odious tricking business at Chiswick. That pattern of art (Elizabeth Foster) has written me a note to inform me of an event which ought forever to prevent the request

G

she makes of my continuing to call her by the endearing title of "Lady Liz"!'

After her delicate son was born, sometimes Caroline left him at Holland House. '. . . thank you for your care of my boy but cannot live without him, if he does not thrive here (in London) I will take him with me to Brocket Hall. How wicked of them (his nurses?) to make him walk when my last orders were that he never should. I wish I was coming to Hd House instead of Wimbledon where I am this moment going . . .'

None of Caroline's letters is dated so it is impossible to establish the beginning of her romance with Sir Godfrey Webster. But, to quote Lord Ilchester: 'Sir Godfrey's regiment appears to have been brought home in 1809 and, shortly after his return, an introduction to Caroline Lamb proved the precursor to a violent flirtation between them.'

During the early autumn of 1809 or 1810, William Lamb elected to 'go and shoot in the east' and encouraged his wife to go to Brighton 'to get a little sea air and Bathing'. From thence, she writes Lady Holland a very revealing letter, casually mentioning that she has just had 'a letter from one of your sons . . . having so much correspondence with the Branches, I cannot give up the head of the family so that if I have not by some negligence or ignorance offended beyond hope of pardon let me hear from you soon'. She proceeds to give an account of her amusements at Brighton and makes no secret of 'living a very gay irregular life—which with Bathing, riding on the Downs, walking and talking, requires all the health and spirits I possess to bear with . . . Tonight is my benefit at the Ship Tavern. I am pasted up on all the walls and have got attendants to the number of 50 to patronize (*sic*) me including officers and all—this place delights me. I make acquaintance with everyone love and like everyone without taste or discrimination & am in such spirits I can scarcely keep upon the ground—this has only been the case however for one week because I have not time to think, for I have broke through your good rule and shall have been away from my Man the only Man in the world I can call so for near a month—it was his fault not mine and I write to him continually.' Caroline professes her love for her husband. 'He is all perfection and with all my faults he will never get a woman to love and admire him as I do.' But she admits: 'My heart . . . is capacious and there is a superabundance of affection, besides which I am easily flattered never resist professions & sentiments come they from the mouth of Man Woman or Child . . .' Yet, despite this butterfly missive, Caroline professes to be 'at heart very judicious and virtuous' and signs herself 'Yr most sincere, Caroline Lamb'.

Her next letter is in much the same vein, but more domestic. She tells Lady Holland that she has got 'your little girl's bonnets'. And, with unexpected primness, comments: 'So the Chevalier d'Eon is a Man. How extraordinary and how improper.' She ends up: 'Dead or alive I shall be at H'd Hse (in a) very few days & hope you will drive and see me. Your affectionate spectre shaddow (*sic*) & dame d'Honneur, Caroline' (a small lamb caricatured after her Christian name).

The trend of her letters soon changed. Lady Holland did not encourage Caroline's intrigue with her eldest son and her forthright demand that it should cease called forth a letter of pathological violence from Caroline. '. . . I do not know whether Sir Godfrey Webster may think proper to send the letter I desired him to give you, but in case his Mother's prudence steals into his mind, I shall write you another and send it you myself. In the 1st place I beg leave to remark that I told you positively last night that I could not come and therefore your extreme anxiety to prevent me might have been wholly set aside. . . . I will never set foot in any one's house who instead of being happy to receive me thinks it proper to make conditions—you may easily make your choice and I call the God of Heaven to witness I will to my death abide by it—but remember Lady Holland I do not wish to be disrespectful in my manner of speaking to you —however I may think you have behaved towards me as my Mother's friend I shall never offer you any childish or public incivility—but neither by writing or by conversation or by any other means will I from this hour hold the smallest communication with you—I am just and whatever my faults, when I see a person actuated, though against me, by a spirit of rectitude of Religion of *strict* undeviating principles, I bow to an authority which . . . I admire—but when I perceive mere worldly prudence conquers every feeling of affection kindness and humanity, I have done and I would as soon waste my affections on a stone as on such a character . . .' Her vehemence increases. 'No human power shall ever dissolve the friendship or allow the sentiments I feel for him some call your son. But you do well to renounce a Mother's name and to leave him to the false friends and bad company your neglect of him has early brought him to . . . it might be deemed no greater impertinence in me to remind you of the Duties of a Mother than in you to taunt me with those of a wife . . .' She becomes defiant. 'As to the gnats and mites that dare to peck at me let them look to themselves. I will turn upon them before long with the vengeance which one bated and pursued at length is taught to feel and level them to the dust from which they spring. What are these things that dare to speak of me. At best only my equals and (from) what I can find many of them inferior to

me in the satiric powers they would stab me with. Grant me but health
and life and if I chuse it you shall see them flatter and follow me and lick
the dust I tread on. Lady Holland if this is the case I shall be courted by
you—that which is loved becomes lovely in your eyes . . . that I did love
you once I showed you, and to this I attribute the change in your manner
to me. Whatever the cause, from this hour we part and wishing you all
happiness to yourself and your whole family, I remain more sincerely than
you deserve—Yours, Caroline Lamb.'

And, as though this is not enough, a postscript of vituperation runs on
for another page.

Yet, the next day, Caroline writes in breathless contrition from Devonshire House, on unexplained black-edged paper: 'My dearest Lady
Holland, I entreat you to forgive the very very improper letter I wrote last
night that I am miserable for it you may believe by my now writing this
that I think you justified in not wishing me to meet Sir Godfrey there I
acknowledge also, and that by my foolish resentment and anger I only
added to the rest of my very blameable conduct I likewise own—do therefore as you will I will not let another hour pass without asking forgiveness for my offence and I think you most fully justified in refusing me.
I go tomorrow to Brocket (her father-in-law, Lord Melbourne's country
house) and if either of us should die I shall on my death bed be miserable
for the letter I wrote last night . . . Were you to forgive me happen what
would I would gallop over to see you at eleven to-morrow morning before
we set out. Yours however you may treat me, most sincerely, Most
affectionately, Caroline Lamb.'

In quick succession, half a dozen more penitent letters follow, and, in
her own time, Caroline is true to her word. She apologises also for once
using Sir Godfrey's brother, Henry, as intermediary. Her flirtation with
Sir Godfrey comes to an end while she protests that 'no young man ever
yet behaved so well to any woman as your son has to me. . . .'—she feels
sure Sir Godfrey is honourable enough to burn her letters and she declares that 'how wrong I have been William never will know. I do not
think were I to tell him he would believe it . . .' But William begins to
suspect the truth and, in another letter to Lady Holland, Caroline admits
that she has deeply hurt her husband by refusing to return home with him
from a party. 'William Lamb for the first time last night witnessed what
he never before believed—it was our wedding Day (3rd June, 1805) and
as he left me waltzing at 2 o'clock, he reminded me of it, and of the vows
and protestations I had then made and are they all changed in a few years—
no believe me—I remained however till ½ past 5 and as I drove home, my

heart reproached me and tho' tired to death I could not sleep. If my Friends feel pain let them ask themselves whether *de gaieté de coeur* I give them a momentary anxiety which must fall short of what I inflict on myself—I regret the infatuation that seems to have overcome all my principles and right feelings, but if a life of very constant attention and thorough amendment can make up for the past, believe me it shall immediately take place—my husband is angry with me, I do not wonder . . .'

And that Caroline is anxious to make her peace with Lady Holland is shown by the following neurotically effusive letter. (Lord Ilchester dates it 1811.)

. . . The vestal to her Madonna—can I live without you? *Le soleil qui brille pour tout autre est a jamais obscurer pour moi*—dear and beautiful Lady, are you not a little grieved at my absence—that is what comes of mésalliances. I am like a flame of Fire or a lamp of oil & those I attach myself to—ice. Were I a poet I should address you like Cowley with all those pretty metaphors such subjects give rise to, but why freeze a little *Dame d'honneur* for a fault if it be a fault of which the best natures only are capable—I am like a vestal who thought of other concerns than the pure Flame she hoped Heaven would keep burning—do not condemn me to being burned alive. Wait a little and I shall return to dust without any unusual assistance.

Then, with hardly a breath, Caroline proceeds:

. . . tell Ld Holland the Duke of Gloucester with whom we dined yesterday praised him warmly.

And she ends with an hilarious account of her waltzing with His Highness while the band plays 'O Mein Liebe Augustein' (*sic*).

. . . Off we went—an extra step of His Highness put me out. Vainly I remonstrated round and round we turned & I never thought waltzing so criminal in my life— tho' I have always been of opinion and still am that those who like it, like it because it is doubtful . . .

The humming-cum-mocking bird is determined to get back into favour. Yet Lady Holland's accusation, that Caroline likes 'to excite interest and anxiety' in those she loves, is to prove bitterly true.

*

During the Christmas holidays of 1809, while staying with his great-uncle, Lord Upper Ossory, Charles Richard sustained a bad fall out hunting. He had gone out with Lord Ossory's daughter, Lady Anne Fitzpatrick, against the expressed wishes of his mother. Writing to Caroline Fox to excuse her own conduct, Lady Anne describes how, after the accident, Charles was lying in bed, half-asleep, being read to by the

nurse when 'in bounced my Lady and Dr Allen this was certainly enough
to give him a fever and a restless night but he was so well that he slept
perfectly . . .' Even so, Lady Holland's anxiety was understandable.
Charles's pony had lashed out and badly cut the inside of his leg as she
describes 'between ham and knee'. From Woburn, the next day, she visited
him again and saw the wound 'a most dreadful gash, as bad as anything
can be which has not touched a vital part, and may not perhaps do him a
permanent injury'. Running no more risks with such negligent relations, as
soon as possible she removed Charles to Woburn.

Caroline Fox attempts to tell Lady Holland that she is inclined to take
an over-gloomy view of things which charge Lord Holland refutes with
vigour. 'I see by your letter to Lady Holland that you think it is her
disposition to see things *en noir* . . . but the fact is . . . he (Charles) might
have been lamed for life but both Anne and my uncle have an odd way of
making light of such things . . . my woman . . . behaved I assure you much
better on the occasion than many more accustomed to control their feelings
would have done . . .' The seriousness of the wound was confirmed by the
fact that it was not declared 'closed' until 30th January and, inevitably, the
occasion of it strained relations between Lord Ossory, his daughter and
the Hollands.

Charles recovered and, during the summer of 1810, joined the Navy.
He was gazetted to the *Lively*, the ship in which he and his family had
returned to England from Spain, and, under the command of Captain
McKinley, sailed for the Mediterranean. Four months later, the *Lively*
was wrecked on the rocks near Malta, and Charles and the rest of his
companions transferred to another ship. Recording this disturbing event,
Lady Holland comments: 'Captain Stewart of the *Seahorse*, now stationed
at Palermo, to whom Charles was recommended by General Fox and Lord
Keith . . . immediately upon hearing she (the *Lively*) was wrecked sent
express to Malta to order him a supply of money and proper equipment,
and also to secure a speedy passage from thence to him. All this was done
in a most obliging and gentlemanlike manner, so as to leave a strong desire
upon my mind of returning the civility whenever any opportunity should
occur.' But this did not perpetuate in Charles a desire to make the Navy
his career. At the end of three years he badgered his father to let him try
something else, to which entreaty Lord Holland reluctantly gave way.

*

Again, in 1810, extensive repairs to Holland House had to be carried
out. Once more, the Library wall had to be strengthened and rooms were

added to the ground floor, at its north-west corner, for Henry Edward's use. The renovations were not completed until October and, for a month, Lord Holland's uncle, General Fox (now General-in-Command at Portsmouth), lent him and his family Government House. On 30th October the Hollands returned to Kensington.

They found Parliament involved in an unexpected crisis due to a recurrence of the King's illness. When his favourite daughter Amelia died, on 2nd November, he sustained a shock from which he never recovered. Clearly, a Regency was imperative and the hopes of the Opposition ran high. Writing to Lord Granville Leveson-Gower, Lady Bessborough tells him she has just met the Hollands. 'She is in high good humour but *très affairée*, and seems already to have all the cares of office on her. Two such large packets arrived to both of them during the time I saw them, that it only wanted a red box to make me think our old Administration in again.' The caricaturists got busy. In a cartoon entitled *Sketch for a Prime Minister* in the *Satirist*, Lord Holland, wearing skirts, and Lady Holland, wearing breeches, were depicted storming Prime Minister Perceval's house, while Napoleon, bearing a peace-offering money-bag, took cover under her ladyship's cloak.

Alone among his colleagues, Lord Holland saw that one man might stand in the Whigs' way to success: Richard Brinsley Sheridan. To quote Lord Holland: 'The Prince of Wales cautiously or scrupulously abstained from all political concert with the Opposition, till official communications should be made to him from Ministers or from Parliament. He pushed that delicacy so far that he did not see Mr Sheridan, who being to the full as desirous of appearing, as of being, his adviser, was ludicrously anxious to cancel so mortifying a circumstance. I was at pains to inform both Lord Grey and Lord Grenville of this circumstance, but it made them more negligent of Mr Sheridan.'

The same month, the Regency Bill came before Parliament, while Grey was absent in Northumberland for his wife's confinement. In the Commons, Spencer Perceval debated it with ability, and gained a small majority for the restrictions he sought to impose on the Regent's powers. In the Lords, Lord Grenville supported the resolutions, and Lords Holland and Lansdowne were the chief spokesmen for the Opposition. The Prince of Wales resented the restrictions on the Regency proscribed in the Bill and, to quote Lord Holland: 'The Princes of the Blood Royal signed and printed a sort of remonstrance to the measure.'

Even so, on 6th January 1811, Lord Grenville was summoned in audience to the Prince of Wales at Carlton House, ostensibly to be asked his and Lord Grey's advice as to how to draft an answer to 'the address shortly to be presented to him by both Houses of Parliament'. And, four days later, the Prince gave an audience to Lord Grey, covering much the same ground. As a result, both he and Lord Grenville lost no time in drafting the answer to the two Houses for which the Prince had asked them. Unfortunately, Sheridan was present when it arrived and ridiculed it and those who had compiled it so effectively that the Prince asked him to draft another. The two lords withdrew their paper but, injudiciously if understandably, expostulated at the way 'unauthorised advisers' had been allowed to draw up another paper. Again, Sheridan derided them, and the harm was done.

There followed a three-hour session with Lord Holland, at which, marooned on his settee with gout, he was forced to play host to his Royal master in what Lady Holland herself called 'our ... dirty habitation in Pall Mall'. At this meeting, the newly appointed Regent protested that he 'looked forward with eagerness to the two Lords completing their arrangements. But after it he hedged and finally changed his mind. Fearful of involving himself in Whig plans for Catholic emancipation, and with his feelings played upon by his mother Queen Charlotte, who magnified her hopes of the King's return to health, he edged towards a better understanding with Spencer Percival and Lord Chancellor Eldon and decided to leave them where they were. As a result, when Lord Grey and Lord Grenville informed the Regent, on 21st January, that should he so wish and should the King's recovery still be considered improbable, they were ready to form a Ministry, they were coldly received. Soon they heard the news that the Regent had notified the existing Government that he wished it to remain in office.

There, it remained until 11th May 1812, when a madman, nursing a private grievance, waylaid and shot Prime Minister Perceval in the lobby of the House of Commons. And, even then, the Prince Regent continued to avert his eyes from his erstwhile friends, the Whigs, calling on Lord Wellesley (who unsuccessfully tried to form a National Government) and finally on Lord Liverpool to form a Ministry.

*

In October 1811, Lady Holland brought her journal to a close. It had served its purpose. Started as a weapon of defence, it ended up as a chronicle of success. In its first phase, it had shown her rebellious, wilful and selfish; in its second, it portrayed in her a new humility. True, as she came to accept a background of security, some of her domineering qualities returned. But they were received by her second husband with unalterable good humour and he was always there to temper them. For he was the master who coloured her every thought and deed. Anthony Morris Storer had implanted in her the seed of learning and Thomas Pelham had fed it, but Lord Holland was responsible for its final fruiting.

Already, the Dinner-Books had largely taken the place of Lady Holland's journal and therein, on 29th April 1811, Lady Holland had made a note: 'Mr Allen drew the lot of God's Gift in the College Church at Dulwich, of which he became warden of that community. He dined at Dulwich.' With God's Gift College (founded by Edward Alleyn in 1619) Mr Allen was associated until he died.

The Hollands kept open house for the rest of that year, entertaining, in varying proportions, several nights a week. (The entry 'no strangers' occurs about one night in seven.) Two or three large dinners, of sixteen or seventeen people, and smaller ones, of three or four, were the usual order, the guests assembling between six and six-thirty and dining in the Gilt Room. Matthew Marsh, Samuel Rogers, Henry Luttrell, Sydney Smith and Hookham Frere were among the most regular guests.

Triumphantly surviving his tactless first meeting with the Prince of Wales in her house, long since, Sydney Smith had established his affectionate, teasing relationship with Lady Holland. On 23rd May 1811, he comments on Lady Holland's invitation to him.

How very odd, dear Lady Holl to ask me to dine with you on Sunday, the 9th when I am coming to stay with you from the 5th to the 12th! It is like giving a gentleman an assignation for Wednesday when you are going to marry him on the Sunday preceding—an attempt to combine the stimulus of gallantry with the security of connubial relations. I do not propose to be guilty of the slightest infidelity to you while I am at H H except you dine in town; and then it will not be infidelity, but spirited recrimination.

Ever the sincere and affectionate friend of Lady Holland,

Sydney Smith.

Still, the Whig politicians, as typified by Lords Grey, Lauderdale, Lansdowne and Mr Tierney, dined regularly at Holland House, but convivially rather than conspiratorially. On such occasions, they held the table. In Parliament, they were hardly listened to.

G*

CHAPTER EIGHTEEN

Lord Byron

EARLY IN FEBRUARY 1812, Lord Holland was forwarded a letter from young Lord Byron about the Luddites.

Taking their name from one Ned Lud, a lunatic frame-maker of Nottingham, these rioting handicraftsmen sought to destroy the new machinery which threatened them with redundancy. A lot of local opinion backed them and Lord Byron, himself a local landowner, was opposed to Lord Liverpool's repressive Frame-Breaking Bill. Now, he sought Lord Holland's advice (as Recorder of Nottingham) as to how to proceed.

My dear Sir,

With my best acknowledgements to Lord Holland I have to offer my perfect concurrence in the propriety of your question previously to be put to Ministers. If their answer is in ye negative I shall with his Lordship's approbation, give notice of a motion for a committee of enquiry. I would also gladly avail myself of his most able advice, and any information or documents with which he might be pleased to entrust me, to bear me out in the statement of facts it may be necessary to submit to the House. From all that fell under my own observation during my Xmas visit to Newstead (his home), I feel convinced that if *conciliatory* measures are not very soon adopted, the most unhappy consequences may be apprehended. Nightly outrage and daily depredations are already at their height, and not only the masters of frames who are obnoxious on account of their occupation but persons in no degree connected with the malcontents or their oppressors, are liable to insult & pillage.

I am very much obliged to you for the trouble you have taken on my account & beg you to believe me ever yr. obliged & sincere friend,

Byron.

Lord Holland was delighted to provide material to help the discourse of such a philanthropical young man, for which Lord Byron thanked him again in another letter, dated 25th February. In this, he enlarges on the righteous grievances of the workers: '... a much injured body of men sacrificed to ye views of certain individuals who have enriched themselves by those practises which have deprived the frame workers of employment.

He tells Lord Holland that he is desirous of speaking against Lord

186

Liverpool's Bill but that he will 'be silent altogether, should you deem it more advisable'.

Lord Holland urges Lord Byron to express his own view in this 'your first speech in Parliament'. With which encouragement, Lord Byron makes his maiden speech in the House of Lords, on 27th February.

With his usual good humour, Lord Holland unreservedly helped his young friend despite the fact that, in 1809, Lord Byron had satirised the Hollands in his 'English Bards and Scotch Reviewers' written in the belief that Lord Holland had criticised his early poem *Hours of Idleness*, in the *Edinburgh Review*. (In fact, this had been done by Henry Brougham.)

Now, anxious to make amends, Lord Byron sends Lord Holland an advance copy of his new poem: *Childe Harold*, which Lord Holland gratefully acknowledges, on 6th March 1812.

> ... I promise myself great pleasure from Child (*sic*) Harold I am glad to see that it is in a regular stanza and that stanza Spenser's ...

Confined to his rented house in Pall Mall with gout, Lord Holland adds a postscript:

> If you are not better engaged I shall be very glad if you can dine with me on Sunday—you will meet (Samuel) Rogers.

On 8th March, not only Samuel Rogers but William Lamb, too, was at dinner. Caroline was not present, but very shortly afterwards, she started her tempestuous love affair with Lord Byron, whom she met at Holland House.

On 24th June 1812, Lady Holland gave birth to another daughter, which lived only a few hours. Lord Holland informed his sister, the same day: 'Lady Hd. now doing well ... she had a very bad time and the poor little Child hardly breathed after she came into the world ... (Ly Hd.) has behaved very well.'

Unaware of this bereavement, Lord Byron writes to Lord Holland, the next day:

> ... I must appear very ungrateful and have indeed been very negligent but till last night I was not apprised of Lady Holland's situation & shall call tomorrow to have the satisfaction I trust of hearing that she is well ...

But Lady Holland never really recovered from the birth of her tenth child and, although increasingly hypochondriacal, thereafter she was subject to genuine and frequent bouts of ill-health.

That autumn of 1812, Lord Holland sought to provide her with a change of scene by taking a house in St James's Square, away from her children.

But depression still pursued her. In September, Parliament was unexpectedly dissolved and, at the ensuing election, several prominent Whigs lost their seats, among them George Tierney, William Lamb, Henry Brougham and Sheridan. At this point, Lord Grey, already considering retirement from politics, asked Lord Holland to assume the leadership of the party. But Lord Holland refused, on the grounds of his increasing liability to gout and his diffidence in assuming such a forceful rôle. Sir Godfrey Webster was elected for the county of Sussex, 'without a contest'. But his mother and step-father were left in ignorance as to what line his politics would take.

In November, Lady Holland had a relapse and was still 'low' at Christmas. Obviously, she had overtaxed her strength as Caroline Fox (writing on 20th November) says 'the children have had gay doings at Holland House ... Mrs (Bobus) Smith's letters are full of nothing but the pleasant days she has passed there and of Ly Holland's kindness and attention to her and her young ones ...'

News had reached Lady Holland that her Jamaican estates had been devastated by a hurricane; then, her faithful Italian footman, Antonio, died (she was always devoted to her servants); and, finally, to the equal annoyance of Lord Holland as well as to herself, her chef Morel, was lured away by Lord Hertford.

Writing to her brother, on 27th December 1812, Caroline Fox treats the last piece of news rather unsympathetically.

> ... I had not heard of Morel's defection ... so little am I acquainted with your domestic concerns. Who has seduced Morel from his allegiance? He is not however the only French cook in the world, and I should think you might easily meet with his equal. I have heard better judges than I can pretend to be in such matters declare that his talents were on the decay or at least that his dinners were not so excellent as formerly.

Two days later, Lord Holland rises to rhetorical heights.

> ... who gave private advice to the Prince of Wales? The M. of Hertford. Who seduced him from his private friends? The M. of Hertford. Who defeated the prospect of a strong administration? The M. of Hertford—who debauched away my cook? The Marquis of Hertford—

and breaking into Latin:

> Omnia qua vidimus (quid autem mali non vidimus?) si recti rationabimur uni accepto referemus Antonio—

> Everything that we have seen (what of evil indeed is there that we have not seen? we shall credit, if we draw the account correctly to one man—Antony!

Still, despite her fluctuations of mood between gaiety and despondency, Lady Holland remained irresistibly attractive to her husband, as shown by the following poem, written in 1813:

> The morning dawned and by my side
> Spite of impending day
> In sleep, that night and care defied
> My sweet enchantress lay
> Closed were indeed those sparkling eyes
> That set my soul on fire
> But other charms in slumber rise
> To kindle fierce desire
>
> The grace of her reclining head
> That even heaving breast
> And limbs so carelessly outspread
> Ten thousand thoughts suggest.
>
> Yes, passion in my bosom strove
> Unruly at the sight
> And fain my rude and boisterous love
> Had wakened her to delight.
>
> No let the thought, I cried, be check't
> The sacrilege forbear
> Love shall those tender looks respect
> That heavenly slumber spare.
>
> I said then bending oer her charms
> With fondness I explore
> How soft how fair a spirit warms
> The being I adore
>
> For oh her lovely smiles express
> The image of her mind
> She looks, and sure she lives no less
> Calm innocent, and kind—

*

By the summer of 1812, Drury Lane Theatre (burnt down in February 1809 during Parliament's debate on Sir John Moore's campaign in Spain) had been re-built. A new management took it over and Sheridan and his family were bought out. A Joint Stock Company was formed, under the Chairmanship of Samuel Whitbread, and Lord Holland became a member of his Committee. Unwisely, the Committee decided to offer a prize for an inaugural address and Lord Holland was commissioned to ask Lord Byron to write one.

On 10th September, Lord Byron writes to tell Lady Melbourne that he has refused Lord Holland's request:

> . . . as all Grub St. seems engaged in the contest, I have no ambition to enter the lists, and have thrown my few ideas into the fire.

He confirms his action to Lord Holland, on 15th September, and adds:

> I think you have a chance of something much better for prologuing is not my forte & at all events either my pride or my modesty won't let me incur the hazard of having my rhymes buried in next months magazine under essays or the murder of Mr Perceval & 'cures for the bite of a mad dog' as poor Goldsmith complained on the fate of far superior performances . . .

Lord Holland replies that he is much concerned that Lord Byron has burnt his verses as he has not had 'any address so good as yours'. And, on 21st September, he returns to the attack more than ever regretting this hasty action 'after wading through the trash which it was allotted to me to peruse'. Now, he is authorised by the Committee to tell Lord Byron, confidentially, that none of the other one hundred competitors will do. He appeals to 'your friendship' to extract the Drury Lane Committee from a difficult situation. 'Pray let me entreat you in the name of Drury Lane and her Committee of Thalia and Melpomene to take pity on us.' He has no objection to a compliment to Mrs Siddons, or a slap at Young Roscius (the brilliant child-actor, now grown up and just castigated for his adult poor performances by Lord Byron, under his proper name of Mr Betty). And he would like a compliment paid to Sheridan, 'our Manager and so was Garrick . . . the first actor and the first Comick writer of the Country have managed Drury Lane . . .'

Lord Byron could not resist Lord Holland's tactful appeal and replies to his letter next day.

> In a day or two I will send you something which you will still have the liberty to reject if you dislike it . . . too happy if I can oblige *you* though I may offend 100 scribblers and the discerning public.
>
> Ever yrs,
>
> B.
>
> Best respects to Lady H.

Thereafter, he shows endless good humour while dozens of his intended addresses go back and forth for Lord Holland and his Committee to '*cut— add—reject—*or *destroy* . . .'. He only makes one stipulation, that his name 'shall not transpire till the day is decided'. And he begs the favour of 'a

good *deliverer*. I think Elliston should be the man or Rosse—not *Raymond*
I implore you by the love of Rythmus! . . .'

He adds a postscript: 'My best remembrances to Ly. H . . . tell Lady H.
I have had sad work to keep out the Phenix (*sic*). I mean the *fire* office of
that name—it had insured the theatre and why not the address!'

Between 22nd and 24th September, Lord Byron sends Lord Holland
five alternative stanzas for his approval, and in his last letter he declares:
'I am ashamed to include any more remembrances to Ly. H. in upon you:
but you are fortunately for me gifted with patience already too often tried.'

Lord Holland replies, on 25th September:

Your verses are better and better every time I read them & you & we may set
the poetasters at defiance—Whitbread . . . was delighted with them though he had
not such a horror of the 'Phoenix' as you and Ldy Holland . . . the verses on
Garrick and Sheridan are admirably executed & make me quite vain of having
hinted their names to you. Whitbread has some apprehensions of *future flame*—the
Ladies he says will call for their carriages . . .

He defers to Lord Byron's choice of a 'deliverer'.

Elliston or Miss Smith—which would *you* prefer—you have a clear right to chuse
your speaker . . .

On 26th September, Lord Holland writes again, criticising certain words
of Byron's and proffering others: 'Intellectual' is a heavy abstract Scotch
metaphysical word & as such most repugnant to the language of the Muses
—who have I suspect a very female dislike to most *feelosife* . . .' He does
not like 'genius—gifted' or 'many coloured' and suggests 'multicolor'.
He ends: 'Lady H begs me to say that remembrances are certainly *unnecessary*—but always flattering and agreeable. She begs most kind ones in
return.'

By some miracle of quick posting, Lord Byron replies the same day,
slightly nettled by Lord Holland's conscientious but persistent criticism.
He explains his reasons for the Garrick lines:

I always scrawl in this way . . . & latterly I can weave a nine line stanza faster
than a couplet, for which measure I have not the cunning. When I began 'Childe
Harold' I had never tried Spenser's measure, & now I cannot scribble in any other.
After all, my dear Lord, if you can get a decent address elsewhere, don't hesitate
to put this aside; why did you not trust your own Muse? I am very sure she would
have been triumphant, & saved the Committee their trouble . . .

But, pacified by a further 'very kind letter' from Lord Holland, Byron's
good humour returns, and, on 27th September, he continues:

... As to remarks I can only say I will allow & acquiesce in anything. With regard to the part which you wish to omit I believe the address will go off *quicker* without it though like the agility of the Hottentot at the expense of one testicle.

He puts the onus of choosing him to write the address firmly back on to the Drury Lane Committee:

As there will probably be an outcry amongst the rejected—I hope the Committee will testify (if it be needful) that I sent in nothing to the Congress whatever with or without my name ... All I have to do with it is with & through you ...

He chooses Elliston to declaim his verses (as it transpires, unfortunately).

Lord Holland replies asking Lord Byron to make 'a long fair copy' and the process of submission and selection continues as before. On Tuesday 29th September, Lord Holland starts off on a four-day visit to Bowood and begs Lord Byron to deliver the address (for Ellison to 'conn by rote') the following Monday. But he changes horses at Maidenhead and takes the opportunity to send the hapless poet eight more pages of 'fault' finding. Then, he suggests meeting Lord Byron at Lord Jersey's on the Saturday, and sends a postscript. 'Lady H. is delighted at your verses & at your good nature in letting them be spoken—she congratulates you on your happy escape from the Phoenix.'

Lord Byron continues with his Herculean efforts, still making desperate but unavailing attempts to keep certain lines. All this time he is writing from Cheltenham where he is taking the waters for stone. On 30th September, he writes Lord Holland:

I send you the most I can make of it for I am not so well as I was

and later that day he writes:

... I am just recovering from a smart attack of the stone. What a pleasing posthumous hope for a man to be able to have his monument carved out of his kidneys ...

On 2nd October, Lord Holland acknowledges the receipt of the shortened corrected copy and sends Lord Byron his congratulations. He has shown his address to Lord Lansdowne who proclaims himself 'an ardent admirer'. Lord Holland himself pronounces it 'far the finest address that has been spoken from the stage since the Monody'.

On 10th October 1812, Drury Lane Theatre re-opened and Lord Holland left his box especially to scribble a few encouraging lines to Lord Byron, still obstinately out of reach, at Cheltenham.

I write from the box to catch the post. It has succeeded admirably. Elliston repeated it well at least that part of it which he was *perfect* in. His only fault was not knowing it by heart and the cry for silence put him out. He substituted here and there some vile epithets—but it succeeded admirably and will more and more every night . . .

As Lord Byron had guessed, there was some sharp criticism of the 'partiality' of his selection, in the newspapers. And four days after the opening, the indignant son of one of the contestants (Dr Busby) as Lord Holland says 'jumped on the stage to read his papa's nonsense . . .' But Lord Holland assures Lord Byron that 'the Committee were not content but proud of the address you gave them and have not thought it proper to answer the nonsense that has appeared in the papers . . .' However, he has to admit that the choice of Elliston, as 'deliverer' of the address, has been a mistake. On 15th October, he writes:

. . . I fear by what I hear he has continued to murder rather than recite it . . .

While on 20th, he says forthrightly:

There is no fault to find with you but the choice of the man to deliver it who really murdered it worse than he did Polonius in the play.

Lord Byron is obviously upset by the criticism of Perry, editor of the *Morning Chronicle*. But Lord Holland comforts him.

Perry is a coxcomb on verses &, as he printed a song of Tierney's once like prose, is not to be considered as an oracle.

*

The Hollands' friendship with Lord Byron was now firmly enough established to ignore the mounting scandal associated with his name.

In November 1812, Caroline Lamb threatened Lord Byron with suicide and, on 5th July 1813, she appeared to stab herself with a knife at Lady Heathcote's ball. Although Lord Byron was at the party he professed himself ignorant of the affair till afterwards when, with masochistic fervour, Caroline poured out her heart to Lady Holland, imploring clemency.

Lady Holland, hear me—you can add to the agonising tortures I endure, you may serve me. I have never harmed you—it is cruel to trample upon one as wholly ruined as completely fallen as I am. I have no words to make use of and I will never see you, but I do implore you as you hope for mercy, show it—and do not speak of this horrid scene more than you can help and when you must speak of it for the sake of better than I am, make light of it—or deny it—for myself it is of no consequence I have long lost and justly lost the opinion of others, my dishonour is complete . . .

She abjectly praises William Lamb:

> William Lamb has ruined himself by excess of kindness for me.

And at this stage, she exonerates Byron:

> . . . it is asserted by all that my conduct was in consequence of Lord Byron's having *slighted* me—it is said that I sought to renew my wrong attachment with him and that because he would not I attempted to stab myself . . . I do assure you before God that this is utterly false . . . I am told that I wished to ruin him to revenge myself upon him—for what—for being first my lover and since then my preserver and friend—and if even now made my enemy by my present conduct can I wonder or can I blame him . . . now you have often said if I told you anything and I asked you not to repeat it you would not, I now beg of you not to say I have written to you because it is a thing not wished my writing at all—but you can act as you think fit—I am Lady Holland whatever you may be to me
>
> > Ever with respect and affection
> > Yours
> > Caroline Lamb
>
> I had rather you did not answer this letter you cannot write kindly on such a subject—my mind is agitated . . .

Intellectually, Holland, and indeed Lady Holland, and Byron were ideally suited to each other and Byron continued to value both their opinions of his work. In May 1813, Lady Holland gave him a miniature of the portrait painted of her by Louis Gauffier, in Florence, in 1795. She quotes some lines, inscribed on it by Countess d'Albany's lover, the poet Alfieri:

> The lines I enclose were written by Alfieri himself upon the reverse of my picture, they are not very good, and affect more humility than was sincere . . .

A fortnight after what Byron cynically called Caroline Lamb's 'cursed scarification', he was dining, with a party of men, at Holland House where, by the end of the year, he had become established as a family friend. So much so that, like a rich uncle, on 27th November, he took Henry Edward to see a performance of *Nourjahad* wrongly attributed, by the *Morning Post*, to Lord Byron's pen. 'Saturday, I went with Harry Fox to *Nourjahad*; and, I believe, convinced him, by incessant yawning, that it was not mine.'

During 1813, Byron consulted Lord Holland about the proofs of his new poem, *The Giaour* (which, subsequently, he dedicated to him), and *The Bride of Abydos*. 'I have had a most kind letter from Lord Holland on *The Bride of Abydos*, which he likes, and so does Lady Holland.' In this poem, Byron changed his mind, when writing the second canto, and contrived that in it the lovers should discover themselves to be first cousins and not brother and sister as implied in the first canto, declaring that the theme of incestuous love 'is not adapted for this age . . .'

On Sunday, 28th November, Lord Byron makes a note in his journal:

Sunday, I dined with Lord Holland in St James's Square. Large party—among
them Sir S(amuel) Romilly and Lady Ry—General Sir Somebody Bentham, a man
of science and talent . . . Horner—*the* Horner, an Edinburgh Reviewer, an excellent speaker in the 'Honourable House' . . . Lord John Russell, and others, 'good
men and true'. Holland's society is very good; you always see some one or other in
it worth knowing. Stuffed myself with sturgeon, and exceeded in champagne and
wine in general, but not to confusion of head. . . . Why does Lady Holland always
have that damned screen between the whole room and the fire? I, who bear cold
no better than an antelope . . . was absolutely petrified, and could not even shiver
(*sic*). All the rest, too, looked as if they were just unpacked, like salmon from an
ice-basket, and set down to table for that day only. When she retired, I watched
their looks as I dismissed the screen, and every cheek thawed, and every nose
reddened with the anticipated glow.

Although he deprecates 'so many *sets*' Lord Byron likes moving in London
society. He states:

At present I stand tolerably well with all . . . Holland's is the first—everything
distingué is welcome there, and certainly the *ton* of his society is the best.

On 5th December he is at Holland House again:

. . . milady in perfect good humour, and consequently *perfect*. No one more
agreeable, or perhaps so much so, when she will.

He is asked for the following Wednesday, to meet Madame de Staël.
Several times already, Lady Holland had entertained her, declaring her
'very clever but also very tiresome'. Lord Byron had praised her works
which had resulted in her sending him 'a very pretty billet' of thanks.
Now, he thinks he has been asked to dine at Holland House 'out of mischief
to see the first interview after the *note* . . .'

At that dinner, the Hollands pulled out all the stops to impress the
Frenchwoman: the Staffords, the Ossulstons, the Melbournes, Sir James
and Lady Mackintosh. Lord Byron comments:

The Staël was at the other end of the table, and less loquacious than heretofore
. . . She asked Lady Melbourne whether I had really any *bonhomie*. She might as
well have asked that question before she told C(aroline) L(amb) '*c'est un démon*'.
True enough, but rather premature, for *she* could not have found it out, and so—
she wants me to dine there next Sunday.

Living up to Madame de Staël's conception of him, in December,
inscribed in his own hand, in a copybook, Lord Byron sent Lord Holland
the manuscript of his 'wild, rambling, unfinished rhapsody': *The Devil's
Drive*. (This, he had based on a poem he believed to be by Porson but

which was later proved to be by Coleridge and Southey, conjointly. Its title: *The Devil's Walk*.)

After Lord Byron's death, Lord Holland wrote in the cover of the copy-book: 'This poem was given me by Lord Byron in 1813. It was his composition and his handwriting and has not hitherto been published or printed. April 1824. Vassall Holland.'

*

Now, the lurid details of Lord Byron's disastrous marriage to Annabella Milbanke (his 'Princess of Parallelograms') are too well known to need further amplification here. And the well-meaning efforts of Lord Holland to negotiate between husband and wife have been duly recorded, too. But it is less well known that both Lord and Lady Byron and Byron's hapless step-sister, Augusta Leigh, later expressed their gratitude to the Hollands for their consistent kindness.

Lord Byron was married on 2nd January 1815, and, on 13th and 22nd September of that year, he and his wife dined at Holland House. By then, Lady Byron was six months gone with child and a later invitation from Lady Holland had to be refused. Writing from her new home in Piccadilly Terrace, on 10th December 1815, Lady Byron makes her polite excuses:

My dear Madam,
   I must trouble you with an answer to Lord Holland's note as Lord Byron accidentally omitted to write one last night, and your very obliging invitation ought not longer to remain unacknowledged. We regret particularly that it is not in our power to accept it Lord Byron having a previous engagement and I am not able to dine out at present . . .

As her daughter (Augusta Ada) was born later that same day, Lady Byron's good manners withstood not only the agitation of her strained relations with her husband but the pangs of labour as well.

Less than four weeks later, Lady Byron's father wrote to tell Lord Byron that his wife, Annabella, encouraged by her parents, now wanted a separation from him. Thereafter, Lord Byron wrote to his wife, asking to see her and telling her he loved her, but she refused his request. And soon she was consulting her lawyers as to her next move.

One of the barristers she consulted was Dr Stephen Lushington, a friend of the Hollands, who now appealed to Lord Holland to act as intermediary. (At first, Dr Lushington had advised a reconciliation between the Byrons, but more detailed evidence on the part of his client decided him that this was impossible.) Lord Holland was loath to commit himself, but his innate good nature prevailed. On 21st or 22nd February, he writes Lord

Byron saying that he has 'the very best opinion of the head and heart of my friend Dr Lushington. I am persuaded that his motives are most honourable both to his client and to you.'

Byron's reply is dated 23rd February 1816. In it, he declares himself perfectly prepared to state his case in court, and makes no allegations at all against his wife. 'I can attach no blame to *her*. Where there is wrong, it may be fairly divided between her relatives and myself, and when there is right she has the monopoly.' In a postscript to his letter, Lord Byron gives Lord Holland his full permission 'to say whatever you please on this subject to me . . . either from yourself or any other person.'

A plan is evolved between them which provokes no immediate response from the other side but, after barely ten days of waiting, Lord Byron's patience is exhausted. On 2nd March, he writes to tell Lord Holland that, having received no answer to the representations Lord Holland has made on his behalf, he retracts what he first said and now, not only will he not agree to sign a deed of separation but he will not even give his 'verbal permission for Lady B's absence'. In other words, he demands the return of his wife.

Further complications arise but, eventually, Dr Lushington produces good reasons for his original delay. On hearing these, Lord Byron relents and agrees to a separation, but Dr Lushington dares not include in the deed a clause that Lord Byron should renounce his rights to his child.

On 27th March 1816, from Mivarts Hotel, Lower Brook Street, Lady Byron writes Lord Holland a letter of thanks:

My dear Lord

Before I leave town which a final arrangement will probably enable me to do in a few days I wish to offer my thanks however inadequate, for your kindness and consideration in regard to the melancholy business that now occupies me. I hope that at some future time I may be allowed an opportunity of acknowledging to Lady Holland & yourself the obligation which I have received from both during our short acquaintance and which will at least not be forgotten.

My dear Lord
Your very faithful servt,
(No signature).

*

Long since, Caroline Lamb's thwarted passion for Lord Byron had changed to venomous hatred, in which mood she plotted his destruction.

From the first, she had been jealous of Annabella Milbanke, an heiress and Lady Melbourne's niece. Some sixth sense had told her that this well-read self-assured young woman could become her rival, so she thought to beguile her by becoming her friend. And as far back as 1812, Caroline started, very circumspectly at first, to invite Annabella to Melbourne House.

As Annabella writes to her mother, on the first occasion Caroline warned her that Lady Holland would be present 'and she thought it right to mention this, as you were absent, lest I might inadvertently be led to do what you would not approve'. Smugly, Annabella had assured her would-be hostess that she was sure Lady Milbanke would not object to her meeting anyone 'she (Caroline) thought proper' to invite. And she concludes: 'If I am asked to be introduced to Lady Holland's acquaintance I shall certainly decline, but I think you will agree with me that no one will regard me as corrupted by being *in the same room* with her.' Four years later, Lady Holland's kindness to her was going to make her eat her words.

On 25th March 1812, having by then read and interpreted *Childe Harold* to her own satisfaction, Annabella Milbanke met Lord Byron, at Caroline Lamb's. This time, she was slightly waspish about her new friend. 'Lady C. has of course seized on him, notwithstanding the reluctance he manifests to be shackled by her. What a shining situation she will have in his next satire!' The tug-of-war was on.

Four times during that summer season of 1812, Annabella meets Byron. By the second meeting she is afraid 'he has a propensity to coquetry'; at the third, she notes with satisfaction that he 'was very good-natured to me'; but, at the fourth, undoubtedly Lord Byron's 'coquetry' is uppermost when he unstintinglypraises the charms of another young woman of fashion, Betty Rawdon, later Lady William Russell.

Throughout all the gossip and intrigue surrounding the Byrons, the Hollands had maintained their kindly attitude towards them both. After Annabella's departure, there was the occasion, on 23rd January 1816, when Augusta reported to Annabella that Lady Holland had just dropped Lord Byron back from Drury Lane; and Annabella's exulting description (from hearsay) to her mother, on 8th April, of Lady Jersey's party when Mrs George Lamb cut Augusta and Byron, and Henry Brougham and some other men cut Byron. In a subsequent discussion there, on morals, rather surprisingly Annabella declares: '. . . Lady Holland and Lady Bessborough —*pour moi.*'

As can be imagined, Caroline Lamb was in the forefront of the Byron intrigues until April 1816 when unwittingly she opened the flood lights of scandal on to herself. This was when she lost her temper with her page-boy and thrashed him with her riding-whip. As so often before, Lady Holland did her best to silence the gossip, for which Caroline writes with her usual incoherent thanks.

My dear Lady Holland,

I have heard of your good nature and I am obliged to you for it and so is William —*Lady Jersey I will never forgive*—I have often stood by her and her leaving me so shabbily now is not right. However thank God I have many kind and firm friends and I must say I heard with perfect astonishment—that I might still rank you in the list of at least a kind one. William approves of my resentment and therefore I am sure it is just—though at this moment disgraced and lowered let it be remembered—that I can shew my gratitude to such as have served me when fallen— and if I cannot he will.

Yrs. with sincerity
Caroline Lamb.

There follows the inevitable postscript:

Even Lord Melbourne is indignant at Lord and Lady Spencer's conduct—at such a moment any kindness shewn is deeply felt, but to see people attempt to alienate me from my husband—and fail—is disgusting—had she knocked my eyes out I would have forgiven her instantly but this *never*, nor any one who takes part.

This time, Lady Holland puts pen to paper, making two copies of her letter, the second copy dated April 1816, Friday, from a house the Hollands had leased in Savile Row.

Dear Caroline,

If an inclination to disbelieve what I heard and to suppress and soften the story I was at last compelled to believe is kindness I can with a good conscience accept your thanks, but I do not know that on any other score I deserve them on this occasion. Indeed I think that the less you express either gratitude or resentment for people's opinions on this unpleasant subject, or in plain English the less you talk or write about it, the more you will show yourself sensible of the pain you must have inflicted upon those whom you ought to consider beyond all others. The anxiety your Mother, William, and the Melbournes must feel should in my judgement occupy your thoughts much more than anything I, Lady Jersey or anybody else may say or think about you, and I cannot believe that you have leisure to think of other persons, or feel any degree of comfort till you have satisfied them they are not likely to be again exposed to such painful scenes.

Yrs.
E. V. H.

Alas! for Caroline's protestations of gratitude. Lord Broughton reports that when she received Lady Holland's letter '*This she said she could never forgive!*' And, in May 1816, she published a turgid, melodramatic novel, *Glenarvon*, in which she caricatured Lady Holland as 'the Princess of Madagascar'. As Lady Holland complains later to Mrs Creevey: 'Every ridicule, folly and infirmity (my not being able from malady to move about much) is portrayed.' In her turn too, she does not forgive.

In his character of 'Glenarvon' Byron is portrayed as a fiend incarnate but he has the last word. When Madame de Staël asks him how he likes Caroline's portrait of him, he answers: 'Il serait plus resemblant, si j'avais voulu donner plus de séances!'

*

As the world knows, having signed the deed of judicial separation from his wife, on 25th April 1816, Lord Byron left England and never returned.

In April 1823, he met Henry Edward Fox, at Genoa, and wrote an account of him to his friend, the poet, Thomas Moore:

... I always liked that boy—perhaps, in part, from some resemblance in the less fortunate part of our destinies—I mean, to avoid mistakes, his lameness. But there is this difference, that he appears a halting angel, who has tripped against a star; whilst I am *Le Diable Boiteux*.

And, certainly, Henry Edward admired Lord Byron, even in his choice of mistresses for, subsequently, he became the lover of Byron's last mistress, Countess Guiccioli.

A month later, Lord Byron accepted an appeal from the Greek Committee, functioning in London, to represent it in dispensing supplies to its countrymen in their fight for freedom against the Turks. He reached Cephalonia early in August 1823 and, after a worrying year, moved on to Missolonghi, on 5th January 1824. There, he met with nothing but procrastination and disappointment and there, on 19th April, he died of fever.

Augusta Leigh was his heiress and, on 15th August 1824, she writes to Lord Holland from St James's Palace, on black-edged paper:

My dear Lord Holland,
I am much gratified by the very kind manner in which you have received the ring I had taken the liberty of sending you. It will be a great consolation to me to know that my dear Brother's character and feelings were so well understood by one whose friendship and regard he so highly valued.

And, from the same address, she writes to Lady Holland, three days later:

My dear Lady Holland,
The kind manner in which you have expressed yourself about the Portrait will render it doubly valuable to me. I am almost ashamed of the shabby appearance of what I have selected for you from the very few articles I have as yet received of my poor Brother's—and it is really only as having been valued by him that I can ask you to accept it. There are more things coming to England and I hope amongst them I may find something more worthy of your acceptance. All you so kindly say of him is most gratifying to me—more so than I am able to express. I hope you have recovered from your indisposition and I remain ...

Among Lord Holland's papers are some lines written in his own hand:

> Short tho' thy course oh Byron and the date
> Of our strange friendship shorter—yet a throng
> of Thoughts press on me if I read thy song
> Hear but thy name or ponder on thy fate
> Marvellous youth! in fame thou will be great
> In genius wert so—and the random tongue
> of praise and censure does thy memory wrong.

Though shortened, the stanza is Spenser's, beloved of Holland and Byron.

CHAPTER NINETEEN

Imperial Passport

THE TIDE OF WAR was turning against Napoleon.

His invasion of Russia, in 1812, had led to an ignominious retreat from Moscow. Next he planned to beat the Prussians and Russians on German soil, but although initially successful at Dresden, his plans miscarried and at Leipzig (in October 1813) his Saxon troops deserted to the enemy. Four weeks later, the remains of his army had retreated back to the Rhine.

At the other end of the Continent, 1813 saw Wellington's final and victorious march through Spain, where disheartened and weakened by long years of arduous campaigning the French fell back before him until, on 21st June, he won a great battle at Vittoria. On 3rd July, Mr Allen enters in the Dinner Books: 'News of the Battle of Vittoria. H. Webster wounded in the neck by a musket ball'. And Lord Holland conveys the news to Caroline Fox. 'Henry W. has a wound in the neck which threw him from his horse. Lady Hd was overcome but is better.'

The Hollands' reactions to Napoleon's reverses were confused. Writing to Lord Granville Leveson-Gower, on 24th October 1813, Lady Bessborough describes a dinner-party at Holland House, the day before:

We dined at Holland House yesterday; it was very pleasant, except for every now and then that tone of incredulity or indifference to our successes—not in Spain, for I cannot make out the consistency of their views; they would defeat Buonaparte in Spain, and let him defeat the allies in Germany. This is beyond my Politicks, and makes me as cross as it does poor (Robert) Adair (diplomat, and kinsman of Lord Holland's) . . . At H. H. however, he cannot open his lips, for he seems to differ on almost all points, but shakes his head and says in a tremulous tone, almost like Kemble's: 'A-Ah! This is not the true old Whig creed.'

And yet, on 6th January 1814, Lord Holland declares to his sister: 'Bonaparte acts neither grandly nor handsomely he tries to evade peace and yet in making war cants whines and truckles . . .' And, in April, after the abdication, he declares again: 'The whole tone of Bonaparte's proclamation and publick papers is disgusting—he always prefers the cant and nonsense of a regular sovereign to the language which would become the military chief of a free nation.' In other words, Lord Holland admired Napoleon as a great general, born of the people, but not as Emperor of the French.

In February 1814, back on French soil, Napoleon's final campaign, brilliant though it was, was doomed to failure through lack of men. On 30th March the Allies marched into Paris and, on 11th April, Napoleon abdicated.

The Hollands and their friends found strangely lacking in taste the Prince Regent's invitation to Bourbon Louis XVIII (emerging from exile at Hartwell) to process in triumph, through London. His suite, postilions and even soldiers wore the white cockade of the Bourbon kings on their liveries and uniforms and, witnessing the scene, Samuel Rogers wrote an epigram in verse:

> Wear it awhile. Against him led,
> With our own blood you'll dye it red.
> But had your brave forefathers worn it,
> Great Nassau from their brows had torn it.

On 5th May, as Louis XVIII entered Paris, Napoleon went into exile on the island of Elba. There, at least, in an area nineteen miles long by six and a half miles wide, his sovereignty remained unquestioned.

*

On 22nd April 1814, John Whishaw, writing to his friend 'Mr Smith' of Easton Grey, informs him: 'Madame de Staël is going for a short time to Paris, and it seems to me that all the world is doing the same.' At least, his own particular friends, the Lansdownes and Hollands, were also planning to go to France. On 1st May, the Lansdownes left England for a three weeks' visit to Paris, and the Hollands left England, in July.

Charles Richard Fox had prevailed on his father to let him leave the Navy and now (aged eighteen) was cramming with the Rev. William Manning at Diss, in Norfolk, preparatory to studying law at Oxford. Constantly, Lord Holland enjoined Charles to work harder, quoting Cicero's speech 'pro archia poeta', and generally encouraging him to pay attention to his 'grammar and prosody'. Yet, once again, while the situation in Europe began to take precedence in his mind over his son's Latin construes, Lord Holland toyed with the idea of uprooting Charles from his studies, to take him abroad. In April 1814 he pencils Charles a letter.

Dear Charles,

One's head has been in a continual whirl with the strange news of the counter revolution in France. The conduct of the Allied princes has been as creditable to their taste as their military successes have been glorious to their arms. All the rest is disgusting in the extreme. I have no admiration for restoration and no belief in Royal promises or written Constitutions. As an Englishman I feel some sort of satisfaction that our rivals the French have almost blotted from our history the most disgraceful passage in it by the superior infamy and baseness of their restoration.

It was at least less disgraceful to submit to Monck than it is to a foreign foe and to shout and rejoice at the division of a parliament than at the entrance of foreign forces and foreign kings into a Capital . . .

While Charles engrossed himself with his new hobby of collecting 'medals and coins' (which was to make his name famous in after life), Lord Holland perfected his scheme. On 29th June, he writes to tell Charles that he is now determined to take him 'for some little time abroad'. He salves his conscience by making conditions: 'I shall expect from yr. good humour and good sense a more ready submission to advice, not to say authority, with me than with anybody else.' Mr Allen and Henry Edward's tutor, Mr Shuttleworth, are to accompany the Hollands abroad and Lord Holland feels sure 'you will have an opportunity not only of keeping up but of acquiring as much or more real knowledge in all branches of learning, classical or scientifick than you would have anywhere else'. (So much for the tutorial capacity of the Rev. William Manning.) His real objective comes out at the end of his letter: 'I shall have great pleasure in having you, seeing your merry face and hearing your merry voice—that is the truth of it.'

Now, Sydney Smith weighs in, with objections. On 25th June he writes to Lady Holland:

I am uneasy dear Lady Holland, at your going abroad. Consider what a thing it is to be well. If I were you, I would not stir from H. H. for 2 years; and then as many jolts, and frights as you please, which at present you are not equal to. I should think you less to blame if the world had anything new to shew you; but you have seen the Parthian, the Mede, the Elamite and the dweller in Mesopotamia; no variety of garment can surprise you, and the roads upon the earth are as well known to you as the wrinkles in Rogers' face.

Be wise my dear Lady and re-establish your health in that gilded room which furnishes better and pleasanter society than all the wheels in the world can whirl you to . . .

Needless to say, his advice is ignored.

In a letter to John Whishaw, Mr Allen gives 10th August 1814 as the date on which the Hollands, their four children, Lady Affleck, himself, Mr

Shuttleworth and the Hollands' usual retinue of servants arrive in Paris, where they lodge in an hotel on the Ile St. Louis.

From thence, on 13th August, Lord Holland writes to his sister. The previous day he, his wife and Charles Richard had dined with Prince Talleyrand 'who received me and yet more emphatically Lady Holland with a franchise and cordiality, even a kindness which I hardly thought were in his character . . .' Present at the dinner had been Fouché, the Duke of Atranto, the Duc de Lévi, 'the old Bishop of Evreux', two more undecipherable guests, and 'Monsieur Montoron' (Monteron) who, strangely enough, had been a captured prisoner-of-war in Charles's ship. Mons. Monteron claimed that 'he was treated most brutally by every body in the ship but Charles . . .'.

Lady Holland writes to Caroline Fox:

The Duke of Wellington is arrived and he has been received with the ceremonial used when the D(uke) of Shrewsbury came, in 1713. It was the only document they could find for an Ambassador Ex^{ry}. It is not supposed he will remain but that there will be a shuffle for Ld. Wellesley. Ld. Castlereagh arrives tomorrow and stays only a few days, Lady C. means to travel through Switzerland and meet him at Vienna, the Congress opens on 1st October . . .

In 1812 Lord Castlereagh had succeeded Lord Wellesley at the Foreign Office and had now embarked on the ten most distinguished years of his career. At that moment, he was leading the British delegation to the Congress of Vienna.

On 28th August, Lady Holland writes from Fontainebleau, and describes the room in which Napoleon signed his abdication:

. . . from a morbid feeling of curiosity I contrived to drag myself into the fatal room where the act of abdication was signed. It is a small room within one of his bed-chambers, the table is round, upon a pillar which was placed before him and as he signed he sat upon a small sofa . . . the whole apartment consists of small rooms adjoining the magnificent one occupied by Marie Louise, the furniture of hers is beautiful—and in the best style, her initials are everywhere introduced, the furniture in his apartment is very rich, but his choice was always to have sombre colors.

She enlarges on the impression Napoleon had made upon the French.

He was much regretted by the people. He distributed largely to the poor, and he employed the townspeople in the Palace. When he first came there was not a glass in the windows, a bed or a lock . . . alas! alas! why did he go to Russia and why was he so headstrong . . .

Plainly, the image of the fallen idol tugged at her heart. So much so that, two months later, from Florence, she obtained permission from Col. Neil

Campbell, British Commissioner on Elba, to send Napoleon 'some parcels of newspapers.' One of them, the *Courier*, declared that the Congress of Vienna was planning to move him to a place of greater safety, possibly 'the Island of St Lucie'. Which may well have quickened Napoleon's desire to make good his escape from Elba.

Yet, Lady Holland was still prepared to give homage to Wellington. She tells Caroline:

The evening before (26th August) I had the honour of a visit from our hero Wellington. He staid (*sic*) several hours. When he got upon military matters he talked well and his whole countenance brightened, but when upon other topics such as the questions to be discussed at the Congress, and the political state of Spain, he is but an ordinary personage. He seemed to like your brother, and his visit was an act of great civility to me on acct of my inability I conclude to go out and take my chance of seeing him in the world. In the morning I had Talleyrand so to the people of the Hotel I must appear a very great Lady . . .

*

Nostalgically, the Hollands intended to pursue their way through Switzerland to Florence and, from thence, to Rome and Naples.

From Geneva, on 20th September, Lord Holland informs his sister that he has seen Lord Dumfries who had recently been to Elba and who had given 'a good account of his interview' with the exiled Emperor. 'He is soldiering and building. He brought away all the furniture from his Sister's palace at Piombino and has fitted up his own magnificently.' Lord Holland continues: 'King Joseph (late of Spain) lives near this place. I have had a sort of invitation but did not chuse to understand it. I should have no objection to meet him but think it better not to *seek* him . . .'

The Hollands had a safe passage over the Apennines during which they had an unexpected encounter with Caroline, Princess of Wales, at that time also travelling to Italy. On 26th October, from Florence, Lady Holland gives her account of it to Caroline Fox:

We had an adventure with the Princess in a dark stormy night in the Apennines. We thought she was at Modena . . . and flattered ourselves we should reach Florence before her when lo! whilst we were sitting round our fire at a wretched place at Loiano(?) after supper a Dragoon arrived and announced her approach. The children were in bed and their room was divided from ours by the stables through which the passage lay, and we were excessively straightened for room. What was to be done! Wind rain in torrents and no moon. With some . . . difficulty I got your brother to go out and propose that she should come and warm herself by the only fire, and then to see what could be done. Accordingly she came with her Lady, Her Gentlewoman, her Escort . . .

The rest of Lady Holland's letter is missing, but, on 10th November, from Florence, Lord Holland adds some more information about the Princess.

> You have heard of our encounter with H.R.H. in the Apennines. She behaved with great civility and good taste and unaffected good humour. I wrote my name at her door here but have avoided as far as I could and hitherto with success being invited to her parties . . .

During the journey to Florence, Mary Fox had been a prey to 'perpetual nausea and giddiness'. Always prone to see the dark side, Lady Holland tells her sister-in-law: '. . . the motion of a carriage disorders her so thoroughly that a journey would I am confident be fatal . . . however she is now under the (care) of my mother, and the joint attendance of Allen and Dr Holland (physician to the Princess of Wales) who both declare she has no malady, but what has been produced by travelling'. So the Hollands had to prolong their stay in Florence for a week or two.

There were mitigating circumstances to Lady Holland's maternal anxiety. The Hollands were lodged in 'the finest hotel in Europe . . . quite Princely and upon the Arno'. And, in Florence, she was reunited with her old friend, Mrs Wyndham.

In March 1814, she had had a letter from Frances Wyndham, written from Florence, and filling the gap caused by her long absence abroad.

> Dst best of friends
> I long to hear all about you and that Excellent man your Husbd—for eight years I had the happiness of being beloved by a man who much resembled Ld. Holland and I was as happy as it is given to mortals to be. About two years ago he went for a few months into Switzd to see his brother Auguste de Talleyrand who was Min. there. He saw a younger and a handsomer woman than myself and I need scarcely add the rest. He is however in my opinion one of the best of men—we must forgive a little légèretè. He was French therefore it could not be otherwise . . .

Whilst admitting that she still suffered a lot from bad health, Frances Wyndham rightly claimed to have achieved 'philosophy' and was determined to remain in Florence, where living was cheap.

On 3rd November, still from Florence, Lady Holland gives Caroline Fox an up-to-date account of her:

> My old friend is living here very comfortably and is much esteemed and liked, her very small pittance has suffered and she has continued to keep within bounds her whole income has been 650£—reduced by income tax and exchange to 500£ with this she always had a handsome apartment, a carriage, a seat in an open Box (at the Opera) an English maid, a Cook a footman and another servant and is very well dressed. She is far from being altered to the degree she described, tho' her

chief beauty is certainly impaired, her teeth possess no longer their former brilliancy. Her spirits are good but rather forced, her pretty voice is tinctured with a foreign accent and she has learnt of the Italians to scream loud in conversation. It is but within these few weeks she has heard of the death of one daughter and the unfortunate marriage of the other. I hear she was dreadfully affected.

Frances Wyndham was lion-hearted to achieve 'philosophy' at such a price.

Mary Fox continued ailing and the Hollands decided to leave her in Florence with Lady Affleck.

Still in his letter of 10th November, on the eve of their departure for Rome, Lord Holland goes into lengthy details of his impressions of Napoleon and the state of Italy. Already, he had written Caroline a 'paper on Bonaparte' . . . ('I have all through it stretched points in his favour . . . to provoke (Matthew) Marsh . . .') but, now, he writes more seriously.

. . . true it is that the military character of his Government and the prodigious extent of his power were the chief evils, and great ones no doubt . . . In this country, which is Italy, and not Tuscany, I believe his institutions had done more good than harm, and the late change is perhaps for the worse rather than the better. It is certainly very unpopular with the active part of the Community, all of whom if they are to have a Master prefer Bonaparte to any other and France very much to Germany. Notwithstanding the Grand Duke's personal moderation and conciliatory conduct to all individuals his publick encasures are not judicious—he has relaxed the police, let loose the beggars in Florence, reduced all the literary and scientifick establishments and on the miserable plea of economy reverted from the confrontation of witnesses and other improvements in the administration of justice to the old and defective system which all Italians as well as foreigners concur in condemning—Tuscany however is unfeignedly rejoiced at his return and at the recovery of commerce of Leghorn and the nominal independence of a Grand Duchy.

Lord Holland continues:

Bonaparte's party is less strong here than elsewhere but throughout the north and east of Italy it is so formidable that could he appear with the slightest force I have no doubt he would very soon have an army stronger than that with which he defended the interior of France—Murat, if he was driven to despair might play this game and recall him but nothing but despair would make Murat have recourse to such a step—the hatred between them is inveterate. In the meantime Bonaparte is exceeding his little revenue and distressing his little island by unnecessary pomp and splendour. It may be policy but it has a strong appearance of vanity and folly. Murat courts the English in the most marked not to say mean manner . . .

Finally, he deals with the topic of his daughter, Mary's health.

There is no apprehension of lungs, she has no fever nor cough—her appetite is good and she sleeps well—but her little frame is very weak, and her bowels liable to derangement.

Less oil in her diet might have worked wonders.

The Hollands started for Rome on St Martin's Day and eleven days of cloudless sunshine cheered their way. But they arrived there in pouring rain and immediately succumbed, he to an attack of gout and she to a mysterious indisposition ambiguously described by Lord Holland as 'an accidental but lowering illness.' Later, on 17th December, Lady Holland tells Mr Whishaw:

... my health has been wretched, nearly thirty days of severe bilious cholic, attended with the most excruciating pain ... Unwarily, we trusted my precious person to the skill of a Roman physician, who administered very strong acid extracted from tamarinds. I leave you to guess the torture they inflicted ...

To make matters worse, at the outset a suitable house to rent proved hard to find until, on 28th November, Lord Holland confides to his sister:

Louis (Bonaparte, ex-King of Holland) makes way for me this day and leaves the house to which I am to succeed—he is well spoken of—but infirm and I suspect not very bright ...

Still, in mitigation of their troubles, friends were in the offing. The Duke and Duchess of Bedford were due to arrive, and Samuel Rogers and his sister were already in Rome, together with some other congenial English visitors.

In the same letter to his 'dear little sister', Lord Holland describes his contacts in Rome. With amusement, he tells Caroline that Rome is full of ex-Kings: Jerome (King of Westphalia); Louis (King of Holland). He declares that Lucien, Prince of Canino, 'seems to have taken up the fancy of acting the Prince since the rest of his family have been compelled to lay it down. He has Chamberlains presentations and Lord knows what.' But Lord Holland is sincerely concerned about 'old Charles 4th' (of Spain), ... old brute as it is, I should make use of the first strength I have to pay my court to him first because he was very gracious to me in his prosperity and secondly because I am anxious to hear what he and his say of the beloved Ferdinand (his son, now restored to the throne of Spain as Ferdinand VII). He, Fd., has shewn that he does not forget injuries though he has so short a memory of benefits, he has insisted on the Pope's or his father's dismissal of (Godoy) Prince of Peace, and Manuelito is actually at Pesaro with no other consolation than that of sweetmeats and sugar plumbs (*sic*) which the Queen never fails to send him ...'

On 29th November the sculptor, Canova, called on the Hollands and Lord Holland found him 'full of genius and simplicity. As simple as Nollekens but the simplicity of a man of more fancy genius and ability.'

H

On taking his leave, he admired little Georgiana Fox, exclaiming: 'Che bellino bracciuolo!' Subsequently, he returned more than once, and accepted Lady Holland's impulsive commission to model a bust of the exiled Napoleon.

Still from Rome, on 12th January 1815, Lady Holland informs Caroline that she and her husband are intending to proceed to Naples but only for a fortnight as the expense is 'incredible 5 guineas a day they ask for lodgings'. And she writes from there, on the fateful 5th March:

> The Queen (Napoleon's sister, Maria Caroline, married to Joachim Murat) graciously invited me to her Ball which I like a goose declined supposing it would require too much dress and exertion.

Whereupon the usurping Queen Maria Caroline asks Lady Holland to come to be presented which, deprecatingly, she accepts to do. 'Alas! I am compelled to wear the *"long manteau"* otherwise not respectfull . . . treating me like an artist and something unworthy of my condition.'

On 6th March, she adds some hurried lines to her letter.

> Since writing the above the news is come of the departure of *my Hero* (from Elba). I am so flurried (paper torn) cannot add a line oh! that the ('time'? page torn again) may be propitious as it was in 99, but alas! we know nothing here for certain . . .

The 'heroic' Napoleon had become her exclusive property.

On 8th March, Lord Holland expresses much less enthusiasm than his lady at the prospect of Napoleon once more free to arouse the passions of Europe.

> Here's a job Bonaparte escaped from his goal! Where is he going? What are his chances of success? Whatever be the result I think it a misfortune—If he fails he must be sacrificed and who can contemplate the extinction of such genius and activity with thorough indifference? If he succeeds we must have twenty years more war—Here they are making a judicious use of the event before the result can be known proving their sincerity by offering to fulfil their engagements while the success and restoration of Bonaparte are still possible events—Joachim has taken so evident a fancy for me that I think he must have read my character in the Examiner and taken it for Gospel every word . . .

Murat's flattery of a potentially powerful English peer was only part of the dangerous political game he played.

For the Hollands, the prospects of an easy journey home were again complicated but, with sublime complacency, Lord Holland writes to Caroline:

Should war recommence though it may alter my direction I do not think it will quicken my pace. War or peace I shall be to the North of the Alps before end of June and snug in Holland House before the opening of Parliament next year.

By 20th March, Caroline Fox is definitely worried that war may impede the Hollands' return. Perhaps they can escape through Sicily? And, by 21st April, she is on her usual tack. Her brother's absence (from the House of Lords) has been 'fraught with mischief and mischief not easily repaired'. But, for Lord Holland, out of earshot of British politics was out of mind and, at all times, he was more interested in the affairs of Europe.

By the time the Hollands were reunited with Lady Affleck and Mary Fox, in Florence, Lord Holland had referred to 'dreadful events, bella, horrida bella, in Italy'. On 11th April, he admits that fighting has broken out in the neighbourhood of Florence, but assures his sister that 'English visitors will be safe'. He intends to proceed by way of Bologna and Verona and, from Padua, on 28th April, he reports on the confused situation by which 'the Austrians had been received with cordiality by the Florentines and the Neapolitans by the Bolognese'. His party had come by 'the well-constructed mountain road' from Pistoia to Modena and thence, via Mantua, to Verona 'through regiments of Huzzars and Croats, stragglers, ammunition waggons artillery and forts'. (Presumably, by then, sheer fright had cured Mary Fox of carriage-sickness.) On their way, the Hollands had found one of the inns occupied by ex-King Charles IV of Spain, his Queen, Maria Luisa, and the object of her continued affections, Manuel Godoy. They had passed through Vicenza and were now 'in a large clean commodious inn at Padua where we shall wait to wash our linen, rest ourselves and our horses and enjoy the conversation of . . . Manfredini'.

Thereafter, the Hollands had as comfortable a journey as possible, in conditions of war. For, on 20th May 1815, by Imperial decree, a passport was granted them signed by the Minister of Foreign Affairs in Paris, allowing them free entrance into France, at all points, to embark from Calais, for England. To it, Lord Holland attached a memorandum: 'Passport granted to Lord Holland by order of the Emperor Napoleon in May 1815, in consequence of an application from Louis Bonaparte Ex-King of Holland.'

An ex-King in exile might appear slightly ludicrous but, when called upon to help, he might still prove effective. Even if, as Lord Holland had commented: '. . . he is well spoken of—but infirm and I suspect not very bright'.

*

The Hollands continued their journey northwards into Germany, their anxiety mounting about Henry Edward's health. On 13th May, Lord Holland attempts to reassure Caroline by saying that his illness is 'more distressing than dangerous'. But he gets John Allen to write her three pages of medical explanation in which he talks alarmingly of violent headaches, photophobia, 'hysterical paroxysms', palpitations and vomiting. A week later, Lord Holland writes that Henry is better but that they are going to Reviso, for cooler air. He feels sure that Henry will get over these attacks 'but they create difficulties over his habits and his education'. Inevitably, Lady Holland is inclined to despondency as 'she has lately grown so immoderately fond of the dear little boy (now aged thirteen) that she really has not calm judgment'. Lady Affleck is 'a great comfort'. On 29th May, from Bolzano, again Lord Holland writes that Henry is better but that he has to lie up in the heat of the day. 'Our dear invalid wavers between his dislike of leaving Italy and the desire of seeing you.' To keep him interested, John Allen, who travels with him, gives him 'a short and spirited abstract of the historical events of every place'.

Lord Holland's letters from Innsbruck (dated 3rd and 5th of June) are less cheerful. Now, Henry is subjected to daily paroxysms which are 'most excruciating and dreadfully painful to watch'. He sleeps late into the morning so that, rather than disturb him, the Hollands are now reduced to an evening drive. Apparently, Allen's daily bulletin (which has not survived) has been read 'to Henry himself who says it is exact but the expressions too strong and likely to alarm his little Aunty'. And, apart from his morning 'attacks', 'he is cheerful, with a good colour, spirits and appetite and sleeps nine hours every night'.

At this point, Lady Affleck goes on alone to Frankfurt. Lord Holland comments:

> She is about all arrangements and plans as changeable as the winds and not pleasant to advise as she throws all the responsibility on her adviser . . .

He admits that she has been 'not quite well herself', and that 'her attendance on Henry at Venice shook her a good deal'. After nearly seven months of almost unrelieved nursing of sick grandchildren, Lady Affleck had earned herself a rest.

On 16th June (from Augsburg), Lady Holland adds her postscript to her husband's letter: 'Henry suffers from depression of spirits tears and sobs, I am quite ill and unhinged myself . . . he is longing for you now he is out of Italy you are all he looks (for? badly smudged).' On 19th June, Allen sends Caroline another long account. Though they do not last so long, the attacks are as frequent as before and, now, they occur at any time of day. Allen has tried henbane, but this has made Henry Edward languorous. So now he prescribes only 'Aloes and Rhubarb for costiveness and Ether and Camphor when in paroxysm'.

By 23rd June, Caroline has consulted 'Baillie', in England, who does not think the attacks are epileptic but who does not think poor Henry will live long, as he attributes his condition to 'nervous irritability'. He commends Allen for his 'highly judicious' treatment and gives a page of diet and medicines.

*

On 18th June 1815, the Hollands were in transit between Augsburg and Nordlingen. The news of Napoleon's defeat reached them at Aschaffenburg and, when they heard it, they cried. But their coachman, by whom Charles Richard was sitting on the box, comforted him by saying: 'Don't mind, Mr Charles, it's all right. I think it is a very good thing that Boney has been beaten.'

On 27th June, Lord Holland writes to Caroline, from Frankfurt:

... We have heard of the *abdication* but cannot yet understand the nature of it. Peace is my wish, if it comes with the triumph of Kings and restoration of Bourbons it comes as much embittered to my palate as so sweet a thing can be—I am in opinion to the full as violent perhaps more so than in 1793 ...

Then he refers to the battle of Waterloo:

How bloody that 18th seems to have been. We are all anxiety about Henry Webster ...

But, writing the same day, Caroline is able to reassure the Hollands that Henry Webster is safe and thinks they will be able to meet him at Brussels or The Hague.

At last, Henry Edward's health had improved so that, with the exception of his mother (whose 'hydrophobia prevents her trusting herself to the boat'), he and the rest of the party proceeded by boat down the Rhine.

On 4th July, Lord Holland writes:

Lord Wellington's glories have opened our road ... The English have raised themselves in the estimation of mankind for courage heroism and all the virtues which give a nation superiority over others, but (he continues despondently) I wish in a better cause ...

And he goes on to declare that:

If Bonaparte's ambition is a grievous sin he has suffered grievously. I expect to see interminable wars in every part of Europe ...

On 17th July, Lord Holland writes to his 'Dearest little Sister' from Brussels. First, he reports on Henry Edward's continued if slow progress and on Charles Richard's departure for England (to join the 85th Regiment as an ensign). Thereafter, with his usual lack of punctuation, he refers to the battle of Waterloo and its after-effects.

In general the weather has been most favourable the inhabitants most attentive and the Surgeons most skilful all which circumstances combined will enable a larger portion of the wounded to recover than the state of the field, horrible even beyond any description of Ld. Byron's verses can give of it, led the most sanguine to expect.

He gives further details of the contest.

One trait of French civility in the midst of these horrors made us smile—the French wounded who required amputation said to the Surgeons *ce sont, Messrs. les Anglais qui ont le droit d'etre servis les premiers* and begged them not to think of cutting off their limbs while one English leg or arm remained to be dressed.

The Hollands intended to go straight to Calais, but the indisposition of Lady Holland and a return of Henry's giddiness and headache delayed them for two days at Lille. On 4th August 1815, they landed safely back, at Dover, with Napoleon's imperial passport filed unused among their papers.

That summer, Lady Harriet Leveson-Gower describes Lady Holland to her sister, Lady Georgiana Morpeth. 'We went to Holland House to-day, but did not see him. She was seated on the grass with Allen and a plate of Baba, very cross and absurd about Bonaparte "poor dear Man", as she calls him!'

By 1818, Canova's bust of Napoleon had been set up in the Dutch garden, with Lord Holland's translation of some of Homer's verses from the *Odyssey* inscribed on the pedestal:

> He is not dead, he breathes the air
> In lands beyond the deep,
> Some distant sea-girt island where
> Harsh men the hero keep.

CHAPTER TWENTY

Champions for Napoleon

WELLINGTON'S VICTORY AT Waterloo had embarrassing results for the Allies. After Napoleon's first abdication the year before, they had been careful to keep in the background so that the re-establishment of a Bourbon king on the throne of France should be seen to be by the will of the French people. But the Hundred Days put paid to that and, when the victorious Allies entered Paris, they brought Louis XVIII 'in their baggage wagons'. This time, they were less lenient in their terms for peace.

*

The Hollands returned home to find the Opposition in a mood of disunity and indecision. In the Lords, there was a split between Lord Grenville (last of the Ministry of All the Talents, who still aimed at conciliation with the Prince Regent) and Lord Grey, who hardly bothered to conceal his contempt for the Regent's vacillating rule. Privately, each was deciding to retire from politics and showed reluctance to take the lead. In the Commons, Whig members were bowed beneath the recent blow of Samuel Whitbread's suicide. After the Hundred Days, Whig reaction had been varied. Following the Prince Regent, Lord Grenville had begun by being 'furious for war' while Lords Grey, Spencer, and Lansdowne had been for peace.

After Wellington's success at Waterloo (to quote John Whishaw), 'the situation of the Allies is difficult and embarrassing in the extreme'. And he applauds Sheridan's 'very eloquent tirade', at Holland House, against 'the Corporation of Sovereigns combined against the rights of independent nations'.

Many Whigs thought that the treatment of Napoleon had been 'in some respects harsh and rigorous' and Whishaw reports:

Almost everyone who has come into contact with Napoleon has been fascinated by his manners and deportment. No one more so than Capt. Maitland, of the *Bellerophon*, who writes to his friends, that he never met with a man more agreeable and engaging, and few so well informed.

215

But Whishaw himself remains calmly judicious.

> For my own part I must confess that my heart is a good deal hardened against
> this deserter of the cause of freedom, and profligate and inveterate warrior. But I
> entirely disapprove of all unnecessary harshness, such as keeping his friends from
> him, and taking away 4,000 gold Napoleons, lest he should attempt to bribe the
> soldiers.

As for Lady Holland, now that her fallen idol had been elevated in her
mind to martyrdom, she set about canvassing her friends to send him
some more of the comforts she had inaugurated, from Florence.

As far back as June 1814, the Duke of Bedford had expressed his surprise
at the warmth of her feelings for the exiled emperor.

> I am amazed to see how warm a Napoleonist you are grown and I can scarcely
> wonder at it . . . altho' I am no Bourbonist I cannot agree with you in calling
> Bonaparte a great man—an *extraordinary* one he certainly is, but he wants too many
> of the essential qualities of greatness to merit the name you have given him.

Yet, so much is he under Elizabeth Holland's spell (. . . 'there is scarcely
any pleasure greater to me than that of doing what is agreeable to you—')
that, fourteen months later, he is declaring:

> I should most willingly send him (Napoleon) any thing that might be acceptable
> to him in his captivity.

But what? And how?

To which queries Lady Holland has her answer ready. On 14th August
1815, William Warden, Surgeon of H.M.S. *Northumberland*, brings
Lord Holland a message of gratitude from Napoleon for his advocacy
'in the Senate' about which he has read in the papers. With it, Warden
reports that

> Madam Bertrand requested me gratefully to acknowledge Lady Holland's attention
> to her children—Harry and Hortense(s) little toys charmed them.

Ten days after her return to England, and through her lawyer, Lady
Holland had devised a means of communicating with the captive on
St Helena despite the fact that the British Government had refused her
request to send him 'articles likely to alleviate the rigours of his captivity'.

On 28th October, John Whishaw writes to Mr Smith, from Holland
House ('Intending to pass only three days at Holland House, I have been
detained most agreeably for ten days . . .'). And from thence he reports:

> We have had several times Sir Hudson Lowe, the new Governor of St Helena
> an intelligent man and considerable military officer. He will do his duty honourably

and liberally without unnecessary harshness. He is taking out for Bonaparte a considerable collection of books, in which are many of his own particular choice; especially some mathematical works and a complete set of the best French translations of the classics. There are many novels for Madame Bertrand.

On 20th November 1815, the Allies signed the second Treaty of Paris, this time negotiating with the 'Ultra-Royalist' French Government. To quote Lord Holland:

Fouché and Talleyrand were dismissed, and a new Ministry was formed under the Duc de Richelieu, which at once took in hand the prosecution of those men excepted by name from the Acts of Amnesty.

The men to whom he referred were Marshal Ney and General Labédoyère.

Now, as animated against the Bourbon monarchy in France as his uncle had been, Lord Holland made up for lost time abroad by tilting against the windmills of the Establishment at home. Thereby not only did he involve himself in a lifelong estrangement from the Duke of Wellington and the Prince Regent but, by the violence of his views, he alienated himself from some of his own party as well. In the first instance, irresistibly, he was caught up in the drama of the Marshal's execution.

Desperately appealing for clemency for her husband, Madame Ney wrote a letter to the Prince Regent which she asked Lord Holland to convey to him. Lord Holland hoped to deliver it personally, but as the Regent was out of London, he appealed for help to Lord Liverpool (Prime Minister). In two letters dated 24th November 1815, one private and the other official, Lord Liverpool advised Lord Holland to forward Madame Ney's letter to the Regent, by special messenger. (To make doubly sure, she had sent a duplicate letter to the Duc d'Orléans, living at Twickenham, who adopted a similar course.) The letter sponsored by Lord Holland reached the Prince Regent who 'did not feel called to intervene'.

Visiting Paris, at that moment, was Lord Holland's kinsman, Lord Kinnaird, to whom Lord Holland now addressed his own urgent letter begging Lord Kinnaird to intercede with the Duke of Wellington, on Marshal Ney's behalf. The basis of his argument was that, up to the actual signing of the Capitulation of Paris, the Allies were in military possession of it 'and up to that time therefore . . . the inhabitants were entitled to claim impunity for all political opinions and conduct. . . . A promise of security was held out to the inhabitants of Paris: they surrendered the town; and while Wellington and the Allies were still really in possession of it, Labédoyère was executed (on 19th August 1815) and Ney was tried

H*

for political opinion and conduct.' Warming to his subject, Lord Holland
launched into unguarded language.

The worst is, that as nothing but Wellington's name could carry down so foul
a transaction, so the whole odium of the breach will fall on him and him only. He
signed, he interpreted the Capitulation; *and when a construction of a doubtful passage
might have saved one of the first officers of the age, he gave it the meaning least favourable to the conquered party, and left a man with whom he had once coped in the field of
honourable war to be taken off by the hands of the executioner.* . . . When the violence
of the times is gone by, and, above all, when the tomb has closed on their offences,
the transaction will be judged with reference to the character of Wellington and to
the nature of his promise, not to the conduct or misconduct of the sufferers. . . .

'Si ego digna in quam faceres, tu tamen indignus qui feceris, Pamphile. . . .

(If I deserve to be treated by you in this way nevertheless it is unworthy of you
to have done it, Pamphilus.)

Unfortunately, this explosive material arrived the day after Marshal
Ney's execution (carried out on 7th December 1815), and nervous of
handling it, Lord Kinnaird lost his head and passed it on to the Duke of
Wellington! To quote Lord Holland:

He (Wellington) affected to take umbrage at a passage (and here he makes a
note: 'Underlined in the above copy. V. H.') which he erroneously supposed was
intended to convey an imputation upon him as jealous or fearful of the military
superiority of Marshal Ney.

With liberated Europe at his feet, it was not surprising that 'the great
English soldier' 'took umbrage' at this unexpected attack on his integrity.
Two years later, in Paris, he cut Lord Holland dead. On 26th August 1828,
when Lord Holland lay very ill at Holland House, Lady Holland reports
that '. . . the D(uke) of W(ellington) even rode here, wet to the skin, to
enquire . . .' but, as late as 1833, young Lady Salisbury observes to her
journal:

The Duke thinks Lord Holland one of the worst among the Whigs, 'a bad man',
utterly selfish and unprincipled, and popular from the effect of manner only.

Next, Lord Holland shifted his attack to the Prince Regent, accusing
him of 'rancour' against Napoleon.

With whom the cruel expedient of exiling Napoleon originated I do not know. I
have reasons to believe that such a destination for him had been contemplated
before he left the Isle of Elba. . . . The Prince Regent subsequently showed himself
so full of rancour to the very memory of a man who had eclipsed the glory and
assumed, with some of the vices, all the functions of Royalty, without having
been born or bred to any such pernicious office, that the suspicion of posterity will
fall chiefly upon him.

And to this condemnation Lord Holland adds:

He (the Prince) grudged even the asylum our laws afforded to the persecuted adherents of the fallen Emperor . . . and he was bitterly incensed against me because the Duke of Sussex signed a dissentient to the bill for the detention of Napoleon Bonaparte. . . . He imagined, or at least asserted, that both Lady Holland and myself had used very earnest persuasions to prevail on his brother Augustus to sign his name, whereas it so happened that from some little personal motives of vanity, and chiefly at the request of Lady Holland, I had taken considerable pains to conceal my entering the protest till it was too late for him or any other peer to add his name.

(In fact, the Duke of Sussex signed Lord Holland's protest on the third reading of the Bill for Napoleon Bonaparte's detention.)

By it, Lord Holland realised that 'the step I was taking would be peculiarly offensive to the English public'. Yet, he contends:

To the Court it was so, no doubt: to the people, I believe, far the contrary.

But there were some even among his friends who were becoming nervous of his outspoken views. With Lord Grenville and Lord Grey bowing each other off the political stage, a new leader for Opposition became imperative. Brougham suggested the Duke of Bedford 'if the Duchess will let him do the needful'; Lord Althorp and John Whishaw felt that Lord Lansdowne was eminently suitable but, friend though he was, John Whishaw was forced to admit that Lord Holland himself was not in the running.

Lord Holland, it is true, is here, but he is considered as too violent, and an out-cry has been attempted against him, with some success, as a friend of Bonaparte and France.

*

The last four months of 1815 saw the usual crowd of guests at Holland House.

On 11th September, the Duke of York dined with the Hollands; two days later, the Melbournes, their son, Frederick Lamb, Sir James Makintosh, the Byrons and Robert Adair were invited to meet Henry Webster (just returned from Holland), Lady Affleck and Charles Richard Fox. This was the period of the Byrons' brief sojourn together in their rented house in Piccadilly Terrace and, again, on 22nd September, they dined at Holland House, to meet Sir Hudson Lowe.

On 27th September, Mr Allen introduces a foreign element into his dinner list by naming 'Princess Talleyrand', 'M. and Mme. de Bourke (formerly Danish Minister in Spain) and Mr Binda, from Italy'.

This young Italian, a close associate of Foscolo, Italian writer, was invited for a short visit to Holland House in September 1815, but so ingratiated himself with the family that his visit there was prolonged, off and on, to one of five years. We gain the impression that his charm was lost on Mr Allen. On 14th October, Allen comments: 'Mr Binda too late for dinner.' And the following night he comments again:

Lord and Lady Bessborough, Mr and Lady C(aroline) Lamb, Lord Duncannon, Mr (Charles) Greville defended a bad cause, Miss Fox laughed, Miss Vernon seemed surprised, Mr Binda slept and looked melancholy.

Yet, despite this lapse of manners, the night after that Mr Binda accompanied Lord and Lady Holland 'to Keen's Richard', at Drury Lane.

About this time, Joseph Blanco White became a reluctant member of the Hollands' domestic circle, introduced therein by Dr Shuttleworth, as Henry Edward's tutor. The grandson of an Irish Roman Catholic, Blanco White had been brought up in Spain where he had become a priest and was made a subdeacon, at an early age. After that, weakening in his religious beliefs, for a year or two he professed atheism and, in 1810, escaped to England before the advancing French. There, he had the luck to meet Lord Holland when he produced a propaganda magazine (the *Espagnol*) for Spanish consumption, partly backed by the British Government. In 1814, he went to Oxford where, once more, he became a professing Christian, joined the Church of England, and was ordained. Hypersensitive and not a little hysterical, he accepted the post of tutor to Henry Fox with great misgivings. Once installed, he was unable to compete with the sceptical, irreligious atmosphere of Holland House and resigned, after eighteen months. Yet his intellectual intimacy with the Hollands remained constant throughout his life. Two copies of his best-known work, *The Doblado Letters*, found their way to the library at Holland House. But his work, *Evidences Against the Catholics*, was too strong for any of the Hollands' following to digest. As the Duke of Bedford wrote to John Allen:

I see a very absurd, pompous, and in my opinion mischievous advertisement of Blanco White's work. Cannot he be content to change his religion as often as he pleases, without interfering with the rights of 6 million British subjects?

On 19th November, the Hollands entertained the Duc d'Orléans, at dinner, and, on 15th December, Mr Allen records: 'General Flahault to dinner and he appears to stay until 30th Dec.'

Charles-Auguste de Flahault was the illegitimate son of Prince Talleyrand and Madame de Flahault (afterwards, Madame de Souza). As a child, when the Terror was at its height, he had escaped with his mother to England, where he had been educated. In 1800, he had returned to France, to join the army of the Republic. He accompanied the Emperor to Moscow and to Waterloo and was arrested after the Hundred Days. Probably by Talleyrand's contrivance, again he escaped to England where, mindful of his mother's injunction to see 'ce bon, cet excellent Lord Holland', he presented himself at Holland House. With equal enthusiasm, Madame de Souza had spoken of Lady Holland as 'Une personne de coeur, tout-à-fait de coeur'. In 1802, in Paris, Lady Holland had described Charles de Flahault as 'a fine open young man'. So now, in Kensington, all parties were satisfied. At Christmas, at Holland House, General de Flahault met his future wife, Margaret Mercer Elphinstone, daughter of Admiral Lord Keith. After which party Lord Holland declares:

> We are quite delighted with Flahault. In addition to many agreeable qualities, he is frankness itself. How that happens I cannot guess, but so it is.

Also invited by the Hollands, for Christmas 1815, was another of Napoleon's generals, Sebastiani. In April 1816, Lord Holland wrote of him:

> Sebastiani is going back to France; by which I conclude he has made, or thinks he has made, his peace with the powers that be. We have scarcely seen him of late. He avoids the Opposition, and fancies that by so doing he pays his court both at home and here.

*

Among the Holland House papers is a long 'List of Articles' declared despatched, on 1st January 1816, to St Helena 'for the use of General Bonaparte and his attendants'. Surprisingly, from a subsequent statement by the Colonial Secretary, Lord Bathurst, this appears to refer to articles sent out by the British Government and not as a result of Lady Holland's magnanimity.

Linen

2 Pieces Superfine Irish at 7/9 per yd.
3   do   do.   do.
3   do. Super Superfine   8/9 do.
1   do. French Cambric
1   do.   do.
1   do.   do.
    The above were made into 60 shirts
15 Pieces of Super long Cloth at 2/8 per yd. made into 168 shirts
11 Pieces of Super Superfine do. at 3/3 per yd. made into 96 sheets
2 Pieces of Sheer hands
4   do.   Mulled Muslin
2   do.   do.

Hosiery
2 dozen fine white silk stockings at 15/6 per pair
2   "   extra fine   do.   do. 13/6   do.
2   do.   do.   do. 16/-   do.
3   do.   do.   do. 15/-   do.
3   do.   do.   do. 15/6   do.
1   do.   ribbed   do.   do. 15/-   do.
1   do.   do.   do. 17/-   do.

Cloth
35¾ yards Superfine Green Broad Cloth
37¾ yards Superfine White Kerseymere
34¼ do.   do.   Drab   do.

Flannel
46 yards fine flannel at 3/6
59   do. Abergavenny 3/9

Meanwhile, Lady Holland's interest grew apace in any member of Napoleon Bonaparte's family.

In November 1815, Canova had dined at Holland House and had been asked to transmit a gift from Lady Holland to Lucien Bonaparte, Prince of Canino. On 20th January 1816, Lucien writes from Rome to thank her and so begins a long, importunate correspondence with the Hollands asking their help to get him and his family to England.

Madame

Veuillez bien agréer mes remerciements pour votre si aimable souvenir que Canova m'a remis; la confiance que je place dans votre amitié et dans celle de mylord Holland me determine à m'adresser a vous pour obtenir la permission d'aller voyager dans la belle et bonne (?) Angleterre avec ma famille ...

Lucien goes on to say that he is now anxious to move from the neighbourhood of Naples (where Bourbon Ferdinand has been re-established) for two or three years and asks for passports to be provided by the British Government, for himself and his wife.

The same year, Louis Bonaparte (ex-King of Holland) follows the same theme, asking Lord Holland to use his influence to obtain passports and permission for himself and his family to 'live in England' and further asking Lord Holland's help to publish a book in England.

Lord Holland warns both brothers that the time is inopportune for their requests, going so far as to tell Lucien, in May 1817, that the choice of himself, as intermediary with the British Government, might prejudice his cause. Instead, he counsels Lucien's direct communication with Lord Sidmouth (Home Secretary).

On 18th March 1817, Lord Holland moved in the House of Lords for papers connected with Napoleon's treatment, basing his case on a letter of remonstrance from General Montholon (sharing his Emperor's captivity) to Sir Hudson Lowe, and on communications he had had with the Imperial Family. He made three main points. Firstly, that Napoleon's captors had no right to restrict his freedom of movement on St Helena. (He contended that the high ground, at Longwood, was unhealthy.) Secondly, he branded the Governor as gravely at fault in not allowing Napoleon books and newspapers, and in refusing him permission to subscribe 'for such publications as he thought proper'. And finally, he maintained that 'appeals and communications to the Regent in England were intercepted, and that, owing to the reduction of the Parliamentary grant made for his establishment, Napoleon had himself to provide money for the ordinary sustenance of himself and his entourage, and was even driven to sell his plate for the purpose'. (This last contention was corroborated by M. Octave Aubry.)

Lord Holland was careful to avoid any unreliable evidence with which Lord Bathurst (Colonial Secretary) sought to involve him. 'I avoided successfully any exaggeration either of the magnitude or the proof of the hardships he (Napoleon) is exposed to.' And, having made his points, he justified them:

I am afraid that my motion will prejudice many good men against me, and possibly do some little injury to our Party, but I cannot repent having made it. . . . For surely it would be a disgrace to the country that such imputations should be thrown out and not one publick man take notice of them.

He did not divide the House, 'though Lord Darnley, never deficient in natural generosity, showed some disposition to urge it . . .'

The gratitude of the Imperial Family for Lord Holland's chivalrous action was quickly forthcoming.

Just over four weeks after he had spoken in the House of Lords, on 23rd April 1817, Napoleon's sister, Princess Pauline Borghese, writes to him from Rome:

Milord,

Malgré que je n'ai pas le plaisir de vous connaitre personellement, les relations que vous avez eues avec quelques personnes de ma famille et la noble conduite que vous tenez dans les circonstances actuelles m'engagent à m'adresser à vous avec confiance. C'est un besoin pour moi, Milord, de vous remercier de l'intérêt que vous prenez ouvertement à l'Empereur. Sa position, d'après les récits que nous transmettent les journaux est digne de fixer l'attention d'un homme sensible et juste comme vous. J'ai vu avec reconnaissance les efforts que vous avez faits pour l'adoucir et je ne puis croire qu'ils soient sans succès. . . .

But the Princess cannot help thinking of the 'privations' her brother still
has to undergo and begs Lord Holland to find the means of transmitting
'plusieurs choses indispensables au maintien de sa santé' for which she
will reimburse him through the banker, Torlonia, at Rome. She longs to
share Napoleon's exile and declares that she would willingly give all she
possesses ('tout ce que je possède') to alleviate his lot. She ends her letter:

Croyez, Milord, à la vérité de mes sentimens et à ma haute considération
                                            Psse Pauline Borghese.
                                            Rome, ce 23 Avril 1817.

In a postscript, she consigns her letter to Lord Jersey (then on a visit
to Rome) to give Lord Holland, and encloses another, for onward trans-
mission to the Emperor.

On 1st May, the Emperor's mother sends her own tribute of gratitude
to Lord and Lady Holland. Written by a secretary she signs her name in
a shaky hand. While enlarging on the difficulties of getting letters to
Napoleon, she declares:

Milord, votre grand caractère me dispense de vous exprimer les sentimens de mon
éternelle reconnaissance . . . Que Lady Holland veuille bien trouver en l'assurance
des sentimens digne de son coeur, et qu'Elle ne cesse de prendre intérêt a mon fils.
                    Je suis pour la vie
                    Milord
                    Votre très devouée Servante
                    La Mere de l'empereur Napoleon.

Her thanks are followed by those of Cardinal Fesch and Prince Borghese.
Relentlessly, Lord Holland importunes Lord Bathurst on Napoleon's
behalf and, on 15th May 1817, Lord Bathurst agrees to forward Pauline
Borghese's letter to her brother. Further, he does not object to Lady
Holland sending out articles to St Helena provided they go through him,
although he must point out that from the list of things sent out on 1st
January 1816, 'he (Napoleon) does not stand in need of any more.' He
concludes:

As to the Princess' observation on her Brother's treatment, I should be sorry to
have a contention with any lady, and particularly with a very pretty one, but it
may be a satisfaction to her to receive a copy of the last Bulletin transmitted from
St Helena on the subject of her Brother's health, which I therefore enclose.

Lord Holland had won the first round.

Together with others, there is a list in French (presumably from
Pauline Borghese) of articles to send out to St Helena:

Six douzaine de chemises de toile de Hollande
      ,,   ,,   de mouchoirs de poche de Batiste
Deux pieces de la flannelle la plus fine
Quatre douzaines de Madras
Trois pieces de Casimir blanc
Une piece de drap vert fin
Quatre douzaine de bas de soie blanc
Cinquantes petites caisses d'eau de Cologne
Deux caisses de vin de Bordeaux
    ,,   ,,   ,,   Soterne
    ,,   ,,   ,,   Lunel

In addition, Messrs Plummer of 44 Craven Street, Strand, sent out the following consignment of wine and Eau de Cologne (the latter in such quantity that it would appear that Napoleon washed in it).

H. L. to G. & M. Holland

No. la 12	12 Half Chests 72 doz. claret	84/6	£302.	8.	0.
13	1 do. do. 6 doz, Sauterne	75/-	22.	10.	0.
14	1 do. do. 12 doz. Pints Lunelle	42/-	25.	4.	0.
15	50 Cases Eau de Cologne 25d oz.	48/-	60.	0.	0.
15	Chests " "	16/-	12.	0.	0.
			422.	2.	0.

This was directed to General Bonaparte, Long Wood, Shipp'd on board the Lady Carrington A.1. Moore for St Helena.

Ca	422.	2.	0.
5 p ct Disc for cash	21.	2.	0.
	401.	0.	0.

On the back of this was a note: 'This money has been paid by order of Princess Pauline by Torlonia of Rome to Mr Plummer.'

On 18th January 1818, a similar shipment was made by Messrs Plummer to St Helena, which, after allowing rebate on 'draw-back customs' and excise on wine and bottles, amounted to £471.17.11.

On 11th January 1819, Lord Bathurst undertakes to forward to St Helena from Lady Holland 'new publications and a microscope'. Also, he is sending the Duke of Bedford's box containing some medals 'as I presume though the medals are not of a political tendency'. In his letter he assures Lady Holland that there is no reason to suppose Bonaparte's health has deteriorated.

On 18th February 1820, Lord Bathurst plays down, to Lady Holland, Count Montholon's contention that the state of his own health makes it imperative for him to leave St Helena. Instead, Lord Bathurst gives as the real reason the rivalry between Montholon and Bertrand and undertakes to ask Sir Hudson Lowe 'to enquire of Bonaparte' if he wants a replacement of either companion to be sent out to him. (A translation of his letter into French is sent to Pauline Borghese.) Nearer the truth was Count Bertrand's revelation to Lady Holland (in a letter from Longwood, written in June 1819) that Countess Montholon suffered from chronic hepatitis. This was confirmed to her by Barry O'Meara, surgeon in the _Bellerophon_, in July 1820, together with an appeal for help for the Countess to come to England, to drink the waters at Cheltenham.

Lady Holland continued to enlist the help of her friends to supply Napoleon with books and, at the time of his death, in 1821, the amount shipped out to him, by her, amounted to four hundred and seventy-five volumes.

In addition, she persuaded 'our excellent friend the Warden' (John Allen, Warden of Dulwich College) to write an article in the _Edinburgh Review_ reviewing a book by William Warden, called _Letters from St Helena_. His review appeared in December 1816, and a copy of it, unfortunately marked indecipherably, by Napoleon, was given to Lady Holland by O'Meara, after Napoleon's death.

And she was indefatigable in organising help of a more practical kind. When, in December 1820, news came that Napoleon's cook had become subject to fits of apoplexy, she was instrumental in inducing Lord Bathurst to send him out two French cooks 'in the first ship going to the Cape'. But her attempt to send him a machine, newly invented, to make ice, was unsuccessful.

As late as 5th March 1821, Sir Hudson Lowe is writing Lady Holland a seven-page letter, deploring the non-arrival of boats; and assuring her that her orders are always punctually fulfilled. In it, he assures her that he is ever mindful of his duties and obligations to 'the Person in my Custody'.

On 17th March, Count Bertrand, speaking of Napoleon, enlarges on 'l'état deplorable de sa santé'. Six weeks later, on 5th May 1821, Napoleon is dead.

*

Although he never wrote personally to Lady Holland, at his death he bequeathed her a snuff-box bearing the inscription: 'L'empereur Napoleon à Lady Holland, témoignage de satisfaction et d'estime'. And, at her own death, Lady Holland left the snuff-box to the British Museum, together with the aforesaid inscription, written without accents or apostrophes.

Napoleon's gift gave rise to seven critical verses from Lord Carlisle, begging her to reject it. Here are the first three:

Lady, reject the gift, 'tis tinged with gore
Those crimson spots a dreadful tale relate;
It has been grasp'd by an infernal power;
And by that hand that seal'd young Enghien's fate.

Lady reject the gift, beneath its lid,
Discord, and slaughter and relentless war,
With every Plague to wretched men lay hid
Let not these loose to range the world afar.

Say, what congenial to his heart of stone
In thy soft bosom could the tyrant trace?
When does the dove the eagle's friendship own,
Or the wolf hold the lamb in pure embrace!

To Lord Byron, such an opportunity of showing up Lord Carlisle to ridicule was too good to miss. He replied:

Lady accept the box a hero wore
In spite of all this elegiac stuff
Let not seven stanzas written by a bore
Prevent your Ladyship from taking snuff.

His friend, Thomas Moore, added another contribution:

Gift of the Hero, on his dying day
To her, whose pity watch'd for ever nigh
Oh! could he see the proud, the happy ray
This relic lights up in her generous eye.
Sighing he'd feel how easy 'tis to pay
A friendship, all his kingdom would not buy.

As the following two anonymous verses show, the opinion of the man in the street ranged against Lord Carlisle. The first was entitled: 'On reading Lord Carlisle's verses in John Bull, recommending Lady Holland to throw the snuff box into the Thames':

For this her snuff box to resign
A pleasant thought enough
Alas my Lord—for verse of thine
Who'd give a pinch of snuff?

And the second scornfully enquired:

Is this a patriot strain of highborn rage
I blush to hear it(s) vulgar titled railer
You hoot a mighty eagle in his cage
And tune your scrannel pipes to court his jailor.

In a last letter of condolence to Pauline Borghese (written on 11th August 1821), Lord Holland tells her how deeply sensible Lady Holland is of the gift she has received from the great man ('ce Grand Homme'). Insignificant though her own efforts have been, the thought that they have helped to sweeten his cruel exile is one she will always cherish. ('L'idée qu'ils n'ont pas été inutiles et qu'ils ont pu adoucir quelques instans de ce cruel exil est bien la plus chère et la plus flatteuse pour Lady Holland . . .')

CHAPTER TWENTY-ONE

Home Circle

DESPITE THEIR ABSORPTION in the affairs of Europe, the Hollands' interest in their children always came first. Particularly for Lady Holland, as her relations with the children of her first marriage continued unsatisfactory. True, she was on good terms with her second Webster son, Henry, but his elder brother, Sir Godfrey, showed no sign of filial affection. Contrary to Caroline Lamb's spiteful accusation to Lady Holland that, thanks to her neglect, Sir Godfrey had had to turn to 'false friends and bad company', in 1814, he had married a charming and beautiful girl, Charlotte Adamson. But the Hollands were abroad at the time of the wedding. And Harriet's guardians, the Chaplins, continued to bar Lady Holland access to her Webster daughter, to the extent that there is no record that she was present when Harriet married Fleetwood Pellew, son of Lord Exmouth, in 1816.

'The little (Fox) girls' (as Allen usually called them) were obedient and industrious, but Charles Fox showed an inability to settle down to a steady career and Henry Fox, though obviously gifted, seemed unambitious to justify his fond mother's expectations. The correspondence between parents and sons shows an interesting contrast. Few letters remain between Charles and his mother who, clearly, left her husband to discipline his elder son. Such letters are affectionate but lack the intimacy of those between Lady Holland and Henry Fox. And frequently, Charles's casual ways exasperated his mother. But the letters between Lady Holland and Henry run into hundreds and clearly show that she looked on her second surviving son as the counterpart of his father and loved him accordingly. To Charles, as usual, Lord Holland shows himself tough at the outset then gradually weaker. In her letters, Lady Holland never takes up a stand from which she has to climb down. She flatters Henry; treats him as a contemporary; confides in him; sometimes gently exhorts him to work harder; but never confronts him with an ultimatum. It is to the credit of both boys that neither played on their parents' indulgence to gain their objectives.

229

In July 1815, aged nineteen, Charles had joined the 85th Regiment at Chatham under the command of Colonel Thornton. From there, he had proceeded to Weedon Barracks near Daventry, then to Winchester, and, thereafter, to Nottingham and Liverpool. Having admonished Charles for his resentment of criticism; for his extravagance; for his inability to settle; for his already proven disregard for the dangers of too close contacts with the opposite sex (aged eighteen, Charles seems to have contracted venereal disease while at his crammer's, at Diss); Lord Holland teases Charles on his unexpected friendship with the Bishop of Winchester. 'You may wash out your naval, legal and military propensities, but if you once have a bishop's hand on your head the character is indelible and you are a parson for life.'

In April 1816, Lord Holland started his elder son on an annual allowance of £150, by which time Charles was keeping a mare which, almost immediately, sprang a curb. After trying unsuccessfully to sell her, Charles sent her down to Holland House to turn out. Lord Holland tells him that 'the vicinity of Foxhounds is no great advantage to you' and again cautions him against extravagance. Then, after this show of parental severity, when the mare does not improve he sends his own black horse to Charles to ride. But he jibs at buying a tilbury.

The Hollands did their best to further Charles's military career and in May were careful to invite his colonel to meet the Duke of York at dinner. But life as an ensign did not appeal to Charles. He complained of the discomfort of life in barracks (no bedstead or blankets); of the absence of free rations of tea and sugar; of the 'fearful drill 5½ hours have I been trudging the long grass this day; and am to have another hour later . . .' So, the subject of his transfer to a regiment with a quicker chance of promotion came under discussion for several months. Since June, Lord Holland had been parrying Charles's desire to visit London and adjured him to remain with his regiment 'while Col. Thornton is with you'. On 21st August, he writes:

Have the goodness before you do anything decisive . . . to tell Col. Thornton that I agree and approve of the step only on the clear understanding that the Regiment you purchase into is not under orders to the West or East Indies—to the first my objection would be insurmountable and though I might if it came in your way be reconciled to the East Indies I would on no account for so trifling an object as Lieutenancy be instrumental in sending you there. . . .

And, to further strengthen his resolve, Lord Holland adds a postscript:

By your mamma's advice I write to Thornton myself.

But, on 4th September, he is preparing to eat his words:

... the sound of the 60th Regiment generally in West Indies and always abroad appals me—but per contra Thornton's opinion has due weight ...

Five days later, he breathes a sigh of relief on hearing that the purchase may not go through and that Charles may yet remain with the 85th Regiment for another year.

Lord Lauderdale found a way out.

The Hollands spent the Easter of 1817 at Woburn and from thence Lord Holland writes to Charles:

Your mamma has told you of Lauderdale's kindness. I think it very likely he will take you. It will suit you exactly.

Thus it was, that, on 15th May 1817, Charles Fox departed for Corfu 'as supernumary or extra Aide de Camp without pay but with bât de forage' on the staff of Major General Sir Frederick Adam, Commander of the British Division at Malta and on the Mediterranean Station.

Before Charles left, again Lord Holland resisted his desire to go to London.

... the worst possible preparation for your journey would be *incontinent* practises that might procure you a clap—though you will soon be in Corfu il ne faut pas être *encore fou* ...

For once, he was firm.

Charles enjoyed himself in Corfu and wrote back happily. But, in the New Year of 1818, he sustained a serious accident and described it in a letter dated 19th January:

... A Canister of Powder was good enough to explode under my nose and *scarify* my Face to a great degree. My eyes were thank God not materially injured. I am now except a few unhealed sores and eyes a little weak quite well ... I shall ask Adam to let me go Home in about two or three months. He is very well and as usual very kind to me indeed ...

So, by June 1818, Charles was back, on furlough.

But, as she shows in a letter to Henry, by next year he is getting on his mother's nerves—

poor Charles is sadly negligent of the duties of life and will make himself enemies by the foolish questions and remarks he makes, and he appears always to be more deficient in understanding than he really is. He goes to Paris tomorrow.

She apologises to Henry for her irritation about his brother, but complains of Charles's 'great inattention and total want of feeling and propriety', departing as he has in 'one of his flurries' without bidding proper adieux.

*

Aged fourteen, on 10th January 1816, Henry Fox writes to his mother, from Holland House:

Dear Mama

Ten thousand thanks for your *very very* entertaining letter . . . I rode today and have ordered three young pidgeons to be executed they are for Grandmama who is not so very Bourbonick as formerly. She has had a headache a toothache a earache a violent cold and a bad cough notwithstanding she looks very well . . .

Adieu ma *très très* chere Maman et croyez moi votre aimant fils pour toujours et toujours.

H. E. Fox

From Woburn, Lady Holland gives Henry an account of her six-hour journey there in an open carriage; and of 'a masquerade and tableaux in frames in the dress and attitude of pictures . . . Now I have given you an ample acct. of our occupations yesterday, and yet do you know my dearest son, I had rather have seen your cheerful innocent face, than beheld all these beauties.' She gives further details of the Woburn theatricals, after which 'I did not get to bed till half past three and now at ½ past 12 have only just finished my breakfast'. But 'Papa' is in the tennis court with, among others, Lord Apsley . . . 'pompous presumptious entirely disagreeable and I suspect mighty empty'. Dangerously outspoken, to a child.

In another undated letter from Woburn Lady Holland praises Henry: 'You have written admirable letters both as to composition and execution' and calls him 'a delightful correspondent'. Then she tempers her praise:

I delight in hearing from you for nothing gives me half the pleasure that seeing your handwriting does. I was going to say *scrawl* for you do not write as well as you did pray attend to that mechanical labour for it is a useful and necessary one.

From September 1816, for a year, Lord Holland took on Henry's classical instruction himself. On 12th September, he writes to Charles:

Since my return I have been up every morning at eight and read 100 lines of Euripedes before breakfast with Harry whom I am glad to find so much better a scholar than I had imagined.

Charles could always put his father in a good mood by emphasizing his own pleasure in reading. At that time he was reading the historians Tacitus and Montesquieu and making a study of Napoleon's Russian campaign.

Perhaps inspired by his mother's account of the theatricals at Woburn, Henry had a new diversion. He, too, took to acting to which Lord Holland refers, in his letter to Charles of 18th December:

Henry is entirely absorbed in his theatrical preparations. His Grand Performance is tomorrow and he acts in Marsh's room . . .

Henry's health improved sufficiently for him to be boarded out with a tutor and in September 1817 he settled in with his father's old friend, the Rev. Matthew Marsh, in the vicarage of Lord Holland's living at Winterslow. On 7th January 1818, approvingly, Sydney Smith writes to John Whishaw:

I am very glad the Hollands have sent Henry from home: he is a very unusual boy and he wanted to be exposed a little more to the open air of the world.

Though occasionally homesick for his family, from Winterslow Henry writes frequent happy letters to his mother:

I am very happy and comfortable. Mrs Marsh is a very pleasant and kind person without the slight(est) affectation and the only thing against the agreeableness of her conversation is that she talks through her nose. I lye down every day before dinner . . . my leg is rubbed by a little old woman with a long waist and a cracked voice who rubs very well.

He gives his mother an account of his studies:

Tell Papa that I do in the morning a translation from Livy 100 lines of the 7th book of the Odyssey & then ten or eleven lines of the Iliad preparing *every* word. In the evening with husband or wife I read the Georgics . . . on Sunday, I only do a little Greek Testament.

He ends up: 'Pray pray write.'

Lady Holland tells Henry that Gina too (aged nine) has an aptitude for writing:

. . . little urchin she manifests symptoms of writing as good a letter as *you and Charles* . . . but scribbling Misses are dangerous and bad Members of Society so she must confine herself to Themes, historical essays etc etc . . .

She shows her engaging lack of vanity and sense of humour in her reply to one of Henry's anxious letters, hoping that 'her head and face are all right'.

. . . in your letter you are so good as to say 'I am sorry for your head and face, I hope you have got rid of it'. Of which do you mean? My face is certainly forty six years worse for wear yet such as it is, it cannot be spared for ordinary purposes of life, tho it has long ceased to serve for those of attraction and admiration. As to my head, it carries face inclusive and I am not sure whether you destine it to the block or Dr Willis, but I cannot spare it for either yet. Why what a careless boy you are and how oddly you express your kindest wishes, which I conclude were for my recovery. This has been effected by change of air . . .

In February 1818, the Hollands lost a well-loved relation, Lord Upper Ossory. Together with his brother, Richard Fitzpatrick (who had died in 1813), and Charles James Fox, he had supervised the upbringing of his sister's child, Henry Richard, 3rd Lord Holland, and had always preserved close contacts with him. After amply providing for his two legitimate daughters, Anne and Gertrude Fitzpatrick, and for two illegitimate sons and a daughter as well, Lord Upper Ossory bequeathed Ampthill Park, in Bedfordshire, to Lord Holland who had loved the place since his youth. He writes:

All these considerations made it a subject of congratulation from my friends; but it is impossible at first not to feel the loss of the person to whom I owe it, and who certainly was in conduct to me during my long minority, and in affection and advice afterwards, a more judicious useful and tender *father* than most people have the advantage of having.

Lord Upper Ossory remembered Charles Fox too in his will, and left him £5,000.

When, shortly after his great-uncle's death, the news comes that Charles intends to return home from Corfu, Mrs Marsh writes Lady Holland that Henry's joy is 'unboundable'. In due course, Charles arrives and joins his parents with Lord Egremont, at Petworth. From thence, Lady Holland writes to tell Henry that Charles has transferred his boyhood's affections from Mary Wyndham to her sister, Charlotte, but that he is 'not far gone in the tender passion'. Henry is avid for news of him and begs:

Tell me about Charles and how he went to Petworth and whether the sight of Miss M. Windham (*sic*) made his flame return after four years coaling.

He starts to learn French with 'the old French Abbé' and means 'to *apply* and write and in fact do all that is right . . .' But he is anxious about his mother. 'Dear Mamma do write to me and do not be ill, or out of spirits it makes me miserable to think you are so . . .' He makes progress in French and Lady Holland tells him that two people have told her he is 'gaily french spouting . . . I like to hear you praised . . .'

Henry's partiality is for romantic literature and he writes to ask his mother for the collected works of Lord Byron. He tells her, too, that he is finding great pleasure in reading Gibbon 'and never liked any history half as much'. With the assurance of his sixteen years, he continues: '. . . though his style is certainly not good yet there are very eloquent and sometimes very fine passages'. He admits that he has no aptitude for mathematics. '. . . so terribly stupid about Algebra and Fractions that Mr M. has been thrown almost into a passion.'

Charles goes to visit him and Henry reports: 'Charles arrived early placid tacit and agreeable.' But in the same letter Henry's anxiety for his family shows up again: 'I do not like the account of Gina especially of her being so very thin.' He wants more news of her and sends her 'many loves and kisses'.

While still sixteen, Henry decided to keep a journal. The first extract is dated 16th December 1818, from Ampthill, where the weather is 'exceedingly cold—the first hard frost we have had'. Like the page following in the steps of Good King Wenceslas, Henry plods after his father, in his social round:

Papa went to Woburn on Thursday 17th, for a night, to meet the Duke of York and a large party. . . . On the 19th the D^{ke} of York and a large party came over to a déjeuner a la fourchette, and to shoot in the laurels and woods; they shot 266 head of game . . .

His entry of Thursday, 24th (December), begins on a solemn note:

Poor Sir Philip Francis died on Tuesday in St James's Square . . .

Then he reports on a matter of universal conjecture:

His death has excited great curiosity, for it is hoped, if he really is the author of 'Junius' (the anonymously published Letters of Junius) he will have removed all doubts by avowing it. His manner of contradicting the report was not direct and certainly implied that he knew *who* the author was. He said to my mother, after she had told him that the lawyers believed him to be so, 'Well, Madam, I could bring proofs to the contrary in five minutes'. And upon being asked, I believe, by Papa, why he did not contradict the report publickly, (*sic*) he said, 'If they choose to thrust laurels on my head, why there let them stick'.

Good reporting, for a beginner. And, as a diarist, Henry Fox was in good company as the journals of both Charles Greville and Thomas Moore were published in 1818.

In August 1819, Henry seems to have gone for three days to the Lansdownes at Bowood, to attend a ball. Countess Woronzow, the bride of Lord Pembroke's brother, opened the ball and Henry remarks laconically to his mother: 'She is tolerably well looking and a pretty figure. You would admire her though she is a Pole.'

To which, from Ampthill, on 23rd August, Lady Holland makes delighted reply:

I hope you continue as well and happy as heart can wish and by this time returned to the friendly roof under which you are harboured so tenderly. Was your *launch* of

three days into the Gde Monde agreeable? I am dying to hear all about it . . . how
the Ladies looked . . . who was gay (?) and who was painted and who was rouged
. . . I hope Lady L(ansdowne?) was the prettiest woman there.

Another two and a half pages of questions follow before she gives an
account of her own improvements to the house at Ampthill.

. . . the House begins to shape itself into some sort of comfort. My own room is to
be Chinesed all over to a charm, and then the window seats are taken out, and I
can get in close and see the *dog* and the Stubbs and all the arrivals and the various
appurtenances, and the sun shines and the last ray of sunlight comes in and is as
good as you have in your own room at home, there's for you Sir . . .

Then, Lady Holland reverts to praise:

. . . oh! you Rogue! What might one not expect from you if your mind was stored
well with useful learning . . I declare solemnly that my own gratification in you
is not so great even, as the delight of having given life to such a being that does and
will give so much happiness to Papa who God knows deserves every blessing life
can yield and what is greater than to have a good son? dear Boy, dear Boy, you are
his Counterpart et c'est tout dire . . .

*

Shortly after this, Lady Holland writes from Ampthill to tell Henry
that she has been very frightened by Gina swallowing a damson stone.
That, in itself, may not have been serious, but Henry's anxiety about
Gina's health was well-founded. On 14th September, his mother tells him
that Gina is very ill—and that Miss Vernon (Aunt Ebey) and even Henry's
beloved 'little Aunty' are behaving with considerable tactlessness.

. . . entre nous it requires nerves and temper to bear with perpetual rapid lisping
tones assuring one that the child is not half so ill as many others were, especially
Vernon, and your Aunty tittering and seeming to laugh at one's folly of feeling
and fearing. In short it has been the first time since I have known them that I
sincerely rejoiced at their going away which they did yesterday. Gd Mamma also
had a tiff with Miss Vernon for her strange way of talking.

Such levity was badly misplaced. A few days later, John Whishaw
writes to Mr Smith, at Easton Grey:

. . . I have been much distressed by the accounts I have received from Ampthill
respecting the youngest daughter, Georgina, who has been seriously ill several
weeks and lately in considerable danger. Her complaint was originally bilious but is
now inflammatory of the nature apparently of pleurisy. She is now a little better
having been bled five times during a very short period. It is to be hoped her youth
will carry her through it; she has no other chance. The family is in the greatest
anxiety and affliction . . .

The Hollands decided to call in the eminent physician, Sir Henry
Halford, who sanctioned Gina's return to Holland House. On 30th

September. Lord Holland writes to tell his sister that the child has stood the journey well and that 'a good water ice' has delighted her. And, the same day, Lady Holland sends Henry six detailed pages of the stages of Gina's journey back to Kensington, carried out with the precision of a military exercise:

. . . at 9 she set off in my town coach which was fitted up as a Bed that she might lie exactly as she did in her room. In the carriage was Mr Thompson & Agatha, Wm. on the seat, followed. Mr Allen was in a light Hackney chaise . . . Mrs B. carried the refreshments such as toast & water, panada milk etc. In the Coach they had a thermomentor (*sic*) & all orders were written & shewn through the glass. The last stage the Hackney chaise took 4 hours & came at the rate of 13 miles an hour so that they might be in readiness to receive her & place her in Bed. She bore the fatigue very well & is established in your *room* with her face towards the window in order to see the trees & birds. Poor little heart she was in the midst of all this sorely tormented by Gnats, which terrified us as being likely to produce fever in the night. Happily she slept & is much as she was . . .

Lady Holland continues:

My good mother has been quite tender and affectionate to *me*, besides being of the greatest use to the dear child.

And she reiterates:

I told you what a relief it was to hear the wheels of your aunt's carriage going off, they provoked and irritated me beyond my powers of endurance. I cannot bear up when my heart is almost broken to hear fine strung phrases, and talk, upon talk, upon such disciplined minds and feelings. When I am wretched I have no control and I like those best who fluctuate in my hopes & fears . . .

At that time, despite its atmosphere of sickness, Lady William Russell was a guest at Holland House. She was near to childbirth as Henry (writing on 3rd October) asks his mother: 'Is Lady Wm still with you? She will be sadly in your way if she produces *chez vous* . . .' He sends his love to his 'dearest Gina' and now, about to go up to Oxford, ends his letter: 'Good Bye, dearest Mama, I shall be with you in a very few days.'

Before his arrival, Lady Holland has just time to complain of another inconvenient guest:

. . . poor Papa is undergoing a séance with the Duke of Sussex who slipped into the House, these Royalties are mighty troublesome, I mean the Collaterals . . .

But, on 1st November, Lord Holland pens a note to his sister:

It is over. She expired between twelve and one last night. She knew me about 5 was insensible after 7. . . . Her case was most extraordinary.

In fact, Gina died of tubercular peritonitis.

In heartbroken tones, Lord Holland communicates his sad news to Charles, at Corfu:

We have lost our poor child—& I do believe such an angel for temper feeling & understanding never existed . . . much as I always thought of your Mama's goodness of heart & strength of mind her conduct to me & to all of us on this heartbreaking occasion has raised my opinion of it & I adore her more than I ever did . . .

Lady Holland's fortitude is borne out by John Whishaw's letter, of 6th November, to Mr Smith:

Lord and Lady Holland are in the deepest affliction owing to the death of their daughter Georgina and it will be long before they recover a tolerable degree of tranquillity. At present Lady Holland bears the loss with the greater firmness; but she will feel it throughout her whole life.

A further unfortunate misunderstanding arises between her and Caroline Fox who, although practically within earshot at Little Holland House, writes to say she will not think of coming up to Holland House unless invited. Lord Holland deplores her attitude:

Lady Holland feels it must appear awkward neither to see nor write to you when so near.

But to Henry again, Lady Holland unburdens her heart about another far more distressing occurrence.

I have received an anonymous letter full of triumph at my misfortune denouncing the vengeance of God that my darling being (taken) was a judgement upon me for being a worthless mother and tyrant wife and a bad mistress and foretelling that my husband will be snatched from me and you all and that I shall be left in contempt and insignificance such as I deserve. I am at a loss to conjecture who could bear so much malice towards me, or indeed be so full of malice against any human being at such a moment.

Conjecture is useless. But it is worth mentioning that the person who had remained consistently hostile to Lady Holland since Sir Godfrey Webster's suicide, in 1800, and who had deliberately poisoned her daughter Harriet's mind against her since then, was her former sister-in-law and Harriet's guardian, Elizabeth Chaplin.

*

And what of thirteen-year-old Mary?

Lady Holland writes that she has been brought home from Ampthill languid but 'a good well-disposed girl and anxious to please'. And, thereafter, she figures little in her mother's correspondence until she grows up.

Two or three times during the spring and summer of 1820, Lord Holland makes anxious reference to Mary in his letters to Charles, and we get the impression of another delicate daughter. In January ('the bitterest winter since year 13') she too contracts pleurisy and has to lose '35 ounces of blood'. Then, two months later, she develops shingles. And, more than once, Lord Holland comments on Mary's loneliness at Holland House. 'Dear Mary recovered of her shingles pleased I am sure at returning but nervous and unhappy at her solitude.' He assures Charles that 'Nothing can be kinder than she to Mama and Mama to her' and, on 4th April, paints a brighter picture of her. 'She is very pretty' and recovering fast. But, by 2nd May, again Lord Holland voices his anxiety.

Mary improving slowly. Her health confines her to the house and makes her life poor little girl solitary and dark.

And, again, in June, he makes sober comment:

Mary is pretty and good but has not the animal spirits of the family which is unlucky for her.

Yet, away from home, Mary could enjoy herself. In September 1820 Lady Cowper invited her to stay at Panshangar from whence she returned 'delighted with Lady Cowper; the place and her friend Miny (*sic*). She was greeted on her return by her two perroquets who had nearly pined away during her absence. She is grown a beautiful girl but some think she is not yet tall enough.'

Considering Lady Holland's resentfulness of the solitariness of her own childhood, it is inexplicable that she should have brought up her daughter, Mary, in similar conditions. True, Mary had a governess and so did not have to endure the 'days hours and weeks' of solitude her mother had so bitterly condemned. And Lord Holland himself was there, ready to play the part of Anthony Storer in inspiring in Mary that love of learning which had dominated her mother's life. But, the fact remains that, as time went on, Lady Holland developed towards Mary a hectoring, bullying manner she had never shown to her other children. On one occasion, she makes positively cruel comment: '. . . the misfortune that has bowed me down, must fall upon her (Mary) and render her life less gay and more solitary . . .' She must 'amuse herself with books and writing, such was my lot for most of the years of my life and I am not perhaps the worse for it. Next to being an old maid, the life of a young one without sisters or cousins is the most melancholy . . .' Lord Ilchester tells us that Mary bore this treatment in a spirit of Christian submissiveness and that, in that atheistic household, there developed in her a strong religious feeling which remained with her through life.

Lady Holland's harshness towards Mary led to tragedy. For it alienated from her the love of her adored son, Henry Fox.

CHAPTER TWENTY-TWO

Kingdom of the Netherlands, and Paris, *1817*

1817 SEEMED TO the Hollands a propitious moment for a change of scene, with social distress at home being met by Tory legislation which Lord Holland felt would lead 'not to a suspension only but to a complete surrender and extinction of our laws and liberties'. So, hardly had Charles left for Corfu than, on 28th June that year, the Hollands plus their three other children, Henry's tutor Mr Shuttleworth, and Mr Allen left for the newly unified kingdom of the Netherlands (Holland and Belgium), Mr Allen still clinging faithfully to his dinner books, to keep them up to date, abroad. They went via Dover to Calais; Dunkirk, Ypres, Bruges, Ghent, to Brussels; and set off for Holland via Antwerp and Utrecht. On 19th July, they reached Amsterdam; on 23rd went on to Haarlem; and, from the Hague, made lightning excursions to Delft and Rotterdam. On the 29th, they retraced their breathless course, to Antwerp.

Nevertheless, from Bruges, Lady Holland manages to find time to give the Duke of Bedford a treatise on agriculture. He thanks her 'very sincerely for your *agricultural* letter from Bruges . . . very considerate in you to think of *my occupations* in the midst of the hurry and bustle of travelling . . .'

And, from Amsterdam. Lady Holland writes forthrightly to her sister-in-law:

. . . indeed there is too much water in this country for a nervous person . . . this Town is a prodigy of human industry and perseverance as is indeed the whole country. I confess I should have preferred Philip and his Inquisition to Liberty with Calvin in these marshes . . .

But, writing to Charles at Corfu, on 29th July, Lord Holland declares himself delighted with 'our famous journey thro' Holland . . . and Mama would have been but for the ferries . . .' He continues:

Away Rogues you cant come in here

I shall be PRIME

TREASURY

Then I shall be Bang Up there...

Et Moi aussi

Lord Wellington Recall

Status quo om...

Peace offering

Sketch for a *PRIME* Minister or how to purchase a *PEACE*

Photo: John Webb

'Sketch for a Prime Minister', published in the *Satirist* on
February 1st, 1811. Attributed to Samuel de Wilde

Letter from 3rd Lady Holland to Caroline Fox
(Naples, 5th and 6th March, 1815)

While writing this a carriage drives to the door and I hear it to be the Duke of Wellington in his way to the Hague. There seems to be much stir among the Generals and Ministers and I half believe that a good harvest and a revival of commerce would set the world quarrelling again . . .

Three days later, 'at night half asleep', from Brussels he writes again:

In spite of all our resolutions the attractions of Paris and the repulsions of bad inns and dull places will draw us thither and we are going to spend six weeks—we set off to-morrow—but Mama will not go post and we shall crawl as usual. . . . There is a kind of rumour but who can believe it? that my Sister and Aunt Ebey are coming to Paris. Harry looks wise and says he knows it . . .

Lord Holland reverts again to his near-miss encounter with the Duke of Wellington, and elaborates on European politics, with a hit at Lord Castlereagh:

D. of Wellington was not going to the Hague. . . . but examining fortifications of which they say he approves mightily. But if . . . the Allies of the Crown do not march a *third* time to Paris, Belgium is once more a province of France, and all we have done has been in vain—for I declare I never could discover what earthly interest England had in Continental politics but that of keeping Ostend Antwerp Rotterdam etc. etc. out of the hands of the French . . . wiser men than Castlereagh thought the separation of the Low Countries not their union was the way of doing it . . . The two dogs Castlereagh separated the other day could not snarl at one another with more fury or hate one another more cordially than the two countries of Belgium and Holland which he so notably united . . .

The Hollands arrived in Paris, on 13th August, just four weeks after the death of Madame de Staël. Neither of them mentions her death in their letters home. They lodged at the Hotel de Paris, Boulevard de la Madeleine.

Paris was crowded with English visitors, presided over by the British Ambassador, Sir Charles Stuart. The Jerseys, the Granvilles (Lord Granville Leveson-Gower had been made a Viscount in 1815), the William Russells, the Morleys, Charles Ellis, Henry Luttrell, 'Monk' Lewis, Henry Brougham.

Lady Granville gives us details of some of the frustrations Lady Holland experienced in Paris. How she had 'seven hundred pounds worth of goods ripped from a feather-bed'; how she was 'a little discomfited with the mistress of the inn' (the Hotel de Paris) who would not allow her own cook 'even to look into the kitchen'. It is plain that she surmounted these set-backs and Lady Granville declares her soirées to be 'very agreeable'.

To their French friends, the Hollands accorded equal hospitality. Madame de Coigny and General Lafayette they already knew. Now, they made a new friend, Benjamin Constant. And, each day, Lord Holland

I

widened his circle, dipping back delightedly into the brew of European politics.

To Charles he enlarges on the misfortunes of Ayanza, now on the run in Paris, condemned to death in Spain for his adherence to the French; and to Joseph Bonaparte, which fact is only of secondary importance to Lord Holland . . . 'he was very good to me in Granada, is in misfortune and d'ailleurs un homme tres raisonnable'. And, thereafter, despite the fact that Charles himself is under an oath of loyalty to his King and Country, Lord Holland expounds to him his dangerous philosophy.

I make great allowance for publick men in such trying moments as revolutions and the use made by Ferdinand of success in a just Cause, induces me to think that Spain itself was no exception to the rule that honest men may take either side on all great political emergencies.

Clearly, Lord Holland was a law unto himself, with charm enough to surmount his indiscretion in nearly every circumstance. Lady Granville finds him 'adorable', and adds:

There is something so very delightful in the artless, almost childish simplicity of his character, when united to an understanding and mind like this.

But one person on whom his charm was wasted was the Duke of Wellington, a fact relayed from Paris by Lady Granville to her sister, Lady Morpeth. In August 1817 she writes:

Lady Holland dined the other day with the Stuarts, and was very much pleased with Lady Elizabeth (his wife), but there was a very great man there who chose not to acknowledge her or Lord Holland. This has caused much discussion. The great man says they would not bow to him, and the welkin rings with the different versions.

On 15th September, Lord Holland gives Charles his own account of the incident:

D. of Wellington would not speak to me. I understand his reason was the letter I wrote to K(innard) about Ney's business. God knows I wished then and do now for his sake and from respect for his character as much almost as from other motives that he had viewed that himself as I am morally certain posterity will view it, and (had) not lent himself to a transaction which will be a stain upon his character for ever.

Lord and Lady Holland contemplated visiting General Lafayette at his country house, La Grange, near Brie, but gout struck Lord Holland down and the General had to procure him 'a wheeling chair'. Meantime, he moved his family from the Hotel de Paris to a rented house in the rue St

Lazare. On 1st September, his sister and aunt arrived in Paris and he took rooms for them 'at 100 franks a week' at 26, Rue Neuve des Mathurins.

Inevitably, the ladies succumbed to the charms of Paris, as Lord Holland reports to Charles:

. . . my sister and Aunt Ebey too take mightily to the French and to travelling and, after all their wonder at our *likings*, I shall not be surprised if they leave their little Paradise of Kensington pretty regularly at the end of the Summer to take a trip on the Continent . . . The two retired ladies of little Holland House spend all their mornings at Milliners, haberdashers, feather makers and upholsterers, then they dine at Ambassadors and Ministers and go to one or even two spectacles in the evening—that poor little garden will never hold them . . .

And in confirmation of their activities, on 10th September, Mr Allen gives a list of forty-six guests at the British Embassy, in which Caroline Fox and Elizabeth Vernon take their place.

Continued gout delayed Lord Holland's visit to General Lafayette and, on 5th October, he still writes to Charles from the rue St Lazare:

Since we have had a house and table of our own we have seen more frenchmen and more foreigners than at the Hotel de Paris. Of Spaniards, Alava whom I like extremely well . . . Lafayette and Gallois are our most frequent guests . . . (Benjamin) Constant, Girardin, and many agreeable men. During the heat of the elections our Ministerial acquaintances called very seldom but I have seen Molé (now a Minister) Pozzo di Borgo, Barenti and some of the most remarkable men of that stamp.

Then, at last, Lord Holland's attack of gout improves and Allen makes an entry in his Dinner Book: 'Went to La Grange in Brie to visit M. de Lafayette on 12th Oct. and returned on the 14th—M. Gallois went with us.'

On 3rd November, Lord Holland writes indignantly from 'a small but warm lodging' (the Hotel de l'Empire), having been peremptorily ejected from his house by

the Commissaries of the Russian and Prussian armies who had taken a lease of it and conducted themselves 'qualiter ex talibus barbaris facile expectavisses' ('as you might easily expect from such barbarians').

But he and his wife are persuaded to remain in Paris, until after 5th November, 'when the King is to open the Chamber'.

After which, Lord Holland sums up:

The great question . . . on which the nation is really agitated and anxious is the evacuation of France by the Allied troops and the amount of their pecuniary claims . . . I am more than ever pursuaded the Bourbons will not last unless they can do one of two things: wage a successful war or give themselves the air of reigning by the revolution and not in spite of it . . .

This indiscreet letter was entrusted to William Ponsonby who, with his 'Lilliputian wife', was on his way to Corfu.

On 17th November 1817, the Hollands crossed over to Dover from Calais and, two days later, were back at Holland House.

CHAPTER TWENTY-THREE

The Years of Waiting

FROM 1815 TO 1819, outstanding Whig debaters in the House of Commons disintegrated at an alarming rate. Samuel Whitbread committed suicide in July 1815 and, almost exactly a year later, Richard Brinsley Sheridan breathed his last. At his funeral, Lord Holland acted as one of the pall-bearers together with Lord Spencer, Lord Lauderdale, Lord Mulgrave and the Duke of Bedford, and he was laid to rest in Poets' Corner, Westminster Abbey. But despite his distinguished cortège, neither Lord Grenville nor Lord Grey were present to hear his funeral oration, as Sheridan had long since forfeited their trust. Of those who remained, both Francis Horner and George Ponsonby died in 1817, and Samuel Romilly took his own life, a year later. For all his brilliance, Brougham was as unpredictable as a runaway horse. He was too headstrong to lead the Whig party in Opposition, especially as he himself declared it unnecessary to have a Whig leader in the Commons, at that moment. The majority of his fellow-Whigs disagreed with his view, and almost automatically, Lady Holland's devoted admirer, George Tierney, slid into the position left vacant by George Ponsonby's death. Then he, too, collapsed from exhaustion, in 1819.

This calamitous toll among the Whigs was rendered the more disturbing by the fact that, in 1816, George Canning returned to the Government, with a seat in the Cabinet, at the Board of Control. As Lord Holland writes: 'No man was so well qualified as Mr Canning to cope in debate with the established as well as rising orators in Opposition', but, by 1819, the established orators in Opposition in the House of Commons had been reduced to a minimum. Among the rising Whig orators, after his brilliant speech against 'Suspension', in 1818, through ill-health, Lord John Russell had to apply for the Chiltern Hundreds and did not return to active politics for another year.

Tierney's main problem was to insure the regular attendance of Opposition members and to try to inspire some consistent enthusiasm in 'the waverers'. So, in the Commons, before a debate of importance, Lord Duncannon (eldest son of Lord and Lady Bessborough) gradually assumed the responsibility of rounding up the Whig members, while, in the Lords, Lord Holland undertook a similar duty. But George Tierney himself evolved no practical system to facilitate such contacts and, with Lord Grey still making pronouncements by long distance from Northumberland, he merely sat back to 'wait for circumstances'.

In the elections of 1818, the Whigs regained some ground. Lord Grey hoped that 'the popular enthusiasm for retrenchment, economy and reform' would be reflected in the new Parliament and even he, usually so cautious, urged Tierney to cash in on the enthusiasm of the new members. But Tierney would not be rushed.

So, it was the more surprising when (to quote Lord Holland) on 18th May 1819, Tierney suddenly moved 'a Committee on the state of the nation', virtually indicting the Government and demanding its dismissal. His policy of waiting on events flung to the winds, this motion had the effect of rallying 'the waverers' to the Government side with a decisive vote against him. Lord Holland writes: 'Mr Tierney was much disconcerted at this result, and it was not . . . long ere he renounced the leadership which he had assumed.' Later, Thomas Creevey, by then member for Appleby, made a malicious attack on Tierney in the House of Commons, which caused Lady Holland to fly to her friend's defence. Creevey reports the matter to his step-daughter, Elizabeth Ord:

Holland House is the only place I have heard of as being in a state of rage at my attack on Cole (Tierney) . . . Sefton told me last night of a conversation he had had with Thanet. It seems Lady Holland had complained to the latter in the strongest terms of my conduct to Tierney . . . 'What did Thanet do or say?' says I. 'Why' says Sefton, 'he . . . said you was quite right and that the Whigs were little better than old apple-women'.

After Tierney's resignation, Lord Holland concludes:

The guidance of the (Whig) party thus devolved to the guidance of three or four men of weight (such as Lords Althorp and Tavistock) and others stimulated by Brougham, or to that of chance itself.

And, although after the 'Massacre of Peterloo', the way seemed open to bring down the Government, once more the Whigs were too divided to take concerted action. In 1820, the Cato Street conspiracy to murder His Majesty's Ministers shocked Parliament and public alike and the Tory party remained in office for another ten years.

*

To the 'Stalwarts', the Hollands kept open house, but as always, all shades of opinion were freely expressed at their table. By the Tory lords Aberdeen, Minto and Granville; by the diarists Creevey, Greville and Thomas Moore; by the novelist. Sir Walter Scott; by Thomas Malthus, political economist; by painters Sir Thomas Lawrence and David Wilkie. And, once or twice a year, one or other of the Royal brothers, the Dukes of York or Sussex, gave free rein to their opinions too. Now Mr Allen's lists of foreigners covered all parts of Europe: Count Palmella (Portugal), the Duke and Duchess of San Carlos (Spain), Count Pozzo di Borgo (Russia), Madame de Coigny and the Flahaults (France), Ugo Foscolo (Italy).

Now and then, host or hostess was unwell and 'did not dine at table'. Or, Lord Holland stayed late at the House of Lords where, occasionally, Lady Holland listened unseen to a debate, hidden behind a curtain in the Peeresses' Gallery. And sometimes, one or other of them went to the play. (At Drury Lane, Lady Holland always had her own box.) But, provided husband or wife was there to preside, the entertainment at Holland House went on.

Lady Holland had never bothered to mind her words and often spoke impulsively and too freely, sometimes hurting those she held most dear.

There were instances, in 1818 and 1823, when even her happy relations with the Bedfords were in jeopardy, saved by the Duke's unalterable tact and affection for her. In 1818, it reached the Duchess's ears that Lady Holland had complained of the noisiness of her room at Woburn and, that October, the Duke gently admonishes Lady Holland and tells her it would be 'better to put off coming to us till a later period when the house will be less full, and we shall be able to lodge you more to your wishes . . .' And he tells her that 'the Duchess is very much amused with a joke of Lord Eynmouth. The world you know will have it, that you and the Duchess have quarrelled, and about the foolish story of the room. Lord E calls it the Feuds of Elizabeth Queen of England and Mary Queen of Scots.' (The Duchess had been a Gordon.) In 1823, the Duke deals frankly with a further misunderstanding. Prefacing it by declaring that 'the Duchess imagines that both you and Holland have been cold to her' he goes on to say

(she) thinks you propose to *me* to go abroad with you and Holl^d and leave *her* in England!—it is vain that I endeavour to persuade her that it is morally impossible that such a proposal could come from *you*, so you must write to her, yourself, and set her too sensitive mind at rest.

This was the tactful handling of one who loved her but, to the world at large, Lady Holland's imperiousness had long since made her very unpopular. Countless acts of kindness bound her to her intimates, many of them unknown outside her own circle, but to the gossips of the day like Jekyll, Creevey and Greville, her eccentricities made amusing if malicious recording and these have come down to posterity. At this date we can instance the gratitude of such disparate women as 'Madame Mère' and Augusta Leigh and, of men, not only that of half-a-dozen devoted friends like Sydney Smith, John Allen, John Whishaw, Matthew Marsh, George Tierney and Henry Luttrell, but of such contrasting characters as Sir Thomas Lawrence and Napoleon Bonaparte. These grateful utterances remain privately expressed in Lady Holland's papers and, except for the message sent her by Napoleon, they have not yet reached the world.

In 1819, little Gina's death put an added strain on her bearing in public. That year, she gave an impression of gratuitous rudeness to the American, George Ticknor, when, at their first meeting, Lady Holland observed that she understood that New England was first colonised by convicts from the mother-country. This ungracious remark Ticknor countered by declaring that he certainly knew that two memorials in Massachusetts still existed to her Vassall forebears: a house, in Cambridge; and a marble monument to Samuel Vassall, in King's Chapel, Boston, and, later, he acknowledged that Lady Holland took his snub in good part and mended her manners towards him. That he himself was in no position to be critical is proved by Henry Fox in his journal (February 1820). 'Mr Ticknor, the American, is at Woburn, but has offended the Duchess by his rudeness and want of manners . . .'

Joseph Jekyll declared that the Hollands presented the two ends of a magnet: he, the attractive end, she the repulsive. Yet, during the Queen's trial, in 1820, Lady Granville tells her sister:

I went yesterday to Lady Cowper's, and found Lady Holland the only really undisputed monarchy in Europe, sitting in a corner, throne and footstool, courtiers and *dames d'honneur*, all *dans les règles*.

Until Lord Holland achieved office, in 1830, Creevey, the time-server, is at his most waspish in describing Holland House and its mistress. Nicknaming Lady Holland 'Old Madagascar' (after Caroline Lamb's cruel parody of her in her novel *Glenarvon*), he mercilessly criticises mistress and background. Yet, early on, his name features frequently in the Dinner Books, in May 1819 as often as three times in one week. A year later, he has turned against his former friends. He tells his step-daughter, '. . . As for the wretched dirt and meanness of Holland House, it makes me perfectly sick . . .' And a, few months later, he encloses '. . . a little love-letter I got from Lady Holland some days ago. It was preceded by a message to the same effect a day or two before; but, as you may suppose, I have taken no notice of either.' Then, he brags that, as a result of Lord Holland's reproach that he never 'comes near my lady', he is induced to visit Lady Holland, in her husband's company, at Holland House, where she is 'all civility and *humility*'. In 1822, Creevey describes Lady Holland's acquisition of a large and vicious cat which scratches Rogers; is kept at bay, with snuff, by Brougham; and which finally goads good-tempered Luttrell into refusing all further invitations to Holland House until the odious animal has been removed.

In 1824, Charles Greville had some estrangement with Lady Holland and did not return to Holland House for seven years. But, in 1830, he describes a dinner with 'the Chancellor' (Lord Eldon):

> . . . Granvilles, Hollands, Moore, Luttrell, Lord Lansdowne, Auckland . . . very agreeable . . . Lady Holland and I are very friendly; the first time I have met her in company since our separation (for we have never quarrelled). She is mighty anxious to get me back for no other reason than because I won't go.

A year later, he is recording in his journal:

> . . . Dined with Lady Holland, first time for seven years, finished the quarrel, and the last of the batch; they should not last for ever . . .

So, if the opinion of these three men-about-town was initially against her, wherein lay Lady Holland's power to lure them back again? For not even Joseph Jekyll stayed away for long. To this question there appear to be four answers. Firstly, the almost universal acknowledgement of Lord Holland's charm, divided between his sunny personality and his entrancing conversation. Secondly, the high mental quality of the guests he attracted. George Ticknor admits that, in the Holland House Circle, there was to be found 'a literary society not to be equalled in Europe'. Thirdly, Lady Holland's admittedly tyrannical but undoubted skill in playing off her guests. In later years, Sir Henry Holland, her physician and by then one of her greatest friends, so describes her:

> Supreme in her own mansion and family, she exercised a singular and seemingly capricious tyranny even over guests of the highest rank . . . Capricious it seemed, but there was in reality *intention* in all she did; and this intention was the maintenance of power, which she gained and strenuously used, though not without discretion in fixing its limits. No one knew better when to change her mood, and to soothe by kind and flattering words the provocation she had just given . . .

And Sydney Smith had already paid her this tribute:

I*

Some of the best and happiest days of my life I have spent under your roof, and though there may be (in) some houses, particularly in those of our eminent prelates, a stronger disposition to pious exercises and as it were devout lucubration I do not believe all Europe can produce as much knowledge, wit and worth as passes in and out of your door under the nose of Thomas the porter.

The fourth and final answer is by no means the least important: the excellent quality of Lady Holland's food.

Abraham Hayward maintains that this lay in her habit of levying forfeits of meat, game 'or any other edible' on those friends living in districts where such commodities abounded and, in her correspondence, there are many instances to confirm this view.

On the first day of each year, Sydney Smith sends her a cheese. And, despite his modest means, from 1801 onwards for forty years, Matthew Marsh sends her wild duck, partridges, truffles, live eels, trout, Irish salmon, a side of bacon (with instructions not to throw away the gammon), 'grass butter' (a great favourite), honey in the comb, and hams. Again over a period of thirty years or so, less surprisingly, the Duke of Bedford supplies her with grouse, venison, pheasants, woodcock, 'a fine lively turtle', fish, and 'ruffs and reeves'. He sends her recipes: woodcock-pie with truffles; '. . . if you ever eat so vulgar a thing as a Hodge Podge it is excellent made of venison instead of mutton'. And he extols his own chêf's prowess in cooking a turtle though, provokingly, he withholds his recipe for doing so.

For special delicacies from abroad, Lady Holland enlists the help of the Diplomatic Corps. Mr Van de Weyer, Netherlands Ambassador to the Court of St James, procures her half a sheep from the Ardennes; Comte de Bourke, Danish Minister in Paris, repeatedly sends her a ham of wild boar ('jambon de sanglier'); and Lord Aberdeen, who writes from Nice, tells her 'the oil is delicious' and sends her a consignment of it. Also, he gives her a recipe for olives stuffed with anchovies.

To co-ordinate all these delicacies, at one point, the Duke of Bedford recommends a young chef, Dieudonné, sometime in his employ. His talents 'are much beyond mediocre' and although not 'un *cordon bleu*, il ne *gâte pas ses provisions* . . . clean . . . good humoured and willing servant . . . young and capable of much improvement under good direction'. In fact, he is as emphatically in favour of Dieudonné as he is against another chef, Silvestre '. . . lived with me some months . . . but he is a foolish troublesome man and a miserable *chef d'Office* as he knows nothing of this metier—he makes good Ices, but his *confitures* are very bad . . .'

In 1828, Lady Holland writes to tell Henry that the Marquis de

Talleyrand's famous chef, Louis, has come over to England to learn some English dishes. She exclaims: 'Bless the poor man, what can he learn beyond melted butter and raw beef steak.' But she admits that there is one 'a very common and good dish . . . which is good and delicious to those who can eat potatoes, I am not one, called *Irish Stew* . . . It is really good . . .'

*

On 29th January 1820, George III died and, at once, the precarious position of the new King's estranged wife occupied all minds. George IV persuaded his Ministers to bring in a Bill for her divorce and, for the latter part of the year, its passage through the House of Lords riveted public attention.

Preceding and during the Queen's trial, again the Whigs were disunited. To quote: 'Lord Grey and the Old Whigs shrank from espousing the cause of the Queen . . . Holland House held aloof from the movement.' But, in his heart of hearts, Lord Holland's sympathies lay with the Queen, as Creevey points out:

Holland set off at *four* this morning for Oxford, to help Lord Jersey at his county meeting (in support of Queen Caroline). It was with the greatest difficulty my lady let him go, and he begged me not to mention it before her as it was a *very sore subject*.

It was plain that Lady Holland was loath to jeopardise possible advantages accruing to her from the new King's reign and, knowing her imperious temperament, it is easy to understand how she felt. After twenty-four years of ostracism from the Court of George III, during which she had been forced to create a rival if unrecognised court of her own, now, at last, she had the chance to win her way back into orthodox Society, and so she played safe. Even as late as 1824, Creevey is telling his step-daughter:

Would you believe it? Lady H. would not let Holland dine with Lord Lansdowne last week—a dinner made purposely for Mina (a Spanish General, who had served under Wellington), merely because she thought it might not please the King if he heard of it! Nor will she let Mina or any Spaniard approach Holland House for the same reason. Was there ever such a—?

Alas! not for the first or last time, Lord Holland's contentious views cut through his lady's plans.

On 24th February 1821, Thomas Creevey passed on this information to Elizabeth Ord:

. . . I am afraid you don't see the *Times*, otherwise you would read in it Holland's apology for having said in his speech in the House of Lords that the Emperor of

Russia was concern'd in his father's death. Lady Holland has never slept since; Madame Lieven declines all further intercourse with the Hollands, and, in short, the contemptible statement in the *Times*, tho' anonymous, is from Holland himself, and made as his peace offering to the Emperor of all the Russias, the Lievens and the Princess of Madagascar.

Once again, foreign affairs had roused Lord Holland to indiscretion.

In 1815 the rulers of Russia, Austria and Prussia had signed a pact know as the Holy Alliance, which became symbolic of the maintenance of autocratic government in Europe. All European rulers signed it, save the Prince Regent, the Pope and the Sultan of Turkey. In 1820, in Spain, insurrection broke out again, this time against the despotic cruelty of her restored King, Ferdinand VII.

To this new revolt against monarchical tyranny, Lord Holland's favourable reaction was inevitable. He exulted with the Cortes when it forced King Ferdinand into craven submission to the restoration of its Constitution of 1812, specially drafted to limit his authority. And, thereafter, he declared: 'The Spanish Constitution of 1812 ran like wildfire through the south of Europe. It was proclaimed at Naples, where no copy of it was to be found and within a month it was adopted in Portugal likewise.'

Like his nephew in Spain, Ferdinand IV of Naples had to accept the new constitution. But, in 1821, he asked for help from the Holy Alliance, meeting at the Congress of Laybach. As a result, the Austrian army suppressed the revolution in Naples. Neither Britain or France protested against this aggression and Lord Holland hinted darkly that 'George IV no doubt rejoiced in secret at the failure of any endeavours to check the anti-revolutionary intervention of Austria' and, further, that a Cabinet weakened by the resignation of Canning was willing to pander to 'his ruling prejudices and prepossessions'.

During February and March Lord Holland spoke often and violently against the resolutions taken at the Congress of Laybach. On one occasion, he was called to order by Lord Harrowby (Lord President of the Council), thereby, as he claims, distorting the sense of his remarks. What he had intended to say was that

It ill became the Czar Alexander to charge those who derived their power from insurrection . . . with being necessarily accessories after the fact to the perpetration of a crime, when he was himself sitting on the throne reeking with the blood of his own father, and would . . . by a parity of reasoning, be exposed to the unfounded or, at least, questionable imputation of being cognisant of and responsible for the murder.

(On 11th March 1801, the mad Czar Paul had been assassinated in his bedroom in St Michael's Palace, St Petersburg. The news had been communicated to his son and heir-apparent, Alexander, by one of the murderers, both he and Alexander resident in the palace.)

Whatever he had intended to say, the speech 'raised an uproar in Europe' and Creevey is pretty accurate in his interpretation of its effects. Lord Holland himself admits that 'the diplomatic agents of Russia felt or affected great indignation' and, up to the time of the Czar Alexander's death (in 1825), 'they pointedly avoided my society'. Princess Lieven refused all invitations to Holland House and, according to Lord Holland, Prince Lieven, 'a very gentlemanlike man' had ideas of challenging him to a duel. Worst of all, his old friend, Count Pozzi di Borgo, told him he could no longer invite him to his house, or accept his invitations, in return.

The reverberations of his unfortunate speech surged round Lord Holland for another three years. In 1824, Prince Metternich refused to allow him to cross the Imperial frontier into Austria. And, writing from Spa, Lord William Russell thus describes her husband to Lady Holland: 'He is looked upon as a levelling, sanguinary monarch-dethroning savage on the Continent. Lord H.! ! ! !' Small comfort to a lady who was hoping to gain admittance to the Court of her own King, George IV.

But, by 27th March, that year, Lady Holland's fears of offending King George by inviting revolutionary Spaniards to her home seem to have been dispelled. For, on that day, a special banquet at Holland House took place, to welcome Don Agostin Arguelles and General Mina. And, two years later (on 14th June 1826) the Duke of Wellington himself accepted to dine at Holland House, to meet another distinguished Spaniard (who had also served under him), General Alava. A price had been put on the General's head by Ferdinand VII and, in 1823, he had fled to England. 'There, he was welcomed everywhere with open arms, except by the Court.'

Upon which, inevitably, Lord Holland makes his point.

George IV, who wears his crown in virtue of the exclusion of the Stuarts, affected not to forgive a Spaniard for concurring, in a moment of national danger, in the temporary dethronement of a King more unwarlike than James I, more perfidious than either Charles, and more arbitrary and cruel than James II.'

*

In varying degrees, during the seven years from 1821 to 1828, the deaths of five men and two women had their effect on the Hollands' lives. Two of them had been intimate friends of Lady Holland's: Lady Bessborough and T. P. She expresses her feelings about both of them, to Henry Fox.

About Lady Bessborough, who had died in Florence, on 14th November 1821, she writes:

... I have been dreadfully shocked by the acct which arrived this post from Florence, poor Lady Bessborough ... I feel all her great kindness rush upon my recollection so addio dear Boy from (a) very melancholy E V H.

And, on hearing of T. P.'s death (on 4th July 1826) she tells Henry:

Lord Chichester is dead. He was a very old friend of mine; and there was a period in his life, for several years, that he would have sacrificed that life and all he held dear for me. But tho' I esteemed him, I never could return his devotion ...

With her usual candour she ends up:

I have had latterly very little intercourse with him; as his wife disliked his coming, or in any way communicating with me.

*

On 7th May 1821, Napoleon Bonaparte died on St Helena, Princess Pauline Borghese announcing the fact to Lord Holland, in her letter of 11th July. On 10th September, in full uniform, Count Bertrand and General Montholon delivered Napoleon's bequest of his snuff-box to Lady Holland, at Holland House. Other relics followed. On 28th November, Countess Montholon delivered to Lady Holland a crystal locket, containing a thin strand of Napoleon's hair, tied with faded tricolor string; a miniature cross of the Legion of Honour, worn by Napoleon, was presented to Lady Holland by Count Flahault; Napoleon's gold ring, set with an emerald and two small diamonds, was sent her by Countess Bertrand, together with one of his socks, worn at the time of his death. While they were in England, the Bertrands and Montholons dined several times at Holland House. But one former member of the personnel on St Helena was no longer welcome there. When Sir Hudson Lowe called to pay his respects, he was refused admittance. And, later, a letter was sent him declaring that, in future, 'any personal interview was undesirable.'

Fifteen months after Napoleon Bonaparte's death, he who had doggedly held together the Grand Alliance in Europe to achieve its arch-enemy's destruction, died by his own hand. Worn out by overwork and the accumulating fears of a disordered mind, on 12th August 1822, Castlereagh (who had succeeded his father, the year before, as 2nd Marquess of Londonderry) slit his throat.

At home, this hideous act altered the whole political scene, opening up new visions of office for the Whigs.

After Queen Caroline's death, Lord Liverpool made an attempt to bring back George Canning into the Cabinet, which was vetoed by George IV. Nevertheless, he offered Canning the post of Governor-General of India, which was accepted. On the eve of his departure for India, Canning dined at Holland House. There, he and Lord Holland discussed Reform which Canning declared to be inevitable. So much so, that he professed himself glad that he would be away 'while the measure was accomplished'.

He got no further.

On receipt of the news of Castlereagh's death, Lord Liverpool and the Duke of Wellington sought audience with the King and insisted that only Canning could assume the role of Foreign Secretary. Hard though he fought against their view, in the end George IV accepted it, and after an interval of twelve years Canning was back at the Foreign Office.

In February 1827, paralytic illness forced Lord Liverpool to resign the premiership, and for six weeks Government was without a head. Then, in April, despite the King's mistrust and that of many of his own colleagues, Canning formed a Cabinet.

Both Tories and Whigs alike split on the issue. Considering that Canning had neither the wish nor the power 'to force the Catholic question', Lord Grey would not go near him. But on the grounds that if they and other Whigs of similar views took office they would keep the ultra-Tories out, Lord Lansdowne, Lord Palmerston, Lord Dudley, Lord Carlisle and George Tierney joined Canning's government. Lord Holland did not join it, but made it plain that he would support it, as long as Lord Lansdowne was part of the Ministry and took the lead in the House of Lords.

This attitude of mind estranged him, for the first time in his life, from his leader, Lord Grey. And, although Lord Holland quickly sought to reassure his old friend, the Duke of Bedford wrote to tell him that, as a result, he had found Lord Grey 'more than usually low' and 'quite broken-hearted'.

But Canning's premiership was short-lived. By the end of the Parliamentary session he was very ill, and died at the Duke of Devonshire's villa at Chiswick on 8th August 1827.

To her nephew, Henry, Caroline Fox draws a comparison between the deaths of Charles James Fox and George Canning, in the same place, instancing Lady Holland's foreboding that Canning was unwise to accept the Duke's offer.

One and twenty years ago at this season of the year, and in the same house, we were awaiting a like fatal event, but in my partial eyes at least the loss of a much more truly great man. It is strange, passing strange; and your Mamma says with a superstitious fear she deprecated his going to Chiswick, and (which was rather hard) scolded the Duke of Devonshire for offering it to him.

Canning was replaced, as Prime Minister, by Frederick Robinson, Lord Goderich, in whom nobody placed much confidence, least of all the wife of an Opposition peer. Early in 1828, Lady Holland met him dining with Lord Aberdeen, and made it plain that she was not impressed:

What a man for a Prime Minister! It is really laughable, and one cannot wonder any government of which he was the head would speedily melt away.

Although he had been encouraged to do so when Canning formed his Cabinet and, probably, was again approached to do so when Canning died, to Lady Holland's intense annoyance Lord Holland persistently refused to accept office. Furthermore, he slapped down Lord Lansdowne's insinuation that 'a promotion in the peerage . . . was to be had for the asking', declaring that he would not contemplate an approach of that kind. And, so violently did he feel on the subject that, for once in his life, he snubbed his wife. As John Cam Hobhouse relates:

From first to last she (Lady Holland) had wished Lord Holland to take office; and . . . he had requested her to leave him alone, and not give advice either one way or other.

That Lady Holland loudly voiced her disappointment is emphasised by Caroline Fox to her nephew:

Could you by any means pursuade your mama to put a padlock on her tongue, and take up what Tierney calls the dignified line? She would be much more likely to accomplish the object she has at heart than by the course she now pursues . . . If she would neither attend to gossipping hearsay or repeat it, nor while she sneers herself teach the rest to sneer, believe me she would do the State some service and herself too.

Hardly a tactful line with which to uphold Henry's respect for his mother.

In December, 1829, the *coup de grâce* was administered to Lady Holland by an unsuspected hand. From his boyhood up, she had turned to Lord John Russell with a trust in his judgment she had never evinced in that of her own children. Now she asked him why Lord Holland had not been invited to join Lord Goderich's administration. And, with commendable courage, Lord John replied:

If you must know, it is because no man will act in a Cabinet with a person whose wife opens all his letters.

After only four months of office, in January 1828, Lord Goderich resigned the premiership. Which prompts Joseph Jekyll to vent his spleen on Lady Holland:

Lady Holland is the only dissatisfied Minister out of office. She counted on sailing down daily with her long-tailed blacks and ancient crane-necked chariot to sit with Holland at the Secretary's office, to administer the affairs of England and make Sydney Smith a Bishop.

He is more lenient to her husband:

As for him, he never cared two pence about the whole job, and the delightful fellow was very wise in so treating it.

*

On 19th April 1824, Lord Byron died at Missolonghi, and 'le diable boiteux' was transformed, for the Greeks, into a national hero. In England, his friends mishandled his memory. Byron had given his memoirs, written between 1818 and 1821, to his friend, the Irish poet, Thomas Moore, to do with as he liked, and Moore had sold them to John Murray, the publisher, for £2,000. But Byron had also left Moore light-hearted instructions, to show the memoirs 'to the elect'. Using his own discretion, Moore had done this, but had left out Byron's devoted friend, John Cam Hobhouse, a slight the latter never forgave.

At Holland House, Moore was a constant visitor and, when he showed the memoirs to the Hollands, he was taken aback by their reactions. Rather unkindly, he pointed out certain adverse comments on Lady Holland to which, although Lady Holland stoutly declared herself unaffected by them, Lord Holland took exception and condemned the sale to Murray. In this he was joined by Lord Lansdowne, to whose patronage and hospitality Moore was also beholden. Already, Moore well knew how fond Lady Holland had been of Byron. Once, she had declared to him that, whatever his faults, Byron's wife could not have helped loving him. 'He was such a loveable person. I can remember his sitting there, with that light upon him, looking so beautiful.' So now he had second thoughts.

The funeral pyre flared up afresh fed by Medwin's 'Conversations' and other inflammatory biographies, and fanned by Hobhouse's counter-attacks. The history of these and the destruction of the memoirs is well known. By this act of sacrilege Hobhouse hoped to preserve his friend's good name not realising that it released rumour on the world, and silenced for ever irrefutable answers to calumny. Lady Holland thought she had found in the memoirs an admission of Byron's incestuous relationship with his half-sister Augusta Leigh. But, later, Moore managed to convince her that she had been mistaken, and she voiced this opinion in a letter to Henry Fox, dated 16th July 1824.

Distressed and harassed by the scandalous assertions in Medwin, on a Friday evening circa November 1824, Augusta Leigh writes Lady Holland her own views on him, and Hobhouse's pamphlet.

My dear Lady Holland

When you asked me today whether I had heard any more of ye reasons for the suppression of Mr Hobhouse's pamphlet, I quite forgot that I had heard from Mr H. since I had the pleasure of dining with you—and that he had said that 'upon consideration he thought it better not to come into collision with Medwin—that he was not a fit antagonist for any Man of Honour.' Since then I have received a letter from my Brother's Servant who had been in his service 20 years and who had come up from the country upon hearing of or reading this Book of Medwin's, and in the greatest despair at it, being much attached poor man!—He tells me that my Brother was in the habit of sending Mr Medwin from his door and saying he would never see him except out riding when others would be present—this proves I think sufficiently what an Imposter he must be—But I am very sorry that Mr Hobhouse did not proceed. So many disagreeable things will (be) and *are* said in consequence. As you are so kind as to take an interest in the subject I will not apologise for troubling you with this note—for I could not say much to you when I called today. Pray do not torment yourself to answer and believe me

My dear Lady Holland

Very sincerely and obliged

Augusta Leigh.

The vindication of Lord Byron's good name would have been better left to the testimony of his servant.

*

Separated from her husband for the last three years of her miserable, drink-sodden life, Caroline Lamb died in January 1828. After the publication of her novel *Glenarvon*, with its vindictive parody of Lady Holland as 'the Princess of Madagascar', Lady Holland had quietly cut her out of her life. But, a few weeks before her death, Caroline attempts to be reconciled with her former friend. Dated January 1828, she sends Lady Holland a note,

I can only write one line to thank you for your generous conduct. Will you accept from my heart my deep regret for the past—it makes me most unhappy now.

I trust I may see you—if not believe me with every affectionate and grateful feeling.

Yours

Caroline Lamb.

Did this last protestation, one of so many proved worthless, finally soften Lady Holland's feelings towards Caroline? Or did she stick to her grim condemnation of her, made four years before? 'She was not mad, only wicked from temper and brandy.'

*

After Lord Goderich's departure from office, George IV appointed the Duke of Wellington Prime Minister. Upon which there was a general resignation, led by Lord Lansdowne, of the Canningite Whigs in the Government. Anxious to keep them, the Duke bribed them with concessions to their principles and they agreed to serve under him. But a Government with such different opinions could not last. It broke, because of its divergent views as to how to apportion the seat left vacant by the disfranchisement of the borough of East Retford. The Duke and his followers favoured giving the seat to a county: more democratically, the Canningites, led by Huskisson, wanted to give it to a manufacturing town. When these two views remained incompatible Huskisson and the Canningites resigned and the Duke determined to soldier on, without them. But, he, too, was doomed. In 1829, the agitation for Catholic Emancipation was so strong that he was forced to repeal the anti-Catholic laws. And in 1830, the movement for Parliamentary Reform swept all before it. The Duke of Wellington's Ministry went out and, at long last, a Whig Ministry under Lord Grey came in, pledged to Reform.

CHAPTER TWENTY-FOUR

Difficult Sons and Docile Daughter

In June 1818, on leave of absence, Charles wanted to change his job. Now he wanted to transfer from Sir Frederick Adam's staff, at Corfu, to active service in a regiment. Furthermore, he wanted promotion.

As usual, his father pulled every wire he could think of to gratify his wishes, and on 2nd November, he writes Charles to tell him he has purchased him a lieutenancy.

so cheap that I shall not come upon your principal (capital?) or interest for any part of the purchase money . . . Per contra you will scarcely be gazetted as Lieut of the York Rangers but you will be reduced to half pay so that far from improving you will diminish yr. income by your promotion.

Three weeks later, Lord Holland announces that Charles has been gazetted 'first as a Lieutenant in the York Rangers . . . and the day before yesterday as exchanged from said regiment to the 8th now in the Mediterranean'. He adds: 'The Duke of York did this latter most handsomely by which he meant to move you from half pay in the service.'

Lord Ilchester maintains that, throughout his life, Henry Webster was jealous of Charles Fox and that, because of this, the Hollands had to engineer to keep the half-brothers apart. Considering the indoctrination against his mother Henry had received in his childhood, prejudice against Charles Fox probably stuck. His maternal grandmother, Lady Affleck, showed him every indulgence and he was encouraged to treat Holland House as his own home. But there were unpremeditated instances in his life there when his jealousy could have been aroused.

Charles's wire-pulled promotion could have been one of them as Henry's own career, as a regular soldier, had not gone too well, of late. A seasoned campaigner, wounded at Vittoria, fighting at Waterloo and, thereafter, decorated for his service to the Prince of Orange, in September 1817, he had been 'named without application' to Sir Charles Greville's regiment in Ireland and had refused to go, when Lord Holland had written an account of his indiscretion to Charles:

Henry Webster is named without application or expectation to a company in Sr Charles Greville's regiment which I understand to be in Ireland. I hope he will join though it is certainly strange to have named him in that way and is somewhat provoking to him to break in upon a scheme of travel and amusement which he had made up his mind to for two years.

In March that year, Henry had started off abroad armed with letters of introduction from Lord Holland 'and Marshal Saxe's pistols'. But Lord Holland had told him that he thought he had already promised the pistols to Charles so that he, Henry, could only look on them as a loan from Charles. Henry promptly left them behind, in a hackney-coach. Upon which, Lord Holland declared that, if ever found, the pistols would become Charles's 'by double right of previous possession and forfeiture by carelessness'. Eventually they were found but, thereafter, Henry was only allowed to use them 'on loan' by a younger brother who, up till then, had never heard a shot fired. A petty humiliation to a regular soldier calculated to arouse resentment in a jealous person. Probably, Charles's promotion confirmed it.

Lord Lauderdale had been instrumental in getting Charles his original staff appointment to Major General Sir Frederick Adam, at Corfu. And, probably, he had effected this by applying direct to the General-in-Command Mediterranean, Lt. Gen. Sir Thomas Maitland, who happened to be his brother. Hardly had Charles arrived in Corfu (June 1817) than his father warned him that Sir Frederick might change to a command under the Duke of Wellington. But, should he do so, Charles was not to worry. 'I know I can contrive to get you on the staff to Sr Thˢ Maitland or some general under him.'

To his credit, a year as staff officer was enough for Charles and he arrived home (in June 1818) determined on a more active military career. But, where he was keen to see active service, for the moment his half-brother, Henry Webster, had had enough of it. So, after his injudicious refusal to go to Ireland, Henry himself was anxious to get on to Sir Thomas Maitland's staff in the Mediterranean, but failed in his endeavour.

The result was a searing, terrible letter written from Florence to his mother, dated 22nd August 1818. It covers five pages of invective, accusing her of 'tricks and intrigues'; bad conduct towards Henry 'for the last 3 years'; and wants to know

by what authority you refused the offer of Sir Thomas Maitland to take me as his Aid de Camp—what induced you to direct certain relations of his to prevent him from making any propositions that might be favourable to me. In fact doing everything you could devise to make him, and them, fancy that I was a fool incapable and unworthy of serving him, damning by these means my military character, which is mean on your part, injuring my private one, which is equally unkind, blasting my prospects in a profession which I must live by . . . You know you have been guilty of this but your first feeling will be to deny it . . . if you will not acknowledge it, I tell you this conduct is infamous, and in the name of God what have I done to deserve it from you, whom I have treated through life with the sincerest love and affection . . . You will say there are few filial sentiments in this letter, true, but you must not expect love for unkindness, sincerity for double dealing, and affection for those petty crimes which you affect to disapprove (of) so much in others, and constantly practise yourself . . . this my mother is the first time I have been roused, God send it may be the last, for if I feel my nature utterly and entirely changed, you are the sole cause of it . . .

He commands:

. . . You may write to Sir Thomas Maitland—saying that his employing me as his personal staff, would be a favor to yourself and me—that I am *capable* and very well *disposed* to be of service to him . . .

There was much in his letter to remind Lady Holland of the violent fits of rage to which his father, Sir Godfrey, had been prone. And his fluctuations of mood were very much the same. For after five pages of blistering invective, mildly, Henry ends up '. . . do not force me to be otherwise than your affectionate son—Henry'.

Two months later, he realises that he has been wrongly informed, which Lord Holland confirms in a letter to Charles, dated 17th October.

. . . Your Mama meant to answer your letter with which she was much pleased. She had received one from Hry Webster in which he says he hopes she will forget his nonsense and apply to Sr Thomas. I think she will try to do the first but the second will at least be deferred till she is satisfied that he thinks himself quite wrong in his suspicions and will not attribute any exertion of hers to fears of his threatened vengeance. Pray advise him when he feels angry not to put pen to paper for he brandishes his pen as a drunken dragoon does his sword and scarcely knows the things he says. Perhaps they are nonsense but they are a good deal besides nonsense . . .

Ten days later, Henry Webster writes his step-father a letter full of contrition, from Rome. And, from Naples, on 19th November, he writes Lady Holland a letter beginning 'My dearest Mother' in which he agrees to abide by her decision as to when to approach Sir Thomas Maitland, through Lord Lauderdale. '. . . You . . . are the best judge of what ought to be done.' This time, he ends up: 'I kiss you my dear Mother, my love to all'.

Had not Lady Holland kept Henry Webster's letter of 22nd August, we might have been tempted to deduce, from the last one, that the gentle, obedient young man who wrote it was the easiest of all her sons.

Lord Holland's letter to Charles, of 11th December 1818, shows him unable and unwilling to help Henry further.

> Henry Webster writes cheerfully and pleasantly but he mistakes me about you and Sir Thomas. I did not say anything done for him would interfere with his promotion but I did say . . . that after he (Sir Thomas) had promised *you* one thing it would have an appearance of encroaching on a person on whom I have no claims to ask for another favour. However I happen to know indirectly that he (Sir Thomas) would refuse it be it asked by whom it may be but with Henry Webster's wrong head I am afraid of saying so because he would fancy that his mother who has as much to do with Sr. Thomas's decisions as the Great Cham of Tartary was at the bottom of it . . .

But eventually, all ends well, as Lady Holland confirms to Henry Fox:

> Henry Webster desires his next letters to be addressed to Paris. I am glad he is coming homewards, for after all he has a good heart and is affectionate in his nature and very much inclined to oblige those he loves . . .

And, after his return, she writes again:

> Henry Webster is returned in good plight both as to spirits and looks. I hope more prudent else he will be put to great distress.

By December 1820, he had fallen in love with Grace Boddington, the daughter of a rich cotton merchant, Samuel Boddington, M.P. for Tralee. According to Henry Fox, Mr Boddington was 'unrelenting' against the marriage, but this made no difference to his daughter's suitor. His persistence was rewarded as, by the autumn of 1824, the opposition of one to whom Henry Fox irreverently referred as 'the archbore, old Bod' was overcome. At that time, those who had made a fortune in 'trade' were graded very low in Society and Lady Affleck openly declared that she considered the union 'mercantile'. Yet, even so, she settled £10,000 on Henry Webster which Lady Holland considered 'very handsome'.

Having at last accepted the young man as his son-in-law, 'old Bod' did his best for him. Lady Holland reported to Henry Fox that he had made 'all suitable settlements' and would give away his daughter in church. And, on 7th February 1825, she reports further:

> Mr Boddington has now invited Henry W to establish in his House, on his return from Ireland, a good thing for all parties and a great relief to Granny.

On his own merits as a soldier, eventually Henry Webster achieved a colonelcy and a knighthood.

*

In September 1819, Charles Fox reached Genoa, on his way back to Corfu. There he met his kinsman, Lord John Russell, on board the *Glasgow*, recuperating from the illness which had made him apply for the Chiltern Hundreds, the year before. Charles declares him 'a great comfort', and he praises John Russell's recently published life of his ancestor William, Lord Russell, which he much admires.

Before leaving England, Charles had become romantically attached to Elizabeth FitzClarence (a daughter of the Duke of Clarence by the actress, Mrs Jordan). Clearly, his father disapproved for, from Corfu, on 4th January 1820, he hastens to reassure his parent:

... I never could be happy my dear Papa if at variance with you—nothing ever can or ever shall induce me to marry without your full consent ... I no longer correspond as you know and this is the state of the case at present ... I will endeavour to behave as prudently as I can whilst here ... I am sure Miss E herself is most sincere ...

In May 1820, Charles has to admit that, for the past five months, he has been having drastic treatment for venereal disease and is 'still confined by strictures' for the greater part of his time to his room. And, although he tries to parry possible censure by declaring his delight in Ariosto's poems, a week later, he admits that he is lonely and miserable and feels that, because of the heat, his best chance of recovery will be to get into a ship under the care of a ship's surgeon. Thereafter, if he cannot be cured 'by Malta and Genoa', he will return to England for treatment. He is uncertain what Sir Thomas Maitland will wish him to do when he leaves.

Considering that 'King Tom' was feared throughout his Mediterranean command for his 'arbitrary conduct to the services' he seems to have treated Charles's total incapacity to serve him with remarkable leniency. By 30th May, he had given him sick leave and Charles had joined John Russell on board the *Glasgow* there to be treated for his disease by the ship's surgeon, as he had hoped. Now, he writes cheerfully that he should soon 'be well *quite*, a happy thing!' And, despite the painful penalty paid for his recent excesses, on 11th July, from Malta, he refers again to his love for Elizabeth FitzClarence:

I do love that girl with all my heart ... She is a good girl and will if ever I am blessed by getting her make me a good man.

But, Charles's hope of conjugal felicity was short-lived. In his journal of 19th August 1820, Henry Fox refers to the announcement of 'Eliza FitzClarence's' engagement to Lord Errol, and comments:

I really do not know whether I am glad or sorry, but on the whole I think it fortunate, though I fear it will cost dear Charles a pang.

Obviously, and wisely, Sir Thomas had not seen fit to extend Charles's leave to England as, back in Corfu, he wrote home in a dispirited vein. But, his fears of delayed promotion proved groundless. Before the end of the year 1820, he is promoted to Captain, on the understanding that he will join his new regiment in the Cape of Good Hope; in 1821, an exchange is arranged for him into the 15th Regiment of the Line. This is granted at a home station, and (as Lady Holland tells Henry) 'Charles is to arrive in town on 28th Oct. 1822, and is . . . to remain for years.'

Unfortunately, a repetition of his amorous exploits brings back the disease of which he had thought himself cured and, as late as February 1822 Lady Holland is writing to tell Henry, at Oxford:

Charles is still obliged to take sarsaparilla and the blue pill (mercury) so I do not think he is quite well.

As is subsequently confirmed by his childless marriage to Mary Fitz-Clarence (sister of the faithless Elizabeth), by the time Charles Fox returned to England promiscuity and the drastic mercurial treatment, which was the only one then known for venereal disease, had rendered him sterile for life.

But, outwardly, events were turning in his favour.

In 1824, Lord Hastings was appointed Governor of Malta and, in response to Lord Holland's lobbying tactics, agreed to take Charles Fox as his aide-de-camp; and, by 1825, the Duke of Clarence had intervened to get Charles 'a majority in his old Regt the 85th on full pay'. A lucky chance, which nearly did not come off through Lord Holland's inability to pay for it.

Since Parliament had abolished the slave trade, in 1807, for eighteen years Lady Holland's income from her Jamaican estates had been steadily diminishing, and despite their affluent way of living, for many years both parents had been crying poverty to their largely unheeding sons. Now, the purchase money needed for Charles's majority amounted to £3,200, towards which Lord Holland seemed able only to advance a loan of £600. The total was made up by gifts of £1,000 each from Caroline Fox and the Ladies Anne and Gertrude Fitzpatrick, and a further loan of £500 from Mr Allen, both loans to be repaid, without delay, by the sale of Charles's captaincy.

In October 1825, Charles and his wife returned to England, to join his regiment, the 84th, as a Major, in quarters at Dover. Thereafter, needing a more permanent home, they settled in a house in Addison Road, built on his father's estate. There, he set out and added to his collection of coins which, already, had brought him renown.

Thanks to the manipulation of every wire possible, thereafter his military career shaped towards success. In August 1827, he became an unattached Lieut. Colonel, again dependent on his father's charity, and when he was given command of a regiment at Halifax, Nova Scotia, a bond had to be found 'to provide money for his promotion, uniforms and general expenses'. But, when George IV died, on 26th June 1830, Charles Fox's father-in-law became King. And one of the first acts of William IV was to appoint Charles as Equerry to his Queen. By 1832 he was Surveyor-General to the Ordnance and an aide-de-camp to his Sovereign. He became a full Colonel in January 1837, and Queen Victoria kept him on as her ADC. Nine years later, he advanced to Major-General, and to General in 1863. In contrast to his half-brother Henry Webster, wire-pulling served Charles Fox far better than meritorious service.

*

Like his father before him, Henry Fox's life at Oxford passed pleasantly but without distinction. He liked the trappings: the 'tuft' (a tassel in his cap worn by privileged students); and his '20 guinea gawdy gown'. But he disliked work. Even Lady Holland, loath to chide her loved one, hopes that Henry reads and, 'as you despair of Greek, determine to make yourself a capital Latin scholar at least . . .' And she urges:

Ground yourself strongly in history, be good about Algebra and with your natural good taste, you will at least do some *one* thing perfectly well.

Much of Henry's lackadaisical application was due to delicate health, but he was clearly more interested in the activities of the dons and students than in the academic studies they pursued.

Bull is become Proctor . . . Bull is likely to be the *sole* magistrate of the University it has thrown the Dons into a ferment . . .

Up to October 1820, he found Oxford very pleasant, but by November, he is disillusioned and finds 'this place very tiresome'. Some anonymous agitator is industriously circulating 'a flaming abuse of all the college . . . in a disguised hand'. And poor Henry's infirmity is ridiculed in verse:

Turning from thee (Henry's friend, Lord
Ashley) another tuft we find
Feeble in body feebler in his mind

Followed and flattered by a motley race
Less formed to honour than disgrace
That noble name, o'er which no tear is shed
It blooms immortal tho' our Fox be dead.

Which cruel lampoon Henry accepts with fortitude.

The author is unknown. I have my own suspicions but never will say as it is one of the *motley race.*

And he proceeds to give 'a great breakfast' which, he declares to his mother, is

by far the most disagreeable thing to do as it is much more trouble than anything else but I did it in order to protest . . .

Meanwhile, he keeps his journal up to date, with such waspish remarks in it about his elders and contemporaries that an acquaintance rechristens it 'Fox's Martyrs'. And Lady Holland tells him that even 'Papa laughs at your soreness upon criticism when you lay about you so briskly upon others, dear Boy.'

Mother and son wrote to each other regularly, usually two or three times a week and sometimes daily, Lady Holland beginning her letters to Henry in a variety of ways:

'My dear love.'
'My dear little Boy.'
'My dear Boy.'
'My pretty Boy.'

Henry is far more interested in the world of Holland House than the world of Oxford and Lady Holland regularly feeds him titbits of gossip.

. . . the fair Lady Conyngham's influence is greatly on the wane, it has been rumoured some time that a lovely humble youthful lass has supplanted her, the daughter of a Windsor forester . . .

She talks of the 'odious subject' of the Queen (Caroline) concerning which Henry is 'quite furious' about the 'most wilfully blind atrocity' and Brougham's 'mischievous vituperative tongue'. And, needless to say, she points the moral to him in several ways.

On marriage:

. . . romantic poverty is never admired but by the contracting parties in *perspective*, before matrimony and experience prove how chilling an ingredient it is in the ménage . . .

On extravagance:

What a place is Oxford for expenses 149£ since Dec!

And on the perils of incontinence, as applying to Charles:

... of his late mistress the accts are deplorable, the Lover was much misled by his surgeons who assured him he was well, but unhappily he has proved the fallacy of their confidence, as the malady has been communicated to her, and she is in a wretched condition.

Lady Holland gives Henry details of the bad effect of mercury treatment, instancing ladies she has known, infected by their husbands, who have lost all their teeth and their complexions. And, that she does so with a double objective is proved by her letter, a month later:

You are a droll pleasant monkey no grumpy feelings dearest directed towards you, only vexed that your name should be dragged and soiled upon silly gossipping stories ...

For, aged nineteen, Henry Fox's name had already been coupled with that of a married woman, Mrs Baring.

Lady Holland had to step warily as her ewe-lamb was resentful of the slightest criticism. After a visit to Ampthill, while admitting the place was 'in beauty', Henry declares:

I hate the country and feel positive aversion for green fields and bleating flocks.

Which prompts his mother to tease him:

Why love you are like Congreve's fine Lady Mrs Millament who talks of the country and says 'The odious odious trees'. Don't get effeminate whatever you do ...

This provokes a furious reply from Henry, who professes himself sorry that his letters no longer please. He points out that it is Papilla and not Mrs Millamant who says 'odious odious trees'. And he winds up with an attack on Holland House, in winter, which he declares is

dull odious cold hateful melancholy uncomfortable ... I always thought and always shall think Hd Hse in winter is *odious* as it is agreeable and delightful in spring and summer more I cannot say ...

Which outburst Lady Holland answers, admitting her error in misnaming Mrs Millamant and gently chiding Henry: 'You are quite a Sir Peter Pepperpot about it.'

Although, in February 1821, Henry Fox had already thanked his stars that he was 'incapable of ever attempting to get a degree' by April, he admits that he has grown fond of Christ Church 'beyond measure'. So that his parents sat back, still full of hope for his academic future. But nothing came of it and, a year later, Lady Holland is writing rather desperately and incoherently:

I am sorry you still find Oxford so odious. What would you do instead what plan do you propose I hate anything being disagreeable to you, and yet I wish you to learn to do something to make you happy consistent with reason is all I wish.

In May 1822, he left Oxford for good. But, a social life at Holland House promised to be equally unproductive, except in developing Henry's susceptibility to the opposite sex, an urge which led to further touchiness on his part, as is proved by his mother's letter to him, of 7th October:

You are so very captious my Love that it is difficult to touch upon any topick that does not produce a *qui vive* sort of feeling. Lady Jane Peel shall be if you please as youthful as Hebe and (as) all matured Misses of 29 fit for young gentlemen of 20, but as neither you nor I can alter opinions or registers we may as well let them be . . .

Already, Henry's infatuations had followed each other with bewildering speed. First, he had fancied himself in love with Lady Georgiana Lennox (the Duke of Richmond's daughter); then, Harriet Canning, George Canning's daughter, to whom he was only prevented from proposing marriage by the opposition of his entire family; then, Lady Jane Peel, nine years his senior.

A trip abroad seemed the best solution and, accordingly, during the winter of 1823, Henry Fox and his friend, John Wortley, crossed the Channel to the Continent. He followed the same route that his mother had taken, thirty-two years earlier, when, as Lady Webster, she had set out on her first journey to Italy.

She recalls that time, nostalgically.

Marseilles was the first place I ever saw the blue waters of the Mediterranean . . . Antibes I first saw oranges . . . the Estrelle Mts (*sic*) were dangerous from Robbers . . . I staid in the town (Nice) in the last House in the Terrace, the entrance was from the publick walk behind, the first window you see on the Terrace was a little Cabinet in which I used with Dr Drew to study natural history and minerology . . .

Like her son, Henry Fox, Lady Webster too had celebrated her twenty-first birthday on her first visit to Nice. On 10th March 1823, she comments: '. . . so you are 21 years old! eligible to what I have been thinking . . .' After which there follows a very faded passage adjuring Henry to cease being 'so frivolous' and to revert to 'industry and exertion that will make you all we can hope . . .' neither of which qualities had been conspicuous in her own make-up, at the same age.

A fortnight later, still at Nice, Henry tells his mother of a momentous dinner-party he has attended, given by Lord and Lady Blessington.

My dinner went off very well at the Blessingtons. D'Orsay is to marry the daughter who is only 13 and whom he has never seen! ! ! ! ! . . . Ly B abuses like pick-pockets all those old Lords we used to think her Lovers . . . She is not in the least pleasant and anything but clever . . .

He adds a disturbing postscript:

The life one leads here is just one I delight in and I am as happy as the day is long.

Henry pursues his mother's route to Italy. From Genoa, he sends her some macabre news of her poor friend, Mrs Wyndham, who had died, in Florence, the year before.

M(adam)e d'Albany sent for a young German physician who had witnessed poor Mrs Windham's last moments—it happened she was the first person he had ever seen die and he was extremely affected—he expected that Me d'Albany sent for him for some very sentimental reason but what was his horror and indignation when she said 'Vous l'avez vu mourir eh bien! dites moi une chose—est ce qu'elle portait une perruque?'

Also from Genoa, Henry Fox announces his first meeting with one whose personality had intrigued him ever since he was a boy of sixteen, anxious to read his verses.

I am just come from Ld Byron whose delightful conversation has made me late that I have only time to say I never was so flattered and pleased as by his extreme kindness and good nature to me. He told me to give his kindest remembrances to both you and Papa for whom he expresses the warmest gratitude . . .

As we know from Lord Byron's letters to Thomas Moore and Douglas Kinnaird, the pleasure was mutual, at that first meeting. After which, Henry Fox met Lord Byron several times, but does not refer to him again in his letters to his mother.

On 19th June 1823, Henry arrived home to Holland House, and remained in England till the following summer. As before, he lived a philanderer's existence and, this time, contrived to fall in love with Theresa Villiers. On the grounds of his youth, his parents were against this marriage too, and relations with them became strained and uncomfortable, especially as his pursuit of Miss Villiers took him so much from home.

During this time, Lord Holland urged Henry to take up politics, promising to arrange a seat in the House of Commons for him at an early date. But Henry declared that he had 'no ambition to shine in statecraft' and, by 1824, Lord John Russell was telling Lady Holland that he thought her son, Henry Fox, 'a hopeless case'. 'I do not think he will do anything in public. He has not any feeling for it, and still less *Whig* feelings.' Nevertheless, Lord Holland pursued his plans and, at the end of 1825, accepted, on Henry's behalf, the offer of a vacant seat at Horsham, made him by the Duke of Norfolk. And all this, unbeknownst to Henry himself.

By July 1824, Henry was in Paris, still inwardly grieving for Theresa Villiers. Then in August, he returned to England, but only for a fortnight. From Interlaken, he writes to his mother that he can do no good at home and so is once more on his way to Italy. The separation will be painful and he tries to temper the blow.

Dearest Mamma I do sincerely from the very bottom of my heart love both of you and most heartily do wish I was standing at the foot of your bed wishing you good night.

Stoically, his mother accepts his decision and writes:

My heart rather goes pitty pat when the post arrives and a great sinking down when there is no letter.

Forced back on to her home resources, Lady Holland begins to see merits in Charles Fox's bride '. . . less flashy than her sister'. And by 21st September 1824, she is writing to tell Henry that Mrs Charles '. . . is remarkably unaffected and has won his love and entire confidence. She soothes his vanity and makes him and his family her whole object. I really like her much tho' I cannot admire her beauty one particle but handsome is who handsome does. Her health disturbs me . . .'

On 2nd January 1825, from Rome, Henry Fox writes that he is 'woefully disappointed' in the appearance of Countess Guiccioli, the late Lord Byron's mistress. Yet, as though predestined to adapt his own halting gait to the uneven footsteps of Lord Byron, eight months later, on 8th August 1825, he himself becomes Teresa Guiccioli's lover, making a cynical entry in his journal:

She has a pretty voice, pretty eyes, white skin, and strong, not to say *turbulent* passions. She has no other attraction.

The knowledge of his liaison is not communicated to his mother, who, however, knows all about it by February 1826. Then, she tells Mr Allen that she has heard that Henry is 'desperately in love with the Lady to whom Byron was attached'. And she adds: 'She is short fat and carrotty, yet I hope the report is founded in truth and will be a good riddance of other entanglements.'

From Naples, on his way to join Charles in Malta, Henry writes:

How *very very very* lovely it is . . . I do not *much* imagine I shall live in the bosom of the Blessington and D'Orsay set as she bores me so much. D'Orsay I am sorry to own is very agreeable.

On 21st June, he complains of the 'persecution of Lady Blessington . . . I hate bad society and there is something so discreditable and vulgar-mannered and minded in her conversation that I always feel ashamed of myself for being in the company of anything so *low* and dreadfully dull.' But, still, he stays on.

Following the receipt of one of Henry's letters, misdirected to her instead of to his aunt, on and after April 1826, Lady Holland writes Henry three letters of recrimination. One of his letters had accused his mother of spreading scandal about Theresa Villiers and Lady Holland takes great exception to it. In fact she declares that it 'alters the whole style of our correspondence' and is as 'vexed as possible' and 'hurt and angry'.

Not having yet received his mother's complaints, Henry writes cheerfully from Corfu Palace where he is enjoying himself as the guest of Major General Sir Frederick and Lady Adam. Then, having at last received one of her letters, he writes to apologise. And, as Henry Webster had done before him, he too acknowledges his 'unjust unkind unfeeling suspicions and distrust of one whom I love so deeply and sincerely and whom I ought to trust so fully. The good sense kindness and justice of your letters cut me to the quick.' Even so, he still makes no promise not to meet or see 'Miss Villiers', should the opportunity arise.

*

Much to Lord Holland's surprise, in April 1822, he was approached by Sir John Newport (aged 66 and for thirty years M.P. for Waterford) asking him to intercede on his behalf for Caroline Fox's hand. She refused it and Lord Holland declared that he was far less surprised by her reply than he had been by Sir John's proposal.

Meanwhile, Lady Holland had a more important domestic matter to attend to: the launching of her daughter Mary into London society.

Already at sixteen, Mary had a suitor as is proved by a letter from Lady Holland to Henry Fox, written in October 1822.

I have told Mary you will say a kind word to Mr Petre. She will rank him probably among her earliest conquests after all a person might fare worse, but I would not recommend him, tho' the longer one lives the more one is satisfied *good nature* is a jewel of inestimable value and the chief requisite for domestic happiness.

Crazy letter from Caroline Lamb to the 3rd
Lady Holland (undated)

By Lᵈ Byron   Decʳ 9ᵗʰ 1813   2

The Devils' Drive - a sequel to
Porson's "Devil's walk." -

1

[The Devil returned to hell by two
And he stai'd at home till five
When he dined on some homicides done in Ragusa
And a rebel or so in an Irish stew
And sausages made of a self-slain Jew,
And bethought himself what next to do -
And quoth he "I'll take a drive -
"I walked in the morning - I'll ride tonight
"In darkness my children take most delight -
"And I'll see how my favourites thrive

2

"And what shall I ride in? - quoth Lucifer then
"Off I follow'd my taste indeed -
"I should mount in a waggon of wounded men
"And smile to see them bleed

Two verses from *The Devil's Drive*, a poem by
Lord Byron which he gave to the 3rd Lord Holland in 1813

She had grander plans for her daughter's matrimonial future, even repelling the eligible widower, Lord Ellenborough, who was 'brow-beaten almost to rudeness' for making advances to Mary.

On 18th April 1823, Lady Holland writes to Henry:

(Mary) yesterday for the first time in her life dined at table she will occasionally upon great occasions do so but she must keep Mrs Dillon company and when we are alone or in a very small (party) it does not suit (to have) a listener or gazer at table . . .

Shortly afterwards, Mary herself writes to Henry, telling him that she has now dined twice 'at table' and is as frightened the second time as the first. Lady Holland continues her letter of 18th April with the news that, on the following Wednesday, St George's Day,

Mary will be presented to His Majesty by Lady Lansdowne. Then she will be fairly *out*, a *bill upon the door*, to say she is *to be had.*

She has misgivings:

She is terribly undersized, however the beauté du diable and her raven locks with a modest deportment may do something, but her mouth alas is not nice . . .

At the last moment, Mary's Presentation has to be postponed to the following year, because the King has gout.

Aged seventeen, she made her début at a ball at Devonshire House. For it, her dress was 'manufactured' by Elizabeth Vernon, Caroline Fox and Lady Holland's house-keeper, Mrs Brown. Although both Lord and Lady Holland attended the ball 'Lady Lansdowne undertook the charge of Mary'. And, luckily, her mother's misgivings proved groundless. 'Mary looked very pretty and was much admired.'

Lady Holland looked upon the whole process of Mary's début with a business-like eye, for which she sought to enlist Henry's help:

As Mary is *out*, I think it will be better policy to keep her in the eye of the batchelors (*sic*). As you know, my opinion is that her charms consist much in the beauté du diable; and I wish for your assistance to introduce some good *epouseurs* to her notice. Prince Leopold says she is as fresh as Hebe! Accordingly she admires said heavy Prince, who is beginning to play a part as future Regent to the future Queen, his niece.

Judging by the frequent recurrence of his name in the Dinner Books, Lady Holland set her sights on Lord Gower (heir to the Marquess of Stafford) as her future son-in-law. But, by October 1823, Henry Fox is teasing her. 'I know the reason why Lord Gower did not marry Mary and it diverts me.' To which Lady Holland replies, with good humour:

K

... Many reasons might be the cause of the objection to Mary ... *the Great Lady* (Lady Stafford) of course thought the birth and connexions not sufficiently splendid ... political influences might have been dangerous, and that *I* might have interfered upon these matters. God knows *that* would have been an error ... (Mary is) sensible docile and affectionate ... but Lord Gower may have preferred more brilliancy and talent for amusing. (By then, he had married Harriet Howard, Lord and Lady Georgiana Morpeth's third daughter.)

During the summer of 1824, both Mary's full brother, Charles Fox, and her half-brother, Henry Webster, were married, but there were no suitors for her. And, that winter, she developed a serious fever as a result of which she had to cut off her hair. In February 1825, Lady Holland comments: '... Mary has entirely recovered her health. She really looked beautiful last night, rich glowing tints and her pretty black crop.' But, by 2nd March, she has doubts about the hair. 'Her head is not quite to my taste. In a short time her hair can be turned up, in the pole, which will give her a dégagé air.' Then her doubts take a wider sweep.

Mary is looking quite beautiful and is considered so. I wish there were any sparks who would shew their admiration; but it seems odd none do. Lady Georgiana Morpeth's trip to Paris is very unlucky for her. She is without exception the best chaperon from knowing so well all the young men, and their being at their ease with her, which is rarely the case.

That September, the Hollands, Mary, a new doctor (Mr Turner) and a retinue of twenty-one people, crossed the Channel by steamboat and established themselves in Paris, for nine months, where Charles and his bride joined them. From thence, rather testily, Lady Holland writes to Henry Fox: 'Mary has the luck or rather ill luck of always captivating Royalties which is rather troublesome leading to nothing but talk.' And, a little later, 'Mary has been a great expense. I wish she had an admirer ... You must not try to set her against people, as she is getting on, no longer the youngest among the belles ...'

In November 1824, in succession to Sir Charles Stuart, Lord Granville had been appointed British Ambassador at Paris. From thence, a year later, Lady Granville sends her sister Georgiana, now Lady Carlisle, a gently satirical description of Mary Fox's success.

Dearest, what an odd thing life is, and how it ups and downs, and ebbs and flows, rises and sinks for human beings in general, Mary Fox in particular! You know in England she has short legs, looks a little gummy, is taken out as a good work, and Lansdowne and you find her rather a heavy shuttlecock. You are glad when sparks dance and speak. Here she is a Venus—she is 'la plus belle, la plus magnifique, la plus piquante: l'esprit brille dans ses yeux, son âme se voit dans sa charmante figure!' She *debutted* at a little soirée on Monday. Prince Frederick of

Prussia did not admire, he immediately fell head over ears in love. Abercromby, Lord Wriothesley Russell, young Molyneux ditto, Cradock, Gore, complain of the unfair advantage these early acquaintances have over them, that they cannot approach the most beautiful creature they ever saw . . . In short, Mary is a sort of sky-rocket in Paris. I see her with my London eyes. I see her a bright, good amiable little thing—rather too precise, but a perfectly amiable little soul. But . . . the divinity she is considered here makes me laugh, and I think it extremely funny. Seriously, it is delightful, a most charming specimen of *les compensations de la destinèe*. I think (private and confidential) either Ralph Abercromby or Wrio Russell would propose tomorrow, but I believe they would approve of neither. I think Mrs Abercromby would like it of all things, she loves Mary so very much.

A few days later, Lady Granville candidly sums up:

The admiration of Mary is quite wonderful. All the Royalties were *à ses trousses*, but I tremble for the question of real business. Lord Wrio is gone to England, where, I hear, he is attached to Miss Russell. Abercromby, with his usual prudence has *tiré son épingle du jeu* . . . I had hoped that Mary's charms and success would have attracted numberless sparks to the Hotel Meurice, but what with the shades on the candles and the awfulness of the séance, it seems to me nobody goes there but the old *affidés*, Luttrell, Rogers, etc., and a few old *savants*.

By November, she sorrowfully reports:

Mary is still admired with enthusiasm at my soirées, but there is nothing like a prospect. I am sure Lady Holland would scorn the attachés, and her manner has already warned them all off. Mary generally sits between Charles and Mrs Fox— I conclude ordered to do so . . .

The Hollands had rented an apartment in the Rue Grande Batelière, to which Lady Granville refers, on 14th December. 'The Hollands have a good apartment and an excellent cook.' Having commented on the fact that, on arrival in Paris, Lady Holland had become 'a very thin woman' and 'certainly looks older', now, Lady Granville writes: 'She is very well and to me all smiles . . .', but 'To the awestruck world who frequent her house (the most strict, undivorced, and ultra-duchesses now go there) she appears encompassed by a solemnity and state of fan and elbow-chair and shaded light which make them suppose themselves in the presence of Maria Theresa at least.'

In May 1826, Lady Granville expresses a few last thoughts on Mary:

What I meant about Mary Fox is that by nature a little gummy, she is so tied by the leg, watched by the eye, so regulated, so tamed, so told not to say this, not to do that, not to go here, not to stay there, to cut this man, to avoid that girl, that she has lost all effect in society but that of being *gêned* herself and a *gêne* to others . . . She has no spirits, no opinion, no expression, *no* conversation . . . I never saw so many natural advantages thrown away . . .

In Paris, the Hollands and Mary eagerly awaited the arrival of Henry Fox. But a sprained ankle laid him up, for several weeks, of all places, in the Blessingtons' villa, at Naples, causing Lady Holland to observe, tartly: 'I cannot (see) how Ldy Blessington could have foreseen so exactly that you were to be ill before it happened however be all that as it may.'

In no hurry to rejoin his family, Henry dawdled in Rome and only reached Paris on 6th March 1826, and hardly had he set foot in the Hollands' apartment than he was told that he had become a member of the House of Commons!

This news he fought with every weapon in his armoury, finally driving a hard bargain: if his parents agreed to his marriage with Theresa Villiers, then he would take his seat in Parliament. To which ultimatum, always fearing for his health should he become agitated, his parents reluctantly agreed. Perversely, with their lack of opposition, Henry's enthusiasm waned and, by the end of 1826, he himself had broken off his engagement to Miss Villiers, and had informed the Duke of Norfolk that he wanted to resign his seat in Parliament, as well. And this despite Lady Holland's depressing account to him of her West Indian estates and the necessity for him to find a job.

As far back as 1824, Lord Holland had begun selling some of his Kensington property for development. Now, Lady Holland regrets that he did not sell some more of his property, at St. Mary Abbots, as well. '. . . in these times one must live from day to day, and not like our ancestors think of unknown posterity . . .'

During the winter of 1826/27, funds were too short for the Hollands to be able to rent a town house. And Lady Holland writes wistfully to her irresponsible son, idling away his leisure at his parents' expense, in Italy. 'It makes my mouth water when I hear of (friends) abroad, we have no chance till next year.'

Still, while in Rome, Henry Fox made a contact which was to lead to a happy transaction for his parents. He was taken to call on Prince Italinski, the Russian Ambassador, where he found, hanging above the old man's head, Robert Fagan's portrait of Elizabeth Webster, commissioned by him, in Naples, in 1793, and which had accompanied him on all his diplomatic missions for the ensuing thirty-three years. In 1827, the old Ambassador died, and the picture became the property of his successor, Prince Gargarin. Henry Fox negotiated for its purchase and Lady Holland acknowledges its arrival at Holland House in a letter to her son, dated 27th October 1828:

My picture from Italinski is arrived and approved and criticised differently . . . I cannot think that it could ever have been like me, or at all to compare with that at Ampthill by Romney, or Hoppner's in the Blue Drawing room.

Having finally broken off his engagement to Miss Villiers, Henry had departed for Italy in the autumn of 1826 and, thereafter, only his mother's letters are extant until the New Year. Yet, in January 1827, Lady Holland still tries to understand his conception of an ideal wife:

. . . the class you would probably like to select a wife from seems difficult . . . a kind affectionate nature really loving you for your own sake, with creditable connexions . . . bring her to me and with open arms she would be received. If for your own sake she had a few hundreds a year you would be more comfortable, but let her come and share our home and be one of us entirely, if she loved you that would be all I should ask . . . I think a foreigner or a Catholick might not make you quite so happy in yr own country when you have duties of affection and situation to fulfil . . .

Still, she is prepared to overlook every obstacle.

We long for a child in the family . . . so dearest supply this commodity to us . . .

In February that year, Henry writes to ask his parents' consent to his marriage to Natalie Potocka, daughter of a Polish Count. The suddenness of his announcement takes them by surprise, but this time, beyond warning him that his allowance would be small, they do not object.

As usually happened if he found himself without opposition, then, Henry himself began to have doubts. Natalie was so young in years; very young in character; and very uncertain of herself. And he was sure he had a rival. On 1st March, he writes his mother:

I hope you have been prudent to acquaintances and not talked right and left about the possibilities of my marriage as all is uncertain . . .

Which fact is stressed by Natalie's sudden serious illness, in April.

Lady Holland anxiously warns Henry to avoid 'the odious rival' and to run no risk of a dispute or of being jostled at night in a squabble. Then, Henry becomes concerned with protocol and writes: 'I trust *my* father has written to *her* father . . .' to which Lady Holland replies that 'Yr Papa has written a very good and proper letter to Vienna . . .'

June and July pass in a state of uncertainty with Henry remaining out of reach. What is wrong? The langugage. The connexion. Foreign children are disciplined to filial obedience. Finally, Lady Holland loses patience: '. . . a Peerage and landed estate is not to be dismissed . . . yr station is high in the community to which you belong and which without any vulgar bull*ish* boasting is the greatest in civilised Europe . . .' By this time

Natalie Potocka had departed to Warsaw from whence she broke off the match. Five months later, she married one of her own countrymen.

Surprisingly, Lady Holland does not turn against her for jilting her beloved son. In an undated letter to Henry, she says that Natalie has written her 'a very pretty letter . . . such an amiable person. I am sorry and grieved that you have lost the opportunity of settling with an estimable person who apparently would have suited us all . . .'

No doubt fitting into the pattern of his marriage with Natalie, about that time, Henry had told his parents of his desire to go into diplomacy, which, as typifying his tardy wish to earn his own living, must have been accepted by them with great relief. At that moment Lord Goderich was in office, as Prime Minister, with Lord Dudley as his Foreign Secretary. With him, Lord Holland began again happily to pull wires, this time in favour of his second son. But, when, in January 1828, Henry receives news from home 'accepting Petersburg', he declares rebelliously to his journal: 'They may accept what they choose for me, but I will only go to Naples or Florence . . .' So all the wires had to be straightened out, once more.

For the whole of 1828, and until August 1829, Henry remained out of reach abroad, resisting every plea that Lady Holland could put forward to lure him home. In August, she tells Henry that Lord Holland is very ill and that she, too, is ill. He turns a deaf ear.

With hardly a sign of affection, in January 1828 Henry resumed his liaison with Countess Guiccioli, which continued, with one slight interruption, until May 1830. That occurred in Naples in June 1829, when Henry declares to his journal that he cannot in the least blame Teresa 'for taking a fresh lover when I had deserted her . . .' But the presence of a rival gives him a new fillip to stir the dying embers of his love affair. By 28th March 1830, he remarks, laconically: 'She (Teresa) is a goose. We supped and soon dispersed to bed.' And the next day he records: 'A deadly dull day. To have to make love without feeling a particle is sad work, and sad and serious did I find it.'

In the New Year of 1829, again Lady Holland beseeches Henry to return home:

. . . Come come . . . You will indeed find yourself happy with us all, and the world open to you for whatever you choose to do or to see, all will rejoice at yr. return . . .

At last, on 23rd April, Henry writes from Malta to say that he is returning, and hopes to see them all, in August.

With this welcome news, Lady Holland tries to prepare him for the altered appearance of his family. She, herself, is sadly infirm, only moving on crutches:

not venturing in my whiskey 100 yards from the House. I cannot walk at all and am even carried up and down stairs . . . I am grown immensely large and continuing to do so from my total inability to take exercise.

And Henry will find Caroline Fox altered too.

. . . your aunt is altered in appearance by the loss of her teeth but these will soon be replaced.

As for Lord Holland, now almost entirely confined to his wheelchair, she tells Henry she has persuaded him to sit for his portrait, in a small size, to Charles Robert Leslie '. . . astonishingly like'. In August 1829 Henry duly appeared in England and established himself at Little Holland House! But later, he joined his parents at Brighton and managed to remain on good terms with them until he departed back to Italy in February 1830. His great-aunt Miss Vernon died just before he left.

Meantime, at home, Lady Holland had nearly given up hope for Mary. Then, on 9th April 1830, she writes to tell Henry that Mary is engaged to Lord Lilford. 'He has never swerved from the most devoted love for her; and certainly he has not been to her an object of indifference'. She praises Lord Lilford's good qualities: '. . . he was an admirable son, and to a numerous set of brothers and sisters has acted like a parent. He is beloved and popular near his own residence'. She sighs: 'I dread the loneliness of this great house when we are left by all.'

Two weeks later, Mary also writes to tell Henry of her engagement. Yet, even after he has received a second letter from her, he remains undecided to return home. He notes:

My sister does not tell me *when* she is likely to be married, but presses me to come for the ceremony, which I shall not think of doing till I am better informed upon the subject.

So, when Mary is married, three weeks later, her brother Henry Fox is still abroad.

Being a practical woman, Lady Holland takes no chances, and on 24th May 1830, Mary Fox is married by special licence in the library at Holland House.

Only four days before the wedding, Lady Holland writes to tell Henry that Mary is 'quite ill' with disappointment at his non-appearance. And, for once, she does not respond to his excuse of ill health '. . . your lungs are quite sound and all you require is bracing . . .'

Matthew Marsh officiated at the marriage which was attended by 'fifty-one near relatives', the only guests outside the family being the Duke of Devonshire and John Whishaw. The bridesmaids were the Ladies Georgiana and Louisa Russell, Louisa Fitzmaurice and Elizabeth Howard. The company assembled in the Gilt Room, itself supposedly decorated to commemorate a more famous marriage, that of King Charles I with Henrietta Maria, and, after the ceremony, the guests repaired to the Yellow and Green Drawing Rooms where tables were laid 'well covered and beautifully arranged'.

On 22nd June, Lady Holland tells Henry that Mary, still ill, has been confined to her room for nine days. And, although the bridegroom has shown 'great kindness and tenderness' towards Mary, Lady Holland thinks it hard on him to have to act the part of nurse rather than husband.

Even this pathetic picture does not move Henry, who only arrives home on 25th November, six months after the wedding.

CHAPTER TWENTY-FIVE

The Ideal Son

ON 9TH OCTOBER, 1808, the Duke of Bedford had written to Lord Holland that he was prepared to place his son, John Russell, in his hands, 'in the most entire confidence' for his forthcoming journey to Spain and Portugal. And, as we know, John had remained with the Hollands throughout their wanderings in the Iberian Peninsula, from October 1808 to August 1809, by which time he had become an accepted addition to their own family, a position he never lost.

On two counts, in politics and literature, this small, self-composed boy turned into the ideal son both the Hollands would have loved to have. At the age of eighteen, he confirms his undeviating allegiance to Foxite Whiggism, thereby endearing himself still further to Lord Holland. In April 1810, he writes to Lady Holland:

> I do not understand what the Opposition are about at all. I only see that more of them are like Webster easily led astray, and that Lord Holland is almost the only one who still sticks to the old fashion of being a Whig.

In May that year, from Edinburgh (where he is studying at the University), John gives Lady Holland evidence of his intention to take up writing seriously. 'I am going to learn to write, do you not think it will be a good thing?' And, thereafter, while pretending to contradict this intention, he goes through a series of virtuoso exercises which must have delighted Lady Holland and her husband, as well.

First, he serenades the lady, in verse:

> Ah my Lady t'is in vain
> You ask the produce of my pen
> I've given up the trade of writing
> It is as bad as bravely fighting . . .
> So as I know not how to write
> I wish you Madam a good night.

Then, in fifty-eight lines, he proceeds to consider, and reject, all types of verse. Taken at random, here are four of his lines:

Satire! That will never do
Whilst I gain the praise of few
Ten thousand foes will soon combine
Who see themselves in every line.

But, with verse still uppermost in his mind, he proceeds to uphold Sir Walter Scott's *Lady of the Lake* against Lady Holland's criticism, and urges her to read it again.

For, tied to her by affection only and not by filial duty, John Russell could hold an independent view from hers, without fear of reprimand. And, gradually reinforcing it with experience and authority, he became a person for Lady Holland to turn to, in any moment of doubt.

Thus, we find him, as early as October 1809, in cheerful opposition to Lady Holland's concern for Charles's propensity to keep late hours, aged thirteen. (This, on the eve of Charles joining the Navy, as a midshipman.)

I do not see the use of preventing Charles going out to dinner because it may happen once or twice that he stays out too late. The more he is restrained here, the more wild he will be when he goes to sea and all your injunctions will there be useless. I expect to see him shine very much in the profession, tho' he will certainly get into some scrapes at first . . .

From the outset, John Russell seems to have taken on the task of making Lady Holland's two elder sons more palatable to her as, in April 1810, writing from Edinburgh, we find him putting in a word for Henry Webster, too.

. . . Webster is very much delighted with his commission in Col. Fuller's regiment, and is busy in getting the boots which are necessary for a hero of modern times— his head may be easily led astray as you say, but I do not think his heart will get into error . . .

In September 1811, Lord John writes Lady Holland an account of a distressing journey made by him through the poverty-stricken Midlands.

We went to Birmingham, Liverpool, Manchester and Leeds, besides episodes of salt mines and plate glass . . . There is great distress at Manchester, and many are entirely out of employ. All the great manufacturers agree in wishing that Reform may not put them in possession of their natural rights undeniable pretensions etc. They find their interests well taken care of by the County Members, and the gluttony and drunkenness of the men is sufficiently free without a general election. But I am coming to see you and though I hope you will not put many queries I will give answers to those you wish to put, and I am able to resolve . . .

Obviously, the sight of so much hardship, so callously disregarded, greatly affected his kind heart and, thereafter, it may well have shaped his thoughts towards Reform, and betterment.

He ends his letter with a teasing impertinence Lady Holland's own sons were incapable of emulating:

How ill I write but you write much worse.

Yours,

J.R.

In 1813, John Russell accompanied his father and step-mother on tours of Spain and Portugal, finally joining the Hollands, in Rome, to accompany them to Naples. On that fateful day of 5th March 1815, whereon Napoleon Bonaparte escaped from Elba, the Duke of Bedford writes Lady Holland an oddly obtuse letter about his son, John:

I trust you will take good care of him, amuse him well, not allow him to eat too many of Honoré's entrées and entremets and bring him back with you to Rome . . .

The dominant theme behind the Duke's letter is his inability to understand that the person of the greedy little boy he conjures up has grown into a shrewdly observant young man, of twenty-three. And, moreover, one who not only has been elected to Parliament, but who has already made two speeches there. And who has just followed the sightseeing initiative shown by Lords Dumfries and Ebrington by going, on his own, to Elba, to seek an interview with Napoleon.

While still under age, in July 1813, by his father's directions, John had been elected Member of Parliament for the family seat of Tavistock, as a Whig adhering to the uncompromising standards of Charles James Fox. Then, due to ill-health, he had accompanied his father and family abroad and his maiden speech was delayed till May 1814. It was a tragedy that, after his notable speech (on 16th February 1817) against Tory suspension of the Habeas Corpus Act, John Russell's health failed again, forcing him to apply for the Chiltern Hundreds. In fact, so precarious was it that there was talk that he might have to give up politics altogether and his father arranged for him to do a term of duty at sea. About April 1817, Lord Holland tells Charles Fox: 'John is still at Woburn. He will be employed when A(ntony Maitland) has a ship and that will be soon.' On board 'H.M. Ship *Glasgow*, under the command of Captain the Honble Antony Maitland', probably Russell's inclusion as 'lieutenant' on the strength of the ship's company was due, again, to the long arm of Lord Lauderdale, Captain Maitland's brother.

Presumably, he was allowed leave to return home to offer himself for re-election to Tavistock (on 18th June 1818) as the Dinner Books show him as staying at Holland House four times during that month. On 22nd June, he writes from Exeter to tell Lady Holland that there has been little opposition to his re-election. Lord Ebrington 'had the show of hands of course, but they were very greasy ones'.

On 11th September 1819, from Genoa, Charles Fox writes to tell his father: 'The *Glasgow* with John Russell in her (a great comfort to me) is here and we shall sail for Naples directly he arrives.' ('He', being Lieut. General Sir Thomas Maitland, in command Mediterranean, Lord Lauderdale's other brother.)

Thereafter, in the same letter, Charles proceeds to eulogise his friend's talent as a writer, and his integrity as a politician:

I think John's life of his ancestor (Lord William Russell, convicted of High Treason as a participator in the Rye House conspiracy and beheaded, in 1683) a most admirable and entertaining work . . . The character(s) of the different politicians of the time are I think very well drawn. No one of any feeling can read the book without experiencing an enthusiasm for Liberty . . . and an uncontrollable abhorrence for tyrants. God be praised we escaped despotism . . . He (John) has made me a much better Whig than I ever was before . . .

Probably, this was the same book to which John Russell rather indignantly refers, to Lady Holland, in an undated letter (written during the summer of 1819 (?)) from France:

You never mentioned my book after you received it, this is what authors don't like—abuse it if you will—indeed I do not think you can have got thro' it—the first chapter stopt most of my lady friends . . .

On 14th December 1819, he was home again to make the first of his many speeches on Parliamentary Reform.

John Russell's brief but evidently satisfactory career in the British Navy has escaped general attention. That it certainly took place is proved by Charles Fox's letters to his father, from Corfu and on board 'H.M. Ship *Glasgow*', in April, May and June 1820. And that John was quite serious in his consideration of an alternative career in the Navy is also proved by Charles's letters home.

From Corfu, on 4th April 1820, Charles tells his father:

John is as he always was steady good tempered and sensible, there is a something about all the Russells that makes them acceptable, I don't think any of them quick or clever but all of them honourable and steady and good-tempered.

Later, Lord Holland corrects his son's condemnation of the Russells as neither quick nor clever, and adds: 'John too has great industry and knowledge—decision of character—he improves every day . . .'

Charles's gratitude to his kinsman leads him to ask his father to indulge in his favourite pastime of wire-pulling. In May 1820, he writes:

John Russell who is as steady and as much respected and liked as he always was and will be, desires to be remembered to you and begs me to say that you would do him a great favor if you would mention to Sir Graham Moore (just rumoured to be the next Admiral in command in the Mediterranean) that he is out here as, even if he should be unable to assist him in promotion, it is still pleasant to be known and taken notice of by the Admiral of the Station. He is very ambitious for his promotion and if he does not get it at the Coronation Promotion fears that it will be long deferred. I am sure you will do this for his own sake as well as mine.

Ten days later, Charles writes to his father from 'H.M. Ship *Glasgow* at sea Adriatick':

I am living on board with John who is as kind to me as possible. I long to see him commanding a brig and hope the next promotion will take him in.

The most plausible explanation for Russell's wish to build up an alternative career to politics must be that he was afraid his health would let him down again; whereas, at sea, in the sunny climate of the Mediterranean, he had a better chance of building up his strength. Yet, still, he kept one foot on land and one at sea. At the general election of 1820, he was returned to Parliament as Member of Huntingdonshire. But, in the Navy Lists, two years later, John Russell's name features as 'Commander' (29th January 1822).

Meantime he still found time to write, continuing further biographies of his family and telling Lady Holland that the play he had written and discussed with her was now finished.

My play is now printing—it will not have all the alterations suggested by you not from want of deference, but because I am tired of the work . . .

A rare admission, from him.

In his letter to Charles, of 3rd September 1820, Lord Holland relates:

John not content with his speeches pamphlets and letters printed and published in the shyest manner imaginable three months ago a book of essays entitled 'Manners and Life by a Gentleman who has left his Lodgings'. It was read by your Mama and others without the slightest suspicion of the author who told neither father brother nor friend of his employment but was detected by his blushes when your Mama was praising the work as one of the most entertaining and philosophical popular books published in our time. These praises were not beyond its merit. I have seen no book of so small a volume in which so much philosophy is applied so successfully to such a variety of topicks . . .

During the winter of 1820/21, John was in Paris, from thence penning Lady Holland an undated letter:

My father has no right to be *grieved* with my coming here nor you to mention it—he must have given me the roving mania he has himself and you put the faculty in action by taking me to Spain . . .

'PM 18th December 1820', from Paris, John tells Lady Holland that he is delighting in reading Lord Byron's *Memoranda*, which contains 'much sense and less swaggering . . .' And, still from Paris, on 6th January 1821, he continues:

Lord Byron has written more memoirs. I am going to see them to-day—he has 3 printable volumes in Murray's hands . . .

After Napoleon's death, John Russell adds his laudatory verses to those of Lord Byron and Thomas Moore, chronicling Bonaparte's posthumous bequest to Lady Holland of his snuff-box.

Many there were who when his star was high
Were raised to greatness by Napoleon's power
Yet few of all the throng have breathed a sigh
Fearless and grateful in his darker hour.

Many there are who plucking wreaths of fame
In open battle fought his yoke
And yet when fortune smiled upon their claim
No generous spark in victors breasts awoke.

But thou unknownst to him by love by hate
Hast filled the place of victor and of friend
When time has buried long his flattering fate
Thy name with his last days and praise shall blend.

Although transcribed in another hand, these lines are dated, at the bottom, 'Paris July 1821', and noted: 'Lord John Russell to Lady Holland'. But, that he himself was dissatisfied with them is proved by his letter from Woburn, to Lady Holland, of 7th October, that same year: '. . . if you will send me my verses on Napoleon's present I will try to repair and beautify them'.

During this time, the Dinner Books show John's frequent attendance at Holland House, but there are many letters, too, written from Woburn, expressing his anxiety about his father's health (who suffered a paralytic stroke, in 1822), begging Lady Holland to write to him: 'pray continue your letters—they amuse my father very much . . .' And he hopes too that Lord Holland may find time to visit the Duke, at Woburn. 'I think if Lord Holland has nothing else to do his conversation would raise my father's spirits . . .' He spares no opportunity to show the Hollands what an essential complement they are to his father's and step-mother's happiness.

From Woburn, 'pm 28 June 1823', John tells off Lady Holland for creating alarm and despondency in the Whig party:

I am sorry if my liberty displeased you but I am for a free pen as well as a free press. Your reasoning is perfectly good, but your premises are not quite so sound. The fact is you do take part in politics, very effectual to discourage our friends very effectual to raise a cry agst the politics of Holland house but ineffectual for any good purpose—there is nothing I admire so much as a woman who takes no part in politics, but in England it is difficult, and those who say so are generally violent tories. However you shall have my terms.

Capitulation granted to Elizabeth Lady Holland.

Art. 1. Lady Holland shall be allowed to prefer vacillating shabby and adverse politicians if agreeable to dull thick and thin voters—granted.

2. Lady H. shall be permitted to take no part in questions of Currency Taxation and Law of Nations.

Answer—granted.

3. Lady H shall be entitled to prefer persons who sell their talents for a sum of money to all other politicians whatsoever.

Answer—Refused.

4. Lady H shall be at liberty to impute the worst motives of malignity and selfishness to all persons who support Lord Holland's politicks.

Answer—Refused.

5. Lady H shall be at liberty to stop politicians conversation when it becomes tiresome.

Answer—This question shall be referred to commissions—John Allen on the one side, and Lady Cowper on the other.

So much—for nonsense.

It was endearing of Lady Holland to preserve, for posterity, this written equivalent of a stinging box on the ears.

By December 1823 (and probably long before this) all is forgiven and, again from Paris, John Russell is writing to tell Lady Holland that he is bringing her 'the things you wish, always under the direction of her excellency of Bourke (Danish Ambassadress at Paris). . . . The fashion is all in favour of high large toques etc. for the head—so much the better for you whom they become.' Then, ever solicitous of her wellbeing, he adds: 'I saw Chenne about your pillow. Rest upon my zeal as you will do on the pillow . . .'

In September 1825, he finds time generously to praise Henry Fox's 'pretty verses', to Lady Holland. 'Henry improves much like a light wine which often becomes bodied by age . . .' But he is not so confident about Henry's maturity of character or about Lady Holland's methods of achieving it. At the moment Henry was philandering with Teresa Guiccioli, in Southern Italy, and John Russell continues:

When he returns to England he must attend to matters of business and mind you do not discourage and snub him if he tries to learn the meaning of the words committee, finance, privilege, etc. etc. . . .

There followed Lord Holland's negotiations with the Duke of Norfolk to bring Henry Fox into Parliament, about which John Russell did not bother to conceal his lack of enthusiasm.

On 26th March 1826, he writes to Lady Holland:

I should be more rejoiced at Henry's coming into parl^t if he showed the least taste for political pursuits—for these days a quick talent is not enough, industry is required and Wortley, Denison, Stanley, Landon etc. will always be more important than he is—for really they attend to questions and give themselves trouble . . .

Always true to his Foxite principles, on 26th February 1828, under the Duke of Wellington's Ministry but powerfully supported by Henry Brougham, John Russell moved for the repeal of the Test and Corporation Acts which, he claimed, had not been done since Charles James Fox had moved the same motion, in 1790. Although opposed by Robert Peel, William Huskisson and Lord Palmerston, he carried the motion by forty-four votes. Thereafter, his Bill to make it effective was passed by the House of Commons and Lord Holland, uncommitted by any temporary allegiance to the Duke of Wellington, 'took charge of it in the Lords'. On 28th April, the Bill became law, a triumph for its sponsor.

During the brief period of Lord Goderich's Ministry, certain Whigs had decided to join his Administration 'to keep the ultra Tories out'. Lords Carlisle, Lansdowne, Dudley, Palmerston, William Huskisson and George Tierney had agreed to serve with Goderich but, to Lady Holland's intense chagrin, Lord Holland had followed Lord Grey's stern example, and had remained firmly outside it.

In John Russell's letters to Lady Holland, there is one, slightly chastising but on the whole comforting, which, dated 'July 27th' (no year), seems to fit into this period.

Lord Holland is perhaps as well out of Office. We shall make together a very respectable Whig phalanx supporting the Ministers, and never framing a question with the Tories, but at liberty to go our own way when we please. You have a comfortable way of accounting for any blame that people may cast upon you, but I do not quite see why men are at all to (blame for?) their envy of a man by abusing his wife . . .

As has been said, it fell to John Russell bluntly to tell Lady Holland that she herself was the main stumbling-block to Lord Holland achieving office in Lord Goderich's Ministry. And the fact that her confidence in him survived this rebuff proves how completely she accepted his verdict.

For, in contrast to her egocentric sons, who professed their concern only when they had been proved wrong in their suspicions of her good intentions, Lady Holland knew that John Russell was prompted to tell her off by a genuinely affectionate desire to open her eyes to her own shortcomings and so to protect her.

CHAPTER TWENTY-SIX

'A House of All Europe'

CREEVEY REPORTS THAT when, in 1827, Canning was prepared to take Lord Holland into his government, George IV declared that 'he would have no Minister who had insulted all the crowned heads of Europe'. And, until the end of his reign, the King refused to see his erstwhile friend. Then, he died on 26th June 1830 and, within a week, William IV had bidden Lord Holland to an audience at St James's Palace.

There, he told him plainly that while, on principle, he was averse to dining out in private houses in London, Holland House was not in London 'and *there* he should dine'.

As a result, on 30th July, the Hollands invited a distinguished assembly to meet him. His brother, the Duke of Clarence, the Duke of Argyll, Lord George Cavendish, the Carlisles, the Granvilles, Lord Amherst, Colonel Fitzclarence, William Lamb (now, since the death of his father, Lord Melbourne), Lord Nelson's friend, Admiral Sir Thomas Hardy, Henry Luttrell, Lady Affleck, and Caroline Fox.

Beneath this impressive list, Mr Allen added an ominous footnote: 'News arrived of the flight of the King of France to Compiègne. This news premature.' But it served as a reminder to the company comfortably assembled to entertain the new King of England of the still precarious position of the King of France.

Thirteen years had elapsed since November 1817, when Lord Holland had told Charles Fox from Paris that, to survive, he felt that the Bourbons would have to do one of two things: wage a successful foreign war, or 'give themselves the air of reigning by the revolution and not in spite of it . . .'

Despite the violently hostile parties of the ultra-Royalists, the Bonapartists and the republicans, Louis XVIII had ruled successfully. Also successful had been his invasion of Spain to restore his Bourbon kinsman, Ferdinand VII. But his brother, Charles X, had overtipped the scales on the side of the émigrés and ultramontanes. And the issue of his 'four ordinances' sparked off another French revolution against another Bourbon King. His successor was Louis Philippe, Duc d'Orléans, son of the regicide, Philippe Égalité.

The routing of the last despotic Bourbon King of France delighted Lord Holland, particularly as the new King was already his friend:

> We all foresaw that the *ordonnances* would be the ruin of the Ministry and dynasty, and for more than fifteen years many, and among them I, have foreboded that the French revolutions would end sooner or later in their natural euthanasia—a constitutional King of the House of Orleans. But who could have imagined that all would have been effected, and so heroically and happily effected, in three short days?

Now both his alternatives had been achieved. And he also welcomed the appointment of Prince Talleyrand, another old friend, as Ambassador of France to the Court of St James.

But Lady Holland was not so pleased. She still saw Talleyrand as a traitor to Napoleon, a conviction he himself took great pains to eradicate but which he was never able, completely, to do. Still, as relations between Prince Talleyrand and Lord Holland were very close, for the next five years, Mr Allen records in the Dinner Books frequent visits between the Hollands and Prince Talleyrand and his niece and hostess, the Duchess of Dino.

*

In November 1830, Lord Grey was called on by William IV to form a government and, on 19th November, Lady Holland writes to tell Henry Fox that she is worried about the serious deterioration in his father's health. Because of this, she has 'urged him not to accept the seals of the Foreign Office' as she wants him 'only (to) have a quiet office where he will not be called upon for much exertion . . .'

In fact, there is no evidence that Lord Holland was ever offered the Foreign Secretaryship, which was given to Lord Palmerston. And, when the names of Lord Grey's Ministry were announced, Lord Holland had been made Chancellor of the Duchy of Lancaster, with a seat in the Cabinet.

By far the most controversial figure in the new Ministry was Henry, now Lord Brougham. Having been triumphantly elected to Parliament, for Yorkshire, he announced that he intended to bring in his own scheme of Reform and that he had no wish to take the office of Lord Chancellor. Lord Grey sighed to Lord Holland: 'What is to be done with him? *You* could do more than anybody.'

Twenty years before, there had been an estrangement between Brougham and Lady Holland when, so gossip said, his wife would not admit Lady Holland into her house. For eight years, Brougham's name does not occur in the Dinner Books. Then, in 1818, it is back. By 1828, he has long since re-established himself in Lady Holland's good graces and is sending her grouse. And, thereafter, his relations with her are tolerably well maintained until her death.

Lord John Russell's name had not been included in Lord Grey's initial Ministry, but in 1831, Grey made some changes and appointed Russell as Paymaster-General. At this time, he was without a seat in Parliament, and one had to be found for him, in his old constituency of Tavistock. Even then, although not yet a member of the Cabinet, he was allotted the onerous task of piloting the Government's Reform Bill through the House of Commons. Thereafter, he prepared to live up to his interpretation of political office, made to Lady Holland, in 1829: 'A Minister in the House of Commons must be made, not like a pope in conclave, but like the champion of England, in a pitched battle.'

At last things were going better for Lord Grey's party, but he himself was still frequently beset by doubts. And again Lady Holland found it impossible to curb her tongue. As Lord Grey complains to Lord Holland: '. . . I hear of nothing but Lady Holland's croaking; others are as bad.' He adds: 'It is really very provoking that in a difficulty our friends do us the greatest mischief. If this measure (of Reform) is lost it will be their cowardice . . .' And he goes on bitterly to complain of disagreements in the party. The greatest difficulty seems to come 'from those from whom we should most confidently expect support . . .' And he moans on: 'I am full 20 years too old. In short I am miserable.'

The first measure of Reform was introduced into the Commons by Lord John Russell, and passed its second reading, in March. After its defeat in committee Parliament was dissolved, and a general election followed.

Reporting to Lady Holland on Lord John's triumphant progress through Devonshire, Sydney Smith tells her:

. . . the people along the road were very much disappointed by his smallness. I told them he was much larger before the bill was thrown out, but was reduced by excessive anxiety about the people. This brought tears to their eyes.

As a result, Lord John and his fellow-reformers were returned to Parliament with an increased majority.

Even so, Lord Grey worried on about the necessity of creating new peers. On 2nd June, he writes to Lord Holland, from Windsor:

Stanhope would be for Reform if he was here but he is gone abroad.

Harrowby will not come home I am told, if he does he will be decidedly against us.

Scarborough, Teynham with us.

Northland professes to be with us but wants to be an Earl.

Lord O'Neill wants to be a Marquis, and that is the case with nearly the whole Irish Peerage, who thinking we are in distress, press their claims without mercy. Amongst them Lord Donegal who applies for a Dukedom. In short I must repeat that I am not at all sure we should not lose as many as we should gain by new creations.

In August, he is still perturbed about the 'delicate question' of new peerages; about the numbers he would have to make to get a majority; and about the risk, in creating it, that it might cause 'a great outcry, and alienate support'. Obviously, for safety, he would have to create a large number but, on 31st August, he confides to Lord Holland: 'I am afraid I shall not be able to screw my courage up to the sticking place for so large a Creation.' By September, he is admitting that some members of the Cabinet, including himself, are against such a course. If the defeat of the Bill is small, perhaps the Government could be saved but, if large, then the Government must resign. 'I see all the fearful consequences of such a result—but we cannot help it.'

The Duke of Bedford had no such doubts.

Following the Reform Bill's successful passage, for the second time, through the House of Commons, on 28th September, he writes to Lord Holland:

The H. of Commons are now in a state of repose as to the English reform Bill, and John may rest peaceably on his laurels. What will the Lords do? Why they will pass the Bill—they can do no otherwise—or they must be further gone in insanity than I can suppose it possible for any body of men to be. Some people have got an absurd notion, that Lord Grey will resign, if he is defeated in the H. of Lords—impossible! if he did he would be as mad as the Tories who oppose the Bill—he would (plague?) the whole country with convulsions and the Tories would obtain the ascendancy, and their first act would be to impeach Lord Grey. Would the people support him, if he deserts them?

The Duke's robust conviction did not really strengthen Lord Grey's resolve, especially as the King himself, very much under the influence of his strong-willed Queen Adelaide (who was biased, against Reform) was lukewarm in his support of the Bill.

On 30th October 1831, Lord Grey tells Lord Holland that the King receives him but that he avoids his meeting the Queen. In January 1832, he declares that 'the King is polite and will support the present Government' but that, though 'the Queen is civil . . . her civility is as cold as the weather'. And she wishes only two new peers to be created and those two to be confined to the eldest sons of peers.

By 26th April, Lord Grey admits to Lord Holland that he is making no headway at all with the King:

I received John's letter yesterday. I really do not see how I can have more frequent intercourse with the King, could it ever do any good. He does not ask me to Windsor, and I have no business to take me there. Tell John Russell his letter is received, that Grey is obliged to him, and would like his opinion on an alteration to a clause.

Meantime, unperturbed, Lord John had endured a series of successes and rebuffs for his Reform Bill. On 22nd September 1831, it passed through the Commons; on 7th October, it was thrown out by the Lords. On 12th December, for the third time, he introduced it to the Commons. On 7th May 1832, Lord Grey refused to accept a wrecking amendment in the Lords, and, this time, he and his colleagues resigned. However, he realised that there were difficulties for the Tories too, in forming an alternative Government, and when first the Duke of Wellington and then Sir Robert Peel failed to do so, his Ministry was reinstated. Yet, even then, his spirits did not rise.

On 15th May, he writes to Lord Holland: '. . . never was a Captive more desirous of escaping from Prison, than I from my present situation. But I will do my duty.' And, at last, his rectitude was rewarded.

On 4th June 1832, the Reform Bill was read a third time in the House of Lords and, three days later, it received the royal assent. As Lord John declared, to an enraptured populace: 'It is impossible that the whisper of a faction should prevail against the voice of a nation.'

*

In April 1831, Sydney Smith writes to ask Lady Holland whether she can accommodate him at Holland House for a few days, in May. 'I hope I shall find you still Duchess of Lancaster, but shall be quite satisfied with you as Lady Holland.' Call her what he pleased, now Lady Holland was a power, indeed.

A few weeks later, on 26th May, Thomas Babington Macaulay relates that, while talking to Sir James Macdonald at a party at Lansdowne House, he heard a voice behind them say: 'Sir James, introduce me to Mr Macaulay' and, turning, beheld 'a large bold-looking woman, with the remains of a fine person and the air of Queen Elizabeth'. His introduction was followed by an invitation to dine at Holland House, the next Sunday. (Invitations were always issued by Lady Holland herself.)

On that first visit, Macaulay arrived 'in a glass coach, through a fine avenue of elms, in good time for dinner at seven'. He was ushered into the library, a long room, 'with little cabinets for study branching out of it, warmly and snugly fitted up'. He comments: 'The collection of books is not, like Lord Spencer's, curious; but it contains almost everything that one ever wished to read.' Nearly all of it collected and bought by Lord Holland himself. That evening Macaulay carried away vivid impressions of his host and hostess. Of Lord Holland's 'kindness, simplicity and vivacity'; and of his eloquence when talking of politics and literature. And of Lady Holland's 'considerable talents and great literary acquirements'. (This praise came from a young man whose erudite work for the *Edinburgh Review* had already brought him renown.) He admitted that, although Lady Holland was 'excessively gracious' to him there was 'a haughtiness in her courtesy' which surprised him. 'The centurion did not keep his soldiers in better order than she keeps her guests.' But this discipline did not deter him and he accepted another invitation, this time to breakfast, on the following Tuesday.

On this occasion he did a tour of the house and was impressed by a portrait of Lady Holland (by Hoppner, Fagan, or Gauffier?) painted some thirty years before. 'She must have been a most beautiful woman. She still looks, however, as if she had been handsome, and shows in one respect great taste and sense. She does not rouge at all; and her costume is not youthful, so that she looks as well in the morning as in the evening.'

After those first two visits, Macaulay became a regular visitor to Holland House. Although, sometimes, Lady Holland was known to cut into his learned dissertations ('Now, Macaulay, we have had enough of this; give us something else'), mainly, she listened to his erudition with deference, as she had always done to anyone who could teach her. And a correspondence sprang up between them, when they were apart.

When the Reform Bill was in jeopardy, Macaulay echoed the Duke of Bedford's views. In an undated letter, obviously written during the autumn of 1831, he says:

... The question is this—if the Reform Bill is lost, ought the ministers to resign? ... The unanimous sentiment is this—that if the ministers resign they will prove themselves to be unfit for their station—small men unhappily called to power at a great crisis, that they will act unfairly towards the King, and towards the people who have supported them ... If those who are bidden ... will not come to the wedding, we must ransack the highways and hedges. Somewhere men will be found—resolute men—men who will not keep the empire in (jeopardy) for six or seven months and then run away for fear of their own shadow.

Lord Grey was fortunate indeed to have young men of the moral fibre of Lord John Russell and Thomas Babington Macaulay to back his policy of reform.

Lord Holland's health did not improve, but his good humour never left him. ('Lord Chalkstone' was his self-imposed nickname.) To suit his growing disabilities 'Cabinet dinners' were sometimes held under his roof, the first one taking place, on 2nd March 1831, in the house he had taken in Old Burlington Street; the next one, on 8th June, in his own home.

On 23rd June, the King dined again, this time meeting his Prime Minister. With no thought for its incongruity, a fortnight later, Lord Holland gave a dinner for the Bonapartes: Hortense, ex-Queen of Holland, now called the Duchess of St Leu, and her son, Louis Napoleon (afterwards Napoleon III).

To meet them, were invited the Duchess of Bedford, Lord Carlisle, Lord John Russell, the painter David Wilkie, and Miss Fox. Also present was Henry Fox who, in 1827, had been introduced to Queen Hortense, in Rome. As a young man, her brother, Eugène de Beauharnais, had been in love with the Duchess (then Lady Georgiana Gordon) and she and Queen Hortense had been close friends. But (as the latter confided to Henry Fox) the difficulties to their marriage seemed insurmountable and she had encouraged Lady Georgiana to marry instead, as his second wife, the widower, John, sixth Duke of Bedford.

That August, of 1831, Lord Holland was well enough to attend a great dinner of ninety-four persons given by William IV in St George's Hall, at Windsor. But the King gave him special dispensation not to attend his Coronation, in September.

As aforesaid, at Holland House Lady Holland now exercised an almost royal prerogative. But not every guest submitted to it easily. When Lord Dudley (the former John Ward) was asked why he did not dine at Holland House, he said that he did not like being tyrannised, while eating his dinner. Even Lord Melbourne stalked out, one evening, after being shifted from place to place. And Count d'Orsay, having in turn retrieved her ladyship's napkin, her fan, a fork, a spoon, a wine-glass, cheekily addressed the footman: 'Put my *couvert* on the floor. I will finish my dinner there. It will be much more convenient to *miladi*.'

With her usual outspokenness, too, Lady Holland had another way of annoying her guests. To Lord Porchester she remarked, 'I am sorry to hear you are going to publish a poem. Can't you suppress it?' More than once, she took Thomas Moore to task on the quality of his verse. And even to her beloved friend, Samuel Rogers, she is supposed to have said: 'Your poetry is bad enough, so please be sparing of your prose.'

Yet, such was the undefinable fascination of this extraordinary woman that, almost masochistically, people went back to her for more. One day, in March 1832, Lord Dudley appeared, out of the blue, to call on her in Old Burlington Street. Afterwards, Lady Holland declared:

> He said he came with the olive branch in his hand, and asked for forgiveness for all he had said against me for years. His eyes were swimming with tears. We literally embraced. I received him as cordially as possible, being really touched and affected and much pleased.

It is sad to relate, that within a fortnight of this touching reunion, Lord Dudley was pronounced by his doctors to be insane. Despite his fits of momentary exasperation, Lord Melbourne remained Lady Holland's life-long friend. Thomas Moore 'took everything in good part from her'. Samuel Rogers remained her friend, for forty years. And, as John Fyvie writes: 'Undoubtedly, Lady Holland, as a hostess, was of immense service to the Whig Party; and many besides Gifford must have wished that they could only get up a Holland House on the Tory side of the question.'

Once more, diplomats jostled each other to invade her drawing-room. The new Czar's Ambassador, Prince Lieven, and Prince Metternich's envoy, Prince Esterhazy, with Princess Lieven playing her double role of informant to her erstwhile lover Metternich and her Russian brother, General Benckendorf; Baron von Bülow, the Prussian Minister; Mon. Dedel, representing Holland; Mon. van de Weyer, representing Belgium; the Portuguese Ambassador, Count Palmella. Last, but by no means least, Prince Talleyrand and his love-child, Count Flahault, their women eyeing each other (and Princess Lieven) with barely concealed mistrust. While, threading their way through this medley of reigning sovereigns and exiles, of politicians and diplomats, of writers and painters, of wits and reprobates, the gossip-writers, Charles Greville and Thomas Creevey, were back.

Through his packed reception-rooms and presiding at his table, Lord Holland made light of his almost constant pain and increasing immobility. Sometimes, he was too ill to attend Cabinet meetings, but in the main, he managed to carry out his duties conscientiously. And he bore his wife's 'teasing ways' with imperturbable good humour. To quote Lady Granville's son, Frederick Leveson-Gower:

> I can see him now gesticulating and finishing a story, as he was by her orders wheeled backwards by the footman out of the room: and he remained perfectly

unmoved when, as would sometimes happen, she told the footman to take away the unfinished food before him.

To a stranger, this treatment of her invalid husband must have seemed intolerable tyranny yet, to those who knew Lady Holland well, her devotion to him was incontestable. More likely, her drastic treatment was meant to have an astringent effect, and to impress on him that he, too, must preserve his place in the limelight and respond to her expert rules.

Now, Lady Holland was besieged by requests for preferment. And there is no record that these requests were refused.

Maria Calcott (author of *Little Arthur's History of England*) begs her, first, to induce Lord Aberdeen to provide her with a list of Ambassadors to 'the Sublime Port', then, to vouch for her to the Portuguese Ambassador, Count Palmella Barrington Tristam asks her help to nominate his son to the Bombay Presidency. In 1831 Matthew Marsh asks her for introductions for his son, Matt, studying in Paris, to which request Lady Holland applies herself with 'a zeal and a spirit of kindness as if you were acting for a child of your own'. (This 'zeal' pilots Matt over the next eight years, from Paris through Madrid to Berlin until, in 1839, he decides to emigrate to Australia.) This year, too, one of Lady Holland's numerous doctors, J. W. Turner, begs for her patronage towards acquiring the Professorship of Surgery at Edinburgh, which, in 1832, he thanks her for helping him to obtain. Having solicited her successful intercession to Lord Chancellor Brougham, for the appointment of himself as 'Assistant Registrar' under the new Act for a General Registry, in January 1833, J. W. S. Turtle Fisher writes to tell Lady Holland that he finds it 'quite impossible . . . to describe the degree of joy diffused throughout our family' by her 'delightful letters'. And Lady Holland has the temerity to sponsor the diplomatic but slightly erratic career of young Alex Malet, married to Lord Brougham's step-daughter Marion. In 1835, she applies successfully to Lord Palmerston to get Malet transferred from Lisbon back to the Hague, where he was before; and in 1838 undertakes to move him again, 'as Alex merits promotion' and when she thinks Lord Palmerston is 'in a good humour'.

From 1831, onwards, Lady Holland is subjected to a three-pronged attack from some of her own relations, probably descended from a 'Loyalist' branch of the Vassalls, who came over and settled in the North of England, after the War of Independence. On 3rd December 1831, Spencer Vassall writes to her from 'the Royal Naval Club, Bond Street' to thank her for her interest in him and to inform her that he is about to join his ship. This, as a result of her approach to Sir James Graham, First

Lord of the Admiralty who, that November, promised her that he would give Captain Vassall a command 'since you desire it in the first vacancy which from his standing he can fill . . .' Three months later, he writes from H.M.S. *Harrier*, from Plymouth, announcing his imminent departure, for India. He expresses his deep gratitude to Lady Holland for getting him so fine a command in this 'highly desirable ship'. In July 1832, his sister, Honora Georgina Henslowe, is emboldened to ask Lady Holland to get 'a small benefice' for her husband, a chaplain in the Artillery. She sounds a responsive chord in Lady Holland's breast by instancing the entire failure of her family's property, in the West Indies. In 1834, from Tunbridge Wells, the mother of this pertinacious pair (now remarried and signing herself: 'Catharine Chetham Strode') forwards Lady Holland one of Spencer Vassall's letters and declares that it is only through her influence that her 'fine fellow' can secure his captaincy.

Until November 1840, except for two short intervals, Lady Holland took all such acts of patronage in her stride.

And, as Charles Greville points out, in 1832, she did not confine her concern to persons of only one class. That year she was very worried about the health of her page 'Edgar' (real name, William Doggett) who was suffering from a tumour on his thigh. Guests were marshalled indiscriminately into his room, to amuse him, to his embarrassment, as well as theirs.

Charles Greville continues:

Such is the social despotism of this strange house, which presents an odd mixture of luxury and constraint, of enjoyment physical and intellectual with an alloy of small *désagréments*. Talleyrand generally comes, at ten or eleven o'clock, and stays as long as they will let him. Though everybody who goes there finds something to abuse or to ridicule in the mistress of the house . . . all continue to go; all like it more or less; and whenever, by the death of either it shall come to an end, a vacuum will be made in society which nothing will supply. It is a house of all Europe; the world will suffer by the loss; and it may with truth be said that it will 'eclipse the gaiety of nations'.

CHAPTER TWENTY-SEVEN

Compère and Commère again

WITH THE WHIGS in office and with Lord Palmerston Foreign Secretary, at last it was possible to get Henry Fox into diplomacy, and now, he had the sense to accept what was offered to him. On 17th January 1831, Lord Palmerston writes to Lord Holland: 'I shall not fail to bear in mind Fox and your wishes on this subject . . .' And, by the following August, Henry is accompanying the Hollands' old friend, Sir Robert Adair, on a special mission to Brussels.

His incursion into diplomacy receives a fanfare of encouragement from his father and, within a few days of his arrival in Brussels, Lady Holland is telling him that his reports much please his father 'for their clearness and observation' even though Lord Holland finds his writing 'sometimes difficult to decypher'. By 13th September, Henry is telling his mother that he has dined with King Leopold (the night before), who said: 'When you write privately . . . mix a little ink couleur de rose with your black ink, do not let them be so ready to see all my actions in the worst light possible.' To which Lady Holland replies that 'poor Leopold' must be perplexed.

At this time, Henry's and her letters are very amicable, as he is 'looking at libraries' for her, a task they both enjoy (but only for £10 or £15, 'I cannot afford more'); and is taking trouble to please her with the gift of a fan ('very handsome'); and a muff, which she declares to be 'quite beautiful'. And she commissions him to find her a pretty cambric night-cap trimmed with Valenciennes lace, and illustrates her request with a little drawing. But it is not long before the Hollands' current lack of money is back, as an ever-recurring theme, and Lady Holland resists 'a great bargain of 2 long tablecloths and 24 napkins for 400 francs' of 'uncommon beauty', pointing out that, being second-hand, they are not cheap. And she is worried by the loss of £1,100 'through the roguery of Plummer', who had omitted to pay salaries at Holland House and who has gone bankrupt.

On family matters, yet again, in her letters to Henry, she shows her lack of understanding of her daughter, Mary Lilford. On 16th August 1831, she announces that 'Mary expects to be confined very soon; arriving to-day via Ampthill from Lilford'. And, on 9th September, she reports that Mary has been safely brought to bed of a little girl; both well. 'I was spared all anxiety as I did not know of her sufferings till all was over.' Not really a surprising announcement, if the Lilfords valued peace and quiet.

Five months of Lord Lilford, as a son-in-law, had torn the mists of illusion from Lady Holland's eyes and, by October 1830, she was informing Henry that Lord Lilford was 'very very parsimonious' even though she was convinced that, in reality, he was extremely rich as 'the new rail' running through his property would increase its value tenfold.

In October 1831, she comments on Lord Lilford's Court appointment. 'Lord Lilford has behaved well in taking the bed chamber . . . both he and Mary love money dearly and will be glad of the £1000 p.a. and the contact with the Court . . . She is in great beauty, but would be the better for some of your hints about dress.' By November, she is lamenting that she has 'lost Mary for ever and all her social daily intercourse . . .'

By which time, Lady Holland's relations with her son, Charles, had deteriorated, too.

When, in October 1831, the second Reform Bill was rejected by the House of Lords, Charles writes waspishly to his brother. 'Mama's agony at the idea of going out of office was monstrously diverting if it were not one's mother! She said "Your Papa is what I feel about; really I do think it will annoy him very much" ' . . . To which Charles had answered: 'Why, I do not think in two days, if you would let him go to H.H. he would even think of it; you would, I know, be sorry.' Lady Holland had expostulated that Charles was quite wrong as his father would miss the little things: the old recollections, the 'little feeling' of doing good, his power to moderate people and to soften prejudices and, in particular, his and his uncle Charles James's great theme of peace between France and England. To which Charles had retorted: 'Oh, you mean Mama, that he and old Talleyrand are to keep the peace of Europe, don't you?' And after noting that his mother looked angry, and exclaimed: 'Oh, you may hold your father cheap . . .' Charles reports gleefully to his brother: 'My shot told which was all I wanted.' And indeed he had scored a bull's-eye, as Lord Holland was being more than usually indiscreet.

Lord Holland's other prediction of 1817 (that the component parts of the newly created Kingdom of the Netherlands would remain incompatible) had also been proved right; and for a year, the struggle by the Belgians to achieve national independence had been gaining momentum. In the complex diplomacy that ensued, Palmerston never deviated from his desire for Belgian neutrality. As a result, he worked to prevent a French prince from becoming King of the new state, and to remove French troops from Belgian soil in the summer of 1831. He also excluded France from the discussions on the demolition of the frontier fortresses. In December 1831 'Britain, Holland, Belgium and the Northern Powers signed an agreement to demolish all the (Belgian) fortresses except Charleroi and Tournay'.

That Lord Holland gave Prince Talleyrand preliminary warning of this agreement is proved by Lord Palmerston's sharp letter to him, of 22nd December, from Goodwood:

... I return you for Talleyrand the enclosed Despatch, which however is not of much importance as it does not quite tally with communications received from Petersburgh or Moscow by Lieven. Your communication to Talleyrand about our Fortress Convention has been a most unfortunate circumstance, and has called into action all those Faculties of Intrigue of which Talleyrand, Sebastiani and Louis Philippe are such unrivalled Possessors. But it is absolutely impossible to give way to them, and therefore, we have only to regret a Bickering which a few days longer silence might have prevented.

Although lacking a date, a copy of a four-and-a-half page letter from Lord Holland to Lord Palmerston, apologising and seeking to justify 'my indiscretion to Talleyrand', seems to have been his answer to the Foreign Secretary's reprimand. Nowadays, his 'indiscretion' would have led to much adverse publicity, if not to his actual resignation from office. In 1831, Lord Palmerston treated it as he might have done a friendly difference of opinion, at Brooks's Club. Once dealt with, it was forgotten. By January 1833, he is writing to Lord Holland: 'I quite concur in all you say about the necessity of being on really good terms with France and not confining our alliance to outward show . . .'

A year later, Princess Lieven gives her brother, General Benckendorff, in St Petersburg, her impressions of the British Cabinet's reactions to Prince Talleyrand. 'Grey devoted to him, Palmerston detests him, Lord Holland tells him all the Cabinet secrets.'

*

In 1833, Lord John Russell's brother, Lord William Russell, was appointed British Minister at Lisbon. The Miguelite wars in Portugal were coming to an end, and at long last Dom Miguel, uncle usurper of the throne from the legitimate young Queen, Maria II, was losing the contest.

The Russells were regular visitors to Holland House, but in her husband's family (to quote Lord John), Lady William was recognised to be 'long-angered'. There was not much love lost between it and herself, as she was notoriously touchy and, already, on 28th November 1832, Lord John had written to tell Lady Holland that he was glad to have her assurance that she had been 'so cautious' respecting 'William's mission' and would 'be glad to set him right in this respect'. Two months later, he writes reproachfully:

> You have got me into a scrape with Lady William by saying that I told you she wrote letters to me against Hoppner, British Consul at Lisbon. It is unluckily a fact I cannot deny. But I shall be more cautious another time.

Lady William's conduct became a matter for drawing-room gossip. Princess Lieven's version (to Lady Cowper) was that, despite the British Government's policy of strict neutrality, Lady William felt that 'Dom Pedro's cause was not the right one'. As such, she took up the cause of the Miguelites, showing especial favour to 'Mr. Cordova, the Spanish Minister at the Court of Miguel', whom Princess Lieven declared to be 'very handsome and intelligent'. After Dom Pedro's naval force had captured Lisbon, it found some of Lady William's 'little green and pink billet-doux which contained a mixture of politics, literature and other matters', addressed to Cordova. Consequently, she was refused permission to go to Cintra and failed to pay her respects to Maria II. Again to quote Princess Lieven: 'It is the Hollands who are most excited about the affair and since Lady Holland is the only one who has talked about the matter, omitting the amorous side of it which she condones, no harm has come of it all . . .'

But, on 17th June 1834, Sir James Graham writes an anxious letter to Lord Holland:

> Lady William Russell appears determined to make mischief. Johnny Russell told me a few days ago, that this controversy which I thought had died away, was revived; and he asked me whether I had shewn to Lady Holland the letters in question. I told him that I took them to Holland House; that I showed them to you; that I did not think I showed them to Lady Holland; but if she said I did, I was certain she was more accurate than I could be; for my recollection of the whole affair which I considered trivial was indistinct. I had no malicious intention whatever on the subject, and at Holland House I knew I was among friends who never abuse confidence, and who were incapable of intentional unkindness to anyone, least of all a Russell.

An artless letter, indeed, from a politician of his calibre.

The upshot of Sir James Graham's indiscretion and Lady William's calumnies was that Lord William lost his job as, after only a few months at Lisbon, he was transferred to Würtemburg. About which time, Lord John tells Lady Holland, in an undated letter, that

> William gets more and more angry with Hoppner; so it is as well they are parted. His hoisting the colours of Donna Maria on his house (was) . . . to be sure neither neutral nor British.

And later, he adds: 'The fact is Lady William and H(oppner) are both very bilious which Lisbon is bad for . . .'

After this, Lord William switches his attack from the British Consul at Lisbon to Lady Holland in Kensington, telling her that his wife now links Holland House with unkind stories against her.

> . . . I will not enter into the subject you have touched upon—it is too painful and disagreeable and might lead to a lengthy correspondence which had better be avoided, but as long as Lady William is under the impression that the stories put into circulation against her issued from or even passed through Holland House she cannot look upon it as a friendly House. That impression (false I sincerely hope) once dispersed I trust our former friendship may be resumed.

He signs himself: 'Yours sincerely, W.R.'.

Airily, Lady Holland informs Henry: 'Lady William had a quarrel with Papa about Cordova's letters, the Lisbon affair, in which she breathed fire and faggot . . . in wrath with Lord Palmerston and the whole Cabinet for not disgracing poor Hoppner.'

The Duke of Bedford remained quite unmoved. In a letter to Lady Holland, he thinks

> Stutgard (*sic*) a handsome offer from Palmerston for William . . . I have a *very* long letter from her—a sort of justification—but such a farrago, such a tirade! She ends by saying she does not hate Lord Grey or Lord Holland, nor dislike Palmerston . . . but is . . . not sparing in bitter sarcasms . . .

The lure of foreign politics was like a drug addiction to both the Hollands; to him from inheritance, to her from propinquity. And just as dangerous in its after-effects. For, six years later, Lord Holland's obsessive loyalty to his uncle's tenets of fifty years before nearly associated his name with disgrace.

CHAPTER TWENTY-EIGHT

Macaulay, Victoria and Dickens

By 1832, both the Hollands were largely confined to wheelchairs. Yet certainly, it never occurred to Lady Holland to cut down on her social activities.

Out of doors, she was driven round the garden in her whiskey or pushed in her chair, while, on his good days, Lord Holland rode his pony down the Green Lane. But here, with unexpected severity, he warned Charles he would never be permitted to ride. 'None who have legs have ever been allowed to do so. Fish Crawford, Anglesey and myself, and nobody else.'

Although Lord Holland's illnesses far exceeded his wife's, her list of what he called her 'host of leeches' was formidable indeed. At this time, Dr Woolryche headed it, together with Sir Henry Halford, Dr Henry Holland, Sir Benjamin Brodie, Sir Stephen Hammick, Dr Chalmers, Dr Fowler, Dr Thompson 'of Kensington', Dr Prout and Dr Turner.

In the spring of 1832, she suffered a new discomfort.

Writing to upbraid Lady Cowper for letting her down for dinner, on 25th February, Princess Lieven tells her she is three women short: 'You, wicked creature; Lady Dover and Lady Holland, who has broken something in her back . . .' Probably, now, this would be diagnosed as a displaced or impacted vertebra. After dinner, one night at Holland House, Lady Hardy asked her hostess where her back hurt most. In the presence of her male and female guests, Lady Holland turned her page round and put her hand on his behind. 'Here, Lady Hardy,' she said. At that time, her condition was unknown to medical science so, for the rest of her life, she had increasing spasms of pain.

Hypochondriacal she undoubtedly was, but at first Lady Holland was quite unperturbed by the outbreak of cholera which hit London early in 1832. The disease had reached England from the Continent, the year before, first manifesting itself in Sunderland, which had given the Duke of Bedford the opportunity to make a pun. Writing to Lady Holland on 29th November, he declared that Lord Londonderry had just issued a letter from his 'Coal Principality' to say he was not afraid of cholera morbus. 'I fancy he is more afraid of Colliery Mob us.' The infection spread and, by the following spring, there had been several deaths.

On 27th February 1832, Lady Holland writes to tell Henry, in Brussels, that there have been forty-nine deaths from small-pox, at Brighton, and six hundred deaths there from the same disease, since the preceding November. Cholera is a flea-bite, by comparison. On 9th March, she writes that cholera 'does not get into the better classes' and notes that, anyway, bowel complaints are common, at this time of year. But, on 4th April, 'a new maid in the confectioner's room' at Holland House is struck down by cholera and dies, nine hours later.

Hurriedly, the Hollands return to their rented house in Old Burlington Street, but no more cases occur in their household. And, as Caroline Fox writes to Henry, from Little Holland House: 'I think your mother, as she always does in real emergency, acts with sense and feeling and no exaggeration; and I believe will come here next week.'

Quarantine (against bubonic plague) was first imposed in 1374, in Venice and, thereafter, on ships' crews in various ports. But the quarantine of civilians who might have been in contact with infectious diseases was not considered necessary for another five hundred years. People just ignored epidemics and went about their business, in the ordinary way. Consequently, in London, in April 1832, the Hollands visited the new French theatre, off St James's Street; dined with ambassadors; and attended crowded sessions in the House of Lords. And, within a fortnight of the fatal outbreak, they were back, entertaining as usual in the unfumigated reception-rooms, at Holland House.

Early in 1834, Thomas Macaulay called to say goodbye to Lady Holland, before sailing for India to take up his seat on the Supreme Council. Later, he told his sister, Hannah, that he was greatly embarrassed by her reception of him.

She became quite hysterical, paid me such compliments as I cannot repeat, cried, raved, called me 'dear, dear Macaulay. You are sacrificed to your family ... you are too good for them.' Then, when she realised she had gone too far, she apologised profusely. 'I beg your pardon. Pray forgive me, dear Macaulay. I know I was very impertinent ... No one has such a temper as you ... and I am sure you will bear with my weakness.' And, again, she cried.

Macaulay continues:

She storms at Ministers for letting me go ... So much so that at one dinner party, Lord Holland is said to have expostulated: 'Don't talk such nonsense, my Lady. What, the devil! Can we tell a gentleman who has a claim upon us, that he must

L

lose his only chance of getting an independence in order that he may come and talk to you in an evening.'

No letters are extant between Thomas Macaulay and Lady Holland concerning his wise jurisdiction, in India. But, after his return to England, on 3rd May 1839, he writes her a letter which shows that, even then, the faint outline of his great History of England was shaping in his mind.

Dear Lady Holland

Thank you for the loan of Eden's book. It will, I have no doubt, be of great use to me. Lord Fitzwilliam was exceedingly friendly and cordial, and seemed greatly interested about my plan; . . .

My present object is to collect as many facts as I can to illustrate the internal arrangements of private families towards the close of the seventeenth century. I have got the household books of an old Leicestershire family with which I am connected, and here I find full accounts of their income, their expenses, what they gave Lord Rutland's cook when they dined at Belvoir, what the son at Cambridge and the son at Westminster cost them and so forth. Lord Fitzwilliam promises similar information about his own family and some others in a much higher line of life. These are in my opinion, the real materials of history. I have found more historical information in a small receipt book than in a folio of diplomatic correspondence. I hope to get at the very ancient books of one or two of the oldest banks in London. They will no doubt contain much curious information. Whether I shall succeed I cannot tell. But I shall do my best to place my readers in the England of the seventeenth century. I have had so many proofs of your kindness that I need not ask you to suggest to me anything that may occur to you.

I certainly shall not forget Sunday.

Ever dear Lady Holland
Yours most faithfully
T. B. Macaulay.

That Thomas Macaulay should have singled out Lady Holland to tell her his plans for his future great work and, even, to ask for her helpful suggestions concerning it was a supreme tribute to her intelligence.

*

Lord Grey resigned as Prime Minister, on 9th July 1834. He was an old man and the passing of the Reform Bill, two years before, had fulfilled one of his most cherished ambitions. His successor was Lord Melbourne.

The next day, Charles Fox has some acid remarks to make to Henry about his mother.

Her anxiety to see William (Lord Melbourne) you may guess. I believe she wants to make William make Papa Foreign Secretary at least. However it will be as much as he can do to persuade him, I think, to remain Ch. Duchy Lancaster, as he always considered himself yoked to Lord Grey . . .

As it was, Lord Holland was confirmed in his same office, Lady Holland maintaining that he carried on in it as 'a legacy from Grey, made and urged by him'.

A week later, imbued with her elder brother's bias, Mary Lilford continues, in the same vein.

My Lady and Mary (Charles's wife) took a drive late in the evening, the latter not at all knowing *where* she was to go. And who do you suppose they *did* visit? Lord Melbourne, the Prime Minister of three days! They found him extended on an ottoman *sans* shirt, *sans* neckcloth, in a profound slumber.

For four months, all seemed well, with the Hollands dispensing their usual hospitality. In July, they gave two important dinners: one, to the King; the other as a farewell to Prince and Princess Lieven. Ostensibly, Prince Lieven was returning to Russia to take up new duties, 'as governor and instructor' to the young Czarevitch. But it was widely believed that the Czar had recalled him as his Ambassador to the Court of St James in retaliation for Lord Palmerston's unwelcome appointment of Sir Stratford Canning, as British Ambassador at St Petersburg; and that Lord Palmerston had deliberately forced the Czar's hand, in order to get rid of Princess Lieven. Many people in England were not sorry to see Princess Lieven go but now, on the eve of her departure, Caroline Fox writes:

She is become so amiable since her recall, so tender and even affectionate to man woman and child belonging to England, that she would melt the heart of a stone.

On both occasions, Lady Holland had invited past and present Prime Ministers to meet her guests. Had she but known, it was the last time either King William IV or Prince Lieven was to set foot in Holland House.

Now, Edwin Landseer's name appears in the Dinner Books, shortly to do portraits of Charles Fox and Mr Allen. The high level of talk at dinner is regularly maintained by Holland, Melbourne, Sydney Smith, Luttrell and Rogers. So much so that Charles Greville and Thomas Creevey are eager to record such wit, erudition and anecdote, and Charles Greville candidly admits to 'a deep sense of depression' at his own inadequacy as a conversationalist, at Holland House. He is tongue-tied, 'a listener on a lower plane'.

On 11th August, the Irish Tithe Bill was refused by the House of Lords. On 20th, the Hollands repaired for ten days to Ampthill. September and October followed their usual autumn pattern of smaller, more intimate,

dinner-parties, at Holland House. In September, Charles Greville dined
there six times in three weeks.

The year before, Lord Lauderdale had deserted the Whigs for the
Tories, a treachery the Duke of Bedford could not forgive. He ousted
Lord Lauderdale's bust which, as a staunch Foxite, had stood for years in
the Temple of Liberty, at Woburn, and voiced his indignation about
Lord Lauderdale's defection to Lady Holland.

I am amused at your calling him an 'old friend' of Grey's you should rather have
said an old *enemy*—and a most malignant one at that.

The total destruction by fire of the Houses of Parliament, on 16th October,
had an unexpected effect on the Duke. On 27th October, writing to Lady
Holland from his Scottish estate, the Doune, he declares:

I rejoice in the destruction of the two houses of Parliament as no lives were lost
and nothing of value destroyed—they were worthless buildings and a national
disgrace. I never rode up to the *ginger-bread façade* of the House of Lords without
blushing . . . When we have such men as Barry, Smirke, Wyatville . . . we need
be at no loss for an architect.

Alas! for the sensitivity of the Duke of Bedford. Barry rebuilt 'the worthless buildings' exactly as they were before.

On 10th November 1834, Lord Spencer died and, thereby, his son,
Lord Althorp, was elevated to the House of Lords. Four days later, Lady
Holland writes concerning him to Henry Fox.

Your father will tell you all about the dilemma occasioned by the death of Lord
Spencer, and the consequent removal of Lord Althorp from the lead in the House
of Commons. Never was there a more severe blow inflicted on a government than
his loss . . .

Still, another Chancellor had to be found and, on 13th November,
Lord Melbourne went down to Brighton to discuss with the King the
reshuffling of his Cabinet.

On the 14th, the Hollands entertained at dinner Lord Brougham, Lord
Mulgrave, the Master of the Rolls, Lord John Russell, John Cam Hobhouse, James Abercromby (the future Speaker) and his wife, and waited
in vain for Lord Melbourne. And, not until the next day, did the ministers
concerned know that William IV had exercised his royal prerogative to
dismiss his Whig Ministry and to turn, instead, to the Tories.

With alacrity, the Duke of Wellington accepted to form a government,
showing such haste in securing the support of *The Times* newspaper
(which he had just bought) that, three days later, Lord Holland declares
that, by so doing, he is 'kissing the hands of King Press before he did
those of King William'.

On 17th March, Lady Holland and Caroline Fox called on Lord Palmerston, for news. He told the two ladies that 'the Duke holds the Premiership pro tempore' and that every other appointment was provisional until Sir Robert returned from abroad. Which fact was quickly confirmed, when Sir Robert assumed the Premiership and appointed the Duke, Foreign Secretary.

The Holland family was very adversely hit by the sudden change. Not only did Lord Holland lose the Chancellorship of the Duchy of Lancaster but Charles Fox, since 1832 surveyor-general to the ordnance, lost his post as well. Furthermore, this post had entitled Charles to a seat in Parliament, where he sat as member for Tavistock. As his re-election there looked increasingly doubtful, now he put himself as Whig candidate for Stroud.

Nevertheless, as the Whigs still had a big majority in the Commons, government proved impossible for the Tories. So, in January 1835, Parliament was dissolved and a general election was held. With the exception of Lord Palmerston, who lost his seat, the other Whig Ministers were triumphantly returned. As the Whigs still held a substantial majority after a series of defeats, Sir Robert Peel resigned in April and Lord Melbourne resumed office as Prime Minister.

The Hollands were back in business. But, having accepted office as Home Secretary and Leader of the House of Commons, in May, Lord John Russell was defeated when he sought re-election, and Charles Fox, with an unselfishness not previously notable in his character, retired, as member for Stroud, in his favour. At once, *The Times* accused Charles of selling his seat for a Commissionership in Canada, and the Tory press attacked him again when he was appointed secretary to the Master-General of the Ordnance. Though less important than his previous post, a house in London went with the new one. And William IV had not turned against his daughter. In September 1835, Mary Fox was appointed housekeeper at Windsor Castle, with her own apartment near the Norman Gate.

At least, the Duke of Sussex remained true to his Whig sympathies and to his long friendship with the Hollands, even, thereby, establishing a precedent among his brothers. For, on 29th November 1835, Mr Allen notes in the Dinner Books: 'Lord *and Lady* Holland dined with the Duke of Sussex'. (The italics are ours.)

On 19th September 1836, from Windsor Castle, the King's private secretary Sir Herbert Turner, writes, on his Majesty's orders, to express 'to you and to Lady Holland his sincere regret that he cannot meet Her

wish to drive in Her Pony Chaise in Kensington Gardens, without subjecting Himself to much embarrassment, the Privilege having been hitherto
limited to the members of the Royal Family and rarely exercised even by
them . . .'

But William still played for his daughter and son-in-law.

Following the death of Sir William Knighton who, among many other
appointments to George IV, had held the non-political office of Receiver
of the Duchy of Lancaster, Lord Holland (in his capacity as Chancellor)
wrote to King William, suggesting that the salary of this office should be
reduced from £1,200 to about £800 a year, and that Mr Allen should be
appointed to fill it. He dated his letter 11th October, but, the same day,
William IV counter-claimed to him on behalf of 'Lt. Col. Fox'.

At first, Lord Holland hesitated to agree to this, fearing accusations of
nepotism, but when, on the grounds that Charles's salary would be met
from his own private funds and not from public money, the King persisted, Lord Holland gave way. And, still on 11th October 1836, Charles
Fox was appointed Receiver to the Duchy of Lancaster.

*

With increasing frequency, the names of 'Mr and Mrs Norton' and then
'Mrs Norton', by herself, occur in the Dinner Books onwards from
March 1834. A granddaughter of Richard Brinsley Sheridan, Caroline
Norton had inherited much of his wit and brilliance and many of his
more controversial qualities. In 1827, Caroline Fox had attended her
wedding to Lord Grantley's brother, at which Mary Fox had been a
bridesmaid. Thereafter, she had described the bride to Henry:

> Mrs Norton is an extraordinary person, gifted with talents more likely to
> mislead than guide her quietly and securely through life. But allowance being made
> for the eccentricity of her character and the brilliancy of her imagination, I believe
> she has many and great qualities . . .

As one of them, she omitted to describe Mrs Norton's great beauty.

All these qualities were enough to delight Lord Melbourne, so much so
that in 1836, Mrs Norton's jealous husband brought a very flimsy action
against him. His case, of seduction against his wife, was so unsubstantial
that the Prime Minister's political opponents were suspected to have
pressed Norton to bring it, and it was quite easily disposed of. A few days
before it was quashed, Melbourne's nephew, William Cowper, writes to
Lady Holland: 'There is a story going about that the King, when told
that Lord Melbourne would not (after an unfavourable verdict) be fit to
be his minister, replied, "Then I am not fit to be King".'

It was typical of Lady Holland that this adverse publicity did not influence her to repudiate Mrs Norton, whose intellect she admired.

And equally typical was her posthumous praise of Thomas Creevey who, in life, had so often proved himself a back-biting and unstable friend. In February 1838 she writes to Henry:

I am very much shocked at the sudden death this morning of poor Creevey. His life was useful and valuable to many, and his wit and *agrémens* made him a most agreeable member of society. To me and mine he was always friendly.

Then, nervously, she identifies her own condition with the cause of his death.

We used to compare notes upon our *hearts*. He had an affection very like mine, and his remedies were the same. It was of *that* he died. This has shocked and frightened me a good deal.

*

On 20th June 1837, William IV died, to be succeeded by his eighteen-year-old niece, Victoria. Mary Fox devotedly nursed her father until the end, and he died, holding her hand. Already, he had made generous provision for his numerous love-children by Mrs Jordan, and the £10,000, bequeathed to Mary, may have been handed over to her in his life-time.

Lord Holland was not well enough to attend the Queen's first Council meeting but, shortly afterwards, he had to transact some business with her and thereafter writes enthusiastically to Henry:

Our little Queen has made courtiers of us all and of me among the number.

He proceeds to make a poignant simile.

Her reading captivates the most fastidious. She starts with one advantage, the clearest and most touching voice, they say, that has been heard since Mrs Jordan.

By 25th July, Lady Holland is telling Henry: 'Had (Augusta) been here she would have suited the little Queen to a T, and would soon have become prime favourite for her agrémen and talents . . .'

In September, Lord Holland received a Royal Command to Windsor and Lady Holland paints a happy picture of his reception there, to Henry. 'Your Papa was enchanted with the Queen, indeed all who approach her are the same. She lodged him in such a room! and ordered all herself for his comfort.' But she herself was not invited. And Lord Melbourne warned her not even to come to the Castle, to stay with Mary Fox, until after the Queen had left it. He explains:

I know if you do that, it will lead to discussions which you will not like. I believe I do wrong in telling you this, as I know that it will give you a great desire to come; and if I said it did not signify, you would probably think no more about it.

Lady Holland took the hint and controlled her impatience until 7th October, when Mr Allen noted in the Dinner Book: 'Went to Windsor Castle to Lady Mary Fox's apartments at the Norman Gate of the Castle.'

Her ego would have been fortified could she have seen the young Queen's entry in her journal, of 15th February 1838: '. . . Lord Melbourne dines with Lady Holland tonight; I *wish* he dined with me!'

For, from the first, Queen Victoria took a lively interest in Lady Holland, plying Lord Melbourne with questions concerning her. Thus, three days after the above entry in her journal, she adds: '(Lady Holland), Lord Melbourne says, always thinks *first* of herself and then of Lord Holland, who quite obeys her.' Two months later, she is at it again. 'Spoke of Lady Holland, who has been very handsome though he (Lord Melbourne) always remembers her very large; and she has a vulgar mouth and used always to say, "A vulgar ordinary mouth I have".'

The Queen asks Lord Melbourne how he accommodates Lady Holland at Brocket. 'Oh, I give up the whole house to her', he answers. And she jots down meticulous details of what this means. '. . . She twists everything about; not only in her own room . . . Then she swears she has too much light, and puts out all the candles; then too little, and sends for more candles; then she shuts up first one window, then another . . .'

And, of course, Victoria is fascinated by Lady Holland's long-distance infatuation for Napoleon Bonaparte.

I asked if she knew Sebastiani; he (Lord Melbourne) said she did, but didn't like him much, except for his connection with Napoleon 'whom she adored'. She never knew Napoleon . . . but saw him at Paris at the Peace of Amiens. She used to send him things she knew he liked, said Lord M; when he was at St Helena she sent him *gateaux* and chocolate, etc. 'She was half on his side', Lord M. continued, 'if not more'.

One day, the Queen and Lord Melbourne discussed Lady Holland's superstitions.

'She has no religion, but she has every sort of superstition,' said Lord M. I asked if she disbelieved in religion; he said she did . . . Spoke of the book Lady Holland had sent him, which led us to speak of her fear of dying, which Lord Melbourne said was so very great, and haunted her night and day, though she had *no* apprehension as to what was to become of her hereafter. I said I thought people who didn't believe in religion had always more fear of death. 'They generally have,' Lord M. replied.

Another entry in the Queen's journal is as revealing of Lord Melbourne's easy-going nature as of Lady Holland's unflagging curiosity:

... Talked of when my boxes arrived in London, and Lord M. said he always tried to prevent their bringing boxes to him when he was at dinner at Lady Holland's, for that she was always wanting to know what was in it, and would say, 'What's that? Let me see what that is.' That he always made as good a fight as he could, but that it was often very difficult to prevent her.

Even so, Lord Melbourne reveals that Lady Holland has an Achilles heel:

Asked Lord M. if he thought Lady Holland felt her being unable to come to court; he shook his head and said,' Perpetually; oh! she feels it very much.' George IV knew her, he said, but disliked her very much latterly; and she one day was very rude to him ... when he came into her box at the Play ... George IV was excessively fond of Lord Holland, Lord M. said; and Lady Holland rather expected he would have received her, as he used when Prince Regent to go there so often; said, I thought perhaps she mightn't feel the exclusion; Lord M. said, 'Oh! she feels it deeply; there's nobody who doesn't feel it; I have never known anybody who didn't feel it bitterly; many don't wish to go, but they don't like the exclusion.'

Without meeting Lady Holland, thanks to Lord Melbourne, the new Queen was getting a very clear idea of her idiosyncrasies.

*

On 12th August 1838, Serjeant Talfourd took a new young writer, Charles Dickens, to dine at Holland House, and a few days later, Lord Holland describes him to his sister:

We have had the author of *Oliver Twist* here. He is a young man of 26, very unobtrusive, yet not shy, intelligent in countenance, and altogether prepossessing.

Later, Caroline Fox

was much struck with him, and liked everything but the intolerable dandyism of his dress ... but (she thought) it will probably wear away with his youth ...

Dickens himself was ready and willing to be introduced into the intellectual circle of Holland House. On 9th July, he had written to Serjeant Talfourd to tell him that he had 'purposely kept aloof from Sunday engagements in expectation of Lady Holland's most agreeable invite' only to find that, when the 'invite' eventually came, he was unavoidably committed to 'a family anniversary'. A week later, he wrote Serjeant Talfourd again, to say that 'in duty bound', he would present himself to Lady Holland 'at her bidding ... whatever her ladyship may do I shall respond to, and anyway

L*

shall be only too happy to avail myself of what I am sure cannot fail to form a very pleasant and delightful introduction'.

He was careful to start off on the right foot. On 2nd September, as editor of *Bentley's Miscellany*, he writes Lady Holland disclaiming responsibility for the 'business part of the publication' which, that month, had published 'some impromptu of Sydney Smith's, purporting to have been written at your table some years ago, which Bentley, I presume, obtained gratis from some well-informed babbler, and printed accordingly'. He goes on to express his 'abhorrence of printed recollections of private conversations', and his 'detestation of the impertinence and vulgarity which makes them public' and assures Lady Holland that the publication in question had never been authorised by him.

In August 1839, he writes apologising for a muddle in dates due perhaps to his being engaged 'with some imaginary persons (the Nickleby family)'. And, that November, he begs Lady Holland to accept a copy of the same *Nickleby* 'in a dress which will *wear* better than his everyday clothes . . .'

Almost inevitably, Henry Fox takes an opposite view about Dickens' novel. Writing to his mother, he declares: 'I am very glad you did not send me *Nicholas Nickleby*, as I dare say I should not be more successful in reading that, than in getting through the more celebrated and admired of that author's works. I agree completely with what Lady Carlisle said about them. "I know there are such unfortunate beings as pickpockets and street-walkers. I am very sorry for it and very much shocked at their mode of life, but I own I do not much wish to hear what they say to one another." ' And, with self-satisfied prescience, Henry predicts that when the novelty of Dickens' works wears off 'they will sink to their proper level'.

Confined within the limits of his own misanthropy, he failed to appreciate the stimulus, due to humanitarian sympathy with the underdog, which Dickens was injecting into English literature.

CHAPTER TWENTY-NINE

Strained Relations

In 1832, while Lord Grey nervously considered the creation of peers, Lord Holland proposed to Henry Fox that he should send up his name for a peerage, stipulating that Henry must be prepared to carry out his duties, in the Lords. Happily employed at last, Henry was reluctant to let his name go forward and, shortly afterwards, he was sent as diplomatic attaché to Sir Augustus Foster at Turin. In January 1833, he wrote asking his parents' consent to his marriage to Lady Mary Augusta Coventry.

During his earlier sojourn in Italy, despite the disparity of age, Henry Fox had had quite a flirtation with Lady Augusta's mother. For some years, Lady Coventry had been living apart from her husband and had brought up her daughter in Rome, where the habit of mother and daughter to ride 'a-straddle' had shocked Roman society.

The Hollands gave the engagement their blessing, while warning Henry that he could not expect an increase in his allowance of £1,000 a year. But Lady Coventry herself was reputed to be rich and as Lord Lauderdale was her friend 'of long standing', yet again he was appealed to, to help the interests of a Holland son. Without returning to England and despite a severe attack of gout, Henry Fox and his bride were married by the British Minister at Florence, on 9th May 1833. This time, his family paid him back in his own coin, and no member of it attended his wedding.

On 24th November, that year, Thomas Creevey writes to his step-daughter, Elizabeth Ord:

> Yesterday at the Hollands we had Lord Grey and Lord J. Russell, Charles Fox and Lady Mary (who had now been given the title of an earl's daughter, by William IV), Henry and his little bride . . . Lady Holland introduced me to Henry's wife in a very pretty manner as one of Henry's oldest and *kindest* friends. The said Lady Augusta I consider as decidedly under three feet in height. The very nicest little doll or plaything I ever saw. She is a most lively little thing apparently, very pretty, and I dare say up to anything, as all Coventrys are, or at least, *have been* . . .

Despite Lord Lauderdale's efforts to mediate, Lord Coventry refused

315

to give his daughter an allowance. But, Henry hoped Lady Coventry might increase her own allowance of £500 p.a., to make up for her husband's stinginess. She did.

Henry elaborated on Lady Coventry's lack of maternal affection. 'I never saw more deeply rooted dislike and thorough indifference to her daughter's future fate.' But his mother-in-law liked the marriage, was flattered by the connections, and was fond of him. 'Which makes my little wife cling more affectionately to me as she has no friend to love and cherish her at home and longs to get away.'

Even before his marriage, Henry was urging his mother to 'put her shoulder to the wheel and get from Palmerston a promise of Florence should it become vacant'. But Lord Palmerston was determined to make Henry work for his promotion. On 24th December 1833, he makes this plain to Henry's father.

. . . all I mean about Fox is to make him comprehend that he is not to take matters quite so cooly (*sic*) and cavalierly as he seems inclined to do; and that Ministers have a Duty to Perform. But he is an able man and if he will go on (at) a steady pace constantly, instead of standing still for a year, and galloping for a week, he will I am sure do credit to himself, and his name, and render good service to his country.

So, first, Henry had to do a term of (as it turned out distinguished) duty in Vienna and thereafter in Frankfurt, until 1838, when Lord Palmerston promoted him 'downwards, according to our scale' to Florence, as Minister Plenipotentiary.

During her first visit to England, as Henry's wife, Augusta set out to charm her way into his parents' hearts. Her visit was brief (from October 1833, to the New Year of 1834) but, by 4th February 1834, Lady Holland is writing to tell Henry that there have been many enquiries about Augusta. 'She is a little meteor that has blazed among us, and alas! vanished.' And Augusta sends her mother-in-law affectionate messages. 'Your little wee daughter, dearest Lady Holland, has been working day and part of the night . . . (getting into her house in Turin). Dearest Mamma—are you angry at my exchanging Lady Holland for a more tender name? but I feel tender towards you . . . Farewell I should like to embrace you and Pappy.'

To her father-in-law, she writes:

Dearest Pappy. Whereas when we left England you had promised some excellent Wiltshire cheese, and whereas you were pleased to break your word and let us go without. I Mary Augusta *Fox* call upon you, in lieu of the cheese, for some more *Amptill* lace . . . I must have it . . .

She got it.

The Hollands were enchanted with their 'little doll' and Lady Holland writes to Henry and Augusta collectively as 'my dear Children', but, on 26th July, she gets the usual stinger from Henry. This is because he accuses his mother of preventing 'dear Little Aunty' from visiting himself and Augusta, at Turin. 'I wonder you could find it in your heart to put an end to the project except upon your universal principle of never allowing people you can sway by fair or foul means to do what they wish.' To which Lady Holland begs the question by replying mildly that 'Aunt' is at Bowood and she herself is lonely. And, at that moment, her mother is ill . . . 'She has always been essentially to me and mine a tender Parent however many little spurts of temper may intervene occasionally.'

*

In contrast to her rather strained relations with her three Fox children, in May 1833, Lady Holland's Webster daughter, Harriet, and her husband, Admiral Pellew, together with their daughter, also called Harriet, came to dine at Holland House. (For some years, Henry Fox had been on affectionate terms with his half-sister and probably he effected her introduction to his parents.) Lady Holland comments:

She was very affectionate, and seemed delighted to see me. She is pretty and cheerful. Her daughter will be prettier than she is now. In short, it gives me sincere pleasure to have seen her so friendly and warm to me.

Thereafter, the Pellews and Harriet, together with their son and daughter-in-law ('Capt and Mrs Pellew'), moved easily and comfortably into the home circle at Holland House.

*

On 16th February 1835, Lady Holland tells Henry that her own mother, Lady Affleck, 'is declining fast. Too weak to use her trumpet but speaks herself. Great fortitude; she has arranged all the Melancholy Ceremonies.' At the age of eighty-eight, Lady Affleck died later that very day, leaving her small house, 33 South Street ('a nutshell'), to her daughter.

On 24th March, Lady Holland informs Henry that Lady Affleck has left Augusta 'the thick gold chain she always wore and two glasses one magnificent . . . but only when she comes to England . . .' She continues:

We shall occasionally come to the dear little House in South Street . . . My kind mother years ago made it larger for servants and with a very good kitchen . . . able to manage very comfortably tho' the House is no more than a *closet* and a *cupboard* so small are the rooms.

Later, she goes into more detail. She has made 'a beautiful Nook in the dining-room, with a charming view. It holds Papa's chair. It is like a bird cage and very gay and light.' And 'the nutshell' has another advantage. It is only five doors down, in South Street, from Lord Melbourne who, preferring to live in his own home rather than 10 Downing Street, drops in on his way back from the office.

On 30th March, Henry writes to his mother 'quite unhappy at not hearing from her' and fearing he has offended her. He is delighted she will be in South Street 'instead of that gloomy dirty old hospital in Burlington Street for which you used to pay so exorbitantly . . .' No word of regret for his grandmother and the rest of his letter details Augusta's recurring ill-health.

Back in the Foreign Office, at the end of June, Lord Palmerston made Henry Fox a firm offer of the Secretaryship at Vienna, with an increase of £400 in pay, on Turin. And, as the British Ambassador, Sir Frederick Lamb (Lord Melbourne's brother), was on leave in England, Lord Palmerston pointed out that Henry would find himself *chargé d'affaires*, on arrival at Vienna. Henry accepted, but owing to medical treatment Augusta was only able to rejoin her husband, two months later.

The success of the young couple was instantaneous. Henry Fox overcame Prince Metternich's instinctive distrust of a son of Lord Holland and, by the end of the year 1835, Lady Holland is writing to tell him:

> Your ears ought to have *tingled* last night. Esterhazy spoke of you in a way most gratifying to parental ears. of your talents, *tact* and success. He backed his opinion very strongly by what Metternich thought and said, who says he never met a person of your age so formed to be distinguished in your present career . . . As to Augusta, Esterhazy is full of praise, in which he adds that all Vienna join(s) . . .

And Lady Holland is delighted when she hears that Henry and Augusta are called 'les petits Renards', taking this as evidence of their popularity with the Viennese.

As Sir Frederick Lamb showed no sign of returning to his post, in December, Henry Fox decided to move himself and Augusta from his lodgings ('the cage') to the Embassy, for which presumption he was severely reprimanded by Lord Palmerston. But, as Sir Frederick raised no objections, Lady Holland encouraged Henry's move, only warning him to be careful about Sir Frederick's china as 'it makes him *mad* to have it broken'. On 17th December, Henry writes to tell his mother that he is giving a Christmas dinner for 30 or 40 of the English colony, with a party afterwards but no dancing, as it is Advent. And, characteristically, he grumbles at such a corvée. He gives his mother a cynical recipe for success with the Viennese. 'Give (them) a fiddle to waltz to, a supper to eat, and treat them with an indifference approaching to insolence and you will be adored.'

*

In 1835, the Hollands lost one and regained another old friend, both diplomats. Boasting that he had lived to cement the alliance between France and England, 'and to establish it by treaty', aged eighty-one, Prince Talleyrand resigned as French Ambassador to Great Britain; and Count Pozzo di Borgo succeeded Prince Lieven as the Czar's Ambassador. An intimate of Talleyrand's since 1791, Lord Holland mourned his departure more than did his lady. But both were delighted to welcome 'Pozzo' back into their midst. By August, Lady Holland is writing: 'Pozzo has taken a house at Tunbridge for his niece, and will hover between it and London. He is almost a suppléant for Talleyrand, as he often comes at night and stays sociably long.'

Following Charles Fox's altruistic action in surrendering his Parliamentary seat to Lord John Russell, for nearly a year Russell and Lady Holland were on bad terms. In April 1835, he married Adelaide, widow of 2nd Baron Ribblesdale (and mother of four children). On 21st May, he writes Lady Holland a crisp letter in a new vein, that of an irate husband. Lord John regrets that his conduct has displeased Lady Holland as he had accepted 'an offer from Charles' assuming that his family knew of the step he was taking. And he regrets '. . . still more that you should have thought it right to vent your feelings when I was absent, in the presence of my wife who had done nothing to offend you'.

Always, when Lord John stood up to Lady Holland she stood down, and a reconciliation was effected, three days later. Thereafter, when in January 1837, Lady John contracted measles from her elder children, Lady Holland eagerly invited her baby daughter to Holland House, writing, rather tactlessly, to announce this fact to Henry. 'John Russell's sweet baby is coming to be out of the way of its mother's measles, it is a lovely child. I could become very fond of her, as she is so very merry and good tempered.' But tragedy attended the birth of the next baby. On 21st October 1838, Lord John reports its safe advent 'both doing well'. Yet, his wife died and, on 6th November, he writes, from Brighton: 'I can only express my gratitude for your kindness and sympathy in this great calamity.'

*

In 1835, Lord Holland rather tartly reminded Henry Fox that 'he had not passed ten months with his parents in ten years'. As a result, for a few weeks that year, Henry returned alone to England, visiting his family, in South Street. He reports to Augusta:

Mamma is certainly grown visibly older. She is a little deaf, and tho' she will not use spectacles or glasses, her eyes are not so able to read small print . . . It is the fashion in the family to think Mamma very ill. I do not . . . Papa said to me when we were alone, 'You will find us grown much older.' I protested 'No, no.' 'I do not mean in looks, but in character, particularly your Mamma. She is *become*! ! ! irritable and peremptory, and even a little selfish, which she was never before! ! ! ! ! !'

While in England, Henry got a shock. That spring, Lord Holland had made a new will and made no secret of its intentions, to him. He had left Holland House and Ampthill Park to Lady Holland for life, 'with a large measure of control'; and the contents of both houses were to be hers, absolutely. After Lady Holland's death, Ampthill was to go to Charles and, thereafter, back to Henry. To Henry himself were to be left the bare bones of both estates, after his mother had had the pickings.

Henry might have protested. Instead, in 1837, he and Augusta made a joint visit to England, to spend Christmas at Holland House. The following January (1838), Henry tells his mother that 'our happy fortnight with you . . . has given me the greatest pleasure . . . God bless you and pray believe in my sincere thanks for all your kindness and love to me and still more to my little wife.'

*

1836 saw the death of Lady Holland's eldest son, Sir Godfrey Webster. On one occasion, he had written to ask Lord Holland for money, which had been refused. Estranged from his wife, whom Lady Holland referred to as 'a charming woman', for many years he had lived out of touch with his family, under an assumed name. Lady Holland staunchly upholds the merits of her daughter-in-law. 'By great personal sacrifices and diligence, she has brought up a fine family of four boys with credit and success. She has kept the property and house as far as she could very advantageously together.'

Lady Holland's grandson succeeded his father as Sir Godfrey Webster, 6th Baronet. For him also Sir James Graham had found promotion in the Navy, in 1831. From 1838 onwards, his name, and that of his mother's, occurs in the Dinner Books, at Holland House.

*

After four years of marriage, Augusta Fox was not yet with child so, on 10th November 1837, Lady Holland sends her some grisly details of a current operation performed by a Dr Locock. Convinced that a misplaced uterus is the cause of all Augusta's troubles, Lady Holland tells her that Dr Locock has a very ingenious method of re-placing the uterus 'not with a wooden instrument' but with something which can be inserted 'with scarcely any inconvenience or pain'. Augusta hastily refutes any idea that her uterus is misplaced; gives it as her opinion that her liver is at fault; and declares that she is getting better.

In April, that year, Lord Palmerston offered Henry Fox high promotion for a diplomat of only six years' service: to become British Minister at Frankfort. While reluctantly accepting his offer, neither Henry nor Augusta showed any gratitude or enthusiasm for it and Henry asked his mother not to congratulate him or his wife 'upon an appointment which is extremely disagreeable to us both'. After presenting his 'letters' at Frankfort, he intended to take Augusta back to Florence (where she had an English doctor, Playfair, in whom she had great faith), and hoped she would be able to join him, in the summer. From Frankfort, on 3rd June, after a preamble concerning some red chestnut trees he hopes to send his mother, casually, he announces that Augusta is pregnant, a fact he has already communicated to Caroline Fox. (Without rancour, his mother confirms this: '. . . we *both* resisted the temptation of opening the letter to your Aunt which conveyed it . . .')

Lady Holland tells Henry that 'the great event of Augusta's condition makes me so happy . . .' And she is delighted to hear that Augusta is disposed to come home to have the birth with her with 'good attendance and comforts'. But, as usual, she is mainly concerned about Henry's health and, although feeling that his current disorder is probably 'only bilious', recommends him to consult a physician in Frankfort.

At last, Caroline Fox manages to visit her nephew in one of his diplomatic posts abroad and, on 20th August 1838, she writes from Frankfort announcing that now she is 'under dear Henry's roof'. She emphasises 'his anxiety about his little wife . . .' and declares that her condition 'preys upon his mind'. She also enlarges on Henry's own bad health and, while announcing that 'the event will take place in January', declares that he himself is averse to Augusta making the journey to England.

By now, the Hollands have decided to visit Paris, in September, where Lady Holland is set on Henry meeting them. So, on 24th August, not only does she tell Henry that she hopes to see him there, but she declares that, by then, 'it would be perfectly safe for Augusta to move, as I apprehend the critical time must be about over and moving very comfortably à ma façon does good instead of harm afterwards . . . I shall be content with either sex.' In a letter headed 'Tuesday', she pursues this point . . . 'dear little Augusta will I hope follow her inclination of coming towards us . . .' Then she gives vent to her superstitious fears.

. . . I hate to hear of anything born at Florence. I had a child who only lived a few months. Mrs Wyndham the same and the late Lady Aylesbury . . . either Paris or London dearest for the event . . . excuse a grandmother's prosing for g(ran)d-mother to you I will be, (to) the others (presumably to her Lilford and Webster descendants) I dislike the appellation. Goodbye.

Augusta tells her mother-in-law that, in October, she hopes to venture by slow journeys to England 'there to be delivered of my precious burden . . . if I am unfortunate this time I give up the game'. On 29th August, Lady Holland replies with eight pages of advice, adjuring Augusta not 'to fast for a Boy, who will come in time' and to take care of herself. Also, she avers that 'after 5 months, travelling is not injurious at all' and again, declares her antipathy to Augusta's confinement taking place at Florence.

In September, the Hollands went to Paris and while there they heard that, at Frankfort, Henry Fox had had 'a strange fit of the gout in his foot'. Despite the fact that his aunt was with him, on 22nd September, Lady Holland sent off a disastrous letter to Augusta, urging her to 'remember her duties'. She rants on:

What on earth do you imagine induces Aunty to remain with Henry? (Her sense of duty) . . . follow her example my love and give up the agrémens of theatres conversaziones and Cascine to the more substantial pleasures of making others happy and doing what is right affectionate and dutiful . . .

Despite her five-months-old pregnancy, she urges her daughter-in-law to start on her journey to Paris.

Augusta's reply is aggrieved and furious:

. . . It is a hard and cruel thing to receive such letters from you as your last—very hard is it in the midst of bodily fear and pain, mental anxiety about Henry . . . and after *2 months and ½ of solitude* and laying up to be told to give up 'theatres compagnie Cascine' and all for *the duty* of pleasing *you*! for thus do I interpret a journey to *Paris* now! to obtain this *fancy* you are willing to make me run the risk of losing my child and perhaps my own life. I am convinced Henry will be furious when he knows that I have moved but I have written to give him rendez-vous at Genoa. I *will* not move a step further without him . . . I have two jolting days to Leghorn. I shall rest there and then proceed by sea.

She asks her mother-in-law to cease writing to her altogether and feels she is old enough to know her duties. And, probably on the same day (24th September), she thanks Lord Holland for his 'kind little letter from Paris . . . so affectionate and so considerate that I know not how to thank you . . . melancholy letters from my own family and a very unjust one

from Lady Holland has acted as a *nero balsano* . . . I am very nervous of
going from here but shall start off tomorrow or next day if able . . . I am
pretty well but my back feels always weak and painy. I have been bled
once . . . the invisible is tolerably riotous . . .'

By 26th September, Lady Holland has received Augusta's counterblast
and is realising the extent of her tactlessness. She writes that Augusta
must have misunderstood her; and that she must keep quiet. 'You must
not be angry with me . . . anger and moving is not good for you in your
present state . . .' And, three days later, she writes a normal chatty letter,
giving the price of a layette, at 3,000 francs.

But Augusta had started, and announced her arrival at Leghorn, 'tired
but safe', on 6th October. Now she too apologises for writing 'too hastily'
and believes both her mother-in-law and herself were to blame—'you for
saying sharp things to tease me when you know I am in so fretted a state
all alone, *I* for taking them up so seriously . . . Never more will I be
separated from Henry, go he to Botany Bay, and were I to lose 50 children
I follow him . . .'

On 11th October, Lady Holland writes declaring herself very sorry if
any letter of hers has induced Augusta to expose herself to the risks of a
journey to Genoa, and all might have been well had not Lord Holland
entered the lists, as conciliator. On 13th October, he writes to Augusta
from Paris, expressing himself 'astounded and distressed at your thinking
of a journey now'. He feels she must have misread the phrase or date of
some letter of Lady Holland's. 'My dear little Augusta it is quite *an imagination of your own* that we pressed you to come on to Paris *after* we knew
with any certainty of your condition and *after* we knew also that neither
Henry nor my sister would come here . . .'

This well-meaning if unconvincing missive completely obliterated
Augusta's letter of goodwill to her mother-in-law and reacted on her as
violently as had Lady Holland's, of 22nd September. Thereafter she
accused her mother-in-law of 'contriving very ingeniously to turn tables
upon me', and devoted one whole page to underlining the phrase of that
ill-fated missive, prefacing each one with 'has she then forgot?'

Lady Holland's warning against the dangers induced by 'anger' and her
superstitious dread of childbirth at Florence, were justified. On 26th
October, Henry announced 'the terminations of our hopes'.

Gone, forever, were Augusta's happy letters beginning 'Dearest
Mamma'. After her miscarriage, there was a gap in her correspondence
with her mother-in-law. Then, in June 1839, letters began again, but
formally: 'Dear Lady Augusta'. To which Augusta made reply: 'My dear

Lady Holland'. But, according to Caroline Fox, Henry himself was unexpectedly understanding, and declared:

> I shall write kindly to Mamma, for I am sure she will feel the disappointment, and I am sure too that she meant what she wrote kindly tho' I think it was ill judged but there's an end of it. I know she will be sorry as we all are . . .

Caroline Fox assured Lady Holland that 'this was the genuine unprompted dictate of his own heart' and that, as long as her sister-in-law avoided 'all discussion upon controversial points and above all on your Life no word of his Augusta' she saw no reason why all should not be well again between Henry and his mother. But we wonder whether Lady Holland possessed the dubious gift of prophecy which, in 1829, had prompted her to write to Henry: 'The House of Fox shall cease like that of Pitt.'

Luckily, in December, came the welcome news of Henry's exchange from Frankfort to Florence which even a drop in salary of £600 a year did not spoil. In a letter to Lady Holland, Lord Palmerston confesses his relief that, at last, Henry is satisfied. Otherwise, his 'truantism' might have landed him as Foreign Secretary, and the Hollands themselves, in very considerable difficulties.

*

It cannot be said that Lady Holland's relations improved with Charles and her other daughter-in-law either, though some of Charles's bias against her was unmerited.

As we know, since 1824, Lord Holland had been developing building sites on his property bordering Addison Road, and the Uxbridge Road, further west. In February 1839, he embarked on a scheme involving the construction of Holland Villas Road, at its northern end, which affected Charles Fox's amenities.

Charles was up in arms, in an instant, and flatly turned down alternative suggestions that he might be provided with a private road and a lodge to his own house; or, failing 'a satisfactory settlement', that his father should buy him out 'at market value'. He put down all his father's activities to his mother's influence, who, he declared, was bullying everybody in order to increase his father's income. Both Charles and his wife loved their home upon which (so Caroline Fox declared) they had spent 'much time, thought, labour and money upon its embellishment . . .' And, indeed, since she had first gone to live there, in 1826, Lady Mary had expended all her creative energies on the development of the house and garden. To quote Caroline Fox: 'Every shrub and flower in the garden is of Lady Mary's planting, and the plan of her design—one may say too, every room in the house, and every brick in the wall . . .' Rather than see new houses grow up in their hitherto sylvan environment, Charles declared that, much as he and his wife loved the place, now they would prefer to 'sell and clear out'. And he stuck to this pronouncement.

Consequently, the property was put up for sale, and in August, a stream of would-be purchasers crowded into the garden and house. Throughout that summer of 1839, the Foxes refused all invitations to Holland House, which led to an entry in Queen Victoria's journal, dated 31st July:

. . . I talked of Lady Mary Fox's nice house, which he (Lord Melbourne) believes she is going to leave entirely to get away from Lady Holland. Talked of their mutual hatred for one another; and Lady Holland has now padlocked the gates, so as to prevent Col. Fox from going to see his father, the short cut through the Park . . .

At the sale of the Foxes' property, the reserve was not reached which, while not really altering any point of dispute, eased the tension, for the time being. Lady Holland made repeated efforts to heal the breach between the families and, on 30th August, the Foxes dined again at Holland House.

By October 1839, Caroline Fox is describing Lord Holland and his son, Charles, as 'resembling reconciled lovers'. But she makes no reference to relations between mother and son.

CHAPTER THIRTY

'This Wretched Day'

FOR THE CORONATION of Queen Victoria, Lady Holland was offered a place at the Abbey, in the Lord Great Chamberlain's box; but an attack of shingles prevented her accepting it and, eventually, she and Lord Holland viewed the procession from the offices of the Board of Trade.

Lord Holland was well enough to attend several of the big dinners, including the Queen's State Ball, from all of which his wife was automatically excluded. But Lord Palmerston encouraged Lady Holland to invite most of the special envoys from the foreign Courts to dinner, tactfully telling her that they would like to be able to say 'that they had shared the hospitality, culinary and intellectual, of Holland House'. With the result that on 8th July at the end of a dinner-list of eighteen people, Mr Allen adds a footnote: 'The Duke of Nemours and Prince de Ligne called in the evening.'

This summer of 1838, while contemplating his autumn trip to Paris, Lord Holland is careful to apply first to Queen Victoria for permission to go. (The first time in his life he has ever thought of doing so.) No doubt prompted by Lord Melbourne, on 20th August, the Queen replies that she 'willingly consents to Lord and Lady Holland's wish to go abroad and hopes it will be of service to Lady Holland's health'.

Little did either of the Hollands realise that their intended journey abroad had elicited from Lord Melbourne some amusing details with which to divert the Queen which, as usual, she had transmitted to her journal:

Spoke of Lord and Lady Holland's going abroad; of her mode of travelling with her own horses, 15 or 20 miles a day only; and with her own Cook, etc.; and when she got to any Inn, she turned everything upside down, and didn't mind what she paid; though they are far from rich as she spends so much.

Subsequently, the truth of one of Lord Melbourne's statements was borne out by Mr Allen's account of the trip to Paris. The sea voyage, from Dover to Calais, was accomplished 'in the Beaver Steam vessel' and took a mere two hours and forty-one minutes, from habour to habour; but the journey, by coach, to Paris, took five days. Sir Stephen Hammick (Lady Holland's physician for the occasion) accompanied the Hollands and the whole party put up at the Hotel Bristol.

Despite their infirmities, the Hollands embarked on a taxing round of ambassadorial dinner-parties and political receptions, interspersed with visits to the Opera, the Théâtre Français and the Théâtre des Variétés.

Yet, despite these festivities, Queen Victoria notes in her journal that Lady Holland has written to Lord Melbourne, to accuse him of being 'stubbornly silent'. And, on 25th September, she makes another entry, which may well explain the reason for Lady Holland's fatal letter to her daughter-in-law, Augusta, written three days before. This is to announce that, despite Lady Holland having written Lord Melbourne 'a most amusing letter . . .' she 'is ill, and unable to go out, and in a great state'. And the Queen notes: 'She writes to Lord Melbourne: "Please write a line to say you pity me." The 4 last words are repeated twice.'

During his stay in Paris, Lord Holland was flatteringly received by both Louis Philippe and his Prime Minister, Count Molé, who also set out to charm Lady Holland. And this, although she had ridiculed Molé's short ministry of 1837, by calling him 'un Ministre d'Été'. (Count Molé's reply to her jibe had been: 'Dites a Lady Holland que M. Molé est un Ministre des quatres saisons.') Louis Philippe granted Lord Holland a private audience lasting two hours after which, ignoring Lord Palmerston's warning of the French King's 'Faculties for Intrigue', Lord Holland exclaims delightedly:

What a very clever fellow he is! It would be wrong in a Whig to laud a King for too much proficiency in the talent of government, but certainly one talks with no man in this country . . . whose conversation convinces one more that he is qualified to be the Minister of a great nation.

Two years later, his admiration was to cost Lord Holland the esteem of many of his own countrymen.

According to a further entry in Queen Victoria's journal of 25th September, Louis Philippe extended his graciousness to Lady Holland as well. 'Lady Holland says Louis Philippe offered to show her Versailles himself; but she is too ill to go.' And, with evident satisfaction, the Queen notes her Prime Minister's reply: ' "God! if she had embarked in it, what a trouble she would have been to him!" said Lord Melbourne.'

The Hollands found Princess Lieven domiciled in Paris, now permanently estranged from her husband and, at the age of fifty-three, embarking on her love affair with Guizot. On 1st October 1838, she writes to Lady Cowper:

... I see the Hollands a great deal. They appear to be delighted with Paris. She is in very good spirits, flattered by everyone's attentiveness to her. They give dinner-parties for her, my ambassador among others ...'

A fortnight later, Princess Lieven informs Lord Grey:

M. Molé has completely captivated Lady Holland ... Lord Holland dined at Court. Lady Holland did not go; but the Queen sent her all her boxes for the theatres, by which piece of attention Lady Holland appeared to be much gratified.

On 27th October, the Hollands left Paris, on their homeward way. And, that day, there is an illuminating entry in Queen Victoria's journal:

Lord M. showed me a letter ... from Lady Holland, in which she rather complains of Lord Melbourne's being so much here; and as she concludes *will be* at Brighton; for that no one cared about him as much as she did, upon which I said to him, I was sure she didn't care for him *half* as *much* as I did, which made him laugh. I'm *certain no one cares* for him *more* or is *fonder* of him, than I am; for I owe so much to him. I fear alas! Lady Holland will see but too much of him in November, when he must be in London.

On 3rd November she carries on, in the same vein:

Talked of Lord and Lady Holland's coming back; said to Lord M. I couldn't bear Lady Holland's saying that no one cared so much for him as she did, for I was certain *no* one cared for him as much as I did; and that I hoped he didn't believe Lady Holland; he smiled kindly and bowed assent ...

By 5th November, the Hollands were home, and three days later, the little Queen again confides her feelings to her journal. After a ride at Windsor, with Lord Melbourne, Lord Conyngham and Lady Barham, Lord Melbourne had told her he was leaving next morning.

He said: 'I should like to stay (away) Saturday'. 'Must you *really*?' said I, much vexed; 'I want to dine at Holland House; it's as well to hear what he has got to say; I'll come back Sunday,' he replied. 'You *must*,' I said. I was selfish enough to be quite cross inwardly at this announcement ... I said I dreaded Lord and Lady Holland's return, as I knew she would get hold of him; and that Holland House was a great attraction, and that I was jealous of it ...

Until her accession, Victoria had been bereft of paternal companionship, and since then, she had become increasingly possessive with her heaven-sent father-figure. But, on 2nd February 1839, obviously at Lord Melbourne's behest, she obediently sends her 'very best thanks' to the Hollands for the 'pretty contents of the case you forwarded yesterday'. (Probably, a scent-burner for her dining-room, as she notes the directions for burning incense.)

*

1839 showed a marked improvement in Lady Holland's relations with her son, Henry Fox, and her daughter, Mary Lilford.

As Minister Plenipotentiary at Florence, in January Henry had to give a Royal ball there, to celebrate Her Britannic Majesty's coronation. It was attended by young Prince Albert of Coburg, whom even Henry admitted to be extremely handsome and pleasing, with a charming smile 'and so unaffectedly gay and amused'. As host and hostess, Henry told his mother that neither he nor his wife felt that they had acquitted themselves well. But Lady Holland took care to reply that she felt sure that Augusta had done well with 'the example of Lady Coventry' to go by, 'who is (renowned?) for her manners in doing the honours of the house'.

Although still at secondhand, with Henry as intermediary, by February Lady Holland is forwarding Augusta 'a muslin gown' and undertaking to find her 'the exact colour' of 'an abricot colored poplin gown of Mary's' and to send her more Ampthill lace. And, in return, Henry and his wife send her some dresses and pander to her sweet tooth by sending her chocolate, while he tells her of the Florentine fashion for 'iced café à la crème'. Although he does not think iced drinks will catch on, in England, Lady Holland is undeterred and asks for the recipe.

Henry asks for, and gets, 'some of those China seats you have on your little terrace at Holland House' and, when they arrive, he is so pleased with them that he exclaims 'how I should like to see you sitting on one . . . Why not come and see them . . .' And he plans an elaborate itinerary for his mother to start 'in early summer down the Saone and Rhône . . . to embark in fine weather from Marseilles to Leghorn, and on to Lucca . . .' There, he suggests she should rent a villa and come to Florence in the autumn, unknowingly outlining a plan she, as Lady Webster, had adopted in 1795, when Mrs Wyndham and she had formed a romantic quartette with Lord Holland and Lord Wycombe at Lucca. Needless to say, Henry's project does not take shape.

On 12th February, Lady Holland tells Henry: 'Mary (Lilford) has a boy; he is called Victor after his royal sponsor'. So now both Charles Fox and his sister, Mary, are recipients of the Queen's favours.

On 31st August, Henry writes to say that he hopes Papa will at last get down to Lilford, 'a journey he has not yet accomplished in *nine years*! ! ! ' This was undertaken at the end of September, and nearly ended disastrously, in a fire.

At seven o'clock in the morning it broke out in the drawing-room under Lady Holland's bedroom, where, luckily, she was already up, as she and Lord Holland were leaving Lilford that day. To quote him:

Lady Holland was herself as is often the case when the danger is real, much less flurried or agitated in appearance than on slighter occasions.

And even allowing for her own powers of melodramatic description, Lady Holland seems to have come very well through her ordeal.

Everybody behaved well; even *I* did with composure and self-possession. Upon it bursting into my room, I went immediately to Papa, conveyed him in his rolling chair to a distant and safe room, roused Allen from a sound sleep, and remained quiet. Nobody was hurt. Indeed, I believe I was the greatest sufferer, because I quitted my dressing-room about ten minutes after I was out of bed, therefore had very slender *raiment*, only just what one has at first getting out of bed, no shoes, only *les mules*, no *caleçons* nor under petticoats etc., nor had I for near two hours warmer garments.

Even so, the fire effectually thawed Lady Holland's cool feelings for her son-in-law. On 10th October, she writes to Henry: '. . . I have grown to *love* Lord Lilford, he is so good.'

*

Again, Lord Melbourne's Government was in the doldrums and, in May 1839, his majority was so reduced that he resigned.

Proceeding to form a Tory Ministry, Sir Robert Peel found himself firmly opposed by the Queen. When she refused to allow him a free hand with which to appoint her Ladies of the Bedchamber, he, in his turn, resigned, and the Whigs returned to office on a very unusual premise, namely, to uphold the Queen in her stand against her Tory Prime Minister!

During the Whigs' period of crisis, Lord Holland collapsed with a serious attack of gout. Furiously, Lady Holland declared: 'He . . . caught a chill from an open window in the tumble-down Cabinet room. The Conference lasted *five hours*. No power could shut the window.' So, for a month, Lord Holland was unable to attend any meetings. But, after Sir Robert's resignation, he told Henry that he quite agreed with his colleagues that they had to rally to the Queen's appeal to them 'to save her from thraldom'. As a Foxite Whig, he had the grace to add that 'it might *not sound* very *Whiggish* to make the Household the great bulwark of their cause'.

*

Within the space of a year, the Hollands lost three great friends: Lord Lauderdale, the Duke of Bedford, and Matthew Marsh.

Lord Lauderdale died on 13th September 1839, and up to the end Lord Holland tried to induce the Duke of Bedford (through his son, Lord Tavistock) to restore Lauderdale's bust to its former revered position in the *Temple of Liberty*, at Woburn. But he did not succeed.

To Henry Fox, Lady Holland expresses her genuine sorrow at the death of her old (and very useful) friend.

... he was to me the most constant friend any body was ever blessed with, to his friendship active zeal and influence, I owe entirely my station in society, he was indefatigable in carrying through law proceedings in the H. of Lords which enabled me to be what I am in this family, he reconciled Mr Fox and all his connexions to the measure by (supporting?) me and in that I owe him every advantage and comfort I enjoy ... Such a friend of 40 years standing cannot be lost without a pang and a most grateful recollection shall I ever feel towards him. Mr Fox used to say he could not imagine how the world could go on before Lauderdale was born. It is a singular coincidence that these two friends Fox and Lauderdale were born on the same day 24th January died each on 13th September. L. was 10 years junior to Mr Fox.

She got no change out of the Duke of Bedford. '. . . You know perfectly well my opinion of Lord Lauderdale so I will not say a word in reply to your reflections on his death.'

On 3rd June 1838, Queen Victoria transcribed a lively piece of gossip to her journal. 'Lord Melbourne told me something which Lady Holland has done "out of a spirit of perversity", which she certainly has, and which Lord Melbourne says "is really quite unaccountable" . . . The Duchess of Bedford built a room in her house on Camden Hill (*sic*) in order to have a fine view of Harrow; no sooner did Lady Holland find this out, than she ordered her palings to be heightened and quite shut out her view! ! ! This was only done to vex the Duchess . . . The Duke of Bedford is in a perfect phrenzy . . . "Perhaps" he (Lord Melbourne) added, "Lady Holland may think she is paying off old scores to the Duchess", as the Duchess had a little of that in her, never would humour Lady Holland's fancies about rooms, and would put her in the rooms she knew she disliked . . .'

Another version of the story is told by the diarist, Fanny Kemble.

Landseer walking by Lady Holland's wheel chair in the gardens said 'Oh, Lady Holland, this is that part of your place of which the Duchess of Bedford has such a charming view from her house on the hill above.' 'Is it?' said Lady Holland, and immediately gave orders that the paling fence round that part of the grounds should be raised, so as to cut off the Duchess's view into them.

As usual with Lady Holland, the Duke's 'phrenzy' was gallantly muted. Already, on 29th May 1838, from Woburn, he had written to say that he had failed to see her, in London.

... You had so carefully cut off all communications between that Mansion (Holland House) and poor little C. Hill. I saw with regret the formidable *Barricades* you had erected on the top of your park paling, opposite the Duchess's little garden, so as effectively to exclude her view of your beautiful grounds, so we as humble individuals must be content to retire within our own wall(?) ... I am told, also, that you had put a padlock on the gate you formerly had made for my accommodation—notwithstanding all this I shall still hope to find my way to Holland House somehow or other, for I am always

> Yours afft.
> Bedford.

On 3rd June (the date in Queen Victoria's journal) he writes again:

I do assure you that I am most anxious to see you again, and shall make a point of going to see you as soon as I return to town, *nonobstant les Baricades*.

And, thereafter, his easy, affectionate letters to Lady Holland continue uninterruptedly.

In January 1839, he plans a visit for the Hollands to Woburn and, when Lady Holland runs out, he writes good-humouredly:

I will not say I was disappointed in not seeing you here because I never thought that you had the slightest intention of coming here ...

And, later, he writes:

I despair of ever seeing you again at Woburn—however as the mountain won't go to Mahomet, Mahomet must go to the Mountain and I hope very soon for S Street or at H House.

Distinguished arborealist that he was, he took no offence when Lady Holland dismissed his 'large unwieldy Catalogue of Willows' as an 'uninteresting work' and threatened to send her his 'Catalogue of Pines', as its companion.

On 2nd October, he writes to her 'a little angry' that she should have visited Woburn in his absence but very interested in all her comments on the changes he has made there. He believes his collection of cacti to be the finest in Europe, with the exception of the King's Garden, at Berlin. And he adds:

I do not wonder at them *amusing* you they are very whimsical.

From the Doune, on 15th October, he thanks her for 'a very pleasant letter' and looks forward to being her *cicerone* at Woburn, 'to show you my plants and my books, the only things worth your notice in my old ecclesiastical residence ...'

He died at the Doune, five days later.

When Matthew Marsh dies, in July 1840, Lady Holland laments, to Henry: 'What havock death now makes among my nearest dearest old friends within a few months! ! ! '

*

Early in October 1839, Queen Victoria's two young Coburg cousins arrived at her court, to be vetted.

For some time past, her uncle, King Leopold of Belgium, had been working to achieve her marriage to his nephew Albert, and, at sight of him, Victoria flew to her journal. 'It was with some emotion that I beheld Albert—who is *beautiful!*' On 13th October, she announced to Lord Melbourne her intention to marry Albert, and proposed to him, two days later. According to her journal, Albert and his brother Ernest, 'seemed very happy'. And she herself was 'the happiest of human beings'.

Into this atmosphere of bliss, surely it was unnecessary for Lord Melbourne to introduce a dissentient voice, that of Lady Holland's? Yet this he did, deliberately telling the Queen, on the very day on which she betrothed herself to her future husband, that 'Lady Holland had written about it (her engagement) abusing it, and thinking from what the Granvilles had told her, it would not be . . .' This time, he had the tardy discretion not to divulge the actual contents of her letters, of which there was more than one.

By 20th November, the Queen is noting:

. . . Lady Holland don't like my marriage, but liked it better now that it is settled; she, in a great fright lest I should have seen the letters she wrote to Lord M. against it—which he did not show me; her reason against it, that the Family had always had it in their reach . . . Talked of Lady Holland's disliking my marriage, and wishing for a *Prince of Nassau!* ! 'Who did it?' she said, Lord M. told me; 'Is it the Baroness (Lehzen)? Is it the Duchess of Kent?' 'I said' (quoting Lord Melbourne) 'neither of them; it was the Queen herself.'

The Queen's letter to him, written two days later, obviously caused him some uneasiness.

. . . As Lord Melbourne said she might, and that the marriage was in fact no longer a secret, the Queen talked of it to Uxbridge, Albemarle etc. last night . . . They all told the Queen it would be very much liked in the Country, in spite of Lady Holland's disapprobation . . .

To which Lord Melbourne made urgent reply, the same day.

. . . Lord Melbourne has no doubt that the present feeling will be as Albemarle and Uxbridge represented it, but Lord Melbourne hopes that Your Majesty did not mention to them Lady Holland's disapprobation and that it came from Lord Melbourne.

*

Taking a few hours off from the Foreign Office, on 16th December 1839, Lord Palmerston married the now widowed Lady Cowper. Despite the fact that this lady was reputed to have been his mistress for thirty years, Lady Holland manages to imply a marriage of fresh young love, in her description of it:

> It will be the union of two of the best-tempered persons in the world. Never did I see a man more in love and devoted. So there is every prospect of happiness for them, as her family on both sides are friendly and kind upon the subject.

The diplomatic situation was too tense to allow time for a honeymoon and, directly the wedding was over, Lord Palmerston returned to his office.

Deprived of her honeymoon, a week later, the new Lady Palmerston gave her first Christmas party at her new home, Broadlands, in Hampshire. Both Baron Neumann, Metternich's envoy, and Baron Brünow, sent by the Czar on a special mission to England, were her guests.

*

Characteristically, on 1st February 1840, Henry Fox gives his mother his own ribald interpretation of the Penny Post (introduced on 10th January).

> The *improvement* of your Post Office arrangements made the English letters arrive here a day later than they used to do and they cost nearly double the former price . . .

On 10th February, Queen Victoria married Prince Albert of Coburg and, four days later, Lady Holland explains to Henry her despatch to him of an unusual gift. 'Papa has officially a magnificent and really very pretty plum cake.' She explains that she cannot send him the whole cake but sends a large slice, which Henry puts to diplomatic use. On 4th April, he tells his mother that 'it was sent to the Grand Duchess (of Tuscany) while she was at dinner at one o'clock! ! ! She very discreetly only cut about half of it and sent us the rest back after all the Royal Guests had tasted it.'

After her marriage, Lord Holland continued to dine with the Queen and to attend her State balls, to which Lady Holland knew she could never expect admittance. Yet, on 31st July, Mr Allen notes in the Dinner Books: 'Prince Albert made a visit in the morning on Lady Holland accompanied by Col. Bouverie and Mr Anson.'

Neither to Henry nor to Caroline Fox does Lady Holland enlarge on the purpose of this mysterious visit.

*

On 12th May, Lady Holland writes agitatedly to Henry Fox about the murder of Lord William Russell, Lord John's uncle: '. . . I have been so much overwhelmed with horror . . . nothing is proved . . . case very strong against the Valet . . .' Three days later, Charles Greville, too, reports the case which he declares 'has excited a prodigious interest, and frightened all London out of its wits'. The valet, Courvoisier, is tried, convicted and executed.

In her same letter, Lady Holland touches on a different subject, that of the return of Napoleon's remains to be given 'a great state funeral', in France. As a conciliatory gesture, harmless to England, Lord Palmerston had already agreed to it and, on 9th May, had informed the Hollands: 'Napoleon's remains are to be transported to France.' Lady Holland declares:

. . . of course there can be no difficulty made to such a demand. However it is notorious that William IV would have objected, so averse was he to such a possibility that he even ordered Chantrey to make the design of a monument in order as he intended to *secure* the continuance under English control . . .

On 29th, she exclaims 'I cannot say how gratified I feel at the tardy hommage . . .' But, after making tentative plans to meet Henry in Paris, she thinks 'the hurly burly' attendant on the return of Napoleon's remains would be 'anything but suitable to an infirm old couple', and cries off.

By 19th June, she is in a state of agitation again, this time because she is worried that her name is being dragged into public print over something at St Helena. What can they (the newspapers) mean?

Henry enjoys himself, in his reply:

. . . Have you seen the article in the Quotidienne stating that Napoleon's body is *not* at St Helena—that in 1827 Madame Mère and Cardinal Fesch sent an agent to England to *Lady Holland* who prevailed on (undecipherable) to wink at its abstraction, which Bullock undertook to effect and received £20,000 for his pains from Torlonia. How very silently and secretly you seem to have managed the affair. I own I think having got £20,000 out of Madame Mère for her son when dead, when she would not lend him a sou while he was living shews a charming knowledge of character in the writers of the article—the story is said to rest on the authority of an English Baronet—is it Sir R.(obert) Wilson? It is very like one of his tales . . .

Henry's ridicule has a salutary effect, and Lady Holland does not refer to the matter again.

*

A crisis had existed in the Middle East since 1833, when the Pasha of Egypt, Mehemet Ali, had rebelled against his overlord, the Sultan of Turkey, and thereafter had maintained an increasingly successful guerrilla war against him. To keep Turkey as a buffer state between Russian and French aspirations in the Eastern Mediterranean, Lord Palmerston had been negotiating a treaty with the Northern Powers which Russia, Austria and Prussia were willing to sign but from which France held back. Lord Melbourne's Cabinet was not unanimous in its reception of it.

Directly it became clear that although the French were holding back Lord Palmerston was determined to 'bully them into acquiescence', Lord Holland and the new Privy Seal, Lord Clarendon, sharply disagreed with him. As always, the corner-stone of Lord Holland's foreign policy was to preserve good relations with France; and both he and Lord Clarendon were afraid that Lord Palmerston's project might play into the hands of Russia. Lord Melbourne, himself, was undecided. On the one hand, he feared an Egypt dominated by France; on the other, Russia, controlling Turkey. But most of all, he feared a split in his own party. So (to quote) 'He . . . took up his usual mid-way position and pleaded rather ineffectively to his colleagues for compromise.'

Primed in British politics by his mistress and Lord Palmerston's arch-enemy, Princess Lieven, in the new year of 1840, François Guizot succeeded Sebastiani, as French Ambassador to Great Britain. He had an abortive meeting with Lord Melbourne, who was friendly but non-committal. But, at Holland House he received a warm welcome, as the Hollands and he were old friends.

On two successive days (24th and 25th May) Guizot gives Princess Lieven news of Lady Holland. On 24th, when he describes her gnawing hunger whilst he politely puts back his dinner-hour to suit Lord Palmerston; on 25th, when he tells Princess Lieven that Lady Holland has taken on his education (in English). Discussing the saying: 'The way to Hell is paved with good intentions', she apologises for her impertinence, but warns him that, unless he is quoting Milton, he must never use the word 'hell' in polite conversation. As she gets to know Guizot better, she becomes more revealing in her remarks. She tells him that she hates solitude and only reads so much because she is so often alone. She tells him of the isolation of old age and of all the friends she has lost. And she tells him that sometimes when she feels particularly lonely, she goes into the library at Holland House and peoples it again in her imagination with her 'amiable friends': '. . . Romilly, on that chair, Mackintosh here, Horner there . . .' Guizot declares that as she speaks she is visibly moved and 'nearly eloquent in

EMPIRE FRANÇAIS.

Nous Ministre des Affaires Etrangères

Prions les Officiers Civils & Militaires chargés de maintenir
l'Ordre Public en France & chez l'Etranger
de laisser passer librement Lord & Lady Holland, traversant
la France pour se rendre en Angleterre par Calais, avec leur
suite, laisser entrer sur tous les points où ils se présenteront.

& donnez lui aide & protection en cas de besoin.
le présent Passeport valable pour
Donné à Paris le Vingt Mai 1815.

Le Ministre des Affaires Etrangères

Par le S Ministre
Chef du 8 du passeport.

Napoleon's passport to 3rd Lord Holland,
dated May 20th, 1815

Dr. John Allen, librarian at Holland House,
painted by Sir Edward Landseer

a very few words'. And he repeats again what he has said before that, of all the women he has met in England, Lady Holland has the best brain. In June, Princess Lieven arrives in London, to stay with the Sutherlands, so Guizot's letters to her cease, until September.

Still the French would not declare themselves and, in July, Lord Palmerston proposed to a divided Cabinet that, without France, Great Britain, Russia, Austria and Prussia should form a new treaty, to help the Sultan. Lord Holland and Lord Clarendon greeted his proposal with threats of resignation. (Greville reports Lord Holland as saying 'that he could not be a party to any measure which might be likely to occasion a breach between this country and France'.) Lord Palmerston countered by threatening his own resignation, were the outline of his new treaty not accepted. Desperately, Lord Melbourne strove to preserve unanimity. 'For God's sake let nobody resign or we'll have everybody resigning!' he cried. Eventually, a Minute was introduced, exempting Lords Holland and Clarendon from responsibility in any proposal with which they did not agree, and Lord Palmerston's new treaty was passed.

On 16th July Princess Lieven dined at Holland House in company with the Clarendons, Lord Camoys, Lady Acton and Thomas Macaulay (now Secretary at War). No doubt her expert questioning of Lord Holland and even of Lord Clarendon helped Guizot to prepare for the oncoming crisis in his country.

For the French, of course, were furious when the proposal for the new treaty became known. And, led by 'their excitable Prime Minister', Thiers, their rage became so vociferous that it looked as if they might actively range themselves on the side of Mehemet Ali, against the Northern Powers. Inside the Cabinet, the pacifists became frantic and even Lord John Russell (now Colonial Secretary and Leader of the House of Commons) became so alarmed by the prospect of war, that he went back on the treaty, 'and changed his mind'. He, the new Duke of Bedford, and Lord Spencer clamoured 'for some compromise with France, before it is too late'. But their agitation failed to impress Lord Palmerston, who cheerfully maintained that the French were bluffing. Lord Melbourne went from one member of his Cabinet to another, urging unity; and even got the Duke of Wellington, in Opposition, to promise him his support.

By August, the Hollands were inviting Princess Lieven and Mons. Guizot together, on an average, once a week. Charles Greville declares that Lord Palmerston was 'very sore' at the open way in which Lord Holland criticised his foreign policy and, certainly, his name appears less often than formerly in the Dinner Books. But Lady Palmerston still comes

M

regularly, usually in company with the Princess and the French Ambassador.

In September, Charles Greville dines several times at Holland House, observing, on 5th September:

> I have been more in the way of hearing about the Eastern question during the last week than at any previous time, though my informants and associates have all been of the Anti-Palmerston interest—Holland House, and Clarendon, Dedel who objects to the *form* more than to the *fond*, and Madam de Lieven, who is all with Guizot, because he is devoted to her, and she feels the greatest interest where she gets the most information . . .

'Clarendon says that whatever his opinion may have been, now that they are fairly embarked on Palmerston's course, he must as earnestly desire its success as if he had been its original advocate? But' (Greville continues) 'both he and Lord Holland have been so vehemently committed in opposition to it, that, without any imputation of unpatriotic feelings, it is not in human nature they should not find a sort of satisfaction in the frustration of those measures which they so strenuously resisted, and this clearly appears in all Lord Holland said to me and in Lady Holland's tone about Palmerston and his daring disposition.'

On 3rd October, Mr Allen notes: 'Lord Holland prevented from going to the Cabinet at Claremont by an attack of vomiting in the course of last night.'

Four days later, Charles Greville describes a dinner-party which had taken place, on 4th October:

> Dined at Holland House on Sunday, Palmerstons, John Russell, Morpeth, etc., all very merry, with sundry jokes about Beyrout, and what not . . . Lady Holland was plaintive (to Palmerston) about an article in the 'Examiner', in which Fonblanque had said something about H. H. taking a part against the foreign policy; . . . they talked together amicably enough.

Albany Fonblanque, editor and proprietor of the *Examiner* had sent 'his most abject apologies' to Lady Holland for 'the impertinent story' she referred to, which, he declared, 'had slipped into his paper', without his knowledge.

Describing his visit to Holland House, on 5th October, Guizot, too, refers to the article. He tells Princess Lieven that he found his host worried and crestfallen ('troublé, interdit'). Lady Holland had declared herself extremely hurt by it, as she knew the author of it and had always shown him kindness. Guizot had felt that Lord Holland was not built to withstand attack, only challenge, and that, in future, the writer of the article had better keep out of Lady Holland's way. But, as a Frenchman, he tells

Princess Lieven that the article suits him perfectly. And he boasts that now he has the British Government where he wants it. On the one hand, he manipulates 'the old Whigs', through Holland House; on the other, the radicals and, thereby, he stirs up trouble in the Cabinet. ('J'agite l'intérieur du Cabinet'.)

On 18th October, Lord Melbourne feels it necessary to write Lord Holland a sober letter, in which he produces evidence that accounts of matters debated in the British Cabinet are 'being conveyed, from Paris to a banker in Vienna'. Lord Holland himself is reputed to be the source from which they come and 'the material was believed in and acted upon by Metternich'. Tactfully, Lord Melbourne continues:

The probable truth is, that intelligence is written from London to Paris, which is obtained, or said to be obtained, at Holland House, from whence the transition of its being actually furnished by you is ready, easy and natural.

You have a great many people of various descriptions at Holland House, most of them connected with politics, some of them with the City and Bourse. It is impossible to say who or which of the many make this sort of use of what he may hear.

I know not what can be done except to take care that as little of political affairs transpires in conversation as possible; but this is inconsistent with a *salon*, which has many advantages but some disadvantages, and more particularly when matters of great importance are pending.

On 13th October, Lord Holland was unwell again, but recovered and, on 18th, 19th and 20th, he and his wife entertained, as usual. On the morning of 21st, he awoke ill and feeling 'very uncomfortable'. Three doctors, Holland, Chambers and Sir Stephen Hammick, were called in but they could do nothing and, that day, Lady Holland transcribes the word 'Illness—Illness' in the Dinner Books, twice repeated, in a trembling hand.

Lord Holland died, early on the morning of 22nd October. And that day, too, Lady Holland makes an entry in the Dinner Books:

This wretched day closes all the happiness, refinement and hospitality within the walls of Holland House.

Augusta Fox's future adopted daughter, Princess Liechtenstein, declares that, a few days before Lord Holland died, he wrote some lines in verse, which were found on his dressing-table. No reference to them appear in his family papers, but they were 'widely circulated' at the time:

> Nephew of Fox, and friend of Grey,
> Enough my meed of fame.
> If those who deign to observe me say,
> I injured neither name.

＊

The Times printed no obituary of Lord Holland. (It had already castigated the *French faction in the Cabinet* in its leader of 16th October.) The *St James's Chronicle* and the *Morning Post* were not complimentary. Both referred to Lord Holland's opposition to Lord Palmerston's foreign policy, as it applied to his negotiations with France.

The *St James's Chronicle* declares:

Lord Holland was a Cabinet minister and Chancellor of the Duchy of Lancaster. It is pretty well known that in the Cabinet he lately headed a party opposed to Lord Palmertson's foreign policy . . . If Lord Holland is replaced by a person of the same opinions Lord Palmerston may find himself embarrassed by a more energetic opposition than heretofore; should a minister of more *English* views . . . succeed, the negotiation with France will be much simplified . . .

The *Morning Post* is yet more explicit:

The death of Lord Holland is perhaps of more political importance at the present moment than it would have been at any former period of his public existence. He has been generally understood to have led a sort of Cabinet opposition to Lord Palmerston upon the Turkish question, and to have not only favoured but vehemently seconded, the objects of the French Minister upon that question. He has even been lately pointed at by a Ministerial journal which espouses the Palmerston views of foreign policy as intriguing with M. Thiers for the defeat of that policy which the majority of the British Cabinet had determined upon.

*

In their analyses of Lord and Lady Holland's characters, François Guizot and Charles Greville reached the same conclusion. Lord Holland was a light-weight, of superficial attachments; Lady Holland had more heart.

Writing from Windsor, on 23rd October, unexpectedly, Guizot takes the sentimental view.

If I knew what the word grief meant, I would say that poor Lord Holland's sudden death yesterday, was a grief to me. So good and kind! . . . I am shocked, really shocked, at the indifference with which the news (of his death) has been received, around me (here). This is a hard people. I have heard old soldiers speak of their comrades who have died beside them in battle: they were more moved . . .

At this moment of crisis among her Majesty's Ministers, British phlegm had to appear invulnerable, before the French Ambassador.

On 31st December 1840, Charles Greville reviews the events of the past year. He declares that the one which 'had made the deepest impression on society' is Lord Holland's death.

I doubt from all I see whether anybody (except his own family, including Allen) had really a very warm affection for Lord Holland, and the reason probably is that he had none for anybody. He was a man of inexhaustible good humour, and an ever flowing good nature, but not of strong feelings; . . . I remember to have heard good observers say that Lady Holland had more feeling than Lord Holland—would regret with livelier grief the loss of a friend than this equable philosopher was capable of feeling . . .

PART THREE

Wings

CHAPTER THIRTY-ONE

'A Wretched Being'

HENRY AND AUGUSTA sent Lady Holland pretty protestations of sympathy and affection, but although Lord Palmerston gave Henry immediate leave of absence, he did not avail himself of it until 20th November and so missed his father's funeral at Milbrook Church, on 28th October. There, by the late Lord Holland's especial request, his funeral was entirely private and he was laid to rest beside his little daughter, Georgiana.

On 22nd October, Lord Melbourne writes from Windsor Castle, referring to 'this stunning blow . . .' He goes on to say 'I am charged by the Queen to express her very deep concern, and I can say myself that I am sure that she truly and really feels it . . .' Four days later, he reiterates: 'The Queen makes continual enquiries after you . . .' And, where William IV had refused Lady Holland permission to drive in her pony-carriage in the Park, his niece is more compassionate, commissioning Lord Melbourne to tell her (on 23rd December) that '. . . she did it with the greatest pleasure'.

In Lord Melbourne's letter of 26th October, he says 'I fear that the Physicians are right and that the anxiety of his (Lord Holland's) mind upon political affairs must have had its share in hastening this event . . .' Which opinion Lady Holland endorses at considerable length, stoutly proclaiming her husband's loyalty to his Sovereign:

The Queen's condescension in thinking of such a wretched Being as I now am is kind, and I give her credit entirely for what you say of her being deeply concerned at his loss. She ought to have liked him, for in her whole Dominions there is scarce another who felt to the extent he did such tender devotion and admiration of her. It was really remarkable how she had interested and captivated him . . . the Physicians ascribe it to over nervous excitement upon a frame not naturally strong, he had suffered mentally very much these last few weeks upon publick affairs feeling uncomfortable from his strong opinions on the injustice, as well as impolicy regarding War, which made his position in the Government irksome and he almost thought dishonourable this certainly preyed upon his mind, yet when his mind began to wander Syria Egypt Metternich Palmerston etc. were the words he dropped . . .

Lady Holland winds up:

As you may suppose my interest now in Politicks is extinct, but not so in your responsibility, for it will hurt me excessively to hear you blamed when it has been and may still be in your power to avert the calamity of War. You are too confiding and passive—you and John Russell are my only objects . . .

A note is written upside down on this epistle:

Lady Holland thanks for his kindness and the Queen's (concern?) at Lord Holland's death it proceeded partly from anxiety about the Eastern question.

Despite his knowledge that Lord Holland had tried to baulk his foreign policy at every turn, generously, Lord Palmerston writes:

Though I am sure you know all that I must feel, yet I cannot refrain from sending one word to bring myself to your mind and as a Token of my deep sorrow and sincere sympathy . . .

Other lifelong Whig associates and loving relations write too: the Greys; Lord Spencer; the Carlisles; the Duke of Devonshire; the Richmonds; the Lansdownes; 'Chattering Georgy B' (widow of the 6th Duke of Bedford), together with her step-sons, Francis (7th Duke) William and John Russell. His former feud with her forgotten, William now writes with all his old affection, telling Lady Holland that 'My father and Lord Holland were two of the links that chained us to the endearments of life and these two links are broken almost at the same moment.' He hopes she will consider him 'amongst the friends that remain to you' and thereafter keeps her regularly fed with news. And John, writing, on 23rd October, from Bowood, conveys a son's solicitude:

. . . if you think my being with you be any comfort pray tell Hammick (her doctor) or some one to write me a line and I will be in town on Monday early.

Again, in sharp contrast to dilatory Henry.

Sydney Smith tells Lady Holland that he is ready to come to her 'whenever you wish . . .'

Immediately after Lord Holland's death, Lord Melbourne offered Lady Holland Brocket Hall to go to, but instead, she accepted the Duke of Sutherland's offer of West Hill. There, she repaired with the Lilfords, Charles and Mary Fox, Caroline Fox, Sir Stephen Hammick and Mr Allen. On 3rd November, she writes to Henry:

On Saturday, I left the roof under which for forty-two years happiness without alloy except for health, had been my fortunate lot to enjoy.

Caroline Fox tries to give a fair account of her sister-in-law's grief, to Lady Calcott:

Poor Lady Holland has lived a life of excitement and so *out of acquaintance* with herself on the resources of her own mind, that she needs perpetually the excitement of society and the aid of others. I deeply and sincerely feel for her; tho' her way of feeling is so different from my own, it is not less profound and perhaps more incurable.

She cannot understand that where her own interests are concentrated in her family, Lady Holland needs Europe and indeed the whole world for essential mental stimulus.

On 23rd October, before returning to France, François Guizot addresses Lady Holland an almost lover-like letter of affection and sympathy, asking her to look upon him as one of her most devoted, faithful friends, and to keep him posted with her news. He ends: 'Adieu, dearest Lady Holland, mille tendres et profonds respects—Guizot.' Apparently, Lady Holland answers him by messenger, probably elaborating again on 'the Physicians' ' diagnosis as the next day Guizot thanks her for 'une telle marque de confiance'.

A tide of condolence flowed towards her across the Channel. From Baron Dedel, Dutch Ambassador; Baron Bülow, Prussian Ambassador; Prince Esterhazy; Comtesse de Bourke, widow of a former Danish Ambassador, now living in Paris; Princess Lieven; Comtesse de Flahault.

For once, Princess Lieven's letter (dated 29th October 1840) shows the marks of real emotion: '. . . J'ai versé des larmes sincères, bien sincères. J'admirais, j'aimais, de tout mon coeur l'homme incomparable que nous avons perdu . . .' In her concern for Lady Holland's future, Princess Lieven wonders whether Paris might not offer her relaxation and some pleasant distractions '. . . délassement et des ressources assez douces . . .' If so, how happy she would be to have the opportunity of showing Lady Holland her gratitude for her constant kindness and welcome on the 'charming occasions' she had spent in her company.

Madame de Flahault's letter of 30th October, also from Paris, emphasises another point.

No event ever occasioned more general mourning and here it has been regretted not only as a private loss among his friends but as public calamity by all who knew the value of his liberal and conciliatory disposition towards this unhappy country wh. had so much need of his protecting voice at this moment . . .

All these letters Lady Holland preserved, as equal tributes to her loved one. And others too, ranging from intellectuals like Henry Luttrell, Samuel Rogers, Charles Dickens, Leigh Hunt (who offered her one of his plays), Harriet Grote and Caroline Norton to Mrs Turnbull, sending her a present of butter, and the Rev. Joseph Mansevell, sending her some 'sweet little mountain mutton'. It mattered not from whence the tributes came. Each one contributed to a general eulogy.

Then, a paean of praise gladdened the widow's heart, when, on the last day of October 1840, a private petition, signed by fifty-eight names, went up to Lord Edward Howard, at Norfolk House, asking for 'some Testimony of respect, esteem, and affection' to Lord Holland's memory.

The preamble read:

No man ever lived more honoured and beloved than the late Lord Holland, and no man ever died more sincerely and cordially lamented. It would be a disgrace to Society, that His memory should not be distinguished by some Testimony of respect, esteem, and affection. It is therefore proposed, that such persons, as concur in these sentiments, should send their names privately to Lord Edward Howard, Norfolk House, London; in order, that arrangements may be made for the purpose of giving effect to the general desire of paying a due tribute to such a memory—

Headed by Augustus, Duke of Sussex, lords, commoners, and members of the intelligentsia signed this petition which is given here, in its entirety.

	Augustus F.		Clarendon
	Wellesley		Sutherland
	Lansdowne		W. J. Denison
	J. Russell		Monteagle
5	Norfolk	30	Normanby
	Carlisle		J. Motteux
	Melbourne		Cottenham
	Morpeth		Devonshire
	Bedford		G. Byng
10	Ed. Ellice	35	Rosebery
	Brougham		Spencer
	Grey		J. Hobhouse
	Anglesea		Clanricarde
	Westminster		T. B. Macaulay
15	Fitzwilliam	40	Radnor
	Palmerston		H. Labouchère
	Minto		Jeffrey
	Ebrington		Strafford
	H. Fortescue		J. Gibson-Craig
20	C. Howard	45	W. Gibson-Craig
	F. S. Baring		Panmure
	Duncannon		Leicester (already signed)
	Albemarle		C. Gore
	Grafton		S. Rogers
25	Leicester (who signed twice)		

50 H. Luttrell   55 Fox Maule
    Breadalbane   John Allen
    C. Fitzroy   Robert Adair
    A. Fonblanque   Arran
    Suffolk and Berkshire

Did Albany Fonblanque, editor of the *Examiner* containing the lethal article against Lord Holland, salve his conscience by signing the petition?

*

On 20th November 1840, Henry and Augusta returned to Holland House and, within twenty-four hours of their arrival, Lady Holland's new lawyer, Currey, made Henry a disturbing proposal.

No change had been made in Lord Holland's will of 1837, of which Lady Holland had been made sole executrix. And, although she was only left a life-tenancy in Holland House and Ampthill Park, now she had extensive powers over both properties and the contents of each house were hers, unconditionally. Yet, she was imbued with anxiety about her affairs (Caroline Fox called it 'poverty on £5,000 a year') and was convinced that both Holland House and Ampthill should be let at once, or, better still, that Ampthill should be sold. So, Mr Currey put forward this proposition to Henry.

It did not go down well. Henry and Charles were equally against the idea of selling. Both played for time, and Henry refused to discuss 'anything and everything' with his mother. Some money, to repay a large loan from Coutts' Bank and other commitments, had to be found, and Lord Duncannon was induced to look into the affairs at Ampthill. A decision warmly endorsed by Lord Melbourne, who felt 'Duncannon . . . will be able to judge what is best to do and how to do it.' Thanks to his tact and 'a very fair and reasonable offer' from Francis, Duke of Bedford, the Duke himself bought the estate of Ampthill Park and added it to his property in Bedfordshire.

There remained Holland House, which proved an even bigger bone of contention. Once again, the new Lord Holland fiercely resisted his mother's efforts. On 5th April 1841, before he left again for Italy, he writes to tell her that he cannot consent to any scheme that will destroy the grounds of Holland House. 'Whether I may be able to live there is uncertain and depends chiefly on you.' But he is determined to resist her 'awful scheme', concerning 'the frontage of the Hammersmith Road'.

The disposal of certain pictures from Ampthill Park and Holland House gave rise to further acrimony. And though Lady Holland assured Henry that nothing had been sold out of Holland House, one picture, Leslie's 'Interior of the Library', was given away to Lord Grey. Later, Caroline Fox told Henry she was convinced that Lady Holland spoke the truth when she refuted the allegation that she 'had offered the Library to Mr Holford'.

Another dispute between mother and son was over the future editing of Lord Holland's papers for his *Life of Charles James Fox*. Towards the end of his own life, Lord Holland had enlisted the help of Mr Allen and, at his death, Allen seemed the obvious person to carry on his work. But Henry insisted that 'over and over again', he had heard his father express the wish that his two sons should undertake it. Without consulting either of them, Lady Holland designated Allen for the job and, at first, Caroline Fox approved of her choice. But, when she realised that neither Henry nor Charles had been asked to agree to Allen's appointment she (as also Sir Robert Adair whom Lady Holland had consulted as well) clandestinely wrote to Henry, informing him of his mother's intention. Thus, consciously or not, Caroline Fox continued to fan the flame of Henry's suspicions.

And Charles Richard's relations with his mother were no better. In May 1841, he burst out into one of his usual tirades:

> You know well how you have been towards all your children for years and years, you know the things you have said of them, you know the things you have said of those they love, you know the jealousy you have shewn of their being with him they loved above all the world.

To parry the venom of his attack, Mr Allen was called in as mediator. And when the poor man defended his beloved patroness by observing that she 'had always loved her children too fondly and indulgently perhaps for their good', Charles turned the direction of his attack to him. How dared he speak in this strain? he demanded. Had not Allen witnessed the way his sister, Mary Lilford, had been treated 'from her very birth to her womanhood'? Either Allen had 'no observation at all', or he was ready to 'assert anything as a partisan . . .'

Alas! Lord Holland was no longer there to soothe his difficult sons.

*

By the beginning of December 1840, Lady Holland was back in her 'nutshell', in South Street, and, on 21st January 1841, Charles Greville accepted her invitation to dinner.

He tells his memoirs:

> Everything there is exactly the same as it used to be, excepting only the person of Lord Holland, who seems to be pretty well forgotten. The same talk went

merrily round, the laugh rang loudly and frequently, and, but for the black and mob-cap of the Lady, one might have fancied he had never lived or had died half a century ago.

Greville readily admitted that Lady Holland had produced 'a party well composed for talk, for there were listeners of intelligence, and a good specimen of the sort of society of this house—Macaulay, Melbourne, Morpeth, Duncannon, Baron Rolfe, Allen and Lady Holland, and John Russell came in the evening'. It did not occur to him that an old Lady of rising seventy must still be possessed of extraordinary magnetism to be able to attract to her side eight men of such distinction.

During a debate in Parliament on foreign policy, on 26th January 1841, Lord John Russell delivered his apologia for Lord Holland, carefully wedging it between other matters.

... I very much lament, that in the course of the discussions in the French Chambers, the name of a most honoured friend of mine, lately deceased, has been not infrequently referred to for the purpose of showing that there was disunion in the Cabinet of this country, as to the mode of carrying out the treaty of July. I must say that I think the use which has been made of my noble Friend's name was a most unwarrantable liberty ...

Lord John goes on to stress his Friend's altruistic 'motives connected with the general peace of the world'; his kindness and benevolence; his high sense of honour and unflinching integrity; and the way he had represented 'for a long course of years ... those great principles which were maintained by Mr Fox ...'

On the one hand, Charles Greville reduces to one paragraph Lord John's well-meant efforts to re-establish Lord Holland's good name:

John said something about Lord Holland in the H. of C. but Melbourne could not be prevailed on to say anything in the H. of Lords. Lady H. was satisfied with it, but though it was a prettily turned compliment, it was of no great service in relieving him from the charges which have been levelled at him.

On the other hand, in a letter to Lady Holland dated 27th January, Lord Clarendon takes the opposite view.

J(ohn) Russell's allusion last night was beautiful and produced the effect it deserved, but I had the gratification to find among the numerous persons I talked to that, with respect to the calumnies, it was quite unneccessary. Everyone seemed indignant that such falsehoods shld. ever have been put in circulation.

In May, Macaulay was approached to write an article on the late Lord Holland, for the *Edinburgh Review*. On the grounds that he had only known Lord Holland towards the end of his life, at first he demurred.

There were 'extensive portions of his character' with which he was 'not familiar'; he had never heard Lord Holland speak in Parliament. When finally he accepted the task, he made it plain that he did so 'with unaffected reluctance and diffidence'. His final conclusions were not very complimentary to the Foxes, and called forth some lively criticism. Madame de Flahault wrote to Mr Allen, from Paris, considering it in

singular bad taste to take that opportunity to throw odium upon his (Lord Holland's) grandfather and to criticise the early life of his uncle. I am sure there is no attack upon himself that Lord Holland would not have preferred to this last.

*

Now, to Lady Holland's regular correspondents is added a new one, her daughter, Lady Pellew. Admiral Sir Fleetwood Pellew appears to have represented naval intelligence on Lord Granville's staff at Paris and, from thence, on 17th January 1841, his wife starts her letters to her mother by giving her some social news.

Madame de Flahault had given 'a charming dance . . . a v. v. small sauterie for the younger girls—the third is v. pretty like Emily . . .' The (British) Embassy theatricals had taken place wherein Lady Pellew and Madame de Flahault had performed 'the humble part of figurantes in the tableaux . . .' The next day, she writes again, announcing that she is 'thinking of moving towards London . . . Happy if I cld. find a house in yr. neighbourhood . . .' A sentiment but rarely expressed by Lady Holland's children. On 4th April, she announces her daughter Harriet's possible marriage with Lord Walpole, Lord Orford's heir. 'Sir Fleetwood has still to meet Lord Orford' and, apparently, is in no hurry to do so as 'Sir F. wishes H to marry her cousin Exmouth . . .'

This news was circumstantial enough for Lady Holland to make her other daughter, Lady Lilford, a party to it. And, despite a biographer describing 'her thoughtfulness for others and her kindness to all around her', Mary Lilford's reply (dated 10th April 1841) is decidedly catty.

Poor girl, she has been *v. ill* educated, but has I think naturally an affectionate disposition and some quickness—if Ld. W. is sensible and really attached to her. I hope he will improve her manner and style of talk and she may then become a far more agreeable member of Society. Eventually I suppose she will have a large fortune of her own.

Not only had Lady Holland told Mary Lilford of Lord Walpole's attentions. She interviewed the young man herself! For, on 11th April, Lady Pellew writes to thank her 'for receiving Ld. Walpole'.

She gives details of his depressing prospects: £1,200 a year allowance, with debts of £2,000. 'His father paid up once, won't do so again. So, only present method paying £200 a year to debtors.' As such, it is hardly surprising that 'Sir Fleetwood objects to this, so no official announcement at present.' But Lady Pellew herself seems set on the match and tells her mother that 'Miss Pellew' will have £1,000 a year, of her own, and prospects of £10,000 a year entailed estates. Furthermore, if she herself lives with the young couple she can help with their expenses. Her single-mindedness achieves its purpose and Harriet Pellew marries Lord Walpole on 11th November 1841.

*

In April of that year, after Henry had left for Florence, nostalgia drove Lady Holland back to Holland House. Quite a large party of friends accompanied her, including Charles and Mary Fox, Sir Robert Adair, Henry Luttrell and her old friend, the Belgian Ambassador, Baron Dedel. But, despite her telling Henry that she found 'a melancholy pleasure' in revisiting her old home, she could not stand it for long and, five days later, left it. Thereafter, she tried the expedient of daily visits from South Street to her sister-in-law, at Little Holland House, where she sat in the garden and declared herself happy to be near, but out of sight of, Holland House.

That summer, one event gave Lady Holland real pleasure. Lord John Russell married again. Announcing his engagement to Lord Minto's daughter, Lady Frances Elliot, she tells Henry: 'She is a lucky woman and will I dare say make him happy as he deserves. She is good tempered and sensible.'

Again, a magnet drew her back to the vicinity of Holland House, and she elected in August to stay for a week with her sister-in-law. This entailed elaborate arrangements. Lady Holland's servants were accommodated in the big house but came from thence to wait on her and cook her food. For health reasons, and perhaps for reasons of policy, Caroline Fox made it a rule to dine alone, at five o'clock, each day, after which she joined the other ladies in her drawing-room from half-past seven to half-past ten. (We wonder she had the strength for three hours' solid talk, each evening.) She gave her sister-in-law the full run of her house, allowing her to ask her own guests and to act as hostess.

In September, again Lady Holland tried to return to Holland House. And this time she gladly accepted Caroline Fox's offer to accompany her. Yet she could not endure the drive up to the front entrance and went into the house through a side-door. And only the ground floor was put into commission, with Lady Holland occupying Henry Fox's old rooms. Her usual good friends supported her: the Palmerstons, Lord John Russell and his new wife, Lord Duncannon. And Lady Holland admitted that, temporarily at least, her spirits revived in her well-loved surroundings. 'The gardens are as perfect as ever, the flowers never more brilliant; the Dahlias he so admired shine in every colour.'

Then, melancholy envelops her again when she declares: '. . . a *stillness* strikes at the heart, and drives me away'.

*

In May 1841, Lord Melbourne's Government tottered to its fall and, at a general election, in June, the Tories were returned to Parliament with a majority of seventy seats. This fact lost Charles Fox his post at the Ordnance, but he was lucky enough to be elected to Parliament for Tower Hamlets. Lord Aberdeen now succeeded Lord Palmerston at the Foreign Office, and Henry's diplomatic future looked precarious, so much so that Caroline Fox urged him to resign before he was dismissed. But Lord Aberdeen seemed in no hurry to make any changes, so Henry and Augusta decided to sit it out, at Florence.

Lady Holland had declared to Lord Melbourne that, with her husband's death, her interest in 'Politicks' was now extinct. Yet, a large section of her acquaintance still considered her all-powerful.

In June, Mrs Turnbull thanks her for her application to Sir Halsey Vivien, to get her son admitted to Woolwich. The same month, Charles Dickens thanks her for her valuable introduction to Lord Lauderdale (son of her old friend) on his 'official' trip to Edinburgh, where a dinner has been arranged in his honour. In August, both Lady Keith (Madame de Flahault) and her cousin, Lord Elphinstone, write to ask her to procure for him a British peerage. In September, Lady Howick asks Lady Holland how to get a boy into the Blue Coat School. In October, her granddaughter, Harriet Pellew, on the eve of her marriage, asks her to 'mention Walpole favourably to Lord Aberdeen'. And, before very long, rumour has it that Lady Holland, herself, is lobbying Lord Aberdeen, on behalf of her son, Henry Holland! Which calls forth a timely warning from Lady Palmerston. '. . . the *under people* (at the Foreign Office) are v. spiteful and one of them said to me that you had *asked* Lord Aberdeen to let Henry Fox stay at Florence. This I denied at once and said I was sure it was not true.'

All the same, in May 1842, Lord Aberdeen is assuring Lady Holland that there is no truth whatsoever in the report that Sir George Hamilton is going, as British Minister, to Florence. '. . . Nor can I imagine on what foundation such a report has been propagated.'

*

As early as January 1841, the Duke of Devonshire had written to tell Lady Holland that he thought 33 South Street 'quite unfit for a residence for you therefore you must not let . . . melancholy recollections . . . make you unwilling to leave it'.

Probably his sentiment had contributed to her general unrest as, during her toings and froings to Holland House that spring and summer, her agent had been preparing an ever-lengthening list of houses to take, on lease, in London. Lady Holland had stipulated that she wanted one with a view over Hyde Park but though his list was long, none of the owners mentioned in it seemed keen to let to her.

In Park Street, looking towards the Park, only one householder (Mr W. Beckford) out of twenty-one had seemed amenable.

In Upper Brook Street (at No. 29) Miss Campbell had just refused 800 guineas from Sir Rothway—for the season, and 'will not let for less than £1000 a yr. and *certainly not* for *more* than one yr. at a time'.

No. 21 New Norfolk Street, belonging to Mrs Lambert, seemed the only possible house, out of twelve; in Seamore Place, not one in eight houses was available.

Despite Lady Holland's scornful reference (made in 1828) to 'that swamp called Belgrave Square', the list began to go further afield to Thomas Cubitt's new houses, south of Hyde Park.

Mrs Marx (at No. 81 Eaton Square) was prepared to let, for 280 guineas, 'from now till Easter'; Mrs Thellusson (at No. 88) would let for one year, at 600 guineas, or for £500 'anytime after Xmas till the end of Aug.'. Her house contained three large rooms on each of the best floors and boasted 'beautifully furnished baths etc.'.

Another good house was No. 10 Belgrave Road, in which four rooms were furnished. There, the rent asked was £800 a year, or, alternatively, the lease might be bought.

On none of these houses was Lady Holland prepared to make an offer, so, next, she commissioned Madame de Flahault to find her a house at Brighton. Here again, Madame de Flahault combed through the advantages of half a dozen houses on the Steyne and at Hove, finally recommending Byam House which, though shabbily furnished, contained three bedrooms facing the sea. Rent: 14 guineas a week and up to 18 guineas in October. Madame de Flahault added an interesting footnote. She had

made the journey to Brighton, from London, 'by the railroad' which had
been 'v. progressive', in comfortable carriages under the care of attentive
'inspectors', and which had been accomplished in under four hours.

At Brighton, Lady Holland met again the poet, Horatio Smith, whom
her husband and she had befriended, ten years before. On the eve of her
departure he addressed her a long laudatory poem of which we quote the
first and last verses:

To Lady Holland, on her quitting Brighton,
October, 1841

When sickness, pouncing on its prey,
Immures him in his lonely room,
While storms without, by night and day,
Combine to aggravate his doom,—
Oh! with what eagerness the breast,
Which naught but sympathy can ease,
Responds to every proffer'd test
Of friendship's cherished offices.

Lady farewell! My health is thine,
And time, with all the healing balm
Of friendly sympathies, combine
To renovate thy mental calm.—
Hard is the struggle for the breast
To check the gushing sorrow, when
It mourns the kindest, noblest, best,
Of husbands—patriots—friends—and men!

*

That autumn, Madame de Flahault's enthusiasm for the new form of
transport may have encouraged Lady Holland to visit the Lansdownes, at
Bowood. Isambard Brunel, already celebrated as chief engineer of the
Great Western Railway, directed one of his subordinates to look after her
and her journey to Calne was achieved without mishap.

The return journey was not so easy. Brunel himself intended to accompany Lady Holland, but floods on the line confined him to his office, at
Chippenham. From thence, he scribbles her an agitated note, attempting
to put her off. Already he has personally inspected some of the 'impedi-
ments' and assures her that

the trains continue to run with perfect safety . . . (but) if we should be disappointed
in the hope of a fine night . . . I do not think the journey would be such as your
Ladyship would like. I am obliged to go to another part of the line tonight but I
will return to Chippenham tomorrow morning and shall hold myself and all other
things ready for you but I confess that it will relieve my mind from some anxiety

for your Ladyship, although it may disappoint me to find that you do not intend to travel by the railway.

He ends up:

I hope your Ladyship will pardon this my hasty and I fear almost illegible scrawl but I am keeping a train while I write it.

And he signs himself:

Your Ladyships
devoted servant
I. K. Brunel.

No doubt gratified to think that Brunel had held up a train to convey his apologies, Lady Holland took his hint and posted home, by road, braving Madame de Flahault's scarcely veiled sarcasm:

If yr. nerves are over-excited by it, had you not better come to town in yr. good *coach and four* which *at two miles an hour* wld. be less alarming . . .

*

Of all the friends who rallied to her in her sorrow, none was more solicitious in her attentions than Lady Palmerston. Better than anyone, she realised that, as an antidote to acute depression, Lady Holland had to see people. ('Society is her greatest support in her unhappiness and this is much better than if she shut herself away completely.') As she tells Princess Lieven: 'I visit her practically every day, morning or evening.' And, when she cannot do this, she writes delightful letters, keeping her old friend in touch with the world.

The last social rally of the Whigs was in August, when Francis, Duke of Bedford, entertained Queen Victoria and Prince Albert, at Woburn. Lady Palmerston gives a graphic description of the Queen's rapturous welcome by the Duke's tenants who 'rode like mad not caring whether they broke their necks or covered her with dust . . .' At first, she was surprised by the Dowager Duchess's behaviour in going off 'to take a place in the Park in one of the waggons standing there to see the Queen arrive'. But, thereafter, she describes with great sympathy Georgiana Duchess's brave demeanour, although 'it was all she could do to keep from crying the first day when she came to dinner'.

For Lady Holland's benefit, Lady Palmerston gives the list of the Duke's guests, at dinner each evening: 'Leinsters, Somersets, Sutherlands, Wellingtons, Devonshires, De Greys, Palmerstons, Ld. Melbourne, Tavistock, Dow. Duchess, 2 Bedfords, Ld. Headfort, Col. Buckley Bouverie, Mrs Lyttelton and Miss Cavendish . . .' In the evening, others 'drift in' and there is music, when (Alfred) Panizzi (already keeper of printed books at the British Museum but merely described by Lady Palmerston as 'the Horn player') accompanies 'Miss Masson's voice'.

Out of office, Lord Palmerston went to visit his Irish estates, in Sligo, from whence Lady Palmerston writes Lady Holland her usual lively descriptions. Although he only remains there a couple of months, Lady Palmerston declares that he and she lead a 'Robinson Crusoe life creating everything around us' and that 'P. has done wonders in civilising the people and making a most grateful and contented population'.

On her return to London, she takes up the question of Lady Holland's future residence, subtly whetting her friend's appetite to acquire the Palmerstons' own house, in 'Stanhope Gardens' (9 Great Stanhope Street) by refusing to consider such a proposal.

You don't wish for it for only *one* year. Lord So'ton pays £800 a year for the House (*without* stables). Banting says in that situation it is well worth £900 . . . I am sure yr. servants wld. dislike the offices as much as ours do.

She regrets that it is impossible for her husband to consider Lady Holland as a tenant until he has removed his furniture, pictures and books which are stored in the house.

This cat-and-mouse technique continues until November 1843, when Lady Holland moves into 9 Great Stanhope Street, at a yearly rent of £1,000!

*

Unable to settle, after Brighton, Lady Holland returned to 33 South Street where she remained for the next few months. Then, late in June 1842, following some necessary alterations to the ground floor, she made another big effort to take up her residence again, at Holland House.

CHAPTER THIRTY-TWO

Keeping in Touch

LARGELY CONFINED TO her little drawing-room in South Street, Lady Holland kept in touch with the world: with America, Canada, the Far East, and with her friends and relations, at home.

During the autumn of 1841, on the eve of his departure for America, Lord Morpeth called to bid her farewell and, in December, Charles Dickens did the same. Thereafter, the geographical progress of the two young men round the States was largely similar, Lord Morpeth ahead of Charles Dickens by 'a week or two'.

Lord Morpeth had attained the office of Secretary for Ireland in Lord Melbourne's Government but, having lost his seat in the June elections, he set off on a tour of America starting from New York where Lady Holland was able to provide him with a useful introduction.

About 1750, her maternal grandfather, Captain Thomas Clarke (a retired English officer), had bought a farm on the banks of the Hudson River which, later, was incorporated into the City of New York. Situated between 19th and 28th Streets, 8th Avenue and the river, he had called his property 'Chelsea, as being the retreat of an old war-worn veteran who had seen much service in the British Army'. Before very long, the development of the City of New York around it increased its value a thousand-fold. The eldest of Lady Affleck's two sisters, Charity, now a great heiress, married Benjamin Moore, later Bishop of New York, and it was to her descendants that Lady Holland, matchmaking as usual, introduced the charming heir of the 6th Earl of Carlisle.

Lord Morpeth's letter to Lady Holland, from Boston, is dated 16th December 1841, and, knowing her fastidious palate, first he announces that he is sending her some canvas-backed ducks 'by the Arcadia packet' (presumably, packed in blocks of ice and straw). 'They eat them here rather under-roasted, with their own gravy and currant jelly.' Then, he gives her a précis of his tour:

The Yankees are treating me very well, among others, *Miss Sarah Moore*, was v. benevolent to me at New York, and she shews with great pride the Sheffield knife with the view of Castle Howard which you gave her. You wld. be much pleased (I think) with *Mr Prescott* the historian of Ferdinand and Isabella, he is now with the conquest of Mexico and is well fed with manuscripts and every sort of document from Spain . . . They care most for literature and art in this town, for gaiety, fine furniture and French dresses in New York . . .

He tells Lady Holland he aims to proceed to Washington and Baltimore; is 'astonished' to find she is committing herself to 'a Railroad'; and ends up: 'Affec. yrs. Morpeth'.

Charles Dickens' letter from 'Baltimore, United States' to Lady Holland is dated 22nd March 1842, and, in his opening paragraph, he seeks to refute Lady Holland's prediction that he would become spoilt by his triumphal tour.

I know that I am not mistaken in thinking that you would like to hear from my own lips that I am well, not at all spoiled (you remember that you thought I should be?) and longing, in common with my wife, to be again in our dear old home and among our friends and children . . .

Thereafter he confirms her prediction, in nearly every line.

Perhaps you know something of the Public Progress I am obliged to make in this country—of the ball (attended by three thousand people) which they gave me at New York—and of the festivals of all kinds with which they have received me. Public entertainments were proposed in every town I intended to visit—but I gave public notice that I could not possibly bear it, and have refused all those in contemplation, except one. This originates with the people of St. Louis, a town in the Far West, near the Indian Territory. It is one, two thousand miles from here— quite next door as one may say—and I am going there to dinner. We start the day after to-morrow . . .

Rather tardily, he introduces Mrs Dickens 'who remains well in this perfectly trying climate' and thereafter has the grace to include her in the general ovation:

We were obliged to hold a (Levee?) for all comers every day when we are not travelling. . . . The Queen and Prince Albert can scarcely be more tired—for ours is a perpetual drawingroom. Our crown, too, is not a golden one except in opinion.

The Dickenses had been to Boston, Worcester, Hertford, New Haven, New York, Philadelphia, Washington and Richmond, in Virginia. And, originally, they had meant to go as far south as Charleston 'but the premature hot weather and the sight of slavery turned us back'. Now they were on their way to 'the Forests, Mountains and Prairies of the West' and had taken their passage home in a sailing-ship, leaving New York on 7th June.

More soberly, Dickens continues:

I have made some observations of course. They are not all favourable, for I love England better than when I left her. But I am bound to say that travellers have grossly exaggerated American rudeness and obtrusion. Among all the thousands whom I have seen . . . I have never once encountered a man, woman, or child who has asked me a rude question, or made a rude remark. The best and only passports needed in this country, are frankness and good humour . . .

Dickens tells Lady Holland that he has been 'a week or so' behind Lord Morpeth, who, wherever he has been, 'has won the hearts of all kinds of people. They quite love him . . .'

He ends his fanfare of conceit with disarming humility.

This is a poor letter to send you, Lady Holland, from so great a distance, but if it were only because it is a gratification of heart to me to wish you peace of mind, health and happiness—if I had not the selfish desire of wishing to live in your remembrance—I should be tempted to inflict it upon you. If you charge me with any commission, great or small, I need scarcely say it would be a great pleasure to me to execute it . . .

    I am always
      Yours faithfully and truly
        Charles Dickens.

(He underlines his signature twelve times!)

Many a woman would have been thrilled to get such proof of his esteem.

*

At home, in a letter dated 'Jan. 1842', Lord William Russell gives Lady Holland up-to-date news of a house-party entertaining the Duke of Sussex, at Woburn. The play-acting continues, on a par with its former excellence; and the epicurean standards maintained by his father are now even surpassed by his brother.

Lord William declares:

In point of magnificence it is equal to old days, and in point of comfort there is an excellent improvement, that is all that concerns the Housekeeper's department, is more 'soigneé'. We are 30 at table, great profusion and an admirable cuisine, besides repasts at every hour of the day from 10 to 12 Breakfast—from 2 to 3 Luncheon—from 5 to 6 tea—at 7 dinner, and after Balls and Theatres late suppers, otherwise cold. The Duke of Sussex appears delighted, passes the mornings in his room, and is no 'gène' to anyone. You will be glad to hear that the old Abbey has come out of the fire of its purification with more splendour than ever, but pray consider this as a private communication for yr. own satisfaction and nobody else—

He ends up:

> Ever yrs.
> Wm. Russell.

On a different theme, on 12th January the Duke himself writes from Woburn, telling Lady Holland that he has just renamed some streets and crescents in his London property. Having now acquired the estate of Ampthill Park, he has called them: 'Ampthill Street, Ampthill Place, and Milbrook Place', and hopes she approves. He ends up his letter, 'Yrs. truly and affec.^{ately}, B'.

And, knowing Lady Holland's interest in everything connected with Woburn, later that year he elaborates on the colossal upkeep the property entails. Lord Fitzwilliam had told him that the window tax, at Woburn, was the highest in England and that Wentworth 'stands next to it'. In September, the Duke had estimated to the Duke of Cambridge, that he employed 442 'mechanics and Labourers', exclusive of the House and Stables, but, in three months, that number had increased to 542, with further employment to be found for 'so many out of work, wandering about the country, without the means of support'. He had been obliged to get rid of many 'old and useless Servants and Labourers' which made his list of pensioners a heavy one. But he was making additions to the Park, 'in two or three places', which should give employment to 'a great many Labourers'. Sad to relate, many of his father's improvements to the garden had been made of inferior material and now were 'falling to pieces' and would have to be renewed.

*

From her daughter-in-law, Lady Webster, from Battle Abbey, Lady Holland receives a letter dated 7th April 1842. In this, she reports that her son Godfrey's 'horrible Malta affair' is at an end and that he is very ashamed of it.

> He is conducting himself perfectly well and is v. popular with everybody. Ld Ashburnham (his neighbour in Sussex) cld. not be kinder to him if he were his own brother . . . I am still anxious he shld. be in London this season to make acquaintance with young ladies whom it wld. be proper for him to think of for a wife. I shall not be happy again until he is married in England.

Lady Webster reminds her mother-in-law of her former offer of hospitality at Holland House. Could she 'occupy a few rooms there' with Godfrey finding himself lodging in London, 'on Ball nights'? She has 'no wish to be near him for more than six weeks from the end of April'. But Lady Holland takes up her residence again at Holland House too late in the season to be of use to her daughter-in-law.

Another of Lady Webster's sons, Arthur, seems to have been more stable. On 1st November 1842, he writes to his grandmother from Halifax, Nova Scotia. There, his troopship is anchored in 'Cunard's Wharf' and Mr Cunard himself has come on board to greet the Captain. And also to convey his thanks through the grandson, for various acts of kindness from Lady Holland. 'He seems truly grateful for yr. many little attentions to him when in England.' Arthur ends on an optimistic note: 'I am glad to be able to state that Cunard's is not nearly so bad a business as we fancied in England.'

*

Writing from Hampton Wick, William Fitzgerald claims Lady Holland's attention, as being the uncle of 'Olivia Kinnaird', and asks for her help to launch his daughter in Society. He is anxious that

Geraldine shld. see a little of the world, and will come up at anytime for anything that may offer and have already done so for Ld. Salisbury's and have been to Lady Ailesbury's soirée dansante and am going on Wed. to the French Ambassadress.

We have to thank you for having *lancé* us at Lady Palmerston's, who was most *aimable* to us. If *during the season* you will think of us and kindly help us to get on you will v. much oblige me. Indeed, under your kind auspices we shld. be sure to do well, as there is no person more influential than yr. self . . .

It would be nice to report that Sir Godfrey Webster married Miss Geraldine Fitzgerald, but this double event did not materialise.

*

In 1842, Lady Holland received two letters from two naval officers, Captain Granville Lock and Admiral Sir William Parker, giving her personal accounts of the naval operations in China, which followed the Opium War. Lock's letter (from H.M.S. *Dido*) was dated 23rd June; Parker's letter (from H.M.S. *Cornwallis*) was dated 30th August.

Lock's letter was headed 'off Woo Sung,s.side, . . . in River Yang-Tse Kiang'. He describes the progress of his ship (H.M.S. *Dido*) up the River Yang-tse to 'Chang -hai' (*sic*) '. . . one of the richest if not the richest city in this garden of China', and includes some pages from his diary.

June 18th. Landed with Sir H. Gough and staff, upon which he had given me permission to serve when service was going on . . .

June 19th. Landed at 4 o'c a.m. Artillery horse and foot sappers and miners—49th and 18th under Capt. M . . .

Captain Lock describes the Chinese temples, pagodas and tea-houses, and cheerfully admits some inevitable looting.

... round the fires you saw the soldiers lying on beds formed of the richest sables and cloaks of crape satin and silk, embroidered with gold, which they had taken from the numerous Chinese caught with these pilfered articles about them ...

He seemed quite clear in his mind as to when looting was justified and unjustified.

With his letter of 30th August, as hot news, Sir William Parker (in H.M's *Cornwallis*, off Nanking) includes the victorious 'Peace with China' signed, on 29th August 1842, between the Emperor of China, 'H.M's. Plenipotentiary *Sir Henry Pottinger* and the High Commissioner appointed by the Emperor of China'. All Lord Palmerston's demands were included in the 'Peace', to be put into effect by a Tory Government.

China was to pay an indemnity of 21,000,000 dollars, over three years; the ports of Canton, Amoy, Foochow, Ningpo and Shanghai were to be opened to British trade; the island of Hong Kong was to be given, in perpetuity, to H.M. Queen Victoria and her heirs; all British subjects were to be liberated; an amnesty was to be granted to Chinese subjects 'holding service under the British Crown'; and a correspondence, based 'on terms of perfect equality', was to be established between the two Governments.

Short of holding Cabinet rank in Sir Robert Peel's Ministry, hardly could Lady Holland have been more speedily informed of such a breakthrough for British trade in the Far East.

CHAPTER THIRTY-THREE

Curtain

IN APRIL 1842, three truck-loads of furniture and pictures arrived at Holland House from Ampthill implying that Lady Holland had decided to live there, once more. She made some further alterations to the ground floor and knocked two rooms into one to make an imposingly large drawing-room; *Allen's Room* became her own sitting-room; and *Marsh's Room* was converted back into its original function of dining-room. But, again, she fluctuated between Little Holland House and the big house in a state of tearful uncertainty causing Caroline Fox to consider her as 'incurably unhappy'. Then, she took up her abode again in the big house and remained there, entertaining on much the same scale as formerly, until September.

Now, a recurring source of worry to her was John Allen's failing health. His presence in her life had become as important as an essential piece of furniture, which she expected always to find in the same place. Since that far-away day in 1802, when Dr Allen had been introduced into the Hollands' family circle as resident physician, both Lord and Lady Holland had grown to rely on his judgment in all things so completely that, by 1810, Lord Holland was telling him: 'You are yourself like health. One never feels your value more than when you are absent.' And, in 1814, during one of Allen's infrequent absences, Lady Holland was complaining:

. . . the house is really a blank without you. I do not think I could agree to another long absence again for the remainder of our lives . . .

At times, Lady Holland bullied poor Allen unmercifully, a penance he bore with unwavering patience. But, fundamentally, she was devoted to him and, as always, was receptive of the knowledge he could impart.

In an undated letter, written in 1842, Henry Fox, Lord Holland, writes to thank Mr Allen for a letter he had written him. Always suspicious of Allen's partiality towards his mother, Henry admits that he had been 'much hurt' by Allen's attitude towards him on the occasion of his visit to England, in 1841:

I well know your indulgence in strong expressions, I know too, how easily you adopt on trust the passions and prejudices of others, and how vehemently you support opinions and maintain facts which reflexion and calm investigation must teach you to distrust . . .

But he thanks John Allen for his 'handsome letter' and concludes

as it is most probable our communication will for long, if not for ever, be confined to letters, I feel considerable satisfaction in having received your candid explanation of conduct I thought both unkind and *undeserved*.

Meantime, Allen's duties continued uninterruptedly, keeping the Dinner Books; taking his seat, as carver, at the foot of Lady Holland's table; and accompanying her on her various visits to Brocket, Broadlands and Bowood, always on tap. But one solace he was incapable of providing for her: a sense of religion to comfort her in her moments of despair. An agnostic himself, his healing hands were tied.

On 8th July 1842, Charles James Fox's widow died, aged ninety-two, an event which was not recorded in the Dinner Books. In fact, that evening, Lady Holland entertained a dinner-party of ten people, at Holland House.

The preceding March, Augusta Holland had slipped, getting out of her carriage, and another prematurely born child had only lived for a few minutes. So now Henry (who was heir to the St Anne's estate) decided to return alone, to England, intending to divide the pictures and furniture between himself and Charles. It was hardly a lucrative inheritance as Caroline Fox had a mortgage on the property and there was a further charge of £500 a year on the estate to allow for servants' legacies. But Miss Marston (Mrs Fox's companion) had managed it very competently and Henry and Charles came to an agreeable solution whereby Henry bought out Charles's share.

As usual, Henry spent the minimum of time in England, arriving in August for barely a fortnight and then returning to Paris where he took 'little Aunty' with him.

September 6th to 8th, Lady Holland spent at Brocket with Lord Melbourne and, on 12th September, flanked by Mr Allen, Sir Stephen Hammick, Dr Holland and Sir James Kempt, she set out to visit the Palmerstons, at Broadlands. She did not get beyond the 'Star & Garter' at Richmond, where she was taken ill and, from whence, she returned to South Street next day. Yet, a fortnight later, she attended Covent Garden Theatre on two consecutive days.

In October 1842, Lord Melbourne suffered a slight stroke and Lady Palmerston told Lady Holland that she might find his writing a little shaky. His sister-in-law, Lady Beauvale, reported that his improvement was so slow as to be scarcely perceptible and that he just lay on his sofa near the window 'to look at his lovely place'. But Lady Palmerston assured Lady Holland that her letters were much appreciated by him as 'they always contained some topics that interest him'.

That autumn, Lady Holland rented a larger house, No. 31 South Street, from Lord Kilmaine, where Caroline Fox joined her, on her return from Paris. Miss Marston too became a regular visitor there, though usually she seems to have been left behind when Lady Holland went to the play.

Early in 1843, Abraham Hayward, reviewer in the *Quarterly*, quotes a letter from Sydney Smith.

I am sorry Allen is not well; but the reduction of his legs is a pure and unmixed good; they are enormous—they are clerical! He has the creed of a philosopher and the legs of a clergyman. I never saw such legs—at least belonging to a layman.

Obviously, some dropsical condition had attacked poor Allen but he continued painstakingly to keep the Dinner Books, until 2nd April. Then jaundice developed and, a week later, he died. From 3rd April, his place as chronicler was taken by Lady Holland's page, Thomas Doggett, known to her household as 'Harold'. He always refers to Lady Holland as 'My Lady' and, thereafter, it must be admitted that his chronicles are often more spirited than those of his predecessor.

Letters of condolence for John Allen were almost as numerous as those for Lord Holland and in some cases, the praise was greater. Lord Palmerston writes that none of Lady Holland's friends can sympathise more fully than he; that John Allen was not only a sincere and attached friend 'but a member of your family: irreparable . . .' That it 'was impossible for any Body to supply his place'. And Lord Brougham's eulogy is almost hysterical. 'Fifty years friendship without a break or cloud is a thing not often granted to anyone. He has never been the same man he was since the dreadful loss of 1840. . . . Alone you cannot—ought not—must not think of living. You never knew what it was (and) you cannot now learn it at all . . .' He advises 'a medical man'.

Lady Palmerston, Lord Melbourne, Lady Beauvale, Lady Carlisle and the Duchess of Sutherland (who again offers Lady Holland her own Stafford House to go to) mourn Allen's loss. John Russell hopes that Lady Holland will take a larger house in London, 'to accommodate Charles and Mary Fox . . .'

And Mary Fox herself, writing from Paris, says how pleased she is that Charles was with his mother, at the time of Mr Allen's death. 'He was most anxious to be useful'. The Lilfords remained with Lady Holland until after Allen's funeral. But no record remains, in Lady Holland's letters, that either Henry or Augusta condoled.

Charles Fox and the Hollands' family lawyer, Benjamin Currey, were left as executors of John Allen's will which Caroline Fox describes to Henry as being 'simple and sincere like himself'. She continues:

(He) desires to be buried at Milbrook, as close as possible to the objects of his dearest affection, Georgina and her lamented father; and that on the stone placed over his body these words should be added to his name. 'Buried at his own desire close to the objects of his dearest affection'. He leaves in his will the bust of Gina to you.

As she had acted at the time of her husband's death so Lady Holland acted at the time of Mr Allen's and, from April 15th, dinner-parties, four or five nights a week, were resumed. Charles Fox and the Lilfords continued to be very attentive and a new physician, a young rather shy Dr Dick, was added to the household.

On 13th May, Harold Doggett gives a graphic account of Mr Brunel's uncomfortable experience visiting Lady Holland, at 31 South Street.

To-day was extracted from the throat of Mr Brunel by Sir Benjamin Brodie an ½ sovereign after 3 vain attempts—it having been there for some time. N.B. It was accomplished by placing him on an inclined plane head downwards (at the same time slightly raising the head to prevent that oppression of the brain which had been the effect of a former attempt) and which fully succeeded. Then by slightly touching the back caused him to cough, which brought the piece of money into the gullet—and then to prevent his being choked they cut a slit in the windpipe which gave him sufficient air to cough again, and brought it up.

On 20th May, Harold makes a note that Lady Holland dined with Col. Sir Henry Webster, at Richmond, the first reference made to his new colonelcy and decoration. And, also in May, Admiral Sir William Parker writes Lady Holland (still from H.M.S. *Cornwallis*, Hong Kong) that he has appointed her grandson, Augustus Webster, Lieutenant to his 'Flag Ship'. So Lady Holland's Webster descendants are doing well.

After John Allen's death, she gave up all attempts to reopen Holland House, confirming this to Henry, in July 1843:

Hd. H. is out of the question. I would and might have tried it but for this second loss, which has deprived me of my prop and companion, friend and protector. I cannot travel, to pass solitary dull evenings in an inn. My health is greatly affected by the confinement in this little house. I dine out a good deal; and with persons I like, who give me agreeable society. So that a few hours are thus beguiled away; but the others are sad enough . . .

Not even this piteous letter dislodged Henry from his fastness in Florence.

*

Two letters from the Rev. Sydney-Smith to Lord and Lady Holland

The library at Holland House, painted by C. R. Leslie in 1838. *Left to right:* Lord Holland, Dr. John Allen, Lady Holland, William Doggett (page)

During August 1843, Lady Holland paid some visits away: to Lord Cowper (Lady Palmerston's son), at Panshanger; to Mr Smith, at Cheam; to Lord Lansdowne's villa, at Chiswick. Now, she was more prepared to risk her life on the railway so, from 12th to 27th September she paid her delayed visit to the Palmerstons, at Broadlands.

Faithfully, Harold Doggett chronicles a happily uneventful journey:

Sept. 12th. (By railroad to So'ton).
Lady H—accompanied by:
  Sir Stephen Hammick
  Dr Dick
  Mr Bouverie (and an officer of the Company).
Left the Terminus Nine Elms at one—arr. at So'ton ½ past 4 o'c.
My Lady less nervous and frightened than all expected her to have been. Mr Bouverie returned by next train to town.
Afterwards went to the Dolphin Inn. Dined and slept there. At dinner
  Sir Stephen Hammick
  Dr Dick
  My Lady.
(Sept 13th.) Left So'ton to-day for Broadlands.
Sept 15th. Sir S. H. left B. for London.
   ” *19th.* ,, ,, returned to B.
   ” *20th.* Dr Dick left here to-day for Dover.
   ” *27th.* My Lady left Broadlands to-day for So'ton and London by railroad. Sir Stephen and his daughter Miss Hammick (who came to B. on the 22nd) returned to town with My Lady. Arr: at the terminus Nine Elms at 20 past 5 o'clock, it being 40 mins behind our time, we having left So'ton at 10 mins P.(ast) 1 o'clock. We came to Little Holland House after leaving the terminus.

Here Dr Dick took over again from Sir Stephen Hammick, as Harold lists at dinner:

Sir Henry Webster
Dr Dick
My Lady.

*

As always, Lady Holland's friends kept her informed of current events. In September, Lord Brougham, embarking on a joint life of John Allen with Charles Fox, writes:

The *Statesman* will wait upon you ... All your corrections of course adopted and a print of Allen from that fine likeness which I and Charles have (by Edwin Landseer) but it would have delayed till Xmas. So I kept it for 2nd Edition—if any ...
  N

Again, in September, Thomas Macaulay writes Lady Holland a long, comprehensive description of his tour through France. He is disappointed in Chartres and impressed by Orleans, and finds the town of Bourges 'the strangest old place', untouched by the Revolution and 'cut off by a dreary barren tract of several hours journey from the Orleannois'.

He refers to Queen Victoria's visit to France, to take the waters at Eu, and confesses that he thinks the visit 'ill-timed', giving his reason.

> I fear that Louis Philippe will find it impossible to pay to the Queen the respect due to her rank and sex without irritating his own subjects. A royal guest, particularly a woman, ought to be received with something like homage, and, in the pr(esent—piece missing) temper of the people here, any departure on the pa(rt—another piece missing) of Louis Philippe from the punctilious assertion of equality is considered as a national humiliation. The Nantes papers are furious because a French Band has been ordered on French ground to play 'God Save the Queen'. They are furious because a tricolor-flag has been cut down to the same dimensions with the Eng. flag displayed before H.M. Every galanterie to her is construed into a degradation of France. I wish for my part that she had never come hither, and I hope she will soon take her leave . . .

On 2nd November, Madame de Flahault writes to tell Lady Holland that Lord Shelburne (a widower since 1841) has at last been united in marriage (the day before) with her daughter, Emily, who had kept him dangling for many a month, while she made up her mind. And, the next day, another bridegroom, 'Bear' Ellice, writes on honeymoon from Lyons, having recently married Elizabeth, widow of old Lord Leicester. He proclaims complacently that 'My lady is pleased with everything . . .' and he tells Lady Holland:

> We found your belongings (Henry and Augusta) in good preservation at Florence. They gave us 2 amusing dinners . . . They had given shelter to Mr Watts, the clever artist, who won one of three prizes, by his Caractacus cartoon (a design for the decoration of the new Houses of Parliament) . . . He (Watts) has done credit to their patronage by a great portrait of Ld. H. and two of L^y Augusta, one I thought of great merit, in the style of the *Chapeau de Paille*, from some lady having in a joke put one of the country hats on her head . . .

Watts developed the leech-like tendency shown by Binda to Lord Holland's parents. Invited to stay by him for a few days, at the Casa Feroni, he stayed for several years!

On 11th November, Lady Holland left 31 South Street to take up her residence at Lord Palmerston's house, 9 Great Stanhope Street, where, at first, all was not quite to her liking. For, on 31st December, good-natured Lady Palmerston adds an unusually acid postscript to her letter:

Pray don't speak ill of our House. It is too like a spoilt Child to long and cry for it for two years—and then as soon as you get it to fancy all sorts of demands.

By the New Year of 1844, she has recovered her equanimity and laughs at her caustic postscript as 'only jocular'.

I know you are a spoilt child and so must remain, but don't imagine it was Chas. Greville who reported yr. saying for it was a stranger in Dorsetshire who said to Minny (her daughter, Lady Jocelyn)—'How is it that Ld. P's House is such a horrid one, for I had always fancied it was a very comfortable House—.

*

Both Lady Holland and Caroline Fox spent the Christmas of 1843 at Bowood and, about a week later, Caroline has a seizure and was seriously ill for some days. She recovered and, early in February 1844, was moved back to Little Holland House. There, she improved in health but remained apathetic to her surroundings and ceased altogether to write letters. In June, following the death of one of her great friends, Lady Caroline Greville, she suffered a second stroke.

Her illness galvanised Henry Holland to return home. But he took three months to mobilise himself into action and only returned in September, bringing Watts with him. From 13th to 21st, he stayed at Little Holland House, where Caroline recognised him and showed her delight in seeing her beloved nephew, once more.

On 17th, Lady Holland herself was taken ill 'with acute stomachic pains'. So much so that (to quote Harold Doggett) 'To-day came Lady Lilford from Lilford Hall in order to see her mother and Ld. Holland before he returned to Florence.' Sir Stephen Hammick and a new doctor, Babington, moved in.

On 18th, Harold notes: 'My Lady not sufficiently well to go down to dinner to-day.' But, thereafter, she began to recover.

On 21st, with unconscious irony, Harold records:

To-day, left Ld. Holland on his return to Florence from having come to see his aunt, Miss Fox.

The prime object of his visit had been achieved.

*

On 20th March 1844, Lord Morpeth took it upon himself to try to lighten the burden of Lady Holland's moments of despair. Deeply religious himself, he sought to penetrate the cocoon of agnosticism into which she had wound herself, throughout her life.

... I have had our last conversation in my mind, and it impels me to say a single word upon a topic which I have never touched with you before, and will not again unless you desire it, but which to have left for ever unapproached could have been only justified by indifference about you, an alternative to which I do not wish to be condemned.

You say you are very unhappy; my conviction is that everyone, when the peculiar stimulus and various resources of life fall off, cannot fail to be otherwise; unless he has made a friend of his God—unless he finds something ... to which his mind can always tune, not superseding other occupations but supplying a motive and an end in everything (I am not going to be long about this but you know I have told you I must have it out, once and for all, so here with it.) This is what religious people tell you they find in religion, and with it inexpressible peace and an unfailing interest. Suppose there is nothing else, that all ends here, are not these worth trying for? But you may feel you cannot give your assent to the peculiar views of the gospel, and in that you have the company of many strong and clear minds. These are at all events divided, and I cannot expect or wish to force your judgement, but should you not at all events give a fair hearing to the pretensions of revelation—read Paley or Lardner (credibility of the Gospel) to help you to make up your mind whether you consider them authentic; afterwards you may give attention to the tenor and import of the communication. This would be a pursuit surely not unworthy of your intellect.

Now I have done I shall not resume the subject unbidden; as far as I am myself concerned, I had rather almost that you did not notice in reply what I have written; but I shall earnestly pray for your welfare in all things and ways ...

Lady Holland's reply has not been found.

*

Later on, in 1844, Lady Holland developed a positive urge to travel by train, visiting Mr Baring Wall, at Norman Court, Andover; Lord Spencer, at Althorp; the Bedfords, at Woburn; the Lansdownes, at Bowood; and Lord Melbourne, at Brocket. All intricate cross-country journeys, favourably reported on by Harold Doggett. He was particularly pleased with Lady Holland's trip to Leighton Buzzard, en route for Woburn. 'Everything answered well—even the Tunnel—it being the first of any consequence that my Lady has ever passed through.'

The pattern of her life at home remained the same, dining out, large dinners at home, and frequent visits to the theatre. And she kept up her lively interest in Charles Dickens' work, as is shown by one of his letters.

On 1st July 1844, he and his wife are preparing to go abroad and he apologises that he has been too busy to visit Lady Holland 'at her hours'.

... I am finishing Chuzzlewit, and am this day upon the v. last touches ... I do not expect to finish the book until Fri.; and in the meantime I am obliged to walk about the fields and streets every evening, and to avoid all dinners, otherwise I shld not be steadily enough set upon the dismissal of two of the greatest favourites I have ever had . . . I am delighted to find that Chuzzlewit has risen so highly in yr. estimation and I hope you perceive now why the undertakers appeared; and how the unselfishness of the book is the setting for these little sparklers; and how the influence is intended to refine and improve the rest. It is the great misery of such a form of publication that conclusions are necessarily arrived at, in reference to the design of the story, before the design becomes apparent as complete.

Dickens goes on to say that he intends to send Lady Holland, from Italy, 'a small successor to the little Carol, to appear next Christmas. I wish you may like it as well.' With satisfaction, he tells her that the Carol 'has been a most extraordinary success; and still sells quite rapidly. It has been reprinted eight times . . .' He ends his letter:

Believe me always dear Lady H—
   Yrs. faithfully and obliged,
      Charles Dickens.

(This time his signature is only underlined six times!)

*

On 22nd February 1845, death deprived Lady Holland of another lifelong friend, Sydney Smith. And, in his turn, his brother 'Bobus' died within a fortnight of him.

Sydney's brokenhearted widow writes to thank Lady Holland for her condolence, and says she is trying to employ her thoughts.

When the Eyes and hands are occupied the thoughts are compelled to follow them . . .
The light of my life is extinguished! Of what use is the residue?
God bless you, dear Lady Holland—

Most affec. yrs.

C. A. S.

How touching and afflicting the death of dear *Bobus*! Almost at the same time, and with such a similarity of complaints—Who can hope again to look on two such men.

Hard on this double bereavement came the news of another death, even more closely affecting Lady Holland. That of Caroline Fox, on 12th March.

Since her brother's death she had grown much closer to her sister-in-law and had done her best to understand and help a character completely opposite to her own. Appreciated and admired by its most unlikely intimates, without conscious effort, Caroline Fox had maintained her quiet place in the Holland House circle, inspiring even erratic, brilliant Caroline Norton into laudatory if ambiguous verse.

Sonnet upon an old woman seen reading by a lamp, 1842, describing her, not as she is but as she ought to be and some partial friends suppose her really to be. (The terms 'not as she is, but as she ought to be' seem to cancel out the rest.)

There is a beauty which is all of bloom,
Of coloured brightness and smooth outlined youth;
Another, which the spirit rays attune,
'Beauty of holiness', and that in truth
Beams from the loved and venerable face
(Sister of him whom all our hearts deplore)
As did we know thee less, would awe us more.
But in thy charity the weak rejoice,
Too humbly excellent to be severe,
Thy meek smile cheers, as like the angel voice
Bidding the startled shepherds not to fear,
Who looking eastward saw with troubled eye
The herald star of God clear shining from on high.

                                            Caroline Norton.

By Caroline Fox's will, Henry Holland inherited Little Holland House and became her residuary legatee. Charles Fox was left a legacy of £6,000; Mary Fox, £1,000; the infant school Caroline had endowed £3,000; and Mary Lilford's ten children varying small sums. Vernon Smith was Caroline Fox's executor, and through him, Henry arranged to let Little Holland House to his sister for three months in the summer of 1845, at a rent of £300. Nothing would induce him to sell St Anne's Hill, which Charles Fox urged him to do.

That spring, the scheme for a monument to Lord Holland, devised by Lord Lansdowne, took shape. Many friends contributed to it and the sum collected was £5,000. Edward Hodges Bailey was commissioned to carry out the work, and his design was sent out to Henry by his mother, for his comments, before it was finally accepted.

Some adverse though constructive criticism from him was inevitable.

Bailey I know chiefly by reputation. I have seen some few things of his exquisitely finished, and from all I hear he is considered the best sculptor in England. I have no doubt therefore that the figures will be well executed. My criticism upon them can only be as to the general effect. The male figure of a *genius* is not very original. The two female figures both turn their backs to the spectators, which has a bad effect. What I most dislike is the heavy half-Tuscan, half-Egyptian architecture surmounted by a boat which must be too high to be seen, and which is not in character with the architecture. I do not either like the worn-out affectation of putting a simple name on a monument, especially as I remember his condemnation of such a practise.

Henry's criticisms were listened to.

When Lord Holland's monument was put up, at the West End of the

North Aisle in Westminster Abbey, his bust replaced the boat, and no name whatsoever establishes his identity to the sightseers below.

*

On 20th September 1845, Lady Holland and her party were invited by Charles Dickens to attend Miss Kelly's theatre, Dean Street, to witness Ben Jonson's play *Every Man in his Humour*, and *A Good Night's Rest* performed by amateurs, mainly from the staff of *Punch*. Charles Dickens played a part in both plays and Harold Doggett gives a full list of the cast, which included Dickens, playing the part of Captain Bobadill, and Leech (the *Punch* caricaturist) that of Master Matthew. For Harold, the performance of *A Good Night's Rest* was equally delightful and he sums up: '. . . it was throughout most admirable—not a single drawback of any kind occurring'.

*

In October, Lady Holland attended 'a large and . . . agreeable party' at Bowood, at which Louis Thiers was present. Harold comments: 'Mon. Thiers came for 2 nights. He was considered v. agreeable and v. brilliant'. There, she caught a chill 'which' (quoting Harold) 'brought on a severe bilious attack and prevented her from being latterly as much amused as, had she been well, she wld. have been'.

On 18th October, she returned to London and, on 20th, entertained a notable dinner-party of twelve people, including Charles Greville, Mon. Thiers and Lord Palmerston, who met at last as amicable fellow-guests under her roof.

The first week of November passed with the same full programme. Sixty-two guests entertained to dinner, in eight days! But Lady Holland's devoted servants noticed that she began to lean back in her chair, which they looked upon as a bad sign. On 9th November, with a party of twelve already assembled, she was taken ill, 'and remained in the Dr Room'. Harold reports that Lady Holland had a similar attack to the one at Bowood 'but in a more aggravated form—great stupor and general prostration of strength . . .'

Two consultations followed, attended by Sir Benjamin Brodie, Sir Stephen Hammick, Dr Chambers and Dr Babington.

Harold continues:

At night, none of the symptoms more favourable—everyone much alarmed. The night was passed v. restlessly and my Lady complained of a great deal of pain.

'Nov. 11th. No change.' With two further consultations between the doctors, and later attended, at 10 o'clock that night, by Sir Benjamin Brodie. 'Night—symptoms the same, but rather more spirits. From 12 till 5—less strength.'

That same day, Harold makes this entry:

At 5 o'clock this morning (much to the gratification of everyone) arrived Lady Lilford from Boulogne having come from that place by an Express Steamer to Folkestone and thence to Town—passage exceedingly rough.

For the rest of the day, Lady Holland rallied for an hour or two, then had 'a still greater relapse and prostration'.

The next day, Harold reports Lady Holland as

slightly better and My Lady this morning has taken a slight sustenance ... The Blister which was put on last night, rose v. well and certainly relieved the head. She took some champagne and throughout the day was less tormented, and had more interest in things around her.

At dinner—

Ld and Lady Lilford ⎱
Miss Marston   ⎰ slept
Sir Stephen Hammick
Mr Babington.

That night, the symptoms continued favourable:

... the tongue having become moist and clean drowsiness greatly diminished. Sent for Mr Babington from dinner to tell her what was going on in the world and laughed at Sir Ben Brodie calling Harold the fifth opinion as to her case. Soon after 12 she became a little restless which afterwards increased. She insisted ... on getting in and out of bed without any real reason—has wandered a little.

On the 13th, the restlessness continued. 'She steadily refuses to take any sustenance and begged not to be disturbed in her last moments.' Once, on getting out of bed, she said: 'This is Death.'

At 5 a.m. on the morning of the 14th November, Charles Fox arrived from Paris, whence 'an express' had been sent to recall him. Henry Webster arrived simultaneously and Lady Holland recognised them both at once. Harold continues:

... has evidently perfect command of her Faculties and knows all those who are with her. Her hearing is remarkably acute. She resolutely continues still to refuse sustenance. When not spoken to she lies quietly as if asleep, apparently free from suffering.

That night, the Lilfords, Charles Fox and Henry Webster, plus 'Mr Babington' and Miss Marston, all slept in the house.

On 15th, Harold Doggett reports:

My Lady remains in the same state. When asked ... by Mr Babington if she wished to see anyone she said: 'No—no one at all'.

On Sunday night, 16th, Harold notes: 'My Lady is evidently sinking' and, 'at a ¼ of 2 a.m.' on the 17th, he declares:

All is over. My Lady was calm and tranquil to the last.

He adds, with modest pride:

Thus ends a duty which I have endeavoured (inasmuch as I am concerned) to fulfill with the greatest punctuality and I think I may with perfect truth say: That after the first fortnight of Mr Allen's death when this Book was given me to keep, that it has been kept as accurately as it is possible that a Thing of this kind can be.

Harold

Col. Fox and Ld. and Lady Lilford, Miss Marston and Mr. Babington remain in the house . . . (Lady L. dined in her own room) . . .

On 24th November Harold continues his sober chronicle:

the body of My Lady was this morning taken from Stanhope St. on the way to its last resting-place, Milbrook, Bedfordshire—resting at Luton Monday. Tues. Nov. 25th. We proceeded on our melancholy journey from Luton to Milbrook, remaining a short time at Ampthill.

To the original mourners Harold now adds the names of Sir Godfrey and Sir Henry Webster and Sir Stephen Vassall; Lord John Russell, the Duke of Leinster, 'Mr Currey and Mr Lock'; with 'Mr C. Howard and Mr F. Leveson-Gower meeting the procession at Milbrook and following it to the Church'. 'After the funeral, all, except Ld. John Russell and the Duke of Leinster returned to town by the Railway . . .' For the next four days, Harold chronicles the list of guests dining at 9 Great Stanhope Street. Then, on 29th and 30th he lists:

No dinner
No dinner.

The Sovereign Lady's famous dinner-parties had come to an end.

❋

Although kept informed of her worsening condition, Henry Holland was unmoved by his mother's death. He read the announcement of it in the Italian papers and made no effort to return, to pay his respects.

In death, as in life, Lady Holland was controversial, and Charles Greville and Lord Brougham were quick to condemn her last will and testament.

While admiring the 'philosophical calmness and resolution, and peaceful good humour' with which she had faced death, Charles Greville continues:

She has made a curious will, leaving the greater part of the landed property at her disposal to John Russell for his life, and her jewels to Lady Elizabeth Grey, a poor Parson's wife—bequests severely blamed, and justly . . .

O

And, to Augusta, Lord Brougham gives vehement utterance:

The lies in the will exceeded all endurance. As to that about Lord H's intentions, it is beyond all comparison the stupidest as well as the most groundless invention I can remember, for he *could* not by *law* have done so.

Lady Holland had written:

I hereby declare that the disposition of the Kennington Estate made by my Will in favor of Lord John Russell, is made by me not only from my sincere affection for him but also from an intention formerly entertained by my dear Lord to make a similar disposition of the reversion of Ampthill in his favour and I hope Lord John will accept the gift as a token of affection from both.

But, as 'Bear' Ellice testified to Henry, seven years later, by insuring his life almost from the moment of his inheritance, Lord John signed away his legacy to the Lilfords.

Lady Holland's will was dated 31st May 1845, her executors being Lord John Russell, her lawyer, Benjamin Currey and William Adam Lock.

Henry Holland inherited his mother's Jamaican estates (declared by Lord Brougham to be 'worth exactly nothing'), and an income of £7,000 a year, excluding what he had already. He was left all his mother's furniture at Holland House, plus 'all pictures, Busts printed books Engravings and Portfolios . . .' not otherwise bequeathed. But, for these she asked him to pay £2,000 'to be applied by my Executors for the purpose of my said Will . . .'; otherwise, these objects were to be sold. Lord Holland's portrait by Leslie was left outright to Henry, and a further annuity of £500 was left to him from Lady Holland's property in Kennington. Thereafter, subject to two mortgages, the rest of the income derived from this source was to go to Lord John Russell, for his life, and then to Mary Lilford and her family, 'with a remainder, under certain remote circumstances', to the Granvilles' second son, Frederick Leveson-Gower.

'Bear' Ellice's vindication of Lord John Russell's acceptance of Lady Holland's legacy was too delayed to soothe Henry Holland's injured feelings. Only written on 13th January 1852, its tardy if well-meaning intention lost much of its effect.

I must do justice to John Russell. I was at Edinburgh, when he returned there after your mother's funeral. He told me of the legacy (of £7,000) and of the circumstances that compelled him to accept it—a promise given to your mother, after consultation by her desire with the Duke of Bedford, and to prevent the application of the fund (as I understood him) to another purpose wholly unconnected with her family. He told me also, that the property left to him for his life was destined to the second son of Lord Lilford, burthened with legacies to his children of £15,000:

and assured me . . . that it was his intention to apply his life interest in the legacy to insure his life for the £15,000, so that the property might be enjoyed without encumbrance by Ly Lilford's family. I believe that he effected the insurance . . . with the Offices in Edinburgh; and the amount he must have paid, including the tax on the legacy, must so far have absorbed the whole or nearly the whole amount of the income . . .

Almost more annoying, to Henry, was Lady Holland's bequest to Lord John of 'the Memoirs of Mr Fox put together by Mr Allen from passages written and other documents furnished by my dear Lord . . .' These were to be delivered to Lord John 'with any documents among my papers which may be useful for the continuance of that unfinished work and I urgently request its publication as soon as Lord John Russell may think it adviseable . . .' And Henry Holland growled with rage at his mother's 'contemptuous proviso' that Lord John should give him 'those (papers) relating to the Fox family which he may deem fit'. Yet, surely, Lady Holland had shown wisdom in selecting Lord John to complete the work begun by Lord Holland and John Allen? Already an experienced biographer dedicated to the study of Foxite Whiggism, he could bring an enthusiasm and knowledge to the subject of which Henry Holland was incapable.

Contrary to Charles Greville's assertion, Mary Lilford was left her mother's onyx necklace and bracelet ('it was my dear Lord Holland's kind gift to me in Italy'); all her trinkets, except those disposed of elsewhere, and all Florentius Vassall's plate. And, in a codicil to her will, Lady Holland left Mary 'all my laces black and white and all my furs and pieces of new silk or satin and all my entirely new gowns whether made up or not, and my new articles of dress such as shoes stockings and gloves, and all my eider down quilts and silk quilted coverlets'.

She amplifies the bequest which had so annoyed Charles Greville:

I give to Lady Elizabeth Grey daughter of the . . . Earl of Carlisle whom I fondly loved from her childhood . . . my Pearl necklace Diamond Chain and Cross and all my Toilet Plate.

To all appearances, Charles Fox came off badly. His mother left him £1,000; and left her own collection of coins not to him, but to Henry! But it seems that, during their lifetime, Lord and Lady Holland had given Charles several pictures from Holland House, as these were presented by his widow to the National Portrait Gallery after his death.

Henry Webster was left £200, a silver épergne and Romney's full-length portrait of Lady Holland, the subject of such heated controversy between his father and Lord Holland, at the time of his mother's divorce.

Harriet Pellew was left nothing, and the claims of Lady Holland's three daughters-in-law were equally ignored. But Harriet Pellew's daughter, Harriet Walpole (Lady Holland's god-daughter), was left a legacy of £200.

Outside her family, Lady Holland's most important bequest was to the Queen!

I offer to her Majesty the Queen if she will condescend to accept it the Picture of the Duke of York surrounded by the British Residents and several English gentlemen when His Royal Highness was at Florence.

To Lady Palmerston she left a legacy of £300, her collection of fans and 'a slight sketch by Landseer of her brother, Viscount Melbourne'. To Lady Keith she was particularly generous, leaving her 'my Emerald ring set in Diamonds and my hoop Diamond rings and my Emerald ring'. To the Dowager Duchess of Bedford, she left a silver gilt vase.

Whig Lords Lansdowne, Carlisle and Clarendon, and Tory Lord Aberdeen were all remembered, but not Lord Melbourne. And to Lord Morpeth she left 'the Edition of Pope by Wharton which is valuable from Manuscript Notes in the handwriting of my dear Lord and the copy of Bayle's Dictionary'—her final answer to Lord Morpeth's attempt to convert her to Christian beliefs.

To the Duke of Sutherland, Lady Holland bequeathed two miniatures of 'the Comtesse d'Albany and Vittorio Alfieri' made from their large portraits, by Fabre. And she pointed out to the Duke that, on the back of Alfieri's miniature, he had inscribed two lines to her, in his own hand.

Thomas Macaulay got a small drawing of Prince Talleyrand and two bronze statues of Voltaire and Rousseau; Henry Luttrell got £100; but Samuel Rogers got nothing.

Lady Holland remembered her lawyer and doctors and, at the instigation of Sir Benjamin Brodie, left all her bed-linen to St George's Hospital. She left £300 for a monument of herself to be placed in Milbrook Church beside Sir Richard Westmacott's monument to Lord Holland (then, in the making). And to 'the Poor of Milbrook Parish' she left £200 'and mourning cloathing to the two girls whom I clothe annualy'.

Invariably kind to her servants, Lady Holland went out of her way to study their comforts. (As a result, Mrs Brown, her maid and housekeeper at Holland House for many years, had died in her service and left her all her savings.) So it is not surprising that she was generous to her dependants, in death. To each of her retinue of ten servants she left legacies and annuities varying between £100 and £20. In particular, she left her page, Thomas ('Harold') Doggett, £500 and an annuity of £150, asking Lord

John Russell to find him a job 'as I am much attached to him and he is very meritorious'. And, to his brother, William (Edgar) Doggett, she left £200 and an annuity of £40. To both, she left classical works and 'maps of useful knowledge'.

To the British Museum, Lady Holland left Napoleon's snuff-box and, to David Dundas, all her Napoleonic relics including 'some specimens of Iron Ore from Elba which Napoleon sent to me during his exile in that Island'.

As an act of really Christian forgiveness, she left Albany Fonblanque a legacy of £100.

All in all, the 'Goods Chattels and Credits' contained in Lady Holland's will amounted to £80,000.

*

From Brocket, on 2nd December 1845, in an almost illegible hand, Lord Melbourne answers Queen Victoria's letter.

Lord Melbourne presents his humble duty to Your Majesty, and thanks Your Majesty much for your letter of the 28th ult., which he received yesterday morning . . . Lady Holland's death will be a great loss to many and Lord Melbourne is not only ready but anxious to admit that it will be so to him. The advantage of her house was that she asked almost every body and thus it affected an opportunity of seeing persons whom one wished to see and whom one had no chance of seeing anywhere else. Lord Melbourne always found her a very kind anxious attentive and active Friend . .

BIBLIOGRAPHY

Unpublished Sources

British Museum: Holland House Papers. Add. MSS 51520-51957 (Holland
House) hereafter 'H.H.'. These papers are in course of arrangement.
Archives of the Library of the Athenaeum, Boston, Massachusetts.
Church records of St James Piccadilly and St Marylebone.
Sussex archives at the Public Library, Chichester.
Will of Florentius Vassall lent by Mrs Webster of Battle.
Naval records in the Public Record Office.
Royal Archives at Windsor Castle. (R.A.) By gracious permission of Her Majesty
the Queen.
Somerset House: Principal Probate Registry. Lady Holland's Will.
Archives of the Barbados Museum: Vassall genealogy.

Books Consulted

Abercrombie, L. and others (ed.): 'Revaluations. Studies in Biography'. (OUP
1931).
Acton, Harold: 'The Last Bourbons of Naples 1825-1861', Methuen 1961).
Beckford, William: 'Italy, Spain and Portugal' (Bentley 1840).
Bessborough, Earl of (ed.): 'Lady Bessborough and Her Family Circle', (Murray
1940).
Bessborough, Earl of (ed.): 'Georgiana', (Murray 1955).
Blakiston, Georgiana: 'Lord William Russell and his Wife 1815-1846' (Murray
1972).
Brown, Philip Anthony: 'The French Revolution in English History' (Crosby
Lockwood 1918).
Browning, Oscar (ed.): 'Despatches of Earl Gower 1790-1792' (OUP 1885).
Cecil, David: 'The Young Melbourne' (Constable 1939).
Cecil, David: 'Lord M' (Constable 1954).
Cooper, Duff: 'Talleyrand' (Cape 1932).
D'Auvergne, Edmund B. F.: 'Godoy: The Queen's Favourite' (Stanley Paul 1912).
Elwin, Malcolm: 'Lord Byron's Wife' (Macdonald 1962).
Fitzmaurice, E. G. P. Lord: 'Life of William Earl of Shelburne 1737-1776.
First Marquess of Lansdown', 2 vols. (Macmillan 1912).

Frere, John Hookham: 'Works', 2 vols. (London 1874).

Fyvie, John: 'Notable Dames and Notable Men of the Georgian Era' (Constable 1910).

Godoy, Manuel: 'Memoirs', 2 vols. (Bentley 1836).

Gower, Sir G. L. G. and I. Palmer (ed.): 'Hary-O. The Letters of Lady Harriet Cavendish 1796-1809' (Murray 1940).

Granville, Castalia, Countess (ed.): 'The Private Correspondence of Lord Granville Leveson-Gower 1781-1821', 2 vols. (Murray 1916).

Harris, E. D.: 'The Vassalls of New England' (1862).

Herold, J. Christopher: 'Mistress to an Age' (Hamish Hamilton 1959).

Hibbert, Christopher: 'Corunna' (Batsford 1961).

Holland, Henry Richard, 3rd Lord: 'Memoirs of the Whig Party', 2 vols. (1852-4), edited by his son Henry Edward, 4th Lord Holland.

'Further Memoirs of the Whig Party', edited by Lord Stavordale (Murray 1905).

'Foreign Reminiscences', edited by his son Henry Edward Lord Holland (London 1850).

'Some Account of the Life and Writings of L. F. de Vega Carpio' (Longmans 1906).

Hudson, Derek: 'Holland House in Kensington' (P. Davies 1967).

Ilchester, Earl of (ed.): 'The Home of the Hollands 1605-1820' (Murray 1937).

'Chronicles of Holland House 1820-1900' (Murray 1937).

'Elizabeth Lady Holland to Her Son 1821-1845' (Murray 1946).

'The Journal of the Hon. Henry Edward Fox 1818-1830' (Thornton Butterworth 1923).

'The Journal of Elizabeth Lady Holland 1791-1811', 2 vols. (Longmans Green 1909).

'The Spanish Journal of Elizabeth Lady Holland' (Longmans Green 1910).

Jones, Wilbur Devereux: ' "Prosperity" Robinson' (Macmillan 1967).

Lean, Tangye: 'The Napoleonists' (OUP 1870).

Lecky, W. H.: 'A History of England in the Eighteenth Century', 8 vols. (Longmans 1879).

Lever, Tresham: 'The Letters of Lady Palmerston' (Murray 1957).

Leveson-Gower, Hon. F. (ed.): 'Letters of Harriet Countess Granville 1810-1845', 2 vols. (Longmans Green 1894).

Madol, Hans Roger: 'Godoy, The First Dictator of Modern Times', trans. E. Pidcock (1934).

Marchand, Leslie: 'Byron, a Portrait', (Murray 1971).

Marriott, Sir J. A. R.: 'Castlereagh' (Methuen 1936).

Maxwell, Constantia: 'The English Travellers in France 1698-1815' (Routledge 1932).

Maxwell, Sir Herbert (ed.): 'The Creevey Papers', 2 vols. (Murray 1903).

Medd, Patrick: 'Romilly' (Collins 1968).

Mitchell, Austin: 'The Whigs in Opposition 1815-1830' (OUP 1967).

Moore, Doris Langley: 'The Late Lord Byron' (Murray 1961).

Oman, Carola: 'Sir John Moore' (Hodder & Stoughton 1953).

Oman, Carola: 'The Gascoyne Heiress' (Hodder & Stoughton 1968),

Oman, Sir Charles: 'A History of the Peninsular War 1807-9' (OUP 1902).

Paston, George: 'Lady Mary Wortley Montagu and her Times' (1907).

Pearson, Hesketh: 'The Pilgrim Daughters' (Heinemann 1961).

Plumb, J. H.: 'England in the Eighteenth Century 1714-1815' (1950).

Quennell, Marjorie & C. H. B.: 'A History of Everyday Things in England', Vol. III 1733-1851 (Batsford 1937).

Quennell, Peter (ed.): 'Byron. A Self Portrait. Letters and Diaries 1798-1824', 2 vols. (Murray 1950).

'The Private Letters of Princess Lieven to Prince Metternich 1820-1826' (Murray 1937).

Reeve, Henry (ed.): 'The Greville Memoirs', 8 vols. (Longmans Green 1899).

Ridley, Jasper: 'Lord Palmerston' (Constable 1970).

Sanders, Lloyd: 'The Holland House Circle' (Methuen 1908).

Lady Seymour (ed.): 'The Pope of Holland House 1813-1840' (T. Fisher Unwin 1906).

Smith, Nowell C. (ed.): 'Letters of Sydney Smith', 2 vols. (OUP 1953).

Stanley, Maria Josepha: 'The Girlhood of Maria Josepha, Lady Stanley of Alderley' (Longmans 1896).

'The Early Married Life of Maria Josepha Lady Stanley' (Longmans 1899).

Stirling, Monica: 'A Pride of Lions' (Collins 1961).

Sudley, Lord (ed.): 'The Lieven-Palmerston Correspondence 1828-1856' (Murray 1943).

Thompson, J. M.: 'English Witnesses of the French Revolution' (Blackwell 1938).

Trevelyan, G. M.: 'English Social History' (Longmans 1942).

Trevelyan, Sir G. O.: 'The Life and Letters of Lord Macaulay' (Longmans 1908).

Villiers, Marjorie: 'The Grand Whiggery' (Murray 1939).

Wyndham H. A.: 'A Family History' (1688-1837). The Wyndhams of Somerset, Sussex and Wiltshire (Petworth Papers).

SOURCES

Chapter 1—Child Bride

The Home of the Hollands, ed. Earl of Ilchester
Church Records of St James's, Piccadilly and St Marylebone
Will of Florentius Vassall
Archives of the Library of the Boston Athenaeum
Sussex Archives at Chichester
The Journal of Elizabeth Lady Holland (Journal)
Lady Holland to Her son, ed. Earl of Ilchester
The Vassalls of New England

HH   Affleck and Webster Papers, Add. MSS 51807
      Jodrell Poem, Add. MSS 51944

Chapter 2—Posting Through Europe

Despatches of Earl Gower, ed. Oscar Browning
The English Traveller in France, C. Maxwell
English Witnesses of the French Revolution, J. M. Thompson
Maria Josepha Stanley, Girlhood and Early Married Life
Mistress of an Age, J. C. Herold
Georgiana, ed. Earl of Bessborough

HH   Add. MSS 51705-6

Chapter 3—Neapolitan Holiday

Journal
The Bourbons of Naples, Harold Acton
Maria Josepha Stanley

HH   Letters Thomas Pelham 2nd Lord Chichester, Add. MSS 51705-6

Chapter 4—Widening Hostilities

Journal

HH   Letters with the Duchess of Devonshire and the Bessboroughs Add. MSS
     51723-4
     Chichester Letters

Chapter 5—Introduction to Politics

Journal
Maria Josepha Stanley

HH   Chichester Letters

Chapter 6—Damage Beyond Repair

Journal
Private Correspondence Lord Granville Leveson-Gower, ed. Countess Granville
Granville Letters
Petworth Archives

HH   Chichester Letters, Add. MSS 51705-6
      2nd Lord Lansdowne Letters to Lord and Lady Holland, Add. MSS 51682-
      51685
      Poem by Lord Holland, Add. MSS 51942

Chapter 7—Slow Stages Towards Elysium

Journal
Petworth Archives
Maria Josepha Stanley

HH   2nd Lord Lansdowne Letters, Add. MSS 51682-5
      Chichester Letters
      Letters between Lord Holland and his sister Caroline Fox, Add. MSS
      51731-43

Chapter 8—Elysium Attained

Journal
Home of the Hollands
Journals of the House of Lords
Granville Papers

HH   Caroline Fox letters to Lord Holland
      Chichester Letters
      Bessborough Letters
      2nd Lord and Lady Upper Ossory, Add. MSS 51795-6
      The Affleck Papers and Divorce Papers, Add. MSS 51808-10
      Lord Lansdown, Add. MSS 51682

Chapter 9—Dynasty and a Kingdom

Journal
The Home of the Hollands
Derek Hudson, Holland House

Chapter 10—'Family Involvement'

Journal
Home of the Hollands
Harriet Countess of Granville, ed. Hon. F. Leveson-Gower
Petworth Archives

HH   Chichester Letters
      Duchess of Devonshire, Add. MSS 51723
      2nd Lord Lansdowne letters
      Mrs F. M. Wyndham, Add. MSS 51707-9

Chapter 11—Châtelaine

Journal
Memoirs of the Whig Party, Lord Holland
Holland House, Princess Marie Liechtenstein

HH   2nd Lord Lansdowne
      The Chaplins, Add. MSS 51807-9
      The Websters, Add. MSS 51807
      Dinner Books, Add. MSS 51950-57
      Bunbury Letters, Add. MSS 51542

Chapter 12—Consul of France

Journal
Foreign Reminiscences, Lord Holland
Home of the Hollands

HH   Poem Horace Smith, Add. MSS 51945
      Caroline Fox and Lord Holland
      Caroline Fox and Lady Holland, Add. MSS 51774-7
      Upper Ossory letters, Add. MSS 51795-6
      Dinner Books

Chapter 13—Spain and Portugal 1802-1805

Journal
Spanish Journal
Godoy, Hans Roger Madol
Memoirs of Don Manuel Godoy
Italy, Spain and Portugal, William Beckford

HH   Lord Holland and Caroline Fox
      Lady Holland and Caroline Fox
      H. Chamberlain, Add. MSS 51632

Chapter 14—A Taste of Power

Granville Papers
Letters of Sydney Smith, ed. Nowell Smith
Memoirs of the Whig Party
Holland House, Princess Liechtenstein
Lope de Vega, Lord Holland
History of the Early Part of the Reign of James II, C. J. Fox
Journal

HH   Lord Holland and Lady Holland, Add. MSS 51730
      Lord Holland and Caroline Fox
      Dinner Books

Chapter 15—Spain 1808

Sir John Moore, Carola Oman
A History of the Peninsular War, Sir Charles Oman
Corunna, C. Hibbert
Letters of Sydney Smith
Journal
Spanish Journal
Granville Papers

HH   Letters to Miss Vernon, Add. MSS 51800
      Upper Ossory letters
      6th Duke of Bedford with Lord and Lady Holland, Add. MSS 51661-73
      Henry Brougham letters, Add. MSS 51561-4
      Lord Lauderdale to Lord and Lady Holland, Add. MSS 51691-51704
      Lord Holland and Lady Holland and Caroline Fox
      Lord Paget, Add. MSS 51567
      Sydney Smith, Add. MSS 51645
      Dinner Books

Chapter 16—Compère and Commère

Spanish books as in Chapter 15
Journal
Spanish Journal

HH   Letters to Caroline Fox
      Letters with Bartle and Hookham Frere, Add. MSS. 51615
      Letters with Anglesey, Add. MSS 51567
      Letters to Jovellanos and Spanish Correspondence, Add. MSS 51618-28

Chapter 17—Picking up the Threads

Journal, which ends October 1811
Granville Papers
Memoirs of the Whig Party
P.R.O. Naval records
Home of the Hollands
Letters of Sydney Smith

HH Correspondence Lord John Russell with Lord and Lady Holland, Add. MSS
       51677-80
       3rd Lord Lansdowne with Lord and Lady Holland, Add. MSS 51686-90
       Lord Grey with Lord and Lady Holland, Add. MSS 51544-49
       Lady Caroline Lamb, Add. MSS 51558-60
       Caroline Fox and the Hollands
       Dinner Books

Chapter 18—Lord Byron

Lord Byron. A Self Portrait, ed. Peter Quennell
Lord Byron's Wife, M. Elwin
The Late Lord Byron, Doris Langley-Moore

HH Byron Correspondence in Add. MSS 51639-51640
       Lady Caroline Lamb
       Caroline Fox correspondence

Chapter 19—Imperial Passport

Granville Papers
Home of the Hollands
The Pope of Holland House, ed. Lady Seymour
Sydney Smith letters
The Napoleonists, Tangye Lean
Letters of Harriet Countess Granville, ed. Hon. F. Leveson-Gower

HH Letters with Caroline Fox
       John Whishaw, Add. MSS 51568-9
       Charles R. Fox with Lord and Lady Holland, Add. MSS 51780-90
       Mrs Wyndham, Add. MSS 51790
       Poem from Odyssey: Lord Holland, Add. MSS 51902
       Dinner Books

Chapter 20—'Champions for Napoleon'

Memoirs of the Whig Party
Pope of Holland House
Castlereagh, Sir J. A. R. Marriott
Home of the Hollands

HH Napoleonic Papers, Add. MSS 51525-9
       6th Duke of Bedford
       The Flahault-Keith correspondence, Add. MSS 51718-22
       Dinner Books

Chapter 21—Home Circle

Sydney Smith letters
Journal of the Hon. H. E. Fox

HH Caroline Fox to the Hollands
   Charles Fox to Lord and Lady Holland
   Henry Fox (4th Lord Holland) with Lord and Lady Holland. Add. MSS
      51748-51778
   Rev. M. Marsh to Lord and Lady Holland, Add. MSS. 51711-16
   John Whishaw

Chapter 22—Kingdom of the Netherlands and Paris 1817

The Granville Papers
Letters of Harriet Countess Granville

HH Caroline Fox and the Hollands
   6th Duke of Bedford
   Charles Fox
   Dinner Books

Chapter 23—The Years of Waiting

Home of the Hollands
Memoirs of the Whig Party
Creevey Papers
Letters of Harriet Countess Granville
Greville Memoirs
Sydney Smith Letters
Chronicles of Holland House

HH Sydney Smith Letters, Add. MSS 51645
   Rev. M. Marsh
   6th Duke of Bedford
   Henry 4th Lord Holland
   Lord William Russell, Add. MSS 51676, 51681
   Napoleonic Papers
   Byron Papers
   Lady Caroline Lamb
   Cte de Bourke, Add. MSS 51638
   Lord Aberdeen, Add. MSS 51728
   Dinner Books

Chapter 24—Difficult Sons and Docile Daughter

Chronicles of Holland House
Henry Fox's Journal
Letters of Harriet Countess Granville
Naval records at the P.R.O.

HH Correspondence Charles Fox
   Correspondence Henry Webster, Add. MSS 51807
   Letters of Lord John Russell
   Correspondence Henry, 4th Lord Holland

Chapter 25—*The Ideal Son*

Navy Lists

HH   6th Duke of Bedford
      Lord John Russell
      Charles Fox
      Dinner Books

Chapter 26—*'A House of All Europe'*

Creevey Papers
Chronicles of Holland House
Foreign Reminiscences
Sydney Smith Letters
Life and Letters of Lord Macaulay, Sir G. O. Trevelyan
Notable Dames and Notable Men of the Georgian Era, John Fyvie
Letters of Harriet, Countess Granville

HH   Correspondence Henry Fox, 4th Lord Holland
      Letters Lord Grey, Add. MSS 51544-8
      Letters Lord John Russell
      6th Duke of Bedford
      Macaulay letters in General Correspondence, Add. MSS 51856
      Matthew Marsh letters
      Dinner Books

Chapter 27—*Compère and Commère again*

The Lieven-Palmerston Correspondence, ed. Lord Sudley
The Private Letters of Prince Lieven to Prince Metternich, ed. Peter Quennell

HH   Lord Palmerston to Lord and Lady Holland, Add. MSS 51599-51605
      Henry Fox, 4th Lord Holland
      Lord William Russell
      Lord John Russell
      Sir James Graham and Lord Holland, Add. MSS 51542
      6th Duke of Bedford
      Princess Lieven, Add. MSS 51613

Chapter 28—*Macaulay, Victoria and Dickens*

Chronicles of Holland House
Lieven Letters
Macaulay Letters
Memoirs of the Whig Party
R.A. Windsor Castle

HH   Henry Fox, 4th Lord Holland
      6th Duke of Bedford
      Macaulay Letters
      William Cowper Letters, Add. MSS 51559
      Correspondence Lord Melbourne, Add. MSS 51558-60
      Letters Dickens, Add. MSS 51641
      Dinner Books

Chapter 29—Strained Relations

H. E. Fox Journal
Creevey Papers
Chronicles of Holland House
R.A. Windsor Castle

HH   Letters of Lord Grey
      Palmerston Correspondence
      Henry Fox, 4th Lord Holland
      Lord John Russell
      Sir James Graham
      Augusta Fox, 4th Lady Holland, Add. MSS 51779
      Dinner Books

Chapter 30—'This Wretched Day'

Chronicles of Holland House
Foreign Reminiscences
R.A. Windsor Castle
Lord Palmerston, by J. Ridley
Greville Memoirs
Letters of Princess Lieven
Lord M. David Cecil
Holland House, Princess Liechtenstein
Newspaper Obituaries

HH   Palmerston Correspondence
      Henry Fox, 4th Lord Holland
      6th Duke of Bedford
      Melbourne Letters
      Dinner Books

Chapters 31, 32, 33—'A Wretched Being'
                    Keeping in Touch
                    Curtain

deal with the period after the death of Lord Holland and Dr Allen in

Chronicles of Holland House
Greville Memoirs
R.A. Queen Victoria's Journal
Hansard and Newspapers and the Dinner Books and Lady Holland's Will are all
   valuable

Lady Holland kept up an extensive correspondence with her friends which is contained in

HH Add. MSS 51542-3, 51549, 51559-60, 51569, 51571, 51573, 51575-6, 51582-3, 51589-51591, 51594, 51603-4, 51610-11, 51613-5, 51617, 51632, 51638, 51641, 51644-5, 51647, 51674-76, 51689, 51690, 51716, 51722, 51724, 51727-9, 51747, 51778, 51794, 51802, 51813-4, 51856.

INDEX

Abercrombie, James, 308
Aberdeen, George Hamilton Gordon, fourth Earl of, 247, 250, 256, 354, 380
Aboukir, 105, 112
Acton, Sir John, 24, 25
Adair, Sir Robert, 202, 219, 299, 350, 353
Adam, Major General Sir Frederick, 231, 260, 261, 272
Adam, William, 138
Adderley, Mr (stepson of Lord Hobart), 102-3, 107
Addington, Henry (later Viscount Sidmouth, q.v.), 116, 125; and Peace of Amiens, 117; resigns, 133, 134
Addison, Joseph, 80, 82, 83
Adelaide, Queen, 292
Affleck, Sir Gilbert (Elizabeth's stepfather), 72, 74, 106, 111, 124
Affleck, Lady (formerly Mrs Richard Vassall, q.v.), 106, 133, 204, 219, 260, 289; told of Harriet's existence, 108; care of Elizabeth's children, 111, 147, 174, 207, 208, 211, 212, 237; death, 317
Aix-la-Chapelle, 37
Alava, Don Miguel de, 168, 169, 170, 243, 253
Albany, Louise Princess of Stolberg-Gedern, Countess of, 31, 32, 61, 270, 380
Albert, Prince Consort, 329, 333, 334, 357, 360
Albuquerque, Duque de, 168, 171
Alcobaca, 131
Alexander I, Czar, 252-3
Alfieri, Vittorio, 31, 32, 61, 194, 380
Allen, Dr John, 134, 141, 145, 146, 150, 204, 214, 226, 229, 240, 243, 307, 310, 338; as resident physician and librarian, 117, 118, 125, 207, 212-13, 237, 365-6; warden of Dulwich College, 185; his Dinner Books, 202, 219-20, 247, 289, 290, 309, 312, 326, 334; loan to Charles Fox, 265; and Holland's papers for *Life* of C. J. Fox, 350, 379; failing health, 365; death, 367-8
Almeida, 160, 162
Althorp, 372
Althorp, John Charles Spencer, Lord (later third Earl Spencer, q.v.), 219, 246

Amelia, Princess, 183
Amherst, William Pitt, 57
Amiens, Peace of (1802), 117, 125
Ampthill Park, 234, 235-6, 238, 268, 320, 349, 377, 378
Ancaster, Duchess of, 24, 35, 46
Andréossy, Count, 121
Aosta, 34
Aranjo, Don Antonio de, 131
Aranjuez, 125, 130, 153
Arguellas, Don Augustin de, 145, 146, 253
Armistead, Mrs—see Fox, Mrs Charles James
Arranyolos, 165, 166
Aschaffenburg, 213
Astorga, 155, 161
Aubry, Octave, 223
Auckland, William Eden, first Baron, 137
Augsburg, 212
Austerlitz, 135
Aviso, Baron, 34
Aylmer, Rev. Byrne J., 5

Babington, Dr, 371, 375, 376, 377
Badajoz, 165, 171, 172
Bailey, Edward Hodges, 374
Baillie, Matthew, 213
Baird, Sir David: in Peninsular War, 149, 151, 153, 154, 160; Moore's attempt to join up with, 155, 157
Barcelona, 123
Bathurst, Henry, third Earl, 221, 223, 224, 225, 226
Battle, 8-9, 10, 42; Abbey, 4, 8-9
Battoni, Pompeo, 83
Baylen, 145
Beauclerk, Charles, 53, 54, 55, 56, 63, 85, 100, 107, 174
Beauharnais, Eugène de, 106, 295
Beckford, William, 131
Bedford, Francis Russell, fifth Duke of, 44, 73, 74, 99, 106
Bedford, Francis Russell, seventh Duke of, 337, 346, 349, 357, 362
Bedford, Gertrude, Duchess of, 81
Bedford, Lady Georgiana Gordon, Duchess of, 295, 331, 346, 357, 380
Bedford, John Russell, fourth Duke of, 81, 143

394